FAMILY AFFAIR

FAMILY AFFAIR

What It Means to Be African American Today

GIL L. ROBERTSON, IV

A BOLDEN BOOK

AGATE

Bolden is an imprint of Agate Publishing, Inc.

Printed in Canada.

Library of Congress Cataloging-in-Publication Data

Family affair : what it means to be African American today / [edited by] Gil L. Robertson IV.
    p. cm.
 Summary: "A collection of essays and personal reflections by a variety of African American contributors, including some major public figures and celebrities, on the topic of black identity in America today"--Provided by the publisher.
 Includes bibliographical references.
 ISBN-13: 978-1-932841-35-0 (pbk.)
 ISBN-10: 1-932841-35-0 (pbk.)
1. African Americans--Race identity. 2. African Americans--Psychology. 3. African Americans--Attitudes. 4. Blacks--Race identity--United States. 5. Blacks--United States--Attitudes. I. Robertson, Gil L.

 E185.625F354 2009
 305.800973--dc22
                    2008045716

12 11 10 09   9 8 7 6 5 4 3 2 1

Bolden and Agate books are available in bulk at discount prices. Single copies are available prepaid direct from the publisher. Agatepublishing.com

♦ Table of Contents

♦ Acknowledgments

First, I would like to thank God for making this project a reality. *Family Affair* was born from countless conversations I've shared with friends and associates (of all colors) regarding the themes and issues that define the African-American experience. I thank all of you for the inspiration.

Big thanks to the contributors to this project. Your essays are amazing, and the stories and life experiences you share provide a powerful examination of the African-American experience.

Much love to my family: Mrs. Delmyra Robertson; Jeffery Robertson; my three New York aunts, who I lovingly refer to as "The Council"; my two Southern aunts, who I call my "Soul Sisters"; and an array of funny and always supportive cousins—especially Donald Sherman and Giselle Sykes.

My BEST FRIENDS, Rhonda Hall, Karin Turner, and Rodney Harris—always know that you have a special place in my heart.

A very special thanks to my dear friend Kelley Bass Jackson, for your support, love, and constant inspiration.

Special thanks to Raegan L. Burden. Thanks, girl—let's keep on doing what we do!

Thank you, Ava DuVernay, for being a great friend.

I must extend a special thanks to Bernard Bell for being an invaluable resource.

Much love to Jeaunine Askew and my support staff at Robertson Treatment, LLC.

I've been blessed with an incredible partner for my publishing ventures. Thank you, Doug Seibold and the staff at Agate, for your support and belief.

Thank you to my friends at NABJ, especially Ryan and Patrick, for always providing a brutha with a helping hand!

Thanks to the all the booksellers, whose tireless commitment to reading I truly admire.

Last, but certainly not least, a bountiful thank you to readers for supporting the integrity and vision of this project.

My best regards to you all,

Gil L. Robertson, IV
www.robertsontreatment.com

♦ Foreword

Got up this morning feeling good and black.
Did black things …
Played all my black records and minded my own black business.
Put on my black clothes and walked out my black door.

—**Karin Turner**

Karin Turner is an artist. She resides in Oakland, California. Visit her website at www.karinsart.com.

♦ Preface

Who am I? It's a fundamental question for everyone, of course, but for African Americans, it has particular resonance. Since our history in America is filled with grand contradictions, marginalization, and grotesque lies, African Americans have largely been left alone in the dark to grapple with the issue of who we are. Our shared experiences as people of African descent have been marked by an endless wave of mixed messages, leaving questions that lack finite answers. How do we declare our humanity? How do we begin to construct healthy environments for our lives, families, and communities in the face of chaos and confusion?

The idea for *Family Affair* has been growing for years. It took nothing more than a simple conversation with a good friend to cement my resolve to assemble this collection. Like most upwardly mobile African Americans of our generation who came of age in the aftermath of the Civil Rights Movement, my friends and I consider ourselves representatives of a new breed of brothers and sisters who are blessed with hard-won opportunities. Given that, imagine my surprise when my friend (one of the most generous and pragmatic people that I know) used the term "good hair" when describing a guy she had recently met.

I know the meaning of the expression, and I must say I was stunned by her casual use of a throwback reference that to me represents the dysfunction at the core of African-American identity. Something about it confirmed that my generation was still haunted by the remnants of Black America's historical baggage. I knew it was time for me to do my part to turn things around.

Race has been a dominant theme in American life since the nation was founded. From the virtual annihilation of Native Americans and the introduction of slavery to the Civil Rights Movement, Hurricane Katrina, and the 2008 presidential election, race continues to inform the way in which Americans see and define themselves—and others. Throughout our history, our community has had to fight for equal rights and acceptance, while having our status as citizens questioned. Even today, when most people think of an American, they visualize a white person with blond hair and blue eyes. What can African Americans, the descendants of the slaves who built the infrastructure of this nation and contributed to its wealth, do to restore and create examples that are inclusive of our identity? What can be done to change these stereotypes that continue to put African Americans at a disadvantage?

It begins with understanding the various themes, issues, and circumstances that have influenced and shaped our image and perception of self.

Compiling this book was important to me because the black community is clearly in need of healing. Despite the enormous gains made by our community, a majority of African Americans are consciously and unconsciously holding on to negative self-images. They are living lives scarred by erroneous beliefs, social mores, and scurrilous imagery; many are left with invisible trauma and pain. The lethal behavior we see on the evening news or the front pages of newspapers is the manifested result of internal battles fueled by unfulfilled promises and dreams.

Yet, there is more to the African-American experience than the pain and shock of our past. In fact, if we took the time to closely inspect our history, we'd find that we actually have a lot to celebrate. It all depends on your perspective. As descendants of a people who were enslaved, we must remember that we were strong enough to triumph over that experience and the many injustices our collective psyche has suffered. We are a fortuitous people whose African ancestors helped establish and grow this nation. We don't need to quantify or validate our identities as Americans or Africans. We are both. One reason why African Americans are so poorly misunderstood by others is because we misunderstand ourselves. We must learn to reconcile the anger we hold toward the Establishment, white people, and our past. Most importantly, we must learn to forgive ourselves and stop denying that we, too, are responsible for many of the ills that have befallen our lives, families, and extended community.

Ultimately, African Americans must embrace our past and respect what it represents. There is great wisdom and knowledge to be gained from our journey as we move forward, pulling from that strength and wisdom. We must stop complaining about our circumstances and remember that every segment of humankind has its own issues. It's time for us to get over it, get with it, and move forward!

Family Affair is intended to facilitate conversations, spark dialogue, revive dreams, and free our individual minds. The African-American community has been mentally and spiritually fractured for much too long, and it's in need of revival and honest reflection. The voices included in this book take some steps in that direction. The essays selected for this collection expose truths and share individual experiences that will allow the black community to shed our mental baggage and shackles. (Think of it as opening Pandora's box!) Each contributor shares a variety of opinions, attitudes, and beliefs that reveal the strength and diversity of the black community.

If America is ever to engage in a real conversation about race, all of its citizens must be mentally and spiritually prepared to take part. It's time for all of America's citizens to heal—for all of us to come together, united as one.

—Gil L. Robertson, IV

PART I

FAMILY

◆ **Chapter 1**

The Family Must Stand

AFRICAN-AMERICAN CULTURE, MY GRANDFATHER OFTEN SAID, is truly a way of life. It includes our morals, what we believe, how and what we teach our children, our relation to one another, and the emphasis we place on God. I was reared in a strong extended family. My father, mother, sisters, brothers, and other relatives taught me that I could accomplish any goal if I worked hard to achieve it. They provided the constant guidance, encouragement, and unconditional love that is the wind beneath my wings and allows me to fly as high as I dare to dream. Because of their support, I have an unshakable confidence in and firm knowledge of who I am and to whom I belong.

Although our current state of affairs has been the topic of much dialogue, no one can dispute what I know to be true: *family is our foundation.* However, the concept of family must be more than something we ascribe to size or geographic location. At its core, family is both a state of mind and a work in action. The restoration of this sacred structure is the most effective tool we have to combat both our internal and external conflicts. The family must stand strong!

Know Yourself

Self-love and acceptance are gained by knowing your history, God, and family. Throughout my life, I have been fortunate enough to have been surrounded by people who encouraged me to embrace and explore all three.

My family understood the significance of Africa and its people. As children of the oldest civilization in the world, which started with the beginning of humankind, we are the descendants of kings and queens. Although society does not always advance this perspective, we cannot permit others to diminish our value or define who we are. We must engage, equip, and empower our young people by encouraging them to explore our history. As the adage goes, you must know where you have been to know where you are going. This is what I have taught my children and, now, my grandchildren. We must embrace our history to gain a deeper and clearer awareness of who we are. Our limited knowledge of our history has affected our families and extended communities. We know *where* we are, but we are not sure about *who* we are and what we must do to achieve our full potential. The responsibility for ensuring that African Americans use our collective power to achieve prosperity in America always comes back to us. We would be sound, free, and healthy today if we would do certain things—such as obtaining the best education possible—in our own lives.

A sense of self-worth also comes from understanding our relationship with God. That, too, is a source of our individual discontent. We not only must believe in Him, but we must also understand that He is within all of us. God desires that we see the best in ourselves and others, and that we pass that positive energy on to those around us.

Our families represent one of the mirrors through which we see ourselves. So if the glass is foggy or if the mirror is cracked, how does that affect our children? Our children, who then go on to become mothers and fathers themselves, advance to these new milestones in their lives with an unclear image of who they are.

Nothing substitutes for a strong family. In our society, a family has traditionally comprised a man, woman, and children all living under the same roof. My mother and father raised my brothers, sisters, and me alongside uncles, aunts, cousins, and an extended familial unit that included close friends and neighbors. I witnessed firsthand the many ways in which my family and my extended community helped one another.

Today, many families include a mother, father, or even grandparents, and children. Many children do not experience the benefits of being raised under the watchful eyes and ears of a loving and supportive community. We need to do more of that. Even as we redefine what a family is, it is imperative that we reclaim and rebuild the family unit—and reinforce the role the entire village must play in raising our children. To strengthen our families and our community, the family must stand.

The Role of Policy

My service in government is an extension of my obligation to my family, my community, and my country. Every day, I work to represent the best interests of families across America. Public policy affects our quality of life and shapes our view of ourselves and the world. The issues that I fight for and the decisions that I make are important to the people of Michigan's thirteenth Congressional district, the state of Michigan, and our country. The direction our country takes will determine our success or failure, so I am focused on supporting legislation that will build a strong, solid foundation for American families and our country's future.

Legislation has always either improved or added to the problems facing the African-American community at large; this will continue. Laws will determine whether we have access to good-paying jobs, affordable health care, and quality education. They will also determine the strength of our economy, the length of the war in Iraq, and America's relationship with the rest of the world.

Public policy can dictate from the top down, determining where we should invest our dollars—whether it be in education, health care, housing, or trade—to improve our infrastructure. The priority of many of those in power for most of the last eight years seems to have been to take care of themselves, rather than to take care of America's families. Unfortunately, some of these people believe the laws they've passed and the agenda they've set were good for America. Many have made deals that have strategically directed resources out of our country and allowed some individuals and corporations to amass huge profits. During their tenure, the rich have gotten richer, and the middle class and poor have suffered.

President George W. Bush's policies were unfavorable to our economy and threatened our future. Our foreign policies—particularly the war in Iraq—have eroded our diplomacy around the world. Our educational system is not meeting the needs of our children. China will produce about 700,000 engineers this year, while the

United States will produce 50,000. While countries such as China and India spend more than 60 percent of their federal dollars on education, we dedicate only 2 percent of our federal dollars to education, relying on state governments to finance the rest. Our ability to compete in the global marketplace depends on developing the talent and abilities of our people; therefore, we must increase our commitment to education.

In addition, Bush's trade policies had a debilitating impact on our economy and resulted in the loss of thousands of jobs. China has slowly become a world power. India has emerged as one of our largest trade partners. Because of the amount we have borrowed from these two countries, they virtually own America.

Many of the freedoms African Americans now enjoy were fought and won in the courts. However, when Bush became president in 2000, this third branch of government was marginalized. From 2000 to 2008, Bush's administration turned the judicial clock backward. This regression has weakened most communities, but it's specifically hurt African-American families.

In fact, the United States Supreme Court recently upheld a law in Indiana that requires anyone who wants to vote to have a valid driver's license or federal or state ID. Mandating that voters produce government-issued photo identification will have a negative impact on the ability of many Americans—particularly senior citizens, minorities, and young people—to exercise their constitutionally guaranteed right to vote. Exercising that right, a privilege for which many of our ancestors fought and died, is our most important duty as Americans. When we vote, we have a voice. During this historic season, when Senator Barack Obama became the first African American to be elected president, it is critical that we fight discriminatory practices that prevent instead of promote citizen participation in the political process. Citizens must vote to maintain America's democratic system of government and to ensure that the power stays where it belongs— with the people. In my congressional role, it is my responsibility to fight against these institutionalized barriers. In this capacity, I am fulfilling my role in the family—in both mind and action.

As a community and an extended family connected to one another through our ties to Mother Africa, we got out and voted to make sure that our next president is committed to creating an America where everyone has the potential to achieve the American dream. To build a better, stronger America, the family must stand.

The Task at Hand

In order for our community to continue to make strides, we must strengthen our families. A family—whether it is both parents, one parent, or one or more grandparents—is just what it is: a group of individuals living and working together on one accord, all sharing a strong faith that centers them and a burning desire to help one another succeed.

The best expression of faith comes from adopting principles by which to live. Love one another as God loves us. Treat others the way we want to be treated. These elements are necessary to repair some of the mental and emotional scars that have wounded us.

Next, we must feed our minds. We have to reach beyond ourselves to gain more knowledge. We must learn more about our heritage and our family history. We must talk to one another and pass on information. We must become critical thinkers, taking time to analyze and evaluate all that we read, see, and hear. Our personal development is worth the effort. We all have an assignment to be the best, build bridges of understanding, and bring others with us along life's journey.

Finally, I have learned that if we are individually strong, doing what we need to do, and going in the right direction, then we will achieve all that God has intended for us. Our community is doing great things in this universe. We are strong, and we are ready. We just need to remain focused and to continue doing the work. The family must stand.

—**Rep. Carolyn Cheeks Kilpatrick**

Now in her sixth term serving Michigan's 13th Congressional District, Congresswoman Carolyn Cheeks Kilpatrick's hard work and thoughtful political style have earned her the confidence and respect of her peers, who have appointed her to the powerful House Appropriations Committee. She is the only Michigan Democrat on this important committee, which authorizes spending for all levels of the federal government.

Chapter 2

The Out-House Generation

IKE OTHER TRUE SOUL MUSIC LOVERS, WHEN I HEAR THE
first chords of virtually any R&B song, I can instantly name
it and sing along. While attending a Stevie Wonder concert
last fall in Atlanta, all I had to hear were three organ notes to know
that "Living for the City" was next—and I wasn't the only one. The
crowd of thousands erupted into shouts and screams. *"Sing it, Stevie! Play my song!"* As the lights went up around the arena, I could
see brothers and sisters jumping from their seats and clapping their
hands, eagerly anticipating the first verse.

However, I will never forget what I noticed next. Virtually every
white person in my section remained seated. Even the married couple next to me couldn't decide if they should sit and clap or stand up
in appreciation. As I quickly looked around, I noticed they weren't
the only ones. There were others nervously trying to find a comfortable posture. I'm certain they were unsure of how to respond to
this soulful rhythm, without ignoring—or mocking—the gravity of
Stevie's words.

By the song's end, the arena had become a literal church service,
with Stevie serving as the evangelist! (If you've been fortunate enough
to hear him perform this song live, you *know* I'm not exaggerating.)
There were tears in people's eyes as they belted out the chorus. Men
and women of various ages were sharing this private, yet very public,
moment. As tears rolled down my cheeks, I understood. We all did.

Though beloved by people around the world, "Living for the
City" embodies the valleys and the mountain tops of the African-
American experience. As it characterizes our ongoing fight against
racism, joblessness, and institutionalized poverty, it also celebrates

our endurance and optimism. Since it was released in the early 1970s, this song could certainly be considered an old-school track, but the emotion it generated that night more than acknowledges its timelessness.

Still, I was bothered by the outpouring of emotion that I had witnessed. I kept asking myself, "Can't *we* see that we're still hurting?"

Who Is "We," Anyway?

Well, "we've" been called academically gifted, the "Talented Tenth," or, my personal favorite, "different." Our classroom excellence, preppy appearance, clear diction, worldly knowledge, and full command of the English language have puzzled many fair-hued educators—somehow, they didn't expect all of these qualities from people with brown skin. Need evidence? Mainstream media have referred to Barack Obama as "clean and articulate" more times than I care to count. In fact, the insult isn't just that this view is expressed—it's the *surprise* that I hear underneath the words that really disgusts me!

However, my description is even less sophisticated. I refer to myself and my peers as the "Out-House Generation," a group of black people breast-fed on the music of Stax, Motown, and Atlantic Records. Our childhoods were formed by the successes of the Civil Rights Movement, our teenage Sundays were spent in the pews of small row-house churches, and our young adulthoods were ripe with "I-remember-when" stories told on the porches of our grandmothers. We were never able to fully understand the experiences of seasoned members of our families, because our video-soul-watching, microwave-using, Nintendo-playing selves simply couldn't wrap our modernized minds around it.

We, those babies of the 1970s, represent the last generation of Black America that can describe more than 80 years of our history without even picking up a reference book. Why? Because it is the norm, rather than the exception, that we've talked to relatives who've lived through the Great Depression, the King and Kennedy assassinations of 1968, and virtually everything in between. In my opinion, we are a living transition in African-American history. We're the last group that even knows what an out-house is!

Much of the hard work that was done to remove the systemic barriers to higher education, financial advancement, higher wages, and equal opportunity happened before we were born. It was inevitable that we would accomplish what was once nearly impossible. Yes, most of us are college graduates (many with multiple degrees) who are traveling the world, buying homes, starting businesses, and achieving financial independence. We've been able to realize the middle-class dream that some of our parents never lived to see. Generation Y is already emerging, but we are the bridge. We uniquely understand what those battles and sacrifices have afforded us. Without the sustained effort of our lineage, most of us wouldn't be dining at the trendy restaurants we so regularly patronize. Not only would we have insufficient funds, but we'd also be entering through the back door!

Education = Progression

Education is a God-given right that our ancestors demanded that America provide long before the Civil Rights Movement. In his timeless work, *The Talented Tenth*, W.E.B. DuBois was clear that higher education was the key to our development as a community. He understood that it was not for everyone, as talent, financial ability, and sheer desire varies from person to person and from circumstance to circumstance. However, he wisely predicted that those who could become educated would represent another weapon in a multipronged arsenal. The educated not only improve their own quality of life, but they also work on behalf of the larger community.

When I think about the late 1800s, when so many of our beloved historically black colleges and universities (HBCUs) were founded, I am moved by that collective energy. Men, women, brick masons, carpenters, and many others, worked together to build institutions that most of them would never attend. They weren't motivated by individual gain, but they were determined to establish an educational legacy that their children and grandchildren could benefit from. As a graduate of North Carolina A&T State University, I often wonder if the builders of Aggie Land could've imagined the impact they were making. Despite its start with just one building, this university has educated thousands of men and women during the last century.

The fundamental importance of a college degree hasn't really changed during this time. Unfortunately, our perception of what it stands for has. It has become little more than a status symbol. If progression is marked by educational achievement, then, yes, we are evolving. However, as a noun, "progress" is a one-trick pony. The progression that DuBois, my mother, and many of my college professors spoke of is a verb. It's a word that conveys sustained action and multiple purposes. Progression is always in motion, and it never stops. It simply finds another path to keep traveling on.

If education is viewed in this manner, then a college degree is simply the next step in a lifelong pursuit of excellence—exactly as it should be. Still, many of us great-great-grandchildren of these pioneers have gotten off-track. Some of us have lost sight of what higher education truly means, and we've lost our awareness of the responsibility that goes along with it. For this reason, I have reservations about the successes achieved by some of my Out-House Generation peers.

Advancement = Division

The African-American community is not immune to issues of class. Like many other cultural groups, hue variations have caused just as much division as money, cars, or neighborhoods ever could. Although education did expand the horizons of our forebears, taking them to cities near and far, it didn't sever their connection to our community. Seeing the value in what each of them had to offer prevented division from taking root. While an educated person can explain land deeds, only a farmer can ensure that the land produces a bountiful harvest.

Education has become less about adding value, and more about advancement. Although those two concepts appear to be similar, they couldn't be more different. To add value to a situation, you must collaborate with others. You must find the middle ground and move in agreement. However, advancement is more singular in its execution. The goal is to stand out, get ahead, and obtain a position of power.

Since advancers are collaborative only out of necessity, not as a way of being, they are poised to become dividers.

Some members of the Out-House Generation are using their education as a means of escape from the black community. Am I suggesting they don't have black friends, call themselves African American, or don't like soul food? No. In fact, many of them have attended HBCUs, belong to our revered sororities and fraternities, and attend predominantly black churches. However, there are only "certain" types of black people they will mingle with—anyone who fits the same checklist as they do. Not sure if you've met an advancer? Oh, yes you have!

Advancers are the first to remind you, 'I got mine, so you betta' get yours!" Now, I'm all for hard work and accountability, but to advancers, only people who have attained their same level of success are worthy of any form of respect or information sharing. It's as if they've decided in advance, "Get up here where I am, and then we'll talk." You'll never be able to rely on an advancer in a rough patch, because your problem is just that—your problem. Even more, when negative conversations about African Americans take place within mixed racial circles, they're often quick to say, "I don't know people like that." They offer no contextual analysis, or even a balanced response as to how poverty, drugs, or lack of education have disproportionately affected our community. It would be better if they just went ahead and said, "I'm not one of *those* black people." As a matter of fact, some of them do.

This would probably offend me if I didn't find it so hilarious! Most advancers were raised in paycheck-to-paycheck families. They rose into the college ranks from the ghettos and deep country. When they visit home, most of their family members are living in the same homes they've occupied since the 1970s. In fact, although some advancers have traveled abroad, to places like England and Africa, for example, many of their family members haven't even made it to New York City yet. If they were to sit and reflect on it, only two hands would be needed to count the number of cousins who have graduated from college, or who have even left the small towns they were raised in. Although these advancers are decked out in Kenneth Cole and Donna Karan now, some have waited tables or worked in clothing stores to make ends meet. In effect, higher education became their route to an escape from a blue-collar reality and an opportunity to create an entirely new identity.

Now, before you say I'm being too hard on the advancers, I understand there is no road map for what the Out-House Generation is accomplishing. We don't have generations of this type of upward mobility and experience to draw from. We're figuring it out as we go along. Nevertheless, we can't allow our education to become the only way in which we define ourselves or the way we ostracize others. We're not better or more respectable because we have degrees, and those without degrees are not less worthy or less intelligent. We all have something uniquely powerful to bring to the table.

The Charge

There is only one condition that has been placed upon the Out-House Generation: Doing the most good, for the most people, and not just doing that good for our individual selves.

Regardless of what profession we choose, where we live, or how much money we make, it is imperative that our education must be more than just a bullet point on our resumes. How can we use this talent and achievement to improve our lives and the lives of others? How can we make education a unifying force, rather than a tool of classism and division? These are the questions we have to start asking ourselves. We have no time for superficial characterizations based on whether or not a sister has the newest Louis Vuitton bag or if the guy you're dating will be able to upgrade from a Honda to an Audi by year's end. If the Coach bag from two years ago still looks stylish and the brother's Honda is debt free, these minor details aren't even worth mentioning.

Moving Forward

In order to stay focused on progression (and not advancement), the Out-House Generation must focus on the following four things:

- First, we must understand that our education is a service. It not only provides opportunities for the college graduate, but it also improves everything connected to it—our immediate families, our neighborhoods, and the general perceptions that others have about African Americans.

- Second, we must remain humble. Education is still a privilege, not a guarantee. Challenges, like rising tuition costs and disappearing scholarships and grants, are all around us. Any particular set of circumstances could have conspired to keep us out of college as well. For example, in the late 1980s, my mother decided to take a night course at a local community college. When she showed up for the first class, the white male instructor told her the class was full (despite the fact that there were several empty seats in the room) and turned her away at the door. She tried to move past him, but he blocked her entry. That evening, she came home sobbing; my father pursued her to the bedroom to comfort her. As my sister and I listened to them talk, we looked at each other in disbelief. We couldn't understand why this man would deny her something she was entitled to. Although I was only ten years old, I clearly saw the shift that was taking place for my sister and me. You see, our humility is in recognizing that we were only one generation removed from such obvious discrimination.

- Third, we must begin to recognize our generational position within our families and contemporary black history. When I listen to "Living for the City," I hear my own story in those lyrics. My father worked in a textile plant—most of his days there were fourteen hours long. My grandmother was a maid and cook who scrubbed many people's floors. My mother often reminded me that even though there wasn't a lot of money during her childhood, her clothes were always neat and clean. But when I look around at my peers today, many of us are so relaxed, you'd think the struggle is over. People, we haven't arrived! In reality, we never will. Our agenda is not the same as that of mainstream America. What we are striving for is total eradication of the unfair systems that have been imposed upon minorities, the poor, and the uneducated. There will always be a new devil to face or a cleverly designed scheme to uncover.

- Fourth, we have to check our motives. Why are we trying to achieve the goals we've set for ourselves? Is it all for status, money, and recognition? If our vision is truly that narrow, then that's all we shall have—another educated man or woman with an overinflated ego. These characters could care less about progression. Ego is focused on self, and self doesn't have time to be concerned about the village.

Closing Thought

Contrary to popular belief, our generation is not the crescendo—the best and brightest Black America has ever had to offer. We are simply the next movement in the score. The finished composition is generations ahead.

—Raegan L. Burden

Raegan L. Burden is an Atlanta-based writer/producer and managing partner of Raegan/Robertson Productions, a media development and television production company. Her professional endeavors reflect her passion for exploring contemporary culture, entertainment, politics, and religion. Burden is an alumna of North Carolina A&T State University and holds a master's degree from the University of Georgia. Her byline has appeared nationally through the Robertson Treatment and EURweb.com.

◆ Chapter 3

A Journey for Love

IN THE FALL OF 2007, I CELEBRATED MY FORTIETH BIRTHDAY BY taking a soul-stirring journey to West Africa. I made the trip with a group of American volunteers for Habitat for Humanity. Friends and family members warned me of the dangers of going to Ghana alone without anyone I knew, but that's what appealed to my adventurous spirit. Surprisingly, I was the only African American in the group of fourteen for the three-week adventure in the Motherland; all the others were whites aged twenty-three to sixty.

Because of my experiences as a mid-level manager in corporate America, I am quite familiar with being the only black person on an all-white team. With my Habitat team in Ghana, I made friends and enjoyed an honest, open dialogue each night on topics ranging from slave history to family issues. The exhilarating feeling of being in a Third-World country with what I found was a well-traveled group of humanitarians set me free from my daily grind in the institutional environments of America.

As excited as I was about getting to know my fellow sojourners, all of whom shared similar Christian values about serving others in need, I was concerned that these whites would be perceived as the saviors of poor black Africans. Media images often show whites in African villages surrounded by poverty-stricken black children who praise their victors for lifesaving good deeds. My feelings were ambivalent, ranging from gratefulness to shame. It's a blessing to find anyone willing to make strong efforts to bring aid to the disadvantaged. But I'm not so comfortable thinking that impoverished blacks in Africa will see blue-eyed blonds as the only way to greener pastures.

Some of my heart remains in Ghana when I reminisce about the small villages we visited. My eyes often filled with tears as I witnessed the outward expression of joy and excitement of the village children; their intellect and positive energy was so intense that it never failed to move me. Every day, we were greeted with smiles and well-mannered playfulness. The flashes of our digital cameras received screams of laughter and applause. Self-confident Ghanaians of all ages enjoyed posing for pictures, discussing societal affairs, dancing, and offering us food—even though it seemed they barely had enough to feed their own families. Most surprising was the blatant display of Christian values on everything from the "Holy Blessing Barber Shop" to the "Jesus Reigns" bumper stickers on taxicabs, and even names—in one family, every member was named after a book of the Bible. The relentless spirit in this West African country, which was celebrating fifty years of freedom from British rule, was contagious. "We'd rather try to succeed on our own and fail than remain under the oppressors' rule," was the common sentiment in Ghana.

"Sister," the Ghanaians would call me when they wanted my attention. I felt pride in knowing that I was the only person in my group they referred to with a term of endearment. When one of my white comrades inquired with sincere curiosity about the reference, one young lady simply responded, "She's just like me. She is my sister." In that moment, I felt a smile stretch across my heart. In their gentle spirits and beautiful faces, I saw the resemblance of my friends and family members back home.

"Tell me, what do you young Ghanaians think of us African Americans?" I asked Abena, one of the older teenage girls in the village.

"You're lucky," she responded with a beautiful smile.

During sister-to-sister conversations like that, it became evident how much the media influences their unyielding desire to visit America and furthers their assumption that all African Americans are rich. They admire the materialism of African-American life as seen in rap music videos, the *Oprah Winfrey Show*, and Will Smith movies.

But it is their resilient faith in God, their self-confidence, their joy, and their smiles that never fade that won my admiration. I saw stark contrast between them and African-American youth, many of whom suffer from low levels of self-esteem, motivation, and discipline.

Back home, I'm often asked a disconcerting question by whites: "Why can't blacks just get over slavery?" I always take a deep breath as I dig through my soul to carefully address the ignorance of the question. Dr. Joy Degruy Leary said it best in her book, *Post-Traumatic Slavery Syndrome*:

> One-hundred and eighty years of Middle Passage, 246 years of slavery, rape, and abuse; one hundred years of illusory freedom. Black codes, convict leasing, Jim Crow, all codified by our national institutions. Lynching, medical experimentation, redlining, disenfranchisement, grossly unequal treatment in almost every aspect of our society, brutality at the hands of those charged with protecting and serving. Being undesirable strangers in the only land we know. During the three hundred and eighty-five years since our ancestors were brought against their will, we have barely had time to catch our collective breath. That we are here at all can be seen as a testament to our will-power, spiritual strength, and resilience. However, three hundred and eighty-five years of physical, psychological, and spiritual torture have left their mark.

By the seventh day of building homes in Akumsa village, I had successfully campaigned among my Habitat team members to get the infamous slave castles of the Cape Coast onto our tour guide's itinerary for our last days in Ghana. An animal safari, monkey sanctuary, and cloth-weaving tours were the original preferred destinations. Fortunately, they acquiesced to my dramatic appeals, marketing finesse, and unwavering enthusiasm to experience real-world history by taking a trip to the destination that represents the beginning of my existence as an American.

We rode for seven hours in a bus along a slave-trade route that countless Africans once traveled by foot, chained to their fellow captives. These slave castles were run by the Dutch, Portuguese, and British along the Cape Coast, and we learned how hundreds of thousands of Africans succumbed to illness, fatigue, and violence and died along a hundred miles of dirt paths leading to the Cape. We arrived at our destination and climbed out of the bus.

Suddenly, one of my favorite team members, Anja Bennis, a twenty-seven-year-old from Minnesota, turned to me with a surprising statement. "You know, the Ashantis got rich from the slave trade."

Still musing over my thoughts of the peaceful black folks I encountered during my journey in the Motherland, I reached back into my Howard University education and calmly shot back, "Anya, they never got rich from the slave trade. The Ashanti, who were the most prominent tribe in Ghana, were already rich with their own gold, palm wine, and other natural resources. The only things the Ashanti got from the British were guns and a harsh choice—trade, or be traded."

I proceeded to explain the Ashanti concept of indentured servitude, in which Africans could earn their way out of enslavement and even become part of a royal African family. The slave trade in the Americas, on the other hand, was among the most vile and brutal crimes against humanity for several centuries.

For the equivalent of $1 U.S., we were allowed to take pictures in the Elmina Castle. Our tour guide showed us to the common area where women were raped and freedom fighters—formerly called rebels—were beaten. We gathered in a tiny and miserably hot cell where the rebels were left until they suffocated to death. We walked past live bats in the dungeons where Africans were separated from their tribes, shackled, and laid side by side with other dying captives for months at a time.

Occasionally, one of my white comrades would check in. "How are you doing, Venus?" I'd respond with a smile. "I'm doing well. Thank you." Perhaps they assumed I was getting emotional or becoming angry. Behind the pains of my own childhood and the knowledge of my slave history, I felt at peace as I stood in the slave castle. The tour was a testament to the strength of my character as an African American. There was no room for anger, and no need to break down in tears.

Chapter 4

A Family Moment

L ET'S SEE, HOW AND WHERE DO I START? IT'S A SENSITIVE subject, family. Let's start with an all-American family experience. Late one night, I went out to pick up dinner for myself and my son—Italian food. Since I had phoned in my order earlier, I was pretty sure it would be ready. When I entered the restaurant, a man was paying for his order, and a pregnant woman stood next to him at the counter, looking through the menu. As the other customer left, the cashier looked from me to the pregnant woman. She looked up from the menu and smiled.

"It's okay, go ahead."

I gave my name and handed my credit card to the cashier, and he rang up my order. The pregnant woman looked up from the menu and asked me, "What are you getting?"

"Salmon for me, and spaghetti for my son."

"Salmon. That sounds good. Did you get it with the vegetables?"

"Yes." She looked like she could deliver any day, so I asked, "When are you due?"

"Three months." She rubbed her stomach, acknowledging its size. "I'm having twins. How old is your son?"

"Sixteen."

"Is he your only one?"

"Yes. He's taller than I am. It goes by fast. Do you have any other children?"

"Yes. I had a daughter. She died when she was two."

"Oh." Silence.

"But she's still with me. She taught me a lot about life. These twins will be very loved."

I smiled warmly. Deep in my heart, I hoped it expressed my compassion. She looked at me for a moment and asked, "Do you mind if I ask you a question?"

"No."

"What race are you?"

"I'm biracial."

"Yes, but what?"

"My father is black and my mother is white. I'm told there is some Cherokee thrown in there somewhere."

"Where is your mother from?"

"France. My mother is from France, and my father is Sidney-Poitier-black, from Baltimore."

"You'd never know. I can usually tell. But you could be anything—Latin, Mediterranean, Persian, or South American. You fit in anywhere."

"I know. I love it."

"My husband is Filipino and black, and I tell people I'm Scandinavian, but I'm really just a plain white American. It's good that you're proud."

"Thank you. I am. The twins will be beautiful."

"Thank you."

The cashier handed me my food and asked the mother-to-be for her order. She replied, "Salmon," and our brief social encounter was over. As I started out the door, I turned to say, "It was nice speaking with you."

"You, too." She smiled.

I felt her compassion. As I walked away, I sensed that somehow my existence made her feel safer about the world her twins would be born into.

This was not the first time I had been asked about my race. In fact, conversations like this go on every day in America. The multiracial American population, including members of the Latino community who are multiracial, is approximately 17 million. That number will continue to grow—by at least those two healthy twins before the end of the year.

"What race are you? Are you black? White? What?" That's the deep-rooted social question that eventually confronts all biracial and multiracial children. There are lots of influences that form this social identity; family has the greatest influence. The millions of variables that can make up a family are all part of the American tapestry.

Growing up, I always thought my parents were exceptional. My mother grew up in Nazi-occupied France on a farm in the country. My father grew up in the inner city of Baltimore, on Pressman Street. They met when he was stationed in France, before Charles de Gaulle withdrew from NATO and kicked out the American military. Because my mother lost most of her family to the Nazis and saw fascism firsthand, she is more paranoid of a white-supremacist agenda than my father. She still has concerns about the Hitler youth who have now grown up and come into power.

My father made his career in the military, part of that patriotic brotherhood known as "lifers." He believes in a chain of command, and that if you have more stars and stripes, others will salute you, regardless of your race, religion, or gender. As we moved from base to base, I was asked at each new school what race I considered myself to be. I got into more than one fight by answering, "The human race."

In reality, if I went to a predominantly white school, I was too dark, and if I went to a predominantly black school, I was too light. I've been called n***er, an Oreo, a vanilla wafer, a mellow yellow, and a mutt. My primary defense was language itself; my mother always told me, "Sticks and stones may break my bones, but words will never hurt me." As I got older, my responses got more sophisticated: "It's not what you're called, it's what you answer to," and my father's favorite, "Great warriors wait for great battles."

Most biracial and multiracial people consider themselves African American. In the past, because of the "one-drop" rule, you had no choice—if you had one drop of black blood, you were black. There are the tragic stories of those who tried to pass: *The Autobiography of an Ex-Colored Man, Imitation of Life, The Human Stain.* There is a significant and seldom-recounted historical roll call of biracial people: Frederick Douglass, W.E.B. DuBois, Langston Hughes, and Fredi Washington are some of the more familiar names. Nowadays, it has become acceptable to be biracial; in fact, it has become an endearing staple of pop culture, as personified by the successes of Halle Berry, Alicia Keys, Lenny Kravitz, Mariah Carey, Vin Diesel, Tracee Ellis Ross, Dwayne "The Rock" Johnson, and, of course, Barack Obama.

Barack Obama says he owes his very existence to America. His landmark speech about race had special significance to the multiracial community, those who truly understand the road he is walking as he navigates America's racial divides. The very fact that questions remain about whether Obama, with a white mother from Kansas and a black father from Kenya, is "too black" or "not black enough" shows that America is at a crossroads. Barack Obama's primary appeal is that he represents a new America. It's time to recognize that you can be white and love your black relatives, or be black and love your white relatives—that you can love and accept despite race. American history is filled with countless multiracial heroes who have contributed to American culture. Maybe now these truly unique American stories will be told in their full complexity, thus completing the American tapestry.

I personally identify with the African-American community and our political struggle, but in doing so, I have never denied my white heritage. I am aware that the great battle is to win the recognition that we are all truly equal. You cannot ignore social disparities based on race. Although African Americans make up 13 percent of the nation's population, they hold only 1.2 percent of the nation's wealth. All children, regardless of race, religion, or their parents' economic status, have the right to be fed, housed, and educated. It is morally incomprehensible and a criminal offense that African American, Latino, and poor children of other races are discriminated against and denied these basic rights. All American citizens should be treated fairly by the law, yet African Americans make up a disproportionate part of our prison population. African Americans represent 13 percent of the total population, but 29.5 percent of arrests are of black people. Once arrested, blacks are three times more likely to be incarcerated than whites. The great battle is not about race. It's about mission. It's about an American vision. It's about equality, for all of America's children.

Deep in my heart, where those thoughts reside that lead to long late-night philosophical conversations you only have with friends—thoughts I seldom share because they are embarrassingly idealistic—I don't consider myself black or white, biracial or multiracial. I consider myself multicultural.

I love R&B, jazz, rap, classical, and country music. I love all kinds of food: French, Italian, Japanese, Indian, Mexican, Thanksgiving dinner, and soul. I love basketball, baseball, football, lacrosse, soccer, tennis, golf, and figure skating—actually, I'll watch a championship of any sporting event. I love Langston Hughes, Joseph Conrad, Victor Hugo, Alexandre Dumas, Shakespeare, Eugene O'Neill, and August Wilson.

That is one of the great joys of being an American—the freedom to be multicultural. It allows me to consider everyone on the planet a part of my family. This is not idealism; it's simple math. When you calculate our existence against infinite time, it's hard to fathom the odds that we would be alive on Earth at the same time if we weren't somehow all connected and interrelated. These miraculous moments we share have been billions of years in the making.

There are still two Americas: not black and white, or rich and poor, but separatist and integrationist. There are those who accept and respect other people, regardless of their race, religion, or economic station in life, and then there are those who don't.

The American experience is multicultural. Dr. Martin Luther King, Jr.'s dream forever resonates in my mind: "I have a dream … that my four little children will one day live in a nation where they will not be judged by the color of their skin, but by the content of their character." That's not far removed from the words of John Lennon's "Imagine," "… We hope some day you'll join us …"

—**Vicangelo Bulluck**

Vicangelo (Vic) Bulluck is the first executive director of the NAACP Hollywood Bureau, serving in the role since the office opened in 2002. As executive director, he manages the day-to-day operations of the bureau, which addresses issues of diversity in front of and behind the camera in the entertainment industry. Additionally, the bureau is responsible for lobbying and negotiating with entertainment industry executives to expand opportunities for people of color.

Bulluck has been an independent producer for nearly twenty years and is president of his own production company, Vicangelo Films. He has worked on a wide variety of diverse television and film projects, from the documentary film Alex Haley: An American Griot *to* The Essence Awards *and* Showtime at the Apollo. *He is also one of the executive producers of the hit courtroom reality series* The Judge Greg Mathis Show.

Note: For historical context, it is important to note that this essay was written in May 2008, before both the Democratic convention and the presidential election of 2008.

Chapter 5

DNA Has Memory:
We Are Who We Were

B Y THE TIME THIS ARTICLE IS WRITTEN, EDITED, AND READ, three hundred children will be infected with malaria, and hundreds more will die of it in my newfound homeland of Sierra Leone. Sierra Leone has one of the worst infant mortality rates in the world, and Sierra Leone's under five-years-of-age mortality rate is 284th in the world—160.3 deaths per 1,000 live births. In other words, 28 percent of all children born in Sierra Leone die before they turn five, a percentage rate second only to Angola.

In October 2005, I discovered that I share an ancestry with the Mende Temne people of Sierra Leone on my maternal side and with the Mbundu people of Angola on my paternal side. I researched Sierra Leone for eight intense months, reading one horror story after another about the history of Sierra Leone before and after it declared its independence from British rule in 1961.

But the story that interested me the most was that of Sengbe Pieh, or "Joseph Cinque." Pieh was the Mende leader who led the revolt on the slave ship *Le Amistad*. I thought, "Wow! This guy is one of my ancestors! What now?"

I decided to go see the country and Sengbe Pieh's people—my people—for myself. Mind you, I had no idea how this trip was going to begin to come together, but I prayed and planned to have everything and everyone that I needed to make the journey. Many phone calls and several bizarre coincidences later, I had a budget and the visas I'd need. In May 2006, I boarded a plane bound for Sierra Leone with a camera crew; the Sierra Leonean representative from the Corporate Council on Africa, an organization that strengthens relationships between the United States and African nations; and several other key people.

What I experienced in Sierra Leone has changed and affirmed my life forever. I not only saw in the people of Sierra Leone the "faces" of my family members back in Houston, Texas, but I also found myself publicly pledging that I would help raise awareness of the plight of Salone (local slang for Sierra Leone), provide positive and timely improvements, and help finance the construction of a much-needed school in the Bagbwe Chiefdom village of Njala Kendema.

Afterward, I paused, thinking, "What the hell did I just do?" Again, I had no idea how I was going to do all of this—I just knew that it would get done. With that, I founded the Gondobay Manga Foundation in September 2006. The organization received nongovernmental organization status in June 2007 and 501(c)3 status in August 2007. We finished building the school I'd promised, too: The Chief Foday Golia Memorial School, which serves 150 children, opened on November 15, 2007—ironically, the very same day that the democratically elected president of Sierra Leone, Ernest Bai Koroma, was inaugurated. Anyone who knows anything about starting nonprofits knows that all of this generally takes much, much longer to achieve. Yet it has all happened at lightning speed for us.

As a result of my work in Sierra Leone, I now firmly believe that DNA has memory, and that we are who we were. The Mende name Gondobay Manga has not been used since the original Chief Gondobay Manga of Ngalu (the village where I was welcomed) died in battle protecting his village in the late eighteenth century. He was a fierce warrior who was respected by his chiefdom and feared by his enemies. I am a warrior, too, so I thought it was appropriate to name the foundation after him.

I am now Chief Gondobay Manga II, a man with renewed purpose and passion and with a history in Sierra Leone that I can embrace as my own. I was inspired by the legacy of W.E.B. DuBois to pursue his pan-African dreams of dual citizenship, and now I am proud to say that the Bai Koroma has agreed to give me—and any other African American who can prove his or her connection to

Sierra Leone through DNA testing—full citizenship. Needless to say, this is a historic move that will, I hope, finally legitimize the term "African American." It even supersedes Ghana's Dual Citizenship Act of 2000, because that legislation was based merely on skin color, and not DNA.

Another note to drive home my theory that DNA has memory, and we are who we were: In the past, I have had many dreams of what I now know to be various African "villages," long before I'd seen Alex Haley's *Roots*. Reluctant to talk about my recurring dreams, I often pretended they had never happened. The recurrent dreams featured beautiful African women and children working, playing, and running through heavily wooded areas.

During my childhood in the Independence Heights (Studewood) area of northeast Houston in the 1970s, it was common to take shortcuts through heavily wooded and undeveloped areas to get from one neighborhood to the next. Sometimes I took the "beaten path," and sometimes I created my own paths. For some reason, on the occasions that I made my own way through the woods, I never ran late or got lost. I always arrived before my friends, who couldn't understand why I wouldn't just stay on the beaten path they traveled. I must admit it was sometimes a little frightening to split apart from the group, but I always knew it would work out.

When I arrived in Sierra Leone, I instinctively knew in the same way that it was my home. I had seen it all before in my dreams. I am scheduled to return to Sierra Leone in May 2009 and will bring people who want to see what I have seen, people who share my Mende ancestry, people who want to help, people who have had similar dreams of Africa, people who want to see the homeland of their ancestors.

Although I'd always thought that I was continuing W.E.B. DuBois's dream, my research revealed that I was really following in the footsteps of Edward Wilmot Blyden (1832–1912), an educator, writer, diplomat, and politician who was born in the Virgin Islands but emigrated to Liberia after attempting to enroll in a theological college in the United States and being rejected because of his race. (He also spent many years of his life in Sierra Leone.) As it turns out,

Blyden was already teaching classics at Liberia College when W.E.B. DuBois was born!

No disrespect to my man W.E.B., but I discovered that Blyden is clearly the father of pan-Africanism. Blyden strongly believed that African Americans who were suffering from discrimination in America had to play a major role in the development of Africa by leaving America and returning to the African continent. He was very critical of African Americans who did not want to associate themselves with Africa.

"Hmmm ... sounds a lot like me." Blyden and I even share a birthday—August 3. A stretch, you say? Maybe. Maybe not. To me, it's further proof that DNA has memory, and we are who we were.

—Isaiah Washington

Award-winning actor and philanthropist Isaiah Washington has created memorable characters in both television and film; he was seen most recently on the NBC show Bionic Woman *and stars in the up-coming film* The Least of These. *Washington is also the founder and executive director of the Gondobay Manga Foundation, a nonprofit committed to improving the lives of Sierra Leoneans.*

◆ Chapter 6

A Black Family Living in Japan

W E WALKED TOWARD THE TAMAGAWA RIVER, WHICH separates Kawasaki City from Tokyo, Japan, on a balmy September morning. I glanced nervously at my husband, who returned my concerned look with a reassuring smile. I felt increasing pressure from the little fingers gripping my hand as we approached Furuichiba Yochien; I looked down to see my five-year-old son, Stephen Paul, widen his brown eyes with nervous anticipation. It was his first day attending an all-Japanese kindergarten. As I reached to hug him, standing there in the bright yellow *boshi* (hat) and traditional blue smock worn by all kindergarteners in the Kanagawa prefecture, I reminded him of the fun he would have that day, meeting new friends and learning to speak Japanese. My husband told a joke that made my son laugh. It eased my anxiety—somewhat—yet I still had many questions:

- Would the Japanese children accept my handsome, kind-hearted son, or would he become the object of ridicule?
- Would his *sensei* (teacher) take the time to nurture him and help him learn Japanese, or would he be cast aside for being a brown-skinned, African-American outsider?
- What would the Japanese teachers and parents expect of my husband and me? Would they include us in the various social programs we'd heard about, or would they keep us at arm's length because of language and cultural barriers?

Still more questions came to mind as we stepped through the gates of the kindergarten. However, my thoughts slowly shifted from trepidation to delight as we were greeted warmly by members of the teaching staff. They bowed and welcomed us, inviting Stephen Paul to meet the other children. My husband and I smiled and kissed our son goodbye before he was whisked away into a circle of curious kindergarteners.

Feeling pleased, but still uncertain, we were approached by several of the other childrens' parents, who introduced themselves. The parents assured us that our son would be very happy at Furuichiba. Other parents stood back and closely observed our gestures and behavior. Perhaps they were wondering if we were anything like the African Americans they saw on television. Perhaps they did not know what to make of this African-American family at all.

————————

During that morning of being sized up by Japanese families—and doing our share of sizing up, too—I sensed that we were embarking on a cultural journey that would have far-reaching social and cultural implications. How our son would fare from this experience was our main concern. However, we felt confident, given his above-average intellectual capacity, his outgoing personality, and the support we provided, that our decision to enroll him in a Japanese kindergarten was a good one, and one that would affect each of us in myriad ways.

Having lived in other countries prior to our arrival in Japan, we had some sense of what to expect as outsiders in a foreign land. However, Japan has a unique illusion of homogeneity. Dark foreigners are treated sometimes with adoration, sometimes with disdain, and often with fear. I sensed that our public displays of concern and affection toward our son ran counter to preconceived views the Japanese held about African Americans.

While we stood in opposition to the stereotypical lens through which African Americans are often viewed, we witnessed the erosion of these preconceived views as we opened our home and our hearts to the Japanese families that were becoming our friends and neighbors. If my family subtly began to unravel some of the perceived beliefs the Japanese held about African Americans, how were the thousands of other African Americans living in Japan unconsciously serving as agents of change? How did our presence work to debunk false ideologies and stereotypes as we searched for our own sense of self in such a complex society?

Throughout our four years in Japan, I examined the ways in which African Americans are viewed within conflicting racial ideologies, deconstructing the stereotypes created by the racism and discrimination of white-dominated Western traditions and values. I considered how people of color, like my own family, created their own identities separate and distinct from the labels placed upon them by Japanese society. African Americans living in Japan find themselves in a unique position. They must construct social identities that lie somewhere between the two primary opposing views of *kokujin*, or black foreigners: either a traditional racist ideology that defines blacks as inferior and primitive and equates blackness with sexual and athletic prowess, disease, and violence; or the somewhat fanatical adoration of African Americans by Japanese youth in light of the *kokujin bomu* (black boom) or *kokujin karucha bomu* (black culture boom).

As African Americans living in Japan, my family experienced many of the pervasive stereotypes and negative values placed on black *soto* (others). Each and every day, as I jogged along the Tamagawa River, older Japanese men would stare at me, their mouths open wide with disbelief. Some nearly pedaled their bicycles off the road. It was very rare for my husband to ride the train without seeing an older woman grab her belongings and give up her comfortable seat to avoid sitting next to a black man. While it can be argued that these reactions may be the result of other factors, the subtle discrimination African Americans experience on a daily basis in the United States heightens our awareness of this social phenomenon. The overt discrimination we faced in Japan was much more obvious, and certainly no less painful.

Consider the following sample of African-American films that made their way into the programming lineup of Japan's satellite network and onto Japanese video store shelves at the beginning of the decade: *Colors, Boys in the Hood, Menace 2 Society,* and *Juice.* The movies that featured African Americans were overwhelmingly violent, many of them depicting gang-related themes. These negative representations of blacks create an even wider cultural divide. The Japanese have very little or no understanding of African-American culture. When they see these violent, often misogynistic films disseminated by the white American film industry, it's not surprising that they come away from the experience viewing whiteness as the cultural standard of beauty and progress and accept the message that blackness in America is characterized by frustration, hopelessness, and despair. Obviously, this has broad social significance for African Americans living in Japan. These films substantiate the images of urban violence reported by the news media, making the issue of violence in America an overwhelmingly black phenomenon and giving Japanese cause to fear, misunderstand, and stereotype African Americans that much more.

Ironically, these films are often understood by the youth of Japan in a very different context. In their desire to embrace the *kokujin karucha bomu,* these young men and women view the films' representations of black life and auditory assault of loud hip-hop music as cultural symbolism that begs to be imitated. Japanese youth don't necessarily imitate the violence depicted in the films; instead, they look to these films for cues on what it means to be black in terms of style, dress, and attitude.

By conflating the African Americans depicted in these films with similar images in popular music videos, sports, and entertainment, Japanese youth create and commodify their own definition of African-American culture. You'll see this creation walking the streets of popular areas of Tokyo like Shibuya or Harajuku—young, darkly tanned Japanese men and women wearing dreadlocks, goatees, and *wafferu* (waffle) hair, all considered *kako-ii* (cool) by young Japanese people who embrace black culture.

There is little debate that to teenagers and young adults, being cool is as important in Japan as it is in the West. However, I find it problematic that Japanese youth embrace with such enthusiasm this misperception of African-American culture without really knowing or understanding what it is they are embracing (and sadder still, what they are not embracing). For these young people, African-American culture is a series of static images: the black gangsta they see killing other blacks in violent films, the tall black basketball player they see dunking a basketball, and the black entertainer they see dancing in music videos. While the international success of African-American athletes and entertainers is cause for celebration, those who decide which black realities are to be transmitted abroad, and the Japanese who commodify these black images, ultimately leave no room for images of African Americans whose everyday lives are not that different from those of the Japanese.

———————

When living in Japan, I finally discovered a strong black female voice that strove to deconstruct popular Japanese perceptions of African-American women. This positive voice, which has been all but silenced by the white media and contemporary Japanese society, is created by the collective identity of the African-American women who belong to organization called GirlTalk.

GirlTalk was established in Japan in the early 1990s by a small group of black women in search of a refuge from the pressures of being *soto*. This social and educational network, which during the years that we lived in Japan included more than 250 women, provided opportunities for African-American women to share ideas and information. GirlTalk was a resource: You could find out where to locate good English-speaking doctors and where to get your hair braided or relaxed. You could talk to others who understood exactly how hard it was to cope with overt discrimination in Japanese society.

The members of GirlTalk, an impressive roster of professionals, were a strict departure from the images of black women often transmitted through Western media and film. From attorneys to writers, from Japanese classical dancers to educators, from securities brokers to stay-at-home mothers, these African-American women came to Japan for myriad reasons. Many of these dynamic sisters left the United States in search of a temporary reprieve from the harsh realities of being a black woman in America. Others left in search of a better understanding of their sense of self and their place in the world. Whether with a partner or alone, for many of them living in Japan satisfied a desire to seize opportunities for personal and professional growth and fulfillment that may have been unattainable within America's borders. Though some African-American women in the group had preconceived ideas of what life as a black foreigner was like in Japan, many were shocked to learn how little the Japanese understood black culture, and subsequently how much they feared and/or disrespected black foreigners.

The members of GirlTalk often shared stories of sexual misconduct by Japanese men in public places, including being groped by drunken men or having their breasts touched on a crowded train. But for every account of sexual impropriety, disrespect, or ignorance told by a member of GirlTalk, there were at least ten stories highlighting cultural sensitivity and understanding shared among the group. These positive accounts not only helped African-American women cope with the negative aspects of being black, female, and *soto* in Japan, but they also reinforced many of the reasons they were drawn to Japan in the first place.

If this collective voice of African-American women looked to its members for value and sense of self, how were these values translated into positive images for African Americans in Japanese society? African Americans living in Japan recognize that social identity is about where you feel you have a right to be and where you feel you belong. It's easy to feel like an imposter even when you have not only the right, but also the means, to be in a particular place. For most African Americans living in contemporary Japanese society, shedding racial stereotypes in search of not one, but many, positive social identities has everything to do with finding and feeling a sense of belonging.

———

At the end of that school year, my husband and I sat at the kindergarten graduation among the Japanese families we now counted among our friends. As my son walked across the stage to shake the principal's hand and accept his diploma, I felt that he and our family had achieved a sense of belonging that would last a lifetime.

—**Leslie Bardo**

Leslie Bardo earned a bachelor's degree in advertising from the University of Illinois at Urbana-Champaign and a master's degree in humanities from the University of Chicago. She is a vice president and group director for Burrell Engagement Marketing. Now divorced from her husband, Bardo lives in Chicago with her two sons.

♦ Chapter 7

Return to the Village

*Marriage is a way of taking the call of the spirit further.
It brings two souls, two purposes, two worlds together, and
allows them to bring their gifts forward to benefit the community.*

—Sobonfu Some

I HAVE TWO VIEWPOINTS OF MARRIAGE. ONE IS THE PERSPECTIVE
I held once, as a young, idealistic romantic, and the other is a
more spiritual and enlightened perspective.

I was fortunate to have grown up in a loving household with two
parents and a sister. Our family unit was intact, solid, and secure.
But mine was an atypical household. My mother, a beautician, ran
a beauty shop out of our home, so I guess you could say she was a
stay-at-home mom. My father was a numbers runner.

When I was very young, and my mother was busy with a client,
my father would take me with him on his runs. We'd visit bar after
bar, and he'd sit me atop the bar while he handled his business. Everywhere we went, the bar patrons all knew me.

Although it was nontraditional, ours was a bonding and loving
relationship between father and son. My father was a very strong
presence in my life, always there when we needed him. We shared
family meals together, and our lives were filled with quality time. I
grew up experiencing loving relationships—that's what I got from
my parents. The love my parents gave us was a guideline for me when
I established my own family.

I met my wife at a rehearsal in the basement of the St. James
Theater on Broadway. It all began as the sound of high heels click-
ing against the metal spiral staircase caught my attention. As she
descended, I saw her feet, then her ankles, then her legs, then her

hips. In honesty, I must say the first inkling of feeling toward her was sexual attraction—she was such a gorgeous thing. That was the young man in me.

The first thing she said to me was, "You don't remember me, do you?" She reminded me that we had met years earlier as students at Howard University. My policy had always been not to play around at work, because if things didn't work out, it could cause tension, but our relationship developed anyway. In the arts, you must have talent or brains. Hattie was a gorgeous woman with talent *and* brains, and she was special enough for me to break my rule. Unbeknownst to me, the spiritual philosophy of marriage had taken root:

> Marriage is a way of taking the call of the spirit further. It brings two souls, two purposes, two worlds together, and allows them to bring their gifts forward to benefit the community.

Ours was a natural relationship in that it was not forced. Although we were both cautious, we didn't have to work at our relationship. It fell effortlessly into place. Things weren't perfect for us, but we both wanted it to work. We discussed our desires and focused our attention on that common goal—growing old together.

We determined early on that the number one ingredient for a successful marriage was constant communication. Relationships grow, but we also grow as individuals. I am not the same person I was thirty-five years ago, when I first fell in love with Hattie, nor is she the same woman who fell in love with me.

Love is a funny thing. Love is an experience. You *live* love. Being in love is not strong enough; you have to like the person, too. There's an expression that I've always been fond of: "Love is what's left over when being in love fades away."

Communication is the key. When we see change that could pull us apart, Hattie and I talk about it: "Why'd you do this?" "What made you say that?" Without communication, three or four years could pass before you realize you don't know each other any more.

You can't be selfish, because with two people involved, there must be give and take. I have learned that sometimes you have to do things you don't really want to do. And remember, this unselfishness must be equal. If one person is giving more than the other person, it can create tension and can make the "giver" feel unappreciated.

————————————

Many years ago, Hattie and I appeared on a radio show that focused on couples and relationships. We were there to discuss a strategy we'd devised to help keep our relationship on track. We called it Red Light, Green Light.

Since we led individual lives, we found that often one of us would come home grouchy and ruin the other's evening. We decided our signal for conveying a bad mood would be to say "Red light!" as soon as we walked in the door. Once the situation had been resolved, or there had been enough introspection to remove the pall cast by the bad mood, we'd say "Green light!" On the red-light occasions, the other spouse would have to give time and space to work things out alone.

Hattie and I no longer need that strategy, because we have a different understanding, but it was a practical and efficient rule early on in our relationship. I met many people years later who remembered Red Light, Green Light and told me it had helped them.

————————————

During our thirty-five years together, all kinds of things could and did happen. Now, we're living what we said we wanted to do— growing old together. It's a rarity these days. In today's world, society has programmed "ways out" into relationships (prenuptial agreements, for example). In the past, husbands and wives used to stay together even if they were unhappy, and many wouldn't consider divorce until after their children were grown. There's not a lot of confidence in the state of marriage today. It seems as if marriage is no longer sacred.

Couples who have babies out of wedlock are also a culture shock for me. I ask myself, *Is it wrong, or just different? Is it better to have a lousy dad, or no dad at all?* Many single mothers don't realize the long-term effects of growing up without a father in the early years, especially for boys. Outrageous talk-show episodes about DNA tests and finding out about "baby daddies" are very distressing to me. I'm stubborn, and I'm reluctant to accept these changes. It was a wake-up call for me, and I've found that you don't have to like change to accept it. I've adapted, but it's taken a while.

I may be old fashioned, but I still see the virtues of being married. Having someone that you care about and that you can talk to, feel secure with, and share your ups and downs with are the building blocks of happiness. There's a lot of comfort in knowing that someone is there to share your concerns and your joys, someone is there to develop memories with, and someone is there to receive and offer uplifting words. There's value in that.

Unfortunately, marriage has been trivialized. Family values are virtually gone; they are no longer an intricate part of society, and this has affected everything. Relationships used to be cultivated and nurtured by couples, families, and the community. I've come to appreciate this even more now that it's disappeared from the landscape of society. Things have changed for us as a people because we've lost this spirit of community. It really does take a village. Again, the spiritual philosophy of marriage:

> Marriage is a way of taking the call of the spirit further. It brings two souls, two purposes, two worlds together, and allows them to bring their gifts forward to benefit the community.

Many African Americans have difficulty staying connected in intimate relationships because they've lost their appreciation for family—their connection to each other. As a result, all of us are suffering psychological scars—although some don't realize or understand it, and some even deny it.

We've assimilated into general society, which is a good thing. Unfortunately, along the way we've also lost touch with our African-American history, which should have been passed on from generation to generation. We became ashamed of our Southern heritage.

We felt that we had nothing to be proud of. That, in conjunction with other sociopolitical realities, brought about both positive and negative change. Some feel so little connection to the past that they find they have no foundation to build a life on. It's not impossible, but it is very difficult to build a life around nothing but the present.

In order for us to reclaim a sense of self-respect as a people, we must start with our babies. From birth on, we must teach them about their history, their heritage, and the significance of family. Young parents must accept this charge and begin a new generation of strong, proud African Americans, but it will take a great deal of effort from both young and old.

Once some African Americans become successful, they forget where they came from. Very few of us were born with silver spoons in our mouths. We all have had to work hard, and everyone who achieves success should give back. Throughout my career, I have sought out young people to mentor. For example, I was the first African American to conduct the orchestra at the Academy Awards, and after BET aired an interview with me about that groundbreaking achievement, I got letters from many young people who were encouraged and wanted to study music. They saw possibilities that they could do the same.

We've got to get back to looking at community as family. If every successful black person could grab one young black person and serve as his or her guide, we could really make a difference. I spend a lot of time giving back: On a weekly basis, I receive at least twenty requests to watch the taping of the show *Dancing with the Stars*. I love to let them come and hang out with me, because you never know whose life you might change by reaching back and pulling somebody up. If we all did more of this—giving back—it would go a long way.

A man named Randal Simmons understood this. He was a Los Angeles SWAT officer who was tragically killed in the line of duty in February 2008, but it was what he did off duty that demonstrates my point about giving back. With his own money, he started Glory Kids, an organization for children from lower-income neighborhoods. Glory Kids steered them away from gangs and toward the

Gospel. Simmons bought children bicycles and new shoes for school, took them to Dodgers games, and even slipped their parents money for groceries.

Perhaps most important of all, he gave these children his time. He gave them his presence. He was an ordinary man who understood that his life could mean more, and it is fascinating to see the positive impact he had on so many people. Randal Simmons is a role model for community spirit.

It all comes back full circle. My marriage to Hattie has been a blessing in my life. I believe that our life together has been harmonious because we share the same life purpose. Our marriage is not just for us. It is an affirmation of the grander scale of community—as a way of giving back, as a way of example, as a way of connection. In our own small way, we have returned to the village, and we feel right at home.

—**Harold Wheeler**

Harold Wheeler is an orchestrator, composer, conductor, arranger, record producer, and musical director. He has received numerous Tony and Drama Desk award nominations for orchestration, and in 2003, he won the Drama Desk Award for Outstanding Orchestration for the musical Hairspray. *Wheeler made history when he conducted the orchestra for the 76th Academy Awards ceremony, becoming the first African-American conductor in the Academy's history. Wheeler was also a conductor during the closing ceremonies of the 1996 Summer Olympics. He is currently the musical director on the ABC show* Dancing with the Stars.

◆ Chapter 8

Home Training

I AM NEW YORK CITY BORN AND BRED, THE ELDEST OF GEORGE and Betty Winston's three daughters. My parents met sometime in 1944 in a Harlem nightclub. Let's just say my father didn't exactly charm my mom when he told her, "My women usually buy me drinks."

She replied, "Well, I guess you won't be drinking tonight."

The chase was on, and at some point Mom stopped running. She stayed put, in fact, until my dad died, Father's Day 1983.

I was born in Brooklyn, but spent little time there. I grew up on Manhattan's Lower East Side; later, we moved to East Harlem. My young life was filled with strong people just like my parents, who'd migrated to New York from down South, Europe, the West Indies, and Puerto Rico. My role models were of every hue, including some who spoke very little English. They were hardworking folks, mostly minimum-wage laborers who were blessed with maximum common sense.

It's true that memories often are sweeter than reality, and that some of our most cherished memories are actually the recollections of others that have been repeated so often that you truly believe you remember it yourself. Still, what I know for sure is that my memories of being loved and cherished—abundantly so—are real. I don't remember a single day in my youth when I wasn't doted upon and told that I was smart. If it wasn't my parents saying it, my godmother, Sarah Newkirk, our neighbors, or my uncles and aunts were. Simply put, I was affirmed and reaffirmed.

My father told me practically every day that I was pretty, that I was his "Boopie Girl," his "Nooksie," and his "papoose." One particular Easter Sunday, my Aunt Catherine took one look at me, all dressed up, and proclaimed that I was a black beauty. Another of my aunts became upset about her reference. "Don't call her black," she said.

At that, Aunt Catherine, a small, bright-skinned woman who never backed down, replied, "Well, she is black *and* she is beautiful." Aunt Catherine was emphatic. I was not black *but* beautiful; I was black *and* beautiful.

So imagine my surprise years later, when I went out into the bigger world and discovered that even some black people didn't believe a dark-skinned girl could be beautiful. Fortunately, the Black Power movement settled the dispute: black is beautiful, in all its shades, from café au lait to blue-black.

———————————

The community that nurtured me also wisely counseled that "beauty is as beauty does" and that "ugly is to the bone." I never wished to be ugly. I wanted my elders to know that the energy and love they invested in me went to good use. I wanted to do what most of them had never had a chance to do—graduate from high school and, later, from college and graduate school.

It wouldn't be honest to say that I've never had moments of insecurity; certainly, I have. Like everyone else, there have been times that my self-esteem has taken a licking. But having been raised to love and believe in my possibilities, I've always been able to bounce back, heal, and move on without my spirit suffering too much damage.

I've encountered a lot of people—women, men, and children—who obviously haven't been loved and cherished enough. The evidence bleeds through in the quality of their friendships and the fact that they often work overtime to sabotage whatever goodness comes into their lives. But even the most wretched pasts can be overcome. I've seen it happen to people I know. I've read about it in memoirs and biographies. The wise author bell hooks observed in her book *Rock My Soul: Black People and Self-Esteem* that we can overcome our "bads" by living consciously and purposefully.

Meanwhile, although some insist that black women are strong beyond measure, there are times when we can't work out our hurts all by ourselves. There's no shame in taking all that pain to an objective professional. Just as it doesn't make sense to suffer from a toothache when a simple trip to the dentist could make it all better, it doesn't make sense to live with heartache. As my pastor often says, "You can't fix what you won't face."

Face it, girl. You're beautiful!

—Betty Winston Bayé

Betty Winston Bayé has been an editorial writer and columnist for The Courier-Journal *in Louisville, Kentucky since 1991. She began at* The C-J *in 1984 as a general assignment reporter, and prior to joining the editorial board, she held positions as assistant city editor and assistant Neighborhoods editor. Before moving to Kentucky, Bayé reported on housing and urban affairs for* The Daily Argus *in Mount Vernon, New York.*

Bayé earned a bachelor's degree in communications from Hunter College and a master's degree from the Columbia University Graduate School of Journalism. In addition, Bayé was a Nieman Fellow at Harvard University. She hosted The Betty Bayé Show *on local Louisville television for six years.*

♦ Chapter 9

The African-American Family: Giving the Gifts of Roots and Wings

F EW INSTITUTIONS IN OUR COUNTRY HAVE BEEN UNDER SIEGE as long as the African-American family. The documented arrival of the first Africans in Jamestown in 1619 is the starting point from which the African-American family can begin to trace its roots. In the seventeenth century, Africans taken from their families and tribes found themselves in the New World. Many times in this new and foreign environment, the concept of family had to be reinvented. In many cases, "family" was adopted kin, others who shared similar circumstances or perhaps some tribal connections.

The eighteenth and nineteenth centuries found the African-American family struggling to survive the external destructive forces of slavery. However, the family managed to survive and after the Civil War, the end of the slavery meant that countless newly freed people were left to search for family members who had been sold away. A burning desire to reunite the family, a commitment to retain the family that remained, and a determination to create families without interference from whites were compelling issues for these freed people.

Their success is evident in the continued presence of the African-American family, despite external and internal forces that continue to attack its structure. Through many years of turmoil and strife, the family structure has continued to nurture children raised in a society that devalues them. The harbor of safety created by mothers, fathers, siblings and extended family has functioned beautifully for generations. Passing on cultural and spiritual roots to a child is like giving him or her wings. These wings are strengthened with love and caring, two important anchors of the African-American family. They have been tested by time; in my opinion, they are the reason the African-American family survives.

Cultural and Spiritual Roots

My parents believed it was important to pass on family history. Each year at Christmas, we would gather together and listen to the oldest members of the family as they passed history on from generation to generation. Our mother believed that a family's roots started with remembering, telling, and retelling the actions of our elders. We had to accept that our ancestors were enslaved—not slaves. Only after we fully understood how we'd arrived at our current place in time were we ready for the gift of wings. These wings carry us to great heights and allow us to fly over any mountains that threatened to block our way. The wings allow us to soar.

I believe that our families have an obligation to reconstruct the past and provide a history that details the accomplishments of African-American people, particularly those family members who have passed on. Reunions and other family gatherings are the occasions when this history must be discussed.

Younger members of the family need instruction in how our ancestors withstood trials and tribulations and faced down cruel white owners and taskmasters. These children must know the stories of rebellion and protest in order to make a connection with their forebears who were not free. These stories create a permanence that allows our young people to understand they have a foundation upon which to build their futures. The reinforcement of family history ensures that the contributions of elders will never be forgotten, and it informs the family of the importance and value of its ancestors.

I believe that the many African-American families who are now spending time and money trying to discover their transatlantic roots will benefit greatly from their efforts. When tracing their African ancestors, they will discover more stories that provide new cultural experiences. These connections instill a sense of time and place that provide a road map for younger generations to follow. When we understand that spirituality and a respect and reverence for nature were central to our African ancestors, we can better combat the still-mystifying image often presented of sixteenth- and seventeenth-century Africans. We need to know that our ancestors merged this spirituality with select tenets of Christianity to forge a religion that sustained them.

While there may be families that do not attend church regularly, I was not born into one of them. We were very faithful. In many families, a belief in God is joined with a belief that humankind must be active and useful in the pursuit of God's truth. Our family was no different; in fact, my grandmother told us that preachers were just men who read the Bible in front of a large group of people, and that didn't make them special or more loved by God than any of us. Her father had been a preacher, so she knew firsthand that weaknesses could afflict those who professed to be called to preach. Accordingly, she wouldn't allow any of her family members to place them on a pedestal.

Preparation for the World

Our family life is a training ground that prepares young people to go into the world and become successful and productive citizens. Potential leaders are formed in the family, and training for that role begins with learning the responsibility and discipline that is expected of all members of society.

For example, our second-oldest daughter is deaf. Even though she is classified as having a disability, we have taught her that she can do anything—except hear. We expect her to prepare herself to live independently, and we assure her that we will do everything possible for that to happen. Like most African-American families, we have always wanted to ensure that a minimal amount of deference is extended to family members with disabilities, so we do not have different standards for her. This flies in the face of the commonly held idea in the white world that a disability prevents assigned responsibilities and, more importantly, mandates low expectations. All family members must be productive to the best of their abilities. Everyone is treated equally and expected to do his or her best. Abilities, and not disabilities, are what's important.

The focus has to be on building character and encouraging children, no matter what their abilities may be. I firmly believe that there is a need to shelter the family from the onslaught of the world, but this need for shelter does not supersede an obligation to produce strong, self-reliant persons who are aware of what they'll face after they leave the safety of the family.

Gendering the Family

My parents, like many old-school parents, believed that all their children should know how to run a home, whether they married or remained single. Sharing of household chores and assignment of responsibilities were divided democratically. My father, a professional chef, made certain that my brothers, sister, and I all cooked, washed dishes, cleaned the kitchen, and took out the trash. My mother instructed all of us in the art of making beds, grocery shopping, ironing and washing, folding sheets, and setting the table.

This was all way before the concept of gendering—in fact, there was no gendering of these or any other activities not of a personal nature in our home. Household responsibilities belonged to all of the children on a rotating basis. My parents did not believe that having the ability and skill to be able to function in the domestic arena was a gendered activity. The goal was to make us well rounded, and we were expected to become competent in all of these areas.

Safety

The family structure must continue to be a safe harbor. It is here that protection against physical, emotional, and psychological abuse is formed. Our families, our first line of defense, continue to provide self-esteem, self-confidence, life skills, ambition, and love of education. African-American families are constantly preserving legacies, polishing diamonds in the rough, and praying children through trials and tribulations.

Being the first family member to attend college is still a prestigious title to hold, and my older brother carries it well to this day. Although our parents had little formal education, they were adamant that we would attend college. They made it happen by projecting positive images of education, teaching us to love reading, and wanting us to expand our knowledge of all subjects. They took their job as parents very seriously, and our job, as my father often told us, was to go to school, study, get good grades, and go to college. And he didn't stop there. He believed that we needed to have professions, not jobs.

My mother added another dimension to the challenge, demanding that we help others on their journeys once we attained success. She believed that part of the purpose of an education was to be able to share that knowledge with others. We were to be teachers, even if we never set foot in a classroom. We were to share our knowledge, respectfully, with all who wanted to learn what we knew.

Assisting others by sharing what we had—especially our knowledge—was instilled in us early on by our parents. They did it smoothly and seamlessly. It was in their DNA, and because of that, it became part of our family's DNA.

Roots and Wings

Life has been hard for many of our family members. My ancestors on my mother's side had been born in the South and endured enslavement there. Those on my father's side were enslaved in the West Indies. Each had different ways of passing the history of their ancestors to us. My father rarely spoke of his people and their struggles, but despite the fact that he'd advanced no farther than the third grade, he always made sure that we subscribed to Dr. Carter G. Woodson's *Journal of Negro History* and *Jet* magazine. Our mother, on the other hand, spoke frequently about her family and their interactions with racism, segregation, and discrimination. She had personally experienced the harsh treatment of blacks in early to mid-twentieth century North Carolina, but she refused to allow us to become bitter on their or her behalf. Instead, she wanted us to understand the very real sacrifices that had been made so we could be educated without fear of reprisal.

It was always expected that we would put forth our best effort in school. We were required to participate in church activities. Because of my mother, I probably hold the record for having made the most oral presentations at teas, junior speaker events, and Negro History Week programs. At each of these events, I would tell a story about a relative who made it through the fire and stood ready to shelter those who came after. By telling us their stories and having us retell them, we honored what they did. We gave life to stories of their bravery.

Roots and wings have been the historical gifts of my family. They are always in season; their power does not erode with time; they can be given without material cost; they can be passed down from generation to generation; they never need batteries; and the warranty is infinite. One size fits all. The empowerment of knowing your history and where you come from is matched in magnitude only by the ability to go further and higher.

Today, as a parent, I give the gifts of roots and wings to my children. These gifts, these positive images, keep on giving. Roots, strong and gnarled with age, are anchors that are not easily uprooted. Wings offer the ability and opportunity to explore and discover. Both roots and wings allow those who possess them to know who they are when they find themselves in strange lands. They are also tools to navigate the way home, both culturally and spiritually.

Despite the many declarations of its demise, the African-American family is doing the work necessary to produce, protect, and promote strong citizens of the world. We are giving the transforming gifts of roots and wings.

—Sandra Jowers-Barber

Sandra Jowers-Barber is an assistant professor of history at the University of the District of Columbia in Washington, D.C. Her research interest is in disability history, with a focus on African-American deafness. Jowers-Barber received her doctorate from Howard University and lives in Washington with her husband, John A. Barber, Sr., and their four teenage children.

♦ Chapter 10

Family Affair

The Girlfriend

Daddy had a penchant for skinny white women. This one looked like a model. Tall, lithe, big brown eyes, bouncing and behaving hair, and a personality to match. She was perky as hell—a California girl, through and through. Her flawless olive complexion was not that much lighter than mine, but it was the hair, the legs, and the Valley Girl speech that were a dead giveaway. She was a white girl. A nice, young, skinny white girl.

She was my dad's girlfriend when I was growing up. My siblings and I would go out to L.A. to visit him, and Kathie would always make sure we had a good time. She showered us with attention and was a genuinely sweet and gracious lady. She was as crazy about my dad as he was about her. And she treated us well.

She and I had a special connection. Don't know what it was, exactly, but we bonded. One day, she gave me a gold necklace that spelled out the word "winner." She had had it custom-made for herself, but now she was giving it to me. I asked her why she was giving it to me, and she said, "Because you are a winner."

I never forgot that. And I wore that necklace like it was another appendage. She spoke that word into my life, and I held on to it like it was a part of my name. Part of my birthright. And I believed it.

I am a winner.

I wore that necklace for years, long after she and Daddy broke up. But meeting and knowing her changed my life—in more ways than one.

My Father

I was named after my father's grandmother, Daisy Bass Kelly, who was biracial. I researched her background and discovered that the Census Bureau's classification of her race varied at different periods in time. When she was three years old, she was classified as white; when she was in her twenties, she was classified as mulatto; and by the time she married her second husband, Mr. Kelly, she was considered black.

My father's grandfather, Daisy's first husband, was William Henry Patrick Bass, and my daddy was named after him. He was white. So you can probably imagine that the Basses are some very fair black folks. Most could pass for white, but I don't think any did.

Howard Victor Bass, my grandfather, looked like a white guy. I never met him. He died when Daddy was a boy. Howard Bass, with his blond-haired, blue-eyed self, married a pretty brown woman named Arlene. From this union came my dad and two brothers, and the rest is a family tragedy.

From what I was told a long time ago, Howard died in an insane asylum, Arlene was too sick to raise her children alone, and the boys were divided among the Bass clan. Daddy was given to his grandmother, Daisy, and then bounced around to her other children, Aunt Irene and Uncle Bozo, to be raised.

Once Daddy was taken from his mother, Arlene, he was never returned. Daddy did not grow up with his mother. In fact, he didn't get to know her until he was about thirty years old. I was told that the Basses didn't want Arlene raising Daddy, because she was too dark.

My Mother

My mother was (and still is) a striking beauty. Daddy always said, even to this very day, that my mother is the most beautiful woman he ever met in his life. And he was referring to her unmitigated pulchritude. European features chiseled on Native American skin belied her African countenance and gait. In addition to having a perfect figure, she wore her hair very long. Black, billowy, bouncing and behaving hair. Past her shoulders, down her back, Farrah-Fawcett-meets-Diana-Ross-style hair.

Once upon a time, my mother was a model, a nationally ranked tennis champion, and a class queen in high school and college. She was Miss Ninth Grade and Miss Eleventh Grade at Turner High in Atlanta, Georgia. She would have been Miss Turner High, too, had she not excelled on an early college entrance exam and left high school a year earlier than her peers to attend Fisk University in Nashville, Tennessee.

Smart and beautiful, my mother was voted Miss Glamour while at Fisk. She met my father while there, too. They were just a couple of crazy Catholic kids who decided to elope one day. First came love, then came marriage, then came four babies in a baby carriage.

After my parents moved to Cleveland, Ohio, they had four children, but my parents separated when I was five years old. My father wanted to stay in his line of work, which took him to Los Angeles, and my mother wanted to move closer to her family in Atlanta. At least, that's how the story goes.

A single mother of four, my mother later completed law school while working full time at a law firm. She passed the bar at the age of 40 and started her own law practice. How she did this, I will never know. And I was there.

There were other courageously ambitious moments in my mother's life for which I was *not* there that have defined who my mother was and how she came to be who she is now. She was a student when she participated in the burgeoning, turbulent, and transformative Civil Rights Movement. She sat in on lunch counters in Tennessee and was even arrested once.

She and some friends were traveling to Charleston, South Carolina, from Atlanta one summer day. Before crossing the state line out of Georgia, the group stopped in some small town to use the bathroom. They pulled into a gas station, got out, and ventured inside the station. My mother asked the man inside, "Where is the bathroom?" The man told them they could go out back, and my mother told him he could go to hell.

Before they knew it, police had arrived, and they were truly about to piss in their pants. Hands in the air, knees wobbly, bodies shaking, the officers were yelling at them—calling them all kinds of names. An officer asked where they were from, and they told him Atlanta. As the officers began to shove them into the police car, the gas-station owner shouted, "You can tell that Mayor Hartsfield to go to hell."

"Go to hell" must have been a popular malediction among Georgians.

One of the boys in their group could pass for white. The officers spoke only to him, and he was the only person in the group permitted to speak to them. That boy's father bailed them out. I never found out when and where they finally got to use the toilet.

Around the same time as that incident, when my mother was home from Fisk for the summer, a prominent civil rights activist in Atlanta asked my mother and a couple of other black tennis players to show up at Bitsy Grant Tennis Center to play tennis. It was an unwritten rule, but Bitsy Grant did not allow blacks to play. When my mother and the others showed up, along with the activist and a throng of photographers and reporters, they asked if they could play tennis.

They were told no, because it was about to rain.

My mother replied, "Oh, well. We'll wait until it stops."

It never did rain. They never did play. They never did leave.

My mother's obstinacy landed her and another tennis player on the front page of the *Atlanta Journal*. Needless to say, Bitsy Grant became integrated soon after.

My mother doesn't often share these stories or speak of her accomplishments. I don't think she even sees them as successes. It was just her life, and she played the hand she was dealt the best way she knew how. Always a battle to fight. A struggle to overcome. A game to play. And life doesn't play fair.

The vicissitudes of life bring challenges as well as opportunities. It is up to us to strengthen our resolve with every blow to bounce back and to be the best that we can be in spite of our lot. Because "greater is He who is in me, than He who is in the world."

Me

I never thought I was pretty. And I always thought I was fat. Well, I thought I was fat because my father told me I was fat. He always told me and my two sisters that we were fat. Beautiful—but too fat. Well, how can you be beautiful *and* fat? So we must have just been fat, because if beauty is in the eyes of the beholder, and the beholder is your daddy, then you know he's biased. So we were beautiful, but fat. Just like he said.

He must have been fat, too, because he was always on a diet, always watching what he ate, always counting calories, always talking about weight, and always talking about food—about whether it was fattening or healthy.

We all looked just like him, all four of us. We weren't blessed with our mother's quintessential beauty; we were stuck with the Bass genes. Light, bright, with Afro-Euro-Indo-centric hair. Looking like we were mixed with something, but we were black. Just black. That one drop'll do it.

I had freckles.

"Yellow gone to waste" is what they called girls in the South with light skin and kinky hair. Thankfully, I wasn't a total waste. I was, as they called me in school, mellow-yellow, high-yellow, or red-bone. I wore two long plaits on both side of my head, and the kids would tease me and call me Indian. Back then, it was insult to be called Indian. But I was also called a nigger once.

Two white boys in my kindergarten class pulled one of my plaits and called me a nigger one day. I will never forget it. I can still see their faces. I was puzzled and hurt at the same time. I knew that calling me that name must have been a bad thing, because they did it while pulling my hair and taunting me. Nigger had to be a bad word, because they were pointing at me and laughing.

We moved from the North to the South in 1969. At the time, our neighborhood was predominately white. By 1971, it was predominately black. White folks got the hell out! What happened was notoriously referred to as "white flight" in the upscale community of Cascade Heights in Atlanta. Looks like we arrived right on time.

Kids in the neighborhood, as well as our newfound Southern cousins, used to tease my siblings and me for "talking white" or "talking funny." Well, where I came from, we said "Hi" instead of "Hay," referred to soda as "pop" instead of "drink," and we called our mother "mommy" instead of "mama." They called us Yankees and accused us of acting white. We were just "Northern."

It didn't help that Daddy dated white women. Growing up, we were teased by the whole family about that. They thought it was funny. We didn't see anything funny about it; it just was what it was. What did make it strange, though, was that nobody else we knew had a parent that dated a white person. Of course, nobody else we knew had parents that were separated either. That was uncommon in our community.

We were raised in a single-mother household (with the help of two loving, well-heeled, and well-educated grandparents)—*that* was the strange thing. But Daddy dating white women was not strange. We got used to it. Kathie Lee Romano broke us in.

Not only that, but by the looks of my grandmother, white folks being in the family didn't seem like a farfetched thought. Turns out, Granmommanem (translation: Grandmama and them, as they say in the South) were a mix of Irish and black, too! And my fair grandmother, God bless her, was color struck, too—just like the Basses!

I distinctly remember my grandmother telling us girls (there were thirteen grandchildren, and of that, nine were girls) when we came of age, "Don't be bringing home no black-ass, nappy-headed-ass nigger!" Well, we didn't care about all of that, as long as the boy was cute.

My grandfather, her husband, was definitely brown—a rich, red-dish, brown-paper-bag brown. His people's blood was mixed, both Native American and black. He passed the nappy-headed Negro test when he swept my grandmother off her feet during their courtship. He treated her like a queen, and she never had to work a day in her life.

Grandmama had it going on: a closet full of clothes, furs, hats, and shoes; a vanity full of the most exotic and expensive perfumes and loads of gems and jewelry; trips to Paris and island cruises; and beauti-ful gowns to wear to the most exclusive events. She was the proud wife of an Alpha Phi Alpha man, a Mason, a former player in the Negro baseball leagues, an entrepreneur, and a civil-rights financier.

Well, my grandmother would have been proud of me if she had had the opportunity to meet my first husband. He was light-skinned, with curly hair and hazel eyes. People teased me about having a predilection for light-skinned men, and both of us were taunted about how we would have a "white" baby if we ever had a child. I never did plan to marry a man for his complexion. It just happened that I married a man who people, at times, thought was my brother because we favored each other so much. I have even been mistaken for being his father's daughter, not his daughter-in-law. No, I fell in love with his spirit, his talent, and his creativity.

However, I quickly discovered that that shit don't pay the bills. Which brings me to my grandmother's other worldly advice on men: the mantra, "Cute ain't worth a dime." Clearly, she needed to expound on that maxim.

We eventually divorced, but not before producing a beautiful little girl who looks just like Pocahontas, straight off the reservation! Pure earth-brown skin, long wavy hair and Mongolian eyes. She fools everybody, the perfect blend of our disparate heritage.

Since then, I've dispelled the notion that being color-struck was a part of my character. My grandmother would spin in her grave if she saw my current husband. Not only is he black—he's *black*—he's African. Straight from the Motherland. A gorgeous Ghanaian man. An original man.

She'd be pissed.

Now, it all comes together. I was never fat. I just lost the image of who I really was. It was painted for me by outside influences, and not the influence right in my own home. I became a cheerleading captain, a class queen, a member of my high school and college tennis teams, and a member of the honors class at Spelman College. I went to school on an academic scholarship.

I was a lot like my mother.

When I looked to my father, I had to look through time and space to see him. And when I saw him in person, I saw the white women. They were always skinny. And they didn't look like me. I didn't mind the fact that they were white, but they *were* white. Nobody else's daddy dated white women. Yet they were always there, and they were always a part of our "family" because they were with Daddy. And they were cool!

It just felt as if he chose them over me. Over my sisters. Over my mother. But it wasn't a race thing; it was our whole family affair.

I did not see me. I did not see the original mold from which I was cast. That mold was my mother. My identity, forged by a fractured family, was nestled somewhere in my father's approval. My father, swinging in the land of "stars, movies, women, and cars," got metastasized by Hollywood.

A couple of years ago, I did some modeling for a major retailer. I had lost nearly forty pounds and was flown to New York City for a makeover and photo shoot. My hair was dyed blond and one of the women in the ad campaign, a white woman, remembered me from the year before and told me that at first, she hadn't recognized me. She thought I was a skinny white woman.

God has a sense of humor.

I am not Irish, not Native American, not African, not African American, but a combination of them all.

I am a black woman.

I am the fruit of my family, my society, and my relationship with the Almighty.

I am an advocate, a voice, a spirit, a healer, a teacher, a creator, and a conqueror.

I am "*a chosen race*, a royal priesthood, a holy nation, God's own people ..." (1 Peter 2:9)

I am beautiful, and I am a winner.

—**Kelley Bass Jackson**

Kelley Bass Jackson lives in Atlanta and works as a speechwriter. She has worked as a writer, editor, and communications and public relations consultant for more than fifteen years. She is currently working on her memoir, blogging about politics, and raising her daughter, Isabella Daisy. She can be reached at jacksonwoman@gmail.com and can be found on LinkedIn.

♦ Chapter 11

The Place I Call Home

What was I thinking? How could I have done this to my family?

I AM THE ELDEST OF TWO DAUGHTERS OF AN ARMY CHAPLAIN and a librarian, both now retired. My younger sister was six years my junior, and I really didn't get to know her well until we became adults. I was always away at boarding school.

As a child, my sister and I were raised in a tricultural existence. The military was our primary culture, since we lived on the Army post and attended schools provided for the families stationed there. There, we developed unique bonds with other children. We didn't have race in common (most of them were Caucasian, and they had a complicated time grasping our difficult experiences as we integrated the neighborhood), so that allowed us to share our common issues, such as our temporary living arrangements on the base. There was so much to consider as a part of a military family. We contemplated whether our next move would be out of the country. Would we have to learn a new language and new customs, losing a piece of ourselves in an adopted culture? If war came, would our fathers have to leave us? If they did leave, would they come back the same? Would they come back alive?

Our religious life off the military base (the prominent backbone of an African-American heritage) was our second culture, and that's where we interacted with our African-American friends. These were moments that enriched and strengthened our strong religious values. To this day, we are still in touch with friends from the church of our early childhood. We developed the close ties that often produce "play" cousins, aunts, and uncles, since our extended family members lived so far away.

Our third culture, our "real family," was what we embraced most—blood relatives whom we would visit during the fleeting summers and traditional holidays. It was always a joy for us. Our parents would pack the car with plenty of food, games, and clothes (in the early sixties, the South was still in the grip of Jim Crow; traveling by car meant staying with relatives versus hotels, where African Americans were not welcome). My family and I spent time with people who loved us, looked like us, and shared our ancestral heritage. We shared time looking at memorable photos and indulged in countless food fantasies.

Family is important to us: for years now, more than 800 relatives on my mother's side have gathered in Indiana on the third Sunday of every August. My father's family was based in Baltimore, and our visits with them would inevitably become tremendous musical events. Our uncles, aunts, and cousins joined us in singing our favorite hymns. We also played the piano, organ, and other instruments in accompaniment. My dad, who played the violin, always brought it along on our trips.

This tricultural existence of military, religion, and family ties was the never-ending cadence of life for our family, and I thank God daily that our parents were able to keep it balanced for us. It must have been extremely tough for our remarkable parents, but we never once heard them complain.

When I was five, I began to notice the stark differences between myself and other children in our neighborhood. The only other African-American family in the neighborhood with children our age was the Woods family (Major Earl Woods, who later remarried and fathered Tiger, the famous golfer). Everyone else was Caucasian. Being refused service at diners and not being able to go to Myrtle Beach like my Caucasian neighborhood friends was painful. Years later, while I was attending a primarily Caucasian boarding school, I was threatened with expulsion for wearing an Afro instead of straight hair. The same school later threatened me for asking a brave Caucasian male friend of mine to escort me to a school function. Although this treatment was and is awful, it was unfortunately commonplace in the 1960s.

To make matters worse, the African-American community wasn't exactly accepting of me either. When I attended an all-African-American East Coast academy (one of the many boarding schools I attended), I was once shunned by the female students for an entire week. I'm still not completely sure why they were so hostile toward me, but I believe it was because I was from California—and that was as strange to them as if I had been born on Mars. I wasn't harmed by physical means, but the emotional scars still sting.

My family had been transferred to Europe, and it seemed the African-American prep school would be a good place for me to be in the meantime. But it was not to be. The silent treatment was just one of my problems that year. After a few more incidents at the school, things got so bad that I opted to move off campus to stay with family members—a move that certainly didn't win me any friends. Being ostracized by Caucasian people was a daily occurrence—a hindrance, for sure, but it was to be expected. Being ostracized by my own people was a numbing, pervasive pain that negatively affected my adolescence. The stress of dealing with ridicule from Caucasians, and now African Americans (people from my *own culture*), was a powerful shock to my system. Soon, I left the African-American boarding school to finish my high school education at an all-Caucasian prep school that summer. Later, I joined my family abroad for my freshman year of college.

Europe wasn't the best choice either. The time in which we lived there was the zenith of racism in Europe, and I felt nostalgic for the family and friends I had left behind in America. I transferred to my parents' alma mater, a historically black university in the South, so I could attempt to commune with "my people" once again. I had my differences with the Caucasian culture, and the African-American culture eventually ran me out of the country, but nonetheless I viewed myself as a strong African-American woman who was a survivor. I knew I had to integrate these tricultures and ultimately learn to blend in with my community.

At college, I met my husband; we married two months after graduation. Ironically, we were neighbors as children. Both of our families lived on neighboring army posts; my father was the first

African-American Seventh-Day Adventist chaplain in the Army, and his father served a six-year hitch in order to fulfill his medical-school financial obligations. At the time we lived in the same area, I was a newborn and he was only four years old.

We finally met during my college years; he was attending medical school there. For the first three years we were married, my husband and I lived in the housing compound at an inner-city hospital. Violence in the area was commonplace, but even we were shocked that my husband's very first patient didn't make the five o'clock news: He had been dismembered with a hatchet and left for dead in the trunk of a car. Within three years, however, we bought our first home, in a predominantly Caucasian gated community.

Later, my husband and I stumbled upon a quaint, conservative neighborhood nestled in the foothills of Orange County, California. We decided it was the perfect location to raise our growing family of three girls. We agreed upon a lovely country French home in the heart of the community. Shortly after we moved in, our new neighbors, owners of one of the largest theater chains in the country, threw a lavish gala and invited our family to the bash. As we toured the estate and were warmly welcomed by neighbors and friends, we noticed that among the two hundred guests, we were the only African Americans—once again.

Astounded, I thought of my childhood, and of being required again and again to assimilate into a culture that was not my own. Once again, we were a minority surrounded by Caucasian peers. When I find myself in these situations, I remember the advice of my mother, who instructed us, "Be careful how you present yourself. This may be the only time the person you're talking to has anything to do with an African American." My thoughts raced, and I considered how my children would be affected by their minority status in our new neighborhood. I'd really never lived in one place for an extended period of time, since I came from a military family and my husband's medical career had us on the go for years after he graduated from school.

Raising three daughters in an exclusive, predominantly Caucasian community—where the nearest touchstone of African-American culture was thirty miles away—was a constant challenge. We looked to family functions, such as attending church on the weekends, participating in Jack and Jill meetings, and traveling to the National Medical Association's annual convention, to make strong connections between our daughters and other African-American youth with similar cultural experiences. They ended up in a subculture much like the one I had been raised in. It is simply a case of history repeating itself, unintentionally and paradoxically.

But just as my generation struggled with a cultural identity crisis, young people today have compensated for having to constantly calibrate to their various and influential surroundings. My youngest daughter, Kyndall, tells me she's had few challenges with cultural blending. Her age group seems less apprehensive and focuses more on group socializing and blending cultures in the name of "having a good time."

On the other hand, it also appears that the youth of today have a sense of cultural schizophrenia that was common in previous generations. Reflecting back on it all, the sixties were a unique, evolving moment in time for African Americans. When will our differences ever die? When will the situation ever change? When will the nation ever completely blend, so all our children have an equal opportunity in life? When can we finally do right by our forebears, our ancestors, and properly honor all they accomplished for us? As African Americans, let's uplift each other and celebrate the journeys we have experienced.

Despite all the challenges that my daughters have experienced, I feel confident that my husband and I have successfully raised three strong, African-American, and Christian women through God's divine power, strength, and grace.

—**Cynthia Powell-Hicks, MA, PhD**

Cynthia Powell-Hicks is a psychologist and businesswoman. She resides in Anaheim Hills, California, with her husband and family.

◆ Chapter 12

Loving You, Loving Me

A S I LISTEN TO AND OBSERVE MY BELOVED COMMUNITY, THE most serious problem I see is that many of us don't like who we are. Some African Americans don't like *being* African Americans. We are a unique people, unique in our culture, expression, and language. As we see ourselves through the prism of our African roots, we were always destined to stand out from our European counterparts in America. Our heritage is lively, colorful, and drenched in ebony hues and songs of celebration. Yes, we dress differently, style our hair in a variety of ways, and emanate a certain confidence. That's who we are.

We were taught to believe that these are all positive things, but some of us don't believe they are. Some have been diverted from this path of self-acceptance too easily by the negative messages of those within and outside our community. In effect, many of our brothers and sisters are constantly trying to be somebody else.

This identity crisis has origins in racism. I don't believe our people have determined not to love and accept themselves. A systematic campaign has been waged against us. The history of African Americans in this country is filled with contrasting views. *Yes, you can help build this country, but no, you're only three-fifths of a man. Yes, you have the right to vote, but no, you'll have to fight us to actually do it. Yes, you are an American, but you're classified as a minority.* Black people have been, and continue to be, treated as second-class citizens. There is anger and discontent that even today, in 2008, we are considered inferior members of society.

Our discontent is justified. In the aftermath of Hurricane Katrina, the federal government treated New Orleans like a Third-

World country. Although more than three years have elapsed since it occurred, my anger has not subsided. I am still aghast that our government could be so slow to aid fellow Americans. We were not refugees from a distant land. We were citizens of this country! There is no way that a family in the United States of America should have to stay on their roof for seven days! This was a disgrace for America, especially considering that our government had recently responded so quickly and consistently for tsunami victims on the other side of the world. How can we justify being a source of empathy and aid to other nations and turn our back on our own people? I believe God is going to hold our elected officials responsible for their ungodly acts.

Even now, after so many of our brothers and sisters have suffered, the forces of racism and hate are still in play in New Orleans. Although people are starting to rebuild, a facade remains. The money to build new homes that had been promised has barely trickled in, and many of the promises the government made have yet to come to fruition. How long can men and women be expected to stay away from the land they built their homes on? But this is all part of the plan, a plan to keep black people from returning to the city, a plan to make us tired and weary so we'll just throw up our hands and stay wherever we have landed. It's so wrong! What would New Orleans be without African-American culture—our music, our cuisine, our language, and our hospitality? Yes, *our flavor.*

Unfortunately, Katrina was just the next item on a list of nonaffirming moments for black people. We're dealing with racism, and we're still dealing with ourselves. In a very sad turn of events, the anger we have felt and the pain we have endured has taken root, and we're witnessing our community turning on itself. We are afraid to trust or support one another, and that has had dire consequences. We are killing each other, stealing from one another, and losing the capability to love and respect our brothers and sisters. It's become a generational curse. It's imperative that we take individual responsibility because it's not "them" hurting us—it's *us* hurting *us,* in myriad ways.

Without question, the church has an important role in changing the mental, emotional, and social landscape of the black community. It's a unique environment where the positive and negative aspects of our people intersect. It has to be the place where we can consistently address self-love and provide examples of partnership. It is here, through God's Word, social programs, and outreach, that we can continue those internal and external healings. The church is where our young people should be able to find positive role models if none exist in their homes (although Lord knows there should be). Be it through athletic leagues, rap sessions, or targeted messages, the black church has to be able to provide that alternative to men and women, boys and girls. We give them avenues to express themselves by constantly reaffirming that it is God's will that they be gifted and black. Those two concepts are not mutually exclusive.

We must also address the real issues that our members are dealing with. For example, my ministry has endeavored to dialogue more frequently and provide social programs to serve the needs of persons facing HIV/AIDS. Some in the church might say, "It wouldn't happen if you would get saved and live right!" But it *is* happening, and we've got to deal with that. We have to address prevention, medication, and civil rights. It is imperative that we have ministries to address *all* problems our congregation faces, even the "dirty secrets." It's not enough to hold services on Sunday and then lock up and turn the lights off until the following Sunday. We've got to be a church in action, one that is always extending love and support to our members instead of judgment. The presbytery has to be an example of acceptance and of people with different views, perspectives, and opinions who are able to work together toward common goals.

If we are to restore our self-respect, we must start by appreciating the culture God birthed us into. There's still this place in our minds where we don't like who we are. It's amazing to me that the very things we try to distance ourselves from or downplay are the very things other racial groups emulate about us! They try to sing like us, dance like us, prepare soul food (without the soul) like us, and adorn themselves (right on down to cornrows in their hair) just like us! All of these things are rooted in African culture.

Back in the 1960s, we cried, "*I'm black and I'm proud!*" We've got to get back to that sense of pride again. We can't just talk about it.

It has to be part of our daily lives. We must recognize that we have a place right here, in the United States of America. We built this country, after all! Once we realize that and take hold of our cultural pride and self-esteem, we'll be able to reclaim our position in this country.

If you like yourself, even if other people don't, you'll be fine. Nothing can change the rightness of who you are! In effect, loving you means loving me. That collective love is our strength and our redemption.

—**Bishop Paul S. Morton, Sr.**

Paul S. Morton, Sr. is the presiding bishop of the Full Gospel Baptist Church Fellowship. In addition to his worldwide evangelistic ministry, Morton continues to spread the word of God through his Changing a Generation *daily radio and weekly television broadcasts, which air in several markets nationwide.*

◆ Chapter 13

"Golden" Women of Faith
(Originally Titled
"A Salute to Black Women")

THIS IS A SALUTE TO ME
TO YOU, MY MOTHER, MY SISTER, AUNTIE, COUSIN,
FRIEND
THIS IS A SALUTE TO THE BEAUTY THAT EXUDES FROM
WITHIN
FROM THE SOULS OF GOLDEN WOMEN, CHAMPIONS
WHO DARED TO DEFY THE ODDS, JUST BY LIVING.

THIS IS IN PRAISE OF GOLDEN WOMEN,
WOMEN OF FAITH
SINGING OUR STORY, SINGING OUR SONG
GIVING ME THE GRACE AND CONFIDENCE TO STAND
TO THINK OF MYSELF NO LESS THAN ANY MAN
SISTER, YOU CAUSE ME TO SHINE,
IN THE MIDST OF DARKNESS
YOU ARE …
A PEARL, A QUEEN
RARE ESSENCE, BEAUTIFUL LIKE ME
A GOLDEN GIRL, BLACK GOLD DIVA
GOLDEN SISTA, GOLDEN SHE … IS
BEAUTY, LOVE
SOUL, POWERFUL,
PROUD
P O E T R Y … IN MOTION

STAND UP, AND GIVE PRAISE TO GOD FOR
THE STRENGTH OF THE GOLDEN WOMAN
THE ELEGANCE OF THE GOLDEN WOMAN
THE GRACE AND INTELLIGENCE OF THE
GOLDEN WOMAN
THE SINCERE FAITH OF THE GOLDEN WOMAN.
AND WOMEN, IF NO ONE EVER TAKES THE TIME
TO GIVE YOU YOUR PRAISE, DO NOT HESITATE TO
STOP
AND SALUTE YOURSELF …
FOR YOU WERE FEARLESSLY AND WONDERFULLY
MADE!

—Stacey Evans Morgan

Stacey Evans Morgan is a Los Angeles-based businesswoman and television writer.

Chapter 14

Mourning a Child's Choice

THE "FIVE STAGES OF GRIEF" ELISABETH KÜBLER-ROSS WROTE of in her 1969 book, *On Death and Dying*, were reactions to death—someone else's or one's own. But Kübler-Ross's process also applies to other kinds of tragedy. I went through each of these stages after being greeted with the news that my eighteen-year-old daughter had decided, after her freshman year, to drop out of college.

Denial. Oh, no, you didn't just say that after wasting nearly $20,000, you've decided to jump off the only guaranteed path of success in America to "take a break and find yourself!"

Anger. I will knock you into the middle of next year—just in time to start a new semester—if you persist in this foolishness.

Bargaining. If you just reconsider the negative impact this will have on your life, you will see how big a mistake this is. You want a car? You don't need a car if you're not in college. Do you want a car?

Depression. It must have been something I've done. How could I have stressed education more? Maybe I should have visited her classes more often, helped with her homework each night, kept her at home, and driven her to and from school daily. Maybe I should just lie here on my couch, the couch to which she will return and sleep every day, all day, doing nothing, aspiring to nothing, feeling nothing. I am such a failure.

Acceptance. This is where I am now, three weeks after learning that my beloved daughter—the brilliant actress, artist, singer, writer, veterinarian, and preschool teacher—has decided that she doesn't know what she wants out of life, what to feel about life, or what to contribute to life.

It has been three weeks since I reminded her of the two choices I gave her, the two paths by which she could gain skills, and the consequences of each.

The first: Attend school full-time to learn—wait, not just learn, but master—a trade that will provide the lifestyle you want.

The second: Work full-time now and gain on-the-job skills for the lifestyle you must accept.

There was no third option that included lying around at home and working part-time at McDonald's. Not that there's anything wrong with that. It is respectable employment for those who aspire to it or for those who have settled for less than they can do in an economy that shows no favorites. But I come from a family of educators. My mother was an English teacher. My father was a chemistry professor. My grandmother was a substitute teacher who quit her job to take care of her three grandchildren because her daughter contracted multiple sclerosis at the same time that she lost her husband.

And my grandfather? He was a powerfully built, stocky man with skin the color of coal. He had a sixth-grade education, but he always made sure we could afford good schools and books. That's right. In the structure he built while working in a cotton mill, cleaning up lawyers' offices downtown, and driving a cab, we had a beautiful, loving home with a library of our own. I read our World Book Encyclopedia volumes as much as my Nancy Drew mysteries. I knew the works of Langston Hughes and James Baldwin and Ernest Hemingway. I revered Lorraine Hansberry and Alice Walker. I still remember crying after finishing *A Tree Grows in Brooklyn*.

There was never a time in my life when I didn't know I was going to college. It was not an expectation. It was the law.

I raised my daughter the same way. We journeyed from "Whoville" to the shores of Normandy. I introduced her to *The Cat in the Hat* and Dr. Martin Luther King, Jr. We traversed history and math and science together—all in preparation for the day I'd drop her off on a campus to study these things alone.

The day I did drop her off, I felt like I was living a rerun. I had been here before a thousand times in my head. But in my head, I did not lose her.

That day, as I walked out of her pink-on-pink-on-pink room, watching her watch me, her head slightly tilted and smiling that glorious, goofy grin she gives me when she thinks I'm being silly, I didn't realize I'd lost her. If I had, I would have moved in and embarrassed her royally, but I would have done anything to keep her in school.

Instead, I drove home and pretended that she was grown up. I wasn't there while she made discoveries of her own.

She discovered music and clubs and boys and freedom.

She discovered sleeping until three in the afternoon and having breakfast for dinner.

She discovered a life that didn't involve asking me for permission.

She loved it, and she really hated that school got in the way.

Oh, we all have our freshman traumas. I shall spill neither here, nor to her, the mistakes that I survived when I first made my own rules. But I didn't quit.

When I was four, my mother made me memorize a single phrase to guide my life: "A quitter never wins, and a winner never quits." My siblings and I hated that phrase as much as we hated walking over to her wheelchair so she could pinch us each time we used incorrect grammar. (She especially hated "ain't.")

When my daughter told me she was done with college, she may as well have told me she was pregnant with the child of a gang member on the lam from the FBI for murder, and she'd see me when she'd see me.

OK, maybe not.

But for a moment, the words were in a foreign language. I searched for meaning in her face. I actually thought I had misheard her, and greeted her with that quick, startled sound that parents make when they heard exactly what their child said, but dare him or her to say it again.

"Whah?"

She said it again, telling me that it was my fault, that she had told me she wasn't ready for college, and that I'd made her go anyway. She explained that she now needed a year off.

From the looks of her grades, I told her, she'd already *had* a year off. So what was the problem now?

"College isn't for everybody," she told me, quoting every bad influence she must have met on and off campus. I wanted to hunt them down like dogs, those miscreant influences without ambition who had the nerve to tell her not to excel.

"College is not for everybody," I repeated. "But that does not apply to you."

It does not apply to any of the young people I mentor, regardless of their backgrounds. I've peppered hundreds of journalism students and dozens of foster children with the same lessons, adages, and expectations that I have for my own daughter. I did all of that only to learn that the child I'm closest to was listening the least. I wanted to tell her that, but she stopped me cold in my tracks.

She hit me with the one thing I could not change, the one thing that had never been true before, ever, in our lives.

"You can't make me."

And there it was, lying between us like a chasm that might keep us from touching each other ever again. The emotions were so swirled in me that I could not speak. I imagined saying that to my grandmother.

Well, actually, I didn't. I couldn't imagine that. My mind would not let me go there. She would have heard the first two words, realized where they were going, and consciousness would have ended. I talked back to my grandmother, all four-foot-eleven of her, only once. We were in the kitchen of the house I grew up in, the place where I learned about books and dreams and respect and admiration. She had just told me that I couldn't do something or couldn't have something or couldn't go somewhere. Whatever the "couldn't" actually was is irrelevant. After she spoke, as I leaned on the oak hutch that held her dishes—the good ones with the ring of flowers—I said something back to her, under my breath, with my head down.

Neither my sister nor my brother remembers there being any warning. Of course, I can't either. My grandmother walked away from the stove, black skillet in hand, and hit me. I don't know where she hit me. It had not happened before, and she never had to do it again.

But this is 2008, and one thing I decided when raising my child was that violence was not necessary. Spankings could not accomplish what a good, old-fashioned talking-to might. At that moment, three weeks before now, I wished I had spanked her.

I am growing into this acceptance, and so is my daughter. It is harder for her. You see, I told her that our original agreement applies. So if she decided to forgo the path I'd chosen for her to learn her life skills, then she'd have to take the other path: full-time work and living on her own. I told her that as of that moment, she lived in a different tax bracket, and that she could no longer afford many of the things she had become accustomed to: amusement park trips, beauty salon visits, expensive clothes, or a car.

My daughter is now looking for a job on a bus line and a nearby apartment. She is also considering accepting a part-time job as a nanny with one of my best friends, who, like me, believes in all children. When I told her what happened, she said, "Send her to me." Sometimes being a good parent means knowing when to accept help.

For the first time, my daughter is creating a budget, and she cannot believe how many items are on it. As I listened to her ask about electricity and a phone line and talking about needing neither, I kicked myself for not making her keep up the checkbook ledger I'd gave her when she was eight, the one where I made her write down any of the money I spent on her.

She has so much to learn, and she is hating it. I figure she'll be back in school by January. At least, I hope so. But if not, I will wait for her, patiently, with a "faith that the dark past has taught us," as James Weldon Johnson wrote so brilliantly. I will always believe in her and her future and what she has to give this world. She remains the hope and the dream of the slave. The dream, deferred briefly, will hit her like lightning, and she will find her place.

And as she gets used to the lifestyle to which she now must become accustomed, I'll continue to talk to young girls—including my own—about studying and learning and preparing for the life you want, instead of accepting the life you're given.

That is, after all, what college and parents are for.

—**Rochelle Riley**

Rochelle Riley is an award-winning journalist and a columnist for the Detroit Free Press.

PART II
CULTURE

♦ Chapter 15

Soul Music:
The DNA of Our Destiny

Hello. My name is Scott Galloway, and I am a music junkie—have been all my life.

FOR FORTY-THREE YEARS NOW, MY WORK AND MY LIFE HAVE been about music. I've played music professionally as a drummer in funk-rock bands rehearsing in my family's garage, and I've been a musician-for-hire backing singers in musical revues. I practically lived in record shops, working my way up from counter clerk to buyer of all music merchandise for a major chain's showcase store in Los Angeles. I contributed to one of Los Angeles's best-remembered radio stations, an eclectic FM broadcast laboratory known as KUTE, "The Quiet Storm." There, we turned a blind eye to genre programming and instead used open minds and highly skilled ears to weave an audio blend that stimulated pan-cultural musical explorations. For the last two decades, I've been a music journalist, interviewing artists across a broad spectrum of music, but primarily from what the great soul musician Donny Hathaway poetically dubbed "The Black Pool of Genius."

I suspect I emerged from the womb with ears already tuned to rhythm, harmony, and melody, but I know that a significant factor in the finer tuning of my musical aptitude came from the blessing of having both my parents, and their divergent musical interests, in my life. Dad is the deep one, heavy into post-bop jazz (especially if there are vibes involved—from Lionel Hampton and Milt Jackson to Bobby Hutcherson and Roy Ayers), blues of all hues, and the occasional hit ditty that he couldn't shake from his mind, like country star Johnny Paycheck's "Slide Off of Your Satin Sheets" blaring from a honky-tonk jukebox. My mom prefers the popular stuff, including anything from golden-era Motown, Johnny Mathis, or Gato Barbieri (she just loves a sweet man who can blow a mean horn). She also has a weakness for white boys with a touch of soul, from Tom Jones to Michael McDonald. I'm not sure what's up with that. All I know is she had a jump on the rest of Black America when it came to the Bee Gees. She picked "Nights on Broadway" as a smash the first time she heard it, half asleep one night on a Top 40 station. That was two years before everyone else caught Saturday night fever!

One of my most vivid early memories of being profoundly moved by a piece of music was literally at Mom and Dad's feet. We were all in the living room—they in their respective chairs, and five-year-old me lying facedown on the floor. I was in sheer ecstasy for one simple reason—the stereo was on, and we were listening to an eight-track tape of Isaac Hayes's *Hot Buttered Soul*. Although I'd heard the songs many times before and already loved them, I'd never *listened* to them: fully engaged, rapturously focused, and allowing all the marbles that were my virgin senses to be completely rearranged by their majesty. "Walk on By" was a straight-up soul symphony after Ike had his way with Burt Bacharach's masterful blueprint. "One Woman" was classic Southern R&B, with a pretty piano intro and verses leading to walloping choruses all in service of the story of a man torn between two women (whatever that meant). And "Hyperbolicsyllabicsesquedalymistic" is a preposterous word, of course, *and* a fantastic song where Isaac—backed by the Bar-Kays—turned on, stretched out, and got down to some serious noggin-rockin' F-U-N-K!

But it was the final song that did a real number on me: Brother Hayes's eighteen-minute-long sermonized version of Jimmy Webb's "By The Time I Get to Phoenix." With the drummer sticking away time on the bell of the ride cymbal and the organ droning a world-weary chord, Isaac took his time telling the story of a woman who was making a fool out of a man who kept coming back for more. "Seven times he left this woman," Isaac preached, "and seven times he came back." This being the eight-track, just as the story was getting good, you had to wait for the "beep" pause between Track 3 and Track 4 for the story "to be continued."

Hayes couldn't have had me more hooked if he was dangling chocolate Jell-O pudding before my eyes. By the time he finally started singing about hittin' the road for real "this time," my mom looked down at me with some concern. I was hiding my face in my arms, but my body was giving me away.

"Scotty, what's wrong?" she asked.

I didn't answer.

She nudged me gently with her foot and said, "Did you hear me?"

Slowly, I looked up at her and then my dad. My face was flushed and streaked with tears. Finally, I mustered the strength to respond.

"Why did that lady have to be so mean to that man?" I don't remember getting any kind of real answer, but they got a big laugh!

Beyond the greatness of that music, what I cherish most about that memory is that it was time we shared together. And it wasn't the last time. Attaching such vivid memories to something I loved positively reinforced that passion in me. Today, as media is niched to the nth degree and "personal devices" like Blackberries, cell phones, and anything with ear buds enable folks to reside in their own private mental zip code, moments like the one I just shared are scarce.

However, proactively used, these same innovations can bridge gaps great and small between generations. I don't have children, but if I did, I'd encourage them to share songs and artists that interest them, 'cause I *know* I'd be cueing up Monk and Dennis Edwards–era Temptations for them on my iPod and making them endure clips of the Ohio Players and Max Roach on YouTube.

Black music is a powerful cultural touchstone. Gospel gives us our holy spirit. The blues have our backs when we're down. Reggae gives us righteous uplift. Jazz reminds us of our intuitive freedom. Funk enables us to dance our way out of constrictions, and slow jams are the soundtrack to our sweet sooky-ooky-ooo-wees! It's all soul music that reflects the very definition of anything and everything we are and aspire to be. Our finest music has inspired the way we dress, the way we prepare our meals, what we choose to drive, the way we move, the way we communicate with each other, and the way we just "be."

Very early in life, I learned this firsthand. From when I was age three to age seven, my family was the only black family on our street in Rialto, California. I got along pretty well with everybody, but there were very few kids of color in my school. Since I was quite the little "sponge" for learning, I soaked up all the local lingo—everything from "neato" to "spiff"—but I remained starved for *anything* "solid" or "right on!" I consumed any black entertainment voraciously, waiting on pins and needles for the next episode of *Julia* or *The Flip Wilson Show*. I reveled in the sights and sounds of my people.

Best of all, I couldn't wait for Saturday afternoons and *Soul Train*. The minute the show would end, all that "screamin'-n-hollerin'" music sent me into a breakdownin' funky chicken spaz attack. I'd dance for all the neighborhood to see on the brick wall that bordered the walkway to our front door. I was fascinated by the way we moved, talked, dressed, wore our hair, and naturally expressed our "blackness" with one another (or as freely as Don Cornelius would allow on his nationally syndicated show). It's strange to admit now that there were times I studied the show to figure out how I was supposed to "act" and "be." Thank God we moved an hour west to L.A. in '72.

These days, I am deeply concerned about what I see as our youth's systematic disconnect from cultural pride and history. We see it as arts programs are sliced out of school curriculums. We see it in the music videos and movies that feed them an unbalanced diet of booty, bling, and bloodshed. We hear it in radio programming that segregates artists so severely that kids never hear an artistic adult voice of reason and wisdom, which leads to a record industry that isn't remotely interested in the next Bill Withers or Roberta Flack. When I was growing up in L.A., blacks had more than one station to listen to, with a broad range of representation: the O'Jays and the J5, Stacy Lattisaw and Stephanie Mills, "Tonight is The Night" and "Wishing on a Star," "It's Cheaper to Keep Her" and "Always and Forever."

In a recent issue of *Vibe*, rap pioneer Chuck D hit the Funkadelic nail on the head when he said, "We're living in a youth culture that strays a lot of people away from maturing gracefully." With aging club divas Botoxing and breaking their necks to remain perceived as young, O.G. rappers trying to hang on to a rep way past its prime, and "old-school" R&B vets simply being too old to matter to youth, we are lacking models of leadership in music. Who will be the next Lou Rawls to endorse an important cause like the United Negro College Fund? Which superstars of today will be able to carry their fan bases onto "The Tomorrowland Stage" while retaining the respect of the ones coming behind them? Perhaps it will be Alicia Keys, Usher, Anthony Hamilton, Beyoncé, Jay-Z, Chanté Moore, Kenny Lattimore, classical pianist Awadgian Pratt, upright bassist Esperanza Spalding, gospel's Israel and New Breed, or last-band-standing Mint Condition.

Ultimately, we will have to start with those who have already earned the stripes of respect. Thanks to the easy accessibility of information and entertainment the Internet provides, even people of meager means are able to study the masters in any given genre. It costs next to nothing to study the pioneers: Sammy Davis, Jr., then James Brown after him, then Michael Jackson after him, all the way down to Chris Brown. Young people can begin to delineate excellence from average, sifting and separating true talent's amazing artistry from the tragedies of their reality. They'll learn to embrace innovative musicians and skilled songwriters from the hacks and walking copycat jukeboxes. They'll get back to aspiring toward the unity and collaborative spirit of bands instead of the trappings of self-centered stars.

Now that we have "Baracked the Vote," our country will begin seriously reinvesting in education instead of steadily refilling war chests. Most importantly, there will be homes where—through a natural osmosis of handed-down cultural touchstones, traditions, histories, and ways of being—that task will be lovingly attended by family and community. That's the way it was meant to be.

—A. Scott Galloway

An Ann Arbor, Michigan, native, A. Scott Galloway dedicates his contribution to this book to his family: his parents, Dr. Arnold John Galloway and Beverly Bernice Billups; his maternal grandparents, Dorothy and Frank Williams; his Aunt Pookie; his cousin Berene Miller; his sister, Pamela Joy Galloway; the memory of his paternal grandparents, Charles & Marie Abbott; his extended family—and every neighbor who ever loaned him a record!

Galloway is the music editor of Urban Network *magazine and the composer of more than 200 liner-note essays in CD packages for artists including Quincy Jones, Curtis Mayfield, Minnie Riperton, Donny Hathaway, Billy Cobham, George Benson, Bobby Womack, Bill Cosby, Brenda Russell, Steve Arrington, D'Angelo, and Heavy D.*

◆ Chapter 16

Black Like You

BOTH OF MY PARENTS FELT THE SAME PAIN, THE SAME STRUG-
gle and disenfranchisement that thousands of other people of
African descent felt when they arrived in this country from
Cuba. My mother in particular was very active and politically involved, organizing marches and taking part in protests to bring about
a change for racial equality in this country. Of course, it was much
different here than it had been for her in Cuba, because at least here
she had an opportunity to use her voice without fear of becoming a
political prisoner.

My name is Laz Alonzo, and I am an American actor. I was born
to Cuban parents who immigrated to the United States before I was
born. I am also black, and people are always so surprised to know of
my bicultural identity. It's surprising to me that so many people in
this country—both black and white—are unaware of the array of
racial diversity in this hemisphere.

It's frustrating to me that my talents as an actor have not been
better leveraged to both English- and Spanish-speaking audiences,
but the blame cannot just be placed on prevailing attitudes about
race by Americans alone. You don't see folks who are black like me
on Telemundo or Univision either. A pronounced color line exists
among the Latino population, even though a significant number
of the Latino population is also of African descent. There are black
Mexicans, black Colombians, black Panamanians, and black Brazil-
ians. In fact, blacks in South and Central America and the Caribbean far outnumber the black population here in the States. In those
countries, this behavior is a remnant of Colonial times, when the
Spanish elite associated higher status to those who looked more "Eu-

ropean." I am not alone in making this observation, as I have Latin friends with "indigenous" features and/or darker complexions who I know suffer the same types of prejudice.

There's a lot that African Americans can do to change things, but first they must understand the rich diversity of the global black experience. African Americans must recognize that in Martinique, blacks speak French; in Cuba, Puerto Rico, and the Dominican Republic, they speak Spanish; and in Brazil, they speak Portuguese.

Blacks who work in the entertainment industry can play a key role in spreading information about the rich melting pot of black culture worldwide. Being black is an identity without language barriers, and connecting with *all* the markets can be both culturally enriching and profitable. Consider Tyler Perry's success as an example. Whether you like what he does or not, he has successfully identified an underserved consumer base for entertainment. He deserves applause for making movies and television programs that are relevant to our culture. Perry has has tapped into a huge market with products that speak to the needs of his audience.

As an African-American actor with Cuban roots, I see this country through a much larger lens. I believe my message has the potential be a unifying force for black people—certainly *all* the black people of the Americas. We must open our hearts and minds and expand our understanding of the definition of what it means to be African American.

—Laz Alonzo

Actor Laz Alonzo is a graduate of Howard University who grew up in Washington, D.C. He has a growing body of acting credits on television, the stage, and the big screen.

Chapter 17

What It Means to Be Gullah*

Dats right, I am a Gullah, a saltwater Geechee/Gullah.

ALLOW ME TO EXPLAIN—GULLAH CULTURE THRIVES ALONG the coastal and immediate inland communities of South Carolina, Georgia, southern North Carolina, and northern Florida. The cultural branches of Gullahs (or Geechees, as we're also called)—physical features, dietary practices, language and/or tonality, spirituality, beliefs, crafts, and customs—are rooted in our West African heritage. Like the vibrant, verdant summertime marsh grass of the tidal creeks and swamps of Gullah communities, awareness and appreciation of Gullah culture in the world community has grown apace.

In 2005, U.S. Congressman James E. Clyburn (D-South Carolina) proposed a $20 million bill to protect the Gullah way of life by establishing a Gullah/Geechee Cultural Heritage Corridor. The legislation would provide for three interpretive centers—two in South Carolina and one in Georgia—where visitors could learn about Gullah culture. The bill also included provisions for building restoration and other projects.

In 2004, The National Trust for Historic Preservation named the Gullah coast as one of the nation's eleven most endangered historical sites.[1] Gullah festivals, institutes, conferences, and even operas woo tens of thousands of spectators yearly. A maturing generation of Nick Jr. viewers worldwide, along with their parents and guardians, regu-

---

1. Tibbetts, 11.

* This essay is adapted from the preface of the book *Gullah Branches, West African Roots*.

larly sing along with my wife Natalie and me, "Let's All Go to Gullah Gullah Island," our award-winning show's theme song.

Whereas *Gullah Gullah Island* is imaginary, Gullah culture really exists. And others are echoing sentiments stated by Congressman Clyburn: "The Gullah/Geechee culture is the last vestige of fusion of African and European languages and traditions brought to these coastal areas. I cannot sit idly by and watch an entire culture disappear that represents my heritage and the heritage of those who look like me."[2]

My own personal awareness and appreciation of Gullah culture also has grown since the 1986 publication of my first book, *Reminiscences of Sea Island Heritage: Legacy of Freedmen on St. Helena Island*. (The book's sequel, *Gullah Branches, West African Roots*, documents what I subsequently learned about my heritage.) In the preface to *Reminiscences*, I remarked,

> ... an aesthetic documentation of the lifestyles, customs, superstitions and lore of the St. Helena Island people, which soon may be altogether forgotten. As condominiums and resort communities become as commonplace as the Spanish moss draping aged oaks, and as third and fourth generation Islanders cease to identify with a heritage dear to their forebears, that heritage is being hushed and stilled. This work is a time capsule, presented with Sea Island flavoring. It is a people's story of how they "got over" by surviving the hard times, and how and what they learned about life.[3]

At that time, Gullah was a term used more readily by scholars, linguists, and academicians. Geechee was an invective or insult. Sea Island heritage, however, had become a term of endearment and ownership.

Following the publication of my first novel, my wife Natalie and I packaged oral histories, songs, stories, and historical photographs into a multimedia theatrical performance piece entitled *Sea Island*

---

2. Derrick, Hope. Clyburn (SC06)—Press Release.
3. Daise, xvi.

Montage. As we began a performance at an elementary school in the late 1980s, one student turned completely around in her seat, closed her eyes, and covered her ears. Later, she confided to her teacher that the images were "ugly." She didn't want to hear the songs or listen to the stories because she was unaccustomed to a positive presentation of her own cultural identity. *I've learned that many Gullah people hate being Gullah.*

After a performance at a national conference some years ago, a viewer sought us out as we left the stage. An element of one of our stories had given her an *aha!* moment. An old Gullah belief dictates that one should not comb his or her hair outdoors, because a bird could make a nest in the hair, thus leading to headaches. That caught her attention. She was from California, she told us, and her mother-in-law, who was from a South Carolina island, had recently come to live with her. For some reason, the mother-in-law kept bagsful of hair around the house. Until she'd seen our performance, the woman had written her mother-in-law off as simple-minded, weird, and wacky. *I've learned that many people don't understand Gullah ways.*

I've spoken Gullah during performances and watched as viewers have responded with surprise at how readily they understood a Gullah word or expression (maintaining an air of academic dignity all the while). *I've learned that lots of people who may not have wanted to identify with being Gullah really do.*

On the other side of the spectrum, I've also met white Americans with relatives who were raised in isolated Sea Island communities. In these communities, African descendants greatly outnumbered whites. As a result, their relatives speak Gullah, practice Gullah beliefs and traditions, and respect the culture, they've told me. "Are we not Gullah, or of Gullah heritage?" many have asked. Many *beenyahs* (native islanders) have argued vehemently that *comeyahs* (transplants to Gullah communities) are not and never will be Gullah. *I've learned that Gullah ownership, for some, is a conundrum.*

As the marsh grass grows, some cultural enthusiasts have indoctrinated others with false beliefs, such as that Gullah people:

- Only live in shacks.
- Sing plantation ditties.
- Dress in antebellum or regal West African apparel.

- Only work as farmers, shrimpers, oystermen, sweetgrass basket makers, or craftsmen and women.
- Can't consider identifying with Gullah heritage unless they can document it unequivocally.

During my presentations to groups about the Gullah culture, I cite ten memorable cultural touchstones that readily identify Gullah heritage. I use the tune of "Children, Go Where I Send Thee," a coded song Harriet Tubman used as she led hundreds of slaves along the Underground Railroad, to declare: "Dats Right, I Am a Gullah." The song concludes by stating, "I'm Gullah cause my ancestas came from West Africa."

Many African Americans, I'm aware, are stumped about researching their ancestry. In July 2006, I participated in a DNA testing program sponsored by the National Geographic Society's Genographic Project. I found that my deep ancestral history, with genetic markers reaching back about 60,000 years, is from sub-Saharan Africa. My report stated:

> You are descended from an ancient African lineage. In North Africa, this haplogroup (E3a) is found at frequencies of 5 to 10 percent among Berbers, Tunisians, and Moroccan Arabs. Because it is also predominant in West Africa, many African Americans also trace their genetic history to this line of descent ... The man who gave rise to your first genetic marker in your lineage probably lived in northeast Africa in the region of the Rift Valley, perhaps in present-day Ethiopia, Kenya, or Tanzania, some 31,000 to 79,000 years ago. Scientists put the most likely date for when he lived at around 50,000 years ago. His descendants became the only lineage to survive outside of Africa, making him the common ancestor of every non-African man living today.

Longing to know my ancestral legacy from the period of the transatlantic slave trade, however, I pursued subsequent DNA testing with a firm called African Ancestry, Inc. I, like many African Americans, yearned to trace my heritage to a particular African country or village or clan, where the genetic markers are evident in body language, physical features, and spiritual connection. My sixteen-year-old grandnephew, Kendall Session of Sumter, South Carolina, discovered just such a link when visiting Kenya on a missionary trip with his father, Ernest, during the summer of 2006. Kendall is the son of my niece, Marva Carr Session, the eldest child of my eldest sibling.

"They told me I looked like them!" Kendall said with excitement. "They'd tell me that maybe my family's ancestors had come from Kenya to America to work as slaves. They said my facial features, especially my eyes, looked like theirs. And, yes, my eyes *do* resemble theirs. And I saw baskets like the ones I see on the islands of South Carolina. And the songs they sang—the rhythms and the harmonies—were like the ones sung on the islands. I felt like, yeah, maybe they really are my people!" Interestingly, other nieces and nephews have told me that they're often asked if they're Kenyan.

When I received my DNA report from African Ancestry, I opened the envelope slowly with nervous anticipation. I'd felt at home when I'd visited Ghana and Sierra Leone, but just where were my people really from?

"The mitochondrial DNA (maternal) sequence that we determined from your sample shares ancestry with the Temne people in Sierra Leone today," the report read. "The Y chromosome [paternal] DNA markers that we determined from your sample share ancestry with the Ewe and Akan people in Ghana today."

"So, Daddy," my daughter Sara proclaimed. "You had a family reunion each time you went to Africa and didn't even know it, huh?"

I've learned that being Gullah has become highly esteemed. Such was the opinion of the nearly 2,500 people gathered for a daylong celebration of the release of *De Nyew Testament,* a Gullah version of the New Testament published by the American Bible Society. Ardell Greene, one of the charter members of the Sea Island Translation Team of St. Helena Island, South Carolina, worked on the project in cooperation with Wycliffe Bible Translators. Greene spoke during the festivities.

"In 1979, my husband and I were asked to help to do a Bible in Gullah," she stated. Her husband, Ervin Greene, was pastor of the historic Brick Baptist Church on St. Helena Island. "At that time, if people asked if I was Gullah, I would say, 'No, I am not Gullah!' We told Pat and Claude Sharpe (the Wycliffe Bible consultants), no, we would not help with the project because the educators have said that Gullah should not be spoken.

"But I've grown in [respect for] Gullah," she said in summary of her twenty-six-year project of translating the New Testament. "As we began to translate, I became very excited. When I read Gullah scripture to others now, they get excited, sometimes expressing that feeling in laughter. They can identify with it.

"'People used to ask, 'Are you Gullah?' and I would say, 'No, I'm not!' But now I say, 'Yeah, a Gullah! A Gullah down!'"

Like Ardell Greene, many have shed shame and embarrassment about Gullah culture and are happy to identify themselves as "Gullah down"—that is, truly, authentically, and proudly Gullah.

Most importantly, I've learned from first-hand experience and observation that Gullah and Geechee customs are carryovers from West African heritage. Until I visited West African countries, I had repeated that statement only because I had read and believed it. But now I know for sure! In 2004, I participated in a five-week U.S. Department of Education Fulbright-Hays program entitled Teaching and Learning in Ghana that was administered through Charleston Southern University. My first trip to the Motherland inspired me to write a song, "Nshira Nka Mikra," which in Fante means "My soul has been blessed!" Translated into Gullah, it would read, "My soul been bless!" I saw the links in cultures. I was moved and exhilarated and wrote poetry and short stories and journal entries to tell others about all that I had experienced.

In May 2005, anthropologist, historian, and professor Joseph Opala of James Madison University asked me to serve as a Gullah ambassador during a celebration called Priscilla's Homecoming in Sierra Leone. The historic one-week celebration was a Gullah homecoming for a woman named Thomalind Martin Polite of Charleston, South Carolina. In 1756, her ten-year-old great-great-great-great-great grandmother was kidnapped from her home in Sierra Leone. She was forced onto the *Hare*, a slave ship bound for South Carolina. There, she was sold to Elias Ball II, owner of a rice plantation in

South Carolina. Ball gave her the name Priscilla. Through Priscilla's Homecoming, the Martin family connected with the country of its ancestral legacy.

The event was unprecedented, because the Martin family was able to find written documentation to connect with their past. The Ball family had maintained meticulous records of their slaves, and the records from the slave ship matched the Ball family's records. I made many wonderful connections throughout my participation in this one-of-a-kind historical event, which was almost too phenomenal to actually be real. I recalled the tunes of Gullah spirituals and folk songs and used them to chronicle my daily experiences. As part of the Gullah/Geechee Program Series at Brookgreen Gardens in Murrells Inlet, South Carolina, where I am vice president for creative education, I've shared these songs and information with visitors from around the country.

Reflecting my zeal from my two African sojourns, *Gullah Branches, West African Roots* is an aesthetic documentation of the lifestyles, customs, superstitions, and lore of cultures from which Gullahs and Geechees sprang. It is a collection of writings that identify a heritage closely related to other cultures of the African Diaspora. This work is a time capsule, presented with Sea Island flavoring. Its stories and songs showcase that, indeed, there is a connection! And those who may not be able to witness this connection firsthand can—without doubt—believe, cherish, celebrate![4]

For Gullah/Geechee people, a newness, an assurance, and a liberating essence pervade us when we say with pride, "Dats right, I am a Gullah!"

> Dats right, I am a Gullah
> A saltwata Geechee/Gullah
> This is Reason Number 10
> I look back an rememba my ancestas' strength
> Nine is respect for eldas
> Eight is de Gullah language
> Seven is our spiritual songs about heaven

---

4. Daise, ix–xiv.

Six is sweetgrass baskets
Five is benne wafers
Four is rice and cotton and indigo
Three is beliefs and oral history
Two is hoppin john and other rice dishes, too
One is I was born on an island,
A Carolina/Georgia Sea Island
And my ancestas came from West Africa
I'm Gullah cause my ancestas came from West Africa

—Ronald Daise

*Author and performance artist Ronald Daise is a native of St.
Helena Island, South Carolina, and the costar of Nick Jr. TV's award-
winning* Gullah Gullah Island *children's series. He has documented
Gullah culture and history with books, recordings, and performances
and has been recognized by the state of South Carolina's Order of the
Palmetto and Jean Lacey Folk Heritage awards. He is also the recipient
of the 2008 South Carolina African-American Heritage Commission's
Lifetime Achievement Award. His most recent book,* Gullah Branches,
West African Roots *(Sandlapper Publishing), chronicles cultural connections of language, spirituality, dietary practices, and beliefs. Daise
enjoys songwriting and speed walking. He and his family reside in
Beaufort, South Carolina.*

Bibliography

Daise, Ronald. *Gullah Branches, West African Roots*. Orangeburg, SC:
    Sandlapper Publishing, Inc., 2007.
Tibbetts, John H. "Gullah's Radiant Light," *Coastal Heritage 1993* (Winter
    2004-05). Sea Grant Consortium, Charleston, SC.
Daise, Ronald. *Reminiscences of Sea Island Heritage: Legacy of Freedmen
    on St. Helena Island*. Orangeburg, SC: Sandlapper Publishing, Inc.,
    1986.
Derrick, Hope. "Congressman Clyburn Introduces Gullah/
    Geechee Cultural Heritage Act." News Release. July 12, 2004.
    Electronic document. <www.house.gov/apps/list/press/sc06_
    clyburn/041712Gullahbill.html>

♦ Chapter 18

The Little Red School House

This conversation is for grown folks ... now go to bed!

THE ART OF EAVESDROPPING DOES HAVE ITS PRIVILEGES, especially when you are enlightened or informed about something about which you previously had no clue. Eavesdropping can also arrest an anxious energy in you, like a real desire to add your two cents to a thought-provoking conversation, lend a voice to the "amen corner," or just stick up for the underdog. As children, you sometimes listened through wood doors to the conversations of grown folks cussing, fussing, and yelling about myriad things.

Yes, you learned a lot. As you listened to that whispered, high-pitched dialogue, you were somehow forced to understand some things you really didn't need to know. You never dared to mention the episode or confront an adult about his or her so-called emotional meltdown or tirade. No, you certainly did not lose yourself and forget all manners, boundaries, and spoken rules. As a child, you stayed in your place. Some of you are too young to remember this golden rule: A child should be seen and not heard. But you see, I was raised on this principle, which proved to be a natural remedy for staying clear of a physical shack-up—or smackdown—by anyone who said they loved me.

That's how it was. That was old school.

Almost a decade into the new millennium, I find myself reminiscing about the old-school days. I sometimes think about my days of walking home from school because I'd spent my bus fare on snacks at the corner store.

I remember my fourth-grade teacher, Mrs. Denise Davis. Everybody loved her. She was tough, sharp, knew language arts, and demanded the best from all of her students. Mrs. Davis was much like a surrogate mother. She yelled at us, threatened us, pinched us, got in our faces, and pulled our ears. At school, when she thought you were brazen enough to question her directives, she'd remind you, "Yours is not to question why, yours is just to do or die." If Mrs. Davis thought you were slacking and unfocused, she would embarrass you. And oh my God, if she called home. Mrs. Davis was the kind of teacher who would have parents ending the conversation with, "Go ahead, Mrs. Davis, if you need to take your belt off, by all means, please do."

Whoa. That's just too darn much power. But we loved Mrs. Davis, and our parents did too. After one phone call home from Mrs. Davis, I felt I had been baptized and made over as an orthodox believer of Mrs. Davis and her classroom rules. I was never to sin again—until fifth grade, of course. I believed in Mrs. Davis's expectations of me. I believed that she would have the support of the National Guard if she needed it to keep us in check. But she didn't need all that, she was just a great teacher, and that was enough.

Try that today and you're going to jail.

Corporal punishment is a thing of the past and forbidden by law. But I often wonder what we've gained and thereby lost as a result of it.

Those were my fondest memories of grammar school. Mrs. Davis was a black teacher who took *no* mess. She was tough, but you knew that she cared deeply about her students. Now, thanks to some of our child-protection laws, wonderful teachers like Mrs. Davis would find themselves in the state penitentiary for child abuse. It's called corporal punishment, people! Anybody over the age of thirty should know a little something about hearing a teacher say "eyes, nose, and toes to the wall" or writing "I will not talk in class" a hundred or more times. There were also the times you may have had to stand on one leg with books balanced on top of your extended arms, stand in a lonely coat closet, or miss recess or lunch. Corporal punishment. I was certainly familiar with it.

Back in the 1970s, the days of bell bottoms, platform shoes, "black is beautiful," Vietnam, Watergate, blaxploitation films, Jesse

Jackson's Rainbow PUSH Coalition, Shirley Chisholm's presidential campaign, *Soul Train*, *Jaws*, Patty Hearst, eight-track tapes, O.J. Simpson, *Star Wars*, and *Good Times*, I can tell you that I stood in plenty of classroom corners with my face turned to the wall and away from my classmates and teacher. Standing with my hands at my sides in my Catholic-school uniform, my pigtails momentarily stilled, I remained quiet. It was a time-out for ten or more minutes. It was a time for me to collect myself and reflect on classroom rules. I certainly don't remember my self-esteem being dismantled or crushed in any way from standing in the corner or writing "I will not talk in class" two hundred times.

Actually, I remember finding this time to be an awesome opportunity to pray, asking God that the teacher would not follow this act of discipline with a phone call home to my momma. Trust and believe, people, I was happy and thrilled to stand there until the cows came home. In all honesty, after a while I learned that I didn't want to stand in the corner or miss recess for talking and laughing with my friends. So I learned to pass notes instead. I also learned to exhibit good boundaries and self-control when interacting with my teachers and other adults. Hence, my journey through elementary and secondary school was relatively easy and memorable.

What Happened to Us?

Fast forward to the new millennium, with depressing statistics of juvenile delinquency and violence, alarming teen pregnancy and dropout rates, and sagging test scores under constant debate, I wonder how it is that we've lost the precious pearls and pride of yesteryear. In fact, whatever happened to the spirit of the little red school house? What has really happened to us since *Brown v. Board of Education,* more than fifty-four years ago? I now wonder what happened to the days when our schools were literally seen as the bedrock of our community? What happened to the days when students were just plain *expected* to do their best in school? Years ago, students were well informed that it was unacceptable to miss school or misbehave anywhere near school. What happened? How did so many of our people misplace their minds and a sense of priority and value in academic achievement?

In the 1960s, not too long before my birth, Daniel P. Moynihan (who later became a senator) reported that black families were in a crisis due to discrimination, growth in urbanization, broken traditions in the structure of the black family, and the legacy of slavery.[1] He spoke of the breakdown of the black family and its high rates of illegitimacy, welfare dependency, school dropouts, and crime. And that was before I got here. Now, some forty-plus years later, we are still faced with inescapable brokenness in a number of our communities. Snags in our magnificent tapestry caused by a few shattered men who prefer variety in their women and the places they call home. There are also fractures in our priorities and value systems displaced by a wicked lust for materialistic gain, fast money poppin', and hoop dreams. Perhaps this was the beginning of the schism that prevents countless black children from getting to school on time, every day, prepared to learn, thirsty for knowledge, and motivated to close the proverbial achievement gap.

Now, in defense of those who remember from whence we've come, I applaud you. Over the years, our schools have produced some of the most outstanding stars and pioneering leaders of our times. There's no question about that. Our heritage is rich, colorful, and eclectic. Evidence of our extraordinary talent, skill, and intellectual aptitude can be seen all around us: a newly elected African-American president, successful businesspeople, scientists, authors, clergy, politicians, filmmakers, educators, corporate leaders, military leaders, media tycoons, entertainers, and athletes.

Although we have a sizable amount of this prime social and intellectual capital in the black community today, I am always searching for more. Simply put, I am in pursuit of the discipline, structure, and commitment of yesteryear that every school stakeholder offered to its bright-eyed students, people who believed that education was a tangible gateway to a promising future.

In many schools, the bottom line is that our numbers are just not measuring up anymore. With reams of data to support why the achievement gap is so wide, there's no way we can ignore the elephant who sits in front of the flat-screen television watching reality shows

---

1. Moynihan.

and playing games filled with explicit violence and mature content. We might also snatch the dark shades from the face of another five-ton elephant too busy to volunteer at her child's school or participate in an occasional PTA meeting. And then there are other elephants, those who work side by side with students and yet never learn the simple characteristics—firm but fair, respect, sense of humor, empathy, creativity, and engagement—that are the crown jewels of any successful and unforgettable teacher.

In recent times, there have been countless debates and voices of concern relating to the alarming rate of inner-city kids who aren't making the grade. Some have even argued that disenfranchised children of color aren't doing as well as white kids because they aren't under enough pressure to do so. After all, some scholars have reported that in many of our urban schools, high-achieving black students have been teased, taunted, and accused of "acting white" when they exceed expectations. So to protect their social and street credibility, they play dumb—or worse, they completely extinguish their intellectual edge.

While we struggle to make sense of all the things that need improvement in our schools, I look for answers in the tried and true of yesteryear. That little red school house and all its gleaming beauty, potential, strength, leadership, relationships, and plight to push little black children to become U.S. Supreme Court justices, immortalized civil-rights leaders, educators, doctors, scientists, major-league baseball players, nationally renowned opera singers, and on and on and on. It was then that we soared like eagles and graduated from prestigious colleges in spite of segregation and unequal resources. In that one-room school, black folks understood the importance of discipline, pride, community, respect for elders, and high expectations for school success.

Children didn't go to school and cuss their teachers and blatantly disrespect school rules. Vivian Wilson, an eighty-six-year-old retired teacher in Yazoo County, Mississippi, shared with me some of her personal experiences as a teacher in the one-room school house. Wilson began her career at the age of twenty. In the little red school house, she remembers teaching fifty-six children. Her stroll down memory lane began with a mention of the potbellied wood-burning stove that sat in the middle of the room. In addition to getting their lessons, students were also responsible for gathering the wood for the stove.

"It was a rough time for us," she said. "The children didn't have lunch and they had to walk to school in inclement weather." Back then, Wilson confided, her one-room school only had access to basic reading and math books.

Parents in her rural area of Mississippi generally did not have money for much more than their children's basic necessities. As she worked with the fifty-six students in groups according to their ages and grade levels, Wilson recalled that talking, playing, and minor fighting were typical behavioral infractions at the school. Parents were typically very supportive and cooperative. According to her, teachers had the authority to paddle children when they misbehaved, and parents would often come to the school and paddle their children in front of their classmates. "But that was sixty-six years ago," she says.

As another wise elder shared, "Children didn't go to school and cuss their teachers and blatantly disrespect school rules. It was unheard of. Children knew better, and they feared the inevitable consequences for such rash, inconsiderate, and unflattering behavior." Children apparently also knew that it was customary and quite conventional for any adult to chastise them before they arrived home to their parents. Those were the days when teachers often told students to go outside and get switches for their own punishment; corporal punishment was meted out just as it would be by the children's own parents. Those were the days when the worst thing a student might muster the courage to do was pretty minor indeed: fighting behind the school, stealing a piece of candy, pulling hair, pilfering an apple from a neighboring yard, or daydreaming in class.

Doris Fuqua of Jersey City, New Jersey, is a retired educator who taught for thirty-four years in the Jersey City Public School System. Now an owner of three preschools, she reminisced with me about her childhood days at Parker Elementary School in Bentonia, Mississippi.

"At Parker Elementary, a two-room school, classes took turns being taught by one teacher," she said. "Each class had a scheduled time with the teacher. And although the school had electricity, in the winter, students sat around a wood-burning heater because there was no gas heat. Parker Elementary also received secondhand books from white schools in the city. The students had one set of reference books—encyclopedias. At the end of the year, students were instructed to chalk down the edge of the books to make them look new."

Fuqua also talked about her teachers—one very strict one in particular. "You didn't breathe too hard in her class. Students were afraid of her. She'd beat kids for not having their homework or talking in class. But no one was cursing teachers and talking back like they do now. You could get beat for just talking with your classmates." She fondly remembered another teacher as being creative, challenging, and fun. She confided that this particular teacher was respected most by students and their parents.

While Fuqua was a student at Parker Elementary, her father started a petition for the black students to receive bus service from the county school district. The bus was needed to transport students to the high school, which was located some twenty-five miles away. Around 1953, he prevailed, and the school district supplied black students in rural areas with a school bus. During that time, up to fifty students were being transported to the high school in Yazoo City each day. According to Fuqua, it took an hour or more each way to pick up all the students and drop them off after school. When the district started up its transportation service, parents had to accept responsibility for keeping the bus and driving the students. Initially, Fuqua's uncle was responsible for keeping the bus; later, in 1955, her father assumed management of the bus and kept it parked on his land.

"Parents were very supportive of the school," she reports. "The adults in the community shared responsibility in disciplining, correcting, and chastising the children in the community. That was our way of life. If a child got into trouble, any adult could talk to the child. Then, when the child got home, he was punished again by his parent."

In retrospect, the stakeholders of the little red school house have taught us a lot. As it was, most teachers, parents, and community volunteers were involved, entrenched, and greatly instrumental in helping ensure that their children received a quality education. They carried out myriad tasks, such as building construction, painting, providing transportation, donating land, digging water wells, fundraising for supplies, and reinforcing whatever was taught in the classroom.[2] Teachers were considered esteemed authorities in the school and the community.

In her research, Emory University scholar Emilie Siddle-Walker found that in these little red school houses, segregated Negroes pooled their resources and established "good schools" where children were expected to be nurtured, taught, corrected, supported, encouraged, and punished.[3] In a nutshell, parents, teachers, administrators, and community residents loved their little one-room school houses. Their devotion was evident in the time, service, and advocacy they devoted to school programs and fundraising initiatives. Parents were accustomed to undergirding all that the educators deemed important and critical to a child's growth and development.

Eventually, our own one-room school house later turned into five rooms, and then two floors. Today, it's four floors with a hundred rooms. With all of the advancements, resources, technology, and endless choices that are available, it appears that a few of our stakeholders have abandoned our traditions of thinking of education as a fundamental treasure. Having grown to include magnet programs, after-school programs, free and reduced-cost lunches, free bus transportation, athletic clubs, bands, choruses, and a host of other extracurricular activities, our schools have morphed so much that our integral relationships and ability to collaborate and work cohesively have suffered.

With the highest respect, admiration, and appreciation, I extend a curtsy to the many wonderful parents who are totally invested in the educational experience of their children. You are world-class guardians of what is right, pure, and coveted in our schools today. However, research about the realities of working in today's urban schools suggests that an alarming number of parents have forgotten

---

2. Siddle-Walker.
3. Ibid.

about our little red school house. They've forgotten that the foundation of good schools is the patronage, care, and vision of school stakeholders who believe in the potential and beauty of all children. They've forgotten about the plight, pain, and urgency of helping teachers, administrators, and others to protect and uphold the integrity of having a good school.

As we squint through tear-filled eyes, we see many educators who desperately look for the right answers, the right strategies, the right resources, the right business partners, and the right lessons to fill the canyon left by uninvolved, unsupportive, and detached parents or guardians. What is so compelling is that this phenomenon is not a part of our tapestry as African-American people. As reported in numerous studies, minimal parental involvement in urban schools doesn't speak to our identity as champions of segregated education and the outstanding leaders it produced. Once more, this identity blackout is perpetuated and flaunted in urban music and modes of dress, lack of self-respect, and limited intrinsic motivation to learn that so many young people struggle with today.

When I've asked random teenagers to "keep it real" or "school me" about the plight of their peers and their thoughts about the lack of student interest, accountability, motivation, poor attendance, and marginal scholastic performance, they've confided that many of their peers feel school is a waste of time. They also admit that many of their peers are driven by a list of priorities that include:

- Money
- Sex
- Personal possessions (i.e., cell phones)
- Family
- Popularity
- Education
- Physical appearance
- Media
- Friendships
- Extracurricular activities (i.e., band or sports)

Furthermore, some youths have shared that they believe student success depends largely on parents and their ability to "make" students come to school and do their best. As an educator who works in an urban school populated by more than eighteen hundred African-American youth, I am proud to say that we've made some wonderful strides in our efforts to recapture and reclaim our standing as a national school of excellence, however.

Filling the achievement gap in more schools and in more cities will absolutely require more than teachers, principals, superintendents, and educational scholars finding solutions to what ails us in public schools today. This feat respectfully asks that the entire village step up its game. In particular, younger parents and all other guardians who can must join their schools in helping students first, discover their self-worth; second, identify realistic goals and plans to achieve education and career goals; and third, understand that schools are a sacred place. They must become completely focused on the personal growth and intellectual ascension of the urban child and see the rich legacy of the one-room school house. Students need to hear from someone other than a teacher that the ills of our communities have no place in our schools.

We share a history flooded with memories of African-American parents who were devoted to advocacy, volunteerism, and support for their communities' one-room school houses. Today's big urban schools now cry out for help due to a serious drought of the same. Too many of our potential honor-roll members, doctors, lawyers, businesspeople, corporate leaders, and senators have become confused, frustrated, angry, and unbridled as a result of loose parenting practices. The classroom teacher is the child's second teacher and surrogate parent. Our children must be consistently immersed in encouragement, expectations, firm discipline, structure, visibility, resources, PTA involvement, and unwavering support at home—by their *first teachers.*

If you consider a panoramic view of the modern school, academic progress, improvement, and change is on the horizon. I am persuaded that adopting the traditions of the little red school house will fortify our abilities to grow a stellar generation of buoyant, courageous, self-sufficient, and smart citizens.

—Bridget Isaac, EdD

For the past fifteen years, Bridget Isaac, EdD, has worked with children and families in public schools, social service organizations, mental health agencies, and juvenile correctional facilities. She is a native of New Jersey and resides in Atlanta, Georgia. For more information, please e-mail her at bisaac.edd@gmail.com.

Bibliography

Moynihan, Daniel Patrick. *The Negro Family: The Case for National Action*. Washington, D.C.: United States Department of Labor, 1965.

Siddle-Walker, Emilie. "Caswell County Training School, 1933-1969: Relationships between Community and School." *Harvard Educational Review*, 1993, 161–182. Rpt. in *Shifting Histories: Transforming Schools for Social Change*. Eds. G. Noya, K. Geismar, and G. Nicoleau. Cambridge, MA: Harvard Educational Review Print Series, 1995.

Chapter 19

The African-American Tradition: A Framework for Increasing Educational Outcomes for Our Children

Without education, there is no hope for our people, and
without hope, our future is lost.

—Charles Hamilton Houston

A S I REFLECT ON THE EDUCATIONAL EXPERIENCES AND DECI-
sions I have made, I have become more passionate about
the experiences of African Americans in education and the
role school plays in encouraging or discouraging students to prepare
for and attend college. Immediately, my mind goes back to seventh
grade, when I was not allowed to take a placement test to determine
my eligibility to enroll in Algebra I in the eighth grade. My peers
teased and labeled me as not "smart enough" to take the course. Because I was not very knowledgeable of placement policies, I did not
protest. However, I harbored ill feelings toward my seventh grade
math teacher for not recommending me for the test. I also remember
being placed in a "below-average" section of physical science in my
ninth-grade year of high school; I didn't know that it was a below-
average section until I began to investigate why the students in the
class with me performed as poorly as they did.

As I know now, not taking Algebra I in eighth grade and being
placed in a below-average section of physical science had a negative
influence on my math and science abilities. These situations took
place because my family was not knowledgeable about placement
issues in school. Thus, I was a victim of "tracking," and many years
would pass before I truly understood this phenomenon. Determined
not to let these experiences hinder me from graduating high school
and attending college, I took the courses necessary to graduate from

high school on both a college preparatory and vocational/career technical curriculum. While I successfully overcame these experiences, I deal with vestiges of them on a recurring basis.

I constantly find myself wondering about other students whose parents were not intimately involved in their educational experiences and the subsequent impact on their chances of going to college. How many of these students relied on high school teachers and counselors to assist them in preparing for high school graduation and college—and were ultimately unsuccessful? Further, I also wonder how inequities in K–12 funding and poor teaching affected college preparation for me and my peers. These experiences are amplified for students in predominantly African-American or low-income schools.

I have always felt that I have an obligation to become an advocate for groups of students who have not been able to find advocates at home or in the schools they attend. Thus, it is my life's work to assist the African-American community in promoting the importance of education via the African-American tradition of holding ourselves accountable for the success or failure of our educational outcomes.

Education in the African-American Community

"Without education, there is no hope for our people, and without hope, our future is lost." Those immortal words, spoken by the late NAACP attorney Charles Hamilton Houston, are symbolic of the views African Americans have historically held with regard to education. Education has long been a priority in the African-American community. Realistically speaking, there was never a choice of whether or not an African-American child would attend school. Historically, the question for African Americans has been, "Where will you be attending school?" rather than, "Will you be attending school?" Allen and Jewell stated, "Dating back to when black slaves were forbidden to read and write under the threat of physical harm or death, [African Americans] have invested [education] with mythic qualities, seeing it as our hope and salvation for the future."[1]

Formal education was the chief means by which African Americans could separate themselves from a subordinate status in society.

---

1. Allen and Jewell, 241–242.

It also allowed them to achieve social mobility while defending and extending their new rights as citizens.[2] Since many grandparents of the current undergraduate African-American college-student generation were unable to attend college because of racism, discrimination, economic distress, and a general lack of opportunity, these older African Americans often hold the view that education is the "way out" of the social or economic situation an individual may find him- or herself trapped within.[3]

While the call for education for African Americans was ignored and devalued by members of the majority society prior to the founding of black institutions of higher education in the aftermath of the Civil War, the African-American community nevertheless continued to place great emphasis on it. Education was the same as being literate—not only in terms of showing an understanding of reading, writing, and math skills, but also in terms of survival. To African Americans, both slaves and free persons, literacy became synonymous with knowing what to do and how to survive, including how to help the next generation move closer to the dream of being learned and literate citizens of the African-American community. Literacy also meant comprehending how to get along with whites and helping them understand and value the building blocks needed to establish various forms of literacy for the African-American community without making them feel threatened. The kind of education African Americans in our historical communities sought to establish also included helping children—especially those whose parents believed education would gain opportunities and better survivability both inside and outside the community.

Thus, education for the majority of African Americans still clamoring for it was to be literally holistic. It would ideally teach African Americans intellectually, heal them spiritually, develop them socially, and prepare them economically to survive segregation and discrimination. Teaching children was the highest calling, and the entire community was expected to participate in helping them become literate. Literacy, furthermore, meant that the historical African-American

2. Allen; Allen & Jewell; Anderson; Watkins.
3. Anderson.

community emphasized a broad general learning philosophy that demanded African-American people value education above working in agricultural endeavors or any other wage-earning jobs. Developing comprehensive intellect in children was the ideal goal, second only to their spiritual training.

Consequently, then, when conversations arose concerning whether African Americans wanted to be—or even should be—educated, the African-American community could proclaim it had always valued education and literacy, which included understanding how to use education to survive inside and outside their primary environment. Literacy and education, therefore, became a way the community could establish its identity and autonomy by fostering a kind of education that gave them some control over what their children needed to learn. Literacy was essential, the African-American way of ensuring that the life of the African-American community would be continued and that the history, culture, and values of African Americans would be passed on, even if it was necessary that the education be rudimentary in order to make whites feel less threatened.

According to Hochschild, at the center of the American dream is the conviction that education opens the door to success.[4] Believing that even the poorest American can achieve greatness with talent and hard work is one of our society's cherished cultural ideals. Furthermore, education is an opportunity for African Americans to have a liberated future, which is much better than their oppressive past. Consequently, the pressure on African-American children today to receive an education is a product of the educational aspirations of African Americans of the distant and recent past.[5]

The Historical Context

DuBois contended that African Americans have constantly been in a precarious situation with regard to advocating for a quality education for their children.[6] If African-American parents encouraged their children to attend white schools, it was highly likely

---

4. Hochschild.
5. Feagin, Vera, & Imani.
6. DuBois.

that their culture was ignored in the curriculum and ethos of the school. Conversely, some students who attended all-African-American high schools in the South were fortunate enough to be surrounded by teachers and administrators who "cared" about their educational success. In her study of a segregated African-American high school community in the South, Walker explained how parents and teachers worked together to create a positive learning environment for students.[7] While students had decent physical facilities, there was a shortage of educational resources afforded to African-American schools. Because of the "caring" displayed in these schools, the students had access to a "good" education. Walker wrote,

> In classes, students respect the fact that teachers "didn't play," even when they did not like a particular teacher. They saw the educators' high expectations as an indication that the schoolchildren were "cared about." In other words, if a teacher cared about them, that teacher would expect them to learn—an attitude of Vasquez's reference to effective teachers of students of color as "warm demanders." Outside of class, they appreciated the time teachers took to talk with them individually and in small groups. These conversations were opportunities for them to learn from teachers about broader things than academic content. That teachers took the time to do this with them was considered a form of caring.[8]

After all the struggles of our foreparents, it remains a fact that in contemporary African-American society, students who devote their time to school and studying are labeled as "acting white." Their peers ostracize them, and when they attend college, they are often socially excluded. Contemporary efforts to better understand African Americans and their quest for education must consider their existence in society at large.

It is equally important to have a proper cultural context in which to place this work. As defined by Freeman, cultural context is "in-

---

7. Walker.
8. Ibid, 202.

terrelated characteristics that provide a perspective—frame of reference—for understanding individuals' and/or groups' ways of knowing and being."[9] As a researcher of African-American educational experiences, I remain aware that the theoretical frames selected must take into account the intricacies of African-American culture. Making these cultural considerations allows the researcher to present findings that are proper interpretations of the group under study.[10]

Most importantly, the African-American tradition provides a framework for beginning a conversation on the educational progress and steps necessary to get our community where it needs to be with regards to education. Revitalization of this tradition is the vehicle by which positive and systemic change can be realized. The African-American tradition provides a proper framework for my work. This tradition has tenets related to caring, cross-generational uplift, and faith communities.

The African-American Tradition: Ethics of Care

Contemporary work on care theory is most often based on the work of Carol Gilligan,[11] who defined care as "a web of interdependence, a concept of being there, listening as a moral act, understanding, shared responsibility for another's welfare."[12]

According to Noddings, care "refers properly to the relation, not just to an agent who 'cares,' and we must consider the response of the cared-for."[13] Further, Strike explained, "caring aims at a society and at personal relationships in which nurturance and relationships are highly valued."[14] Noddings also found that as schools respond to the needs of students, there may be a need to design varying types of curricula to carefully guide the students through the web of possibilities.[15]

Differentiated curricula are evidence that those who surround students really care for them. Care, as Noddings put it, forces teach-

---

9. Freeman, 2.
10. Ibid.
11. Gilligan.
12. Shrader, 42–43.
13. Noddings, 13.
14. Strike, 21.
15. Ibid.

ers to look at students closely before remedies are recommended and listen to those whose "aspirations, interests, talents, and legitimate values" may differ from the teacher's.[16] This is better than strict curricular offerings that "produce resistance and weaken the relation." Noddings insists that in addition to caring, students need adults in their lives who "listen, invite, guide, and support them."[17]

In sum, McKeon clarified that caring is doing the right thing "to the right person, to the right extent, at the right time, with the right attitude, and in the right way."[18] Caring is the foundation of the African-American tradition.

Heath explained, "Family relationships, group social interaction, support, and achievement have historically been a part of African-American culture."[19] She added that because of this communalistic portrait, African Americans usually do not define themselves in individual terms; rather, they identify only as a part of the larger African-American community. According to Allen-Hayes, St. John, and Cadray, "the African-American tradition, which emphasizes care and community, provides an important foundation for creating just and caring learning environments in post-desegregation urban schools."[20] The authors go on to state that the ethic of care that was so essential to African-American schooling was nearly lost after desegregation. They explain, "To a large extent, this ethic of care that was experienced in African-American schools prior to 1954 had its origin in the neighborhood school concept through which everyone in the school shared a common view of the world."[21] These schools were effective because they fostered a strong sense of community and family cooperation. Teachers lived and worked in the neighborhood, and thus the school was able to serve as a center of social activity. Because of the association, communication, and trust that developed between parents and the school, it was not uncommon for teachers to stop by a child's home or talk to a parent at church on Sunday.[22]

16. Ibid, 15.
17. Ibid.
18. McKeon, 963.
19. Heath, 24.
20. Allen-Hayes, St. John, & Cadray, 250.
21. Ibid, 251.
22. Ibid.

Walker provided a brilliant example of the African-American tradition. In her book about a segregated African-American high school in the South, she recounted that students were successful because of the relationships that developed between the school and families in the community.[23] Although the white-dominated school board unevenly distributed funds to the African-American school, the school's work was undeterred. There were numerous examples of parents providing much-needed supplies for the school and teachers who went the extra mile to ensure that the students had an excellent learning environment. Walker commented:

> But in spite of these challenges, they forged a system of schooling that emphasized the importance of teacher/student relationships, valued activities as a key means of developing the students' many talents, and believed in the children's ability to learn and their own ability to teach. These beliefs are evident in the institutional structures the teachers and principal created and in the additional responsibilities they assumed.[24]

Cross-Generational Uplift

St. John and Miron stated, "The major social theory of educational and social attainment argues there is a pattern of cross-generation uplift, with gains in parent education and occupational status in one generation having a positive influence on the next generation."[25] As St. John and Miron noted, the primary use of this theory is "that African-American families have aspirations for a better life for their children."[26] Dilworth pointed out that historically, "the quests of African Americans for educational equality were framed around the struggle for racial uplift."[27] It was imperative that those in the African-American community who became educated would "reach back" and share their knowledge and resources with those who did

---

23. Walker.
24. Walker, 201.
25. St. John and Miron, 288.
26. Ibid, 288.
27. Dilworth, 8.

not have the opportunity to do so. This theory makes a strong contribution to research related to high school students in predominantly African-American urban high schools as it relates to college preparation and attendance.

Those parents who have graduated from high school and attended college or have knowledge of the social and economic gains that result from college attendance are more likely to encourage their children to prepare for college. These parents will begin to make the financial commitments necessary for their children to attend college, such as saving, investing, setting up prepaid tuition plans. Further, parents will also make certain their children enroll in the proper academic courses in high school to ensure that they will meet admissions criteria for college.

In addition, cross-generational uplift can even have positive effects on students not fortunate enough to have parents who attended college. Because these parents have not attended college, there are often knowledge gaps that prevent them from offering advice or recommendations to their children to help them prepare for college. Therefore, such parents are often dependent upon the public school system for this guidance. In a community where there is a strong sense of uplift, many others can assist a child in preparing for college.

If the student attends high school where there are numerous African-American teachers (or white teachers, for that matter) who possess characteristics related to the African-American tradition, there is the possibility that the student will be cared for and supported to the point that the student will take the proper courses to prepare for college. Additionally, there might be a chance the student will gain some knowledge of what's needed in order for college attendance to become a reality.

While the African-American tradition is based on the strengths of the African-American experience and prompts us to stick our chests out, it should also prompt us to action. Currently, we face many socially and culturally reproductive forces in our society, which challenge the notion of a strong African-American community and weaken the African-American tradition. These forces, such as illicit sex, drug use and abuse, and the lack of social critique, are killing the African-American community. It is time for us to look inward, critique ourselves, and challenge ourselves—and others—to be better. I'm not talking about a Bill Cosby type of critique, but some real supportive care-type vibe where we can challenge each other, make each other better, and still love everyone just the same.

—Ontario S. Wooden, PhD

Ontario S. Wooden is director of the Velma Fudge Grant Honors Program and Academic Success Initiatives and assistant professor of education at Albany State University in Albany, Georgia. His research interests include school reform, college access and choice, higher education policy and finance, and multiculturalism and diversity in higher education. He holds a PhD in higher education administration from Indiana University–Bloomington.

Bibliography

Allen, W. R. "And Who Shall Control Their Minds? Race Consciousness and Collective Commitments among African-American Students." *African-American Culture and Heritage in Higher Education Research and Practice.* Ed. K. Freeman. Westport, CT: Praeger, 1998. 59–74.

Allen, W. R., & Jewell, J. O. "A Backward Glance Forward: Past, Present, and Future Perspectives on Historically Black Colleges and Universities." *The Review of Higher Education,* 25, no. 3, (2002): 241–261.

Allen-Hayes, L., St. John, E. P., and Cadray, J. "Rediscovering the African-American Tradition: Restructuring in Post-Desegregation Urban Schools." *Reinterpreting Urban School Reform.* Eds. L. F. Miron & E. P. St. John. Albany: State University of New York Press, 2003. 249–275.

Anderson, J. D. *The Education of Blacks in the South, 1860–1935.* Chapel Hill: The University of North Carolina Press, 1988.

Anderson, M. *The Children of the South.* New York: Farrar, Straus, and Giroux, 1966.

Dilworth, P. P. "Competing Conceptions of Citizenship Education: Thomas Jesse Jones and Carter G. Woodson." *International Journal of Social Education,* 18, no. 2 (2003/2004), 1–15.

DuBois, W.E.B. "Does the Negro Need Separate Schools?" *Journal of Negro Education,* 4, no. 3 (1935): 328–335.

Feagin, J. R., Vera, H., & Imani, N. *The Agony of Education: Black Students at White Colleges and Universities.* New York: Routledge, 1996.

Freeman, K. Introduction. *African-American Culture and Heritage in Higher Education.* Ed. K. Freeman. Westport, CT: Praeger, 1998. 1–5.

Gilligan, C. *In a Different Voice.* Cambridge: Harvard University Press, 1982.

Heath, T. M. "African-American Students and Self-Concept Development: Integrating Cultural Influences into Research and Practice." *African-American Culture and Heritage in Higher Education Research and Practice.* Ed. K. Freeman. Westport, CT: Praeger, 1998. 33–42.

Hochschild, J. *Facing Up to the American Dream: Race, Class, and the Soul of the Nation.* Princeton, NJ: Princeton University Press, 1995.

McKeon, R. *The Basic Works of Aristotle.* New York: Random House, 1941.

Noddings, N. "Care, Justice, and Equity." *Justice and Caring: The Search for Common Ground in Education* Eds. M. S. Katz, N. Noddings, & K. A. Strike. New York: Teachers College Press, 1999. 7–20.

Schrader, D. E. "Justice and Caring: Process in College Students' Moral Reasoning Development." *Justice and Caring: The Search for Common Ground in Education* Eds. M. S. Katz, N. Noddings, & K. A. Strike. New York: Teachers College Press, 1999. 37–55.

St. John, E. P., & Miron, L. F. "A Critical-Empirical Perspective on Urban School Reform." *Reinterpreting Urban School Reform.* Eds. L. F. Miron & E. P. St. John. Albany: State University of New York Press, 2003. 279–297.

Strike, K. A. "Justice, Caring, and Universality: In Defense of Moral Pluralism." *Justice and Caring: The Search for Common Ground in Education* Eds. M. S. Katz, N. Noddings, & K. A. Strike. New York: Teachers College Press, 1999. 21–36.

Walker, V. S. *Their Highest Potential: An African-American School Community in the Segregated South.* Chapel Hill: The University of North Carolina Press, 1996.

Watkins, W. H. *The White Architects of Black Education: Ideology and Power in America 1865–1956.* New York: Teachers College Press, 2001.

◆ Chapter 20

Growing Up Creole in Los Angeles

I WAS TEN. ONE EVENING AFTER DINNER, MY FAMILY WAS SITTING around the table as usual, catching up on the events of the day and listening to my father's corny jokes (at least the ones my mother would allow him tell us). Suddenly, my brother announced that from now on, he was going to tell everyone that he was Creole. Without missing a beat, my mother looked him at him sharply with that all-knowing mother-wit expression that all mothers have.

She said, "Hey, you'd better soft-pedal that Creole stuff!"

Seizing the opportunity, my father said, "Oh, so you want to be a Creole, huh? Well, let me tell you what you're in for."

He told us a true story about my grandfather. He was from New Orleans, where my parents, and his parents, and his parents' parents had all been raised. One night, he was forced to walk home from Uptown down Rampart Street to the Seventh Ward because his truck had broken down. It was dark and late, and he was carrying his tool box on his shoulder. Two policemen pulled up alongside him and asked where he was going and if he needed a ride. Perhaps they were sympathetic to the fact that he was clearly straining under the weight of the heavy box of trowels and chisels, or maybe they thought he had just stolen the box.

My grandfather declined their offer, knowing better than to get in the back seat of a patrol car. Doing so could be the last conscious act a colored man made on this earth. At that point, one of the policemen became suspicious and shined his flashlight in my grandfather's face. He asked him, "Hey, are you a nigga'?" Now, like me, my grandfather was about five and a half feet tall with his shoes on, but he was, as my father said before my mother had a chance to chastise him, "one cocky, tough son of a bitch." He looked that policeman in the eye and said something that went right through me, something that I never forgot, something that changed my whole perspective on who I was and what I was and where I came from.

He said, "Beans is beans, and hash is hash, but I'd rather be a nigga' than poor white trash."

The next morning, my father got a jailhouse call from my grandfather. He told him to bring him a clean shirt and a pair of shoes and twenty dollars, which was a whole lot of money in 1943. So my father, all of about fifteen years old, went down to the police station to bail my grandfather out of jail. His head was cracked open, his shirt and pants were stained with blood, and he wore no shoes, no socks, and no belt. He never got his tools back either. They walked to the truck, got it started, and drove home.

"So you be careful," my father told my brother. "Don't be runnin' around tellin' people you're Creole. There's two things the white man don't like: They don't like to be fooled, and they don't like uppity. And there's one thing black people don't like, and that's Creoles."

Growing up Creole meant I could tell from the corner what my mother was cooking for dinner. Growing up Creole meant having red beans and rice on Monday. Growing up Creole meant going to Big Loaf Bakery on Sunday after Mass. Growing up Creole meant all the girls who came to the Autocrats West picnic every year were fine, but you couldn't get to first base with any of them because you were related to all of them. Growing up Creole meant your parents were born, and I mean *literally born*, in the house where they were raised in the Seventh Ward. Growing up Creole meant that you and practically every one else you knew had a French last name. Growing up Creole meant all your parents' friends spoke with that lazy, flat, New Orleans accent.

Growing up Creole in Los Angeles meant hearing endless New Orleans stories about the Circle Market, Anybody's Place, Corpus Christi, Xavier (either the Prep or the University), Patsy Valdeler, Canal Street, Maison Blanche, Gus Mayer, sandwiches at Lavada's, how many streetcars your parents rode to get here and there, and how they had to climb the stairs to sit in the crow's nest at the Saenger Theater. Growing up Creole meant hearing about how my parents were only allowed to go to Lake Pontchartrain on certain days and at certain times; how they had to sit in the back of the streetcar, behind a screen; and how they had to sit in the back of the church in the "Colored Only" section for Sunday Mass, and the white people received Communion first.

Growing up Creole meant being despised, too. It meant that every day of my young life, I was a target because of the way I looked. Four feet ten inches tall in the eighth grade, light-skinned, bright, and damn near white, with a wavy mop of "that good hair," I was the recipient of all manner of race-driven aggression from both blacks and whites.

I remember one day walking home down Santa Barbara Avenue from Transfiguration Elementary School, later renamed in honor of Dr. Martin Luther King, Jr. As I passed a group of girls, one grabbed me around the neck and lifted me off my feet. They laughed as my hands and feet flailed away, as I tried hard not to suffocate. One pulled a steak knife out of her purse, and as she came toward me, I thought for sure she was going to stab me. Instead, she grabbed a handful of my hair and said, "Give me some of that good hair!" as she hacked it off. Another girl yelled out, laughing, "Get some for me, too." As she went in for another piece, a car pulled up alongside us, and a man jumped out and yelled at them. He was a truant officer from Audubon High School just across the street. The girls ran off. The truant officer took me home, and I remember spending the rest of the afternoon dumbfounded, trying to comb my hair back into place and cover the huge spot on top that had been lost. Later that day, my father took me to the barber.

Growing up Creole meant having a heritage I was proud of but rarely discussed with anyone outside my immediate family. Growing up Creole meant being part of a wonderful community of friends and family who loved to get together and socialize on the weekends in each other's homes, or at Ashton's Shatto on Slauson for any one of a number of social events. Growing up Creole meant fish on Fridays during Lent, ham and potato salad, roast chicken and macaroni and cheese (but not out of a box—the *real thing*). Growing up Creole meant learning a trade, handling tools, and working with some of the finest carpenters and plasterers and painters around. Men like Curtiss Gueringer and Bobby Dupre and Ruby Felton and Larry Gordon.

Some people thought of Creoles as an interesting slice of Americana responsible for exotic cuisine. Others knew Creoles to be tomatoes or horses or cigars. To them, "Creole" described an American combination of a little of the Old World and a little of the New.

- A creole tomato is the hybrid fruit of an Old World plant brought to this country and cross-pollinated with one found in the Americas. Hence, they have a unique size, color, texture, and flavor. All along the highways of Louisiana during spring and late summer, you'll see roadside stands selling gigantic creole tomatoes. In Los Angeles, we got them along with other distinctly New Orleans products at the Louisiana Seafood Market on Vernon and Arlington.

- At the race track, a letter "c" next to a horse's name designated it a creole, an animal bred from both Old and New World stock.

- My mother's mother, a petite, strong-willed, and independent spirit, rolled creole cigars for thirty years at L. Trellis Cigar Factory in New Orleans. Thirty years, as that was the only work available to "colored" women at the time. Thirty years! During one of her many visits to Los Angeles, she sat at our kitchen table and demonstrated how she rolled creole cigars, a combination of tobaccos from different growing regions.

Certainly, my grandmother and several of her sisters could have passed for white and found better employment and opportunities on the other side. But my grandmother never considered that as an option. To "pass" would have meant abandoning members of her own family, many of whom were darker than she was—including her own mother. Ostracizing herself from them was too high a price to pay, so she, like so many others considered "high yellow," took her place with dignity and self-respect in the "Colored Only" sections of the Deep South. Not all light-skinned black people are the "tragic mulattoes" of Hollywood lore.

Growing up Creole meant often being the target of black anger and violence. After every encounter, I walked away confused and hurt, sometimes bleeding, often with my property stolen and feeling lucky enough to get away with my life. Once, I was on the Crenshaw bus coming home from high school, and a bunch of dudes got on at

Adams. One of the brothas came down the aisle, wearing a Crip coat hanging off his shoulders, a blue nylon undershirt, and croaker sacks on his feet. He took one look at me, stopped, and put a revolver in my face. I could see the bullets in the chamber—four hollow points staring right at me.

"What set you from, ese?" he asked.

"Ese" is a slang term Latinos use for each other the way we use "brotha" or "homey." I guess he thought I was a Mexican. Fortunately, the night before, we'd taken my dad out to dinner for his birthday at El Torito in Westchester. My father ordered a dish called *arroz con pollo*, rice with chicken. My sister and I made up a cute little song about it on the way home, and it was the only Spanish I knew at the time except for the numbers *uno* through *diez*, *taco*, and *burrito*.

So I looked the young thug in the eye and said, as calmly and coolly and with as much of an accent as I could muster, "*Arroz con pollo*, cuz."

"Right on," he said with a nod. He put the gun back in his pocket, walked on down the aisle, and sat in the back. I got off at the next stop and walked home, wondering if he would have shot me right then and there, on a public bus, if I had answered incorrectly. Chicken and rice saved my ass.

Growing up Creole meant being misunderstood. One afternoon, I was shooting hoops at the local high school playground. After the game, we were sitting around cracking jokes and talking about each other's mama and stuff like that. Naturally, the "n-word" was used casually and with great frequency as it always is among young black men. But when I laughed and said, "Man, you niggas are crazy," one of the cats jumped off the bench and wanted to kick my ass.

"Naw, man! Broyard's cool, he's just light-skinned," said one of my friends, saving me from a sure test of manhood. I learned a valuable lesson from that one. My Afro, and my rolled-up Levi's, and my shell-top Adidas, and the range and accuracy of my jump shot—none of that mattered. I just wasn't one of the fellas. Growing up Creole meant not belonging.

Growing up Creole was to have a white boy in high school ask me, "Hey, Broyard, how come you hang out with the black guys? I mean, you're not *all the way* black, are you?"

Growing up Creole meant having a black guy in high school ask me why I had a black girlfriend. "Broyard likes that dark meat," he said, as he and several others laughed at me. Growing up Creole meant having your choices made for you.

Growing up Creole meant having an elderly African-American woman come up to me in a grocery store with tears in her eyes, saying, "Why don't you let 'em go?"

Now, I had run into the store to get a bag of disposable diapers for the baby, and I wasn't about to let those go, so I asked her, "Let *who* go, ma'am?"

"The hostages," she said.

"I don't have any hostages, dear. Who are you talking about?"

She swore up and down that I was from Iran, and that I must have had something to do with taking the hostages. Apparently, my lighter-than-a-brown-bag skin color is just brown enough and my hair texture is just coarse enough to identify me as Iranian. As conflict continues in the Middle East, I always remember that I must be careful.

Having often been mistaken for a North African, I am especially leery when I travel by air. In fact, several years ago a couple of intoxicated rednecks sitting behind me on a plane began making disparaging comments about Islam, the Taliban, etc., all the while kicking my seat and obviously directing their comments at me. It wasn't until I turned around and showed them my driver's license and several other documents with my photo and proof of citizenship that they cooled off, and the rest of the flight went off without any more problems. Apparently, my overall appearance makes some people nervous in this age of terror. Growing up Creole continues to sometimes be a liability for me, even as a grown man.

Growing up Creole connected me to something truly unique in American culture. It's something that I've always been proud of and interested in. I can't begin to explain the feeling I get when I go to New Orleans. The minute I walk out of the terminal at Louis Armstrong Airport, the thick, pungent air washes over me. Walking the broken brick and cobblestone streets of the French Quarter, the Marigny, the Treme, and the Seventh Ward fills me with an indescribable feeling. The sights and sounds of the streets, the wind in the trees, the smell of the city after a hard rain—it all connects me to home. It's familiar, and I revel in it every chance I get—walking the same streets my father and mother walked, seeing the neighborhoods where their parents lived and worked. This gave birth to Creole culture.

Yet so many people seem to have bizarre and offensive notions of who and what Creole is. I was asked by a young lady at UCLA during a question-and-answer session after a seminar on race and culture in America whether or not it was true that Creole fathers "sleep with their daughters in order to ensure that the skin color and hair texture remains consistent." I walked off the stage without answering. I was told by the mother of a good friend of mine that Creoles are "ignorant." I was asked to contribute an article for an anthology of contemporary African-American voices about Creole holidays—I didn't know there were any. At a lecture on the history of slavery in the Americas, I was pointed out as the product of the defilement of black womanhood by the white man. "Look at this poor brother," the lecturer said as he pointed to me, "Obviously, his great-grandmother was raped by a slave master." My great-grandmothers were Augustine Poree Broyard and Bertha Leal Montegut, neither of whom were slaves, neither of whom were raped, and both of whom lived as colored in the Seventh Ward of New Orleans. Growing up Creole was to be constantly misunderstood, misrepresented, and maligned.

My parents raised my brother, sister, and me to know who we were, what we were, and that we were descended from people of color. My father, a building contractor and a former president of the Minority Contractors Association of Los Angeles, never denied the fact that he was colored, Negro, or African American. In fact, only recently did we discover that the Broyard family has roots in New Rochelle, France; previously, my father was under the impression the our ancestors came from what at the time was known as French Morocco in Northern Africa. This is what his father, and his father's father, had told him about his ancestry.

In fact, even though it would be hard for most African Americans to admit, we are all creolized, in the broadest sense of the word, because we're all mixed with something. My mother never passed for white a day in her life, despite rumors and lies circulated by a so-called friend of hers. She grew up in the Lafitte project in New

Orleans, attended Xavier University, and dedicated her life to educating black children in the inner-city neighborhood where we lived. My mother saw herself as a black woman every day of her life, and I'm proud to say she raised her three children so we weren't under any illusions that we were anything other than the same.

The majority of the racism, anger, and violence I've been subjected to has come from those I always thought of as my own people. This has neither confused me nor made me bitter. I still look in the mirror every day of my life and see an African-American man—a black man with a heritage just as unique as any other.

What I've come to understand is that as a race, we often see ourselves as victims of racism only. Yet as African Americans, we perpetrate quite a bit of racism ourselves, and it's really sad that we often turn it against our own kind. Is it that the scars of racism are so deeply internalized that we must turn on ourselves? Or are we just normal human beings who, like so many others, look for someone to put down to make ourselves feel better about who we are? Consider the Hutus and the Tutsis—they look practically the same, and yet they slaughtered each other.

Growing up Creole is to be connected to something worth cherishing. Growing up Creole is to be proud of my family and what they have achieved. Growing up Creole is to live in the margins and to celebrate that every day of my life.

—**Mark Broyard**

Mark Broyard was born in New Orleans, Louisiana. He is a vocalist, a composer, and a visual and performance artist. For the national stage, he has created and performed the critically acclaimed Inside the Creole Mafia *with Obie-award winning actor, playwright, director, and friend Roger Guenveur Smith. As a visual artist, he has shown his work at galleries and museums from Brooklyn to Oakland. His assemblages have been featured in* The International Review of African-American Art.

Broyard is in constant demand as a vocal soloist, and as a composer, he has set to music poems by Langston Hughes, Countee Cullen, and others. He lives in Culver City, California, with his wife, artist Alicia Galindo, and he is the father of two sons.

◆ **Chapter 21**

Urgent Message: We've Got a Problem Here. Fortunately, It's Never Too Late to Do Something About It

MY PASSION GIVES ME UNWAVERING WILL. WHEN I THINK OF the lost potential of a generation of at-risk youth—black, Caucasian, Latino, and Asian—I am driven to work harder in my quest to let them know they are not alone. It is no longer a theory, speculation, or even rumor. So perilous are the odds stacked against them that everyone thought that somebody else would step in to stop this tidal wave of human devastation. There is no need for a scientific survey. The reasons are clear: A lack of positive role models, a lack of two-parent households, inferior education, little hope for employment, drug-infested neighborhoods, and gang proliferation are all pathways to incarceration.

When I think of innocent bodies entering the world with all the hope and promise of their counterparts in more affluent communities, I prepare myself for the inevitable. All children are born with bright eyes eager and ready to learn, thought processes pure of any negativity, and spirits filled with hope. All babies are born with the ability to be absolutely anything humanly possible, both positive or negative. It is not about IQ or skin color. It is about circumstances.

Many at-risk youth are living in a constant state of crisis because of their environmental circumstances, which impact absolutely everything they experience. Their coping skills are limited to their surroundings. Growing up in an environment of negativity is difficult to change if victims don't understand that it's negative. If negativity is all they know, that's the norm and it's their reference point. Anything else is seen as an unobtainable fantasy. They lack knowledge about how to change things, how to plan constructively, and where to turn for help. If adults have trouble coping, imagine the impact on a child. Our goal should be to help them first imagine, then believe, and then work toward the goal of positive achievement.

It is almost unimaginable, but statistics show that most at-risk youth do not graduate from high school. Even fewer attend and finish college. This situation appears to be a fast track to incarceration. This is the reality we are dealing with, but it does not have to be this way.

I believe, I know, I am sure, I am positive that it is never too late to save a child. So I want to focus on the accountability of the community. Not everyone has equal abilities, but each of us has the capacity to do something. Our community is failing its children when so many of them are at risk. No one can save our children but us, so it is imperative for us to step up. That declarative statement includes input from academia, clergy, psychologists, entertainers, sports stars, businesspeople, health care providers, law-enforcement officers, babysitters, beauticians, carpenters, fathers and mothers, and even ex-cons. We can no longer sit idly by, passively pretending that someone is going to come to the rescue.

URGENT! THIS JUST IN! NO ONE IS COMING TO SAVE US! WE MUST SAVE OURSELVES!

Frightening, isn't it? We must recognize that we are operating in crisis mode, but a crisis means a turning point has arrived, and things can go either way. So now we know. We know what our job is and what our challenge is. The disengagement has to end. First, we must acknowledge that these are our children, and we are responsible for them, including absentee fathers coming home and neighbors taking charge of lost children, as was often the custom in the past. The answers and the cures are so simple that many will not believe change can happen that simply.

The downside is that it won't happen overnight. It will take decades to reverse the catastrophic decline of hope in our community. All we need is the will to accept this challenge of monumental proportions that concerns the future of all of us. At this point, we must first put out the fire and then do some long-term planning for future generations.

For many years, I taught and worked with boys who were not just at-risk but were already felons. I believed in them and worked hard to present more positive aspects of life to them. I brought in guest speakers to enlighten and motivate them. I called them positive names like Intellects, Superstars, and Men of Class—names they embraced and began to call themselves. They played sports with children from private schools so they could get a different outlook on life besides their own environment. They learned the importance of social graces. They, like everyone else, needed encouragement in their lives. My passion for understanding them and their plight brought us close, and I earned their respect. Even though I have retired from teaching, I have not retired from their lives. I gave them tough love, but love it was, and they knew it and felt it.

After apartheid ended, the South African government implemented a program called Reconciliation to help heal and unite the races. We could try something similar to start the process of healing between youth and adults, both disappointed in each other. There are also options that don't require money, such as giving our children time and attention.

Women, gather a group of girls together and talk to them about simple things like cooking, planting flowers, sewing, or old-fashioned etiquette. Men, gather a group of young boys and teach them carpentry, home repairs, how to be respectful toward ladies, and how to respect themselves. Talk to them about being a father. Whatever skills, talents, or gifts you possess, share them with the young people. Many public schools no longer offer music: If you are a musician, mentor someone and teach them your skill set. If you are an entrepreneur, mentor someone about how the business world operates. Athletes, get a group together and clear a field for baseball, basketball, football, soccer, or tennis. And somebody, please step up and teach children how money works, so exploitative businesses, such as pawn shops and check-cashing places, can be driven out of poor communities.

Remember, the results won't be immediate, but they will come. Change will require sacrifice of your time and effort, but it requires no money to implement and can begin immediately. If you don't have time but are financially secure, your money would be appreciated to provide equipment and materials. These building blocks are a potential start for creating a peaceful and prosperous society. We've got to do something now, or we will all go down sooner or later.

Imagine our community as a ship large enough to hold millions of people. The ship is so large that you probably won't come into contact with most of the people onboard, so there is a basic disconnect between pockets of people even in this small universe. You might think that what happens on one part of the ship won't affect you because you don't know anyone who's personally involved.

Now imagine that one portion of the ship does not have access to food. The hungry people can see the food that the people on the rest of the ship can have, but they cannot obtain it by ordinary means. After a while, their hunger drives them to try other means to get the food they need to survive: digging, scraping, and stealing.

Eventually, all of the digging and scraping leads the hungry people to food, but it also creates a small hole in the ship's side. Slowly, a very small stream of water begins to seep in from the miniscule hole. The people nearest the damaged area have wet feet, but at least they now have food, so they adjust. No one pays attention to the hole—especially those on the top deck. Some people notice the hole, but they ignore it because they did not cause it, and it was not affecting them personally. Some of these people look down on the people who made the hole, calling them troublemakers and treating them with scorn.

Eventually, the hole gets bigger and bigger and begins to flood the lower levels. People only begin to take action as the ship begins to sink. Suddenly, they all realize that although some are not responsible for the hole, they will all surely drown if it is not repaired.

We are on that ship. That ship is us. It is not too late to plug that hole. Children want us to steer them in the right direction. They want our guidance, and they know they can't do it on their own. They are only doing what they have to do to survive. They have become hardened to "polite society" as a defense mechanism. You'd be surprised at what a hug will do for somebody, or what hearing the words "I love you" can do for a person. Self-esteem comes from within, but everyone needs "love taps" to help them get there. Everyone needs praise and positive reinforcement.

I want to do more than I've already done. I don't mind doing more than my share. I am not willing to retire from the hope that things can be better. I'm willing to continue my lifelong fight on behalf of young people. I'm sending out a challenge to my peers to join me. I want young people to know that I won't give up if they won't give up. If they give us one more chance, we will do our best to make it right, or at least to make it better. We have to offer young people something to hold on to and something to rally around. We must declare ourselves "heroes and sheroes," and we must pray, pray, pray. But we also must put on our battle gear, prepare to sacrifice, understand there will be hurt and pain, and be aware that there will be no immediate results. Always remember that it is never too late to save a child, because every child is worth saving.

URGENT! URGENT! URGENT! THIS JUST IN! THINGS ARE ABOUT TO CHANGE!

—Geraldine Westbrooks

Geraldine Westbrooks is a teacher, businesswoman, and philan-thropist. She resides in Los Angeles, California.

♦ Chapter 22

Soul Survivor*

THERE WAS NO RUNNING WATER IN THE COVINGTON, TENNESSEE, house I was born in on August 20, 1942. It was a shotgun country-style home, if you will. I guess you could say my beginnings were humble, but I never knew it. As a boy, I picked cotton to make ends meet and never thought twice about pitching in to do my part. That was how we were. Those were our circumstances, and if you didn't know any other way, it was normal to you. We all helped each other. That was the way it was, the code we lived by. I may have been two or three years old when I adopted the cotton fields as both a playground and a workplace, and it was the best playground I knew.

My mother died of an illness when I was very young—so young that I don't even remember her. I was about three years old. My father abandoned my sister, Willette, and me before we could form a relationship, so my grandmother, Rushia Addie-Mae Wade, who lived in Memphis, stepped in to claim us.

Off to Lymon Street we went, and my days of picking cotton were over forever. My aunts and uncles lived on the same street, so they all split up the responsibility of raising us. I went to Grandma Wade's by myself, but Willette and I saw each other whenever we felt like it. I went about finding work wherever I could. I cleaned bricks and shoes, picked up groceries—I'd do anything I could to earn a nickel, dime, or quarter, just so I could pitch in.

I never knew I was poor until I moved to Memphis. I'd always figured that that's how it was for everybody. It was so natural to me. But when I started school and noticed that all the other kids had more than I had, it really kicked in. Our days were long and tiring, but they were full of hope and undying love. We were so poor,

* This essay is based on an interview with the late music icon Isaac Hayes.

we couldn't afford a Christmas tree. Instead, on Christmas morning, Grandma Wade would decorate her sewing machine with nuts and apples, which were Christmas presents for Willette and me.

I eventually dropped out of school out of plain embarrassment. It was hard for me to do, because I really liked school and loved to learn. I always liked reading, and unlike kids today, for me it was anything but an interruption. Instead, it *was* what I wanted to do. But my shoes had cardboard in the soles to cover gaping holes. It wasn't long before the girls noticed, and my self-consciousness grew stronger than my desire to attend classes. I didn't have any clothes that were appropriate for school. In an odd sort of way, I literally couldn't afford to go to school.

What saved me, ironically, was music. My music teachers took a special interest in me, and I took a special interest in music. It was always my salvation. Even when I was picking cotton in Covington, music was an escape from the scorching sun and the laborious tasks I faced. I'd sing a song or hum a tune and imagine myself in another place—a juke joint, maybe—and all the pain would go away. It was a temporary fix, but it worked every time. But by this time, the pain was too deep. It hurt too much.

My music teacher came to the house and explained to my grandmother that I hadn't been attending any of my classes, even music. They called me into the room to discuss my decision to stay away, and I told them the truth. My grandmother sat there, unmoved. Eventually, she turned to my music teacher as if to say, "There's nothing I can do about that right now." And she couldn't. She'd done enough by taking me in and giving me all the love and hope a boy could ask for. She'd moved me to Memphis, away from the cotton fields and into a more civilized state.

Without batting an eyelash, my music teacher confirmed her understanding with a nod and then an offer. "My husband has some clothes that he doesn't wear all that much," she said. "In fact, there's a whole side of his closet that we could free up. He doesn't need them." She turned, looked at me, and asked, "Isaac, would you like them?"

I thought I was going to explode from the inside out, but I held my composure, smiled, and calmly replied, "Yes." The new threads were obviously too big for a high school student, but it didn't matter to me. I felt like something out of a newspaper ad, and that was easily enough to get me back in school. Things really started to happen for me after that. I entered a talent show at Lemoyne College and sang Nat King Cole's "Looking Back." When I finished, the house was on its feet! The next day, the girls who hadn't thought I dressed sharp enough before *all* wanted me!

Things continued to look up. I joined the band and learned to play the saxophone, piano, electric guitar, and flute, all by ear. Ultimately, I was the valedictorian of my class and earned seven musical scholarships. It's safe to say that my music teacher's investment paid off.

Needless to say, I wasn't surprised. I'd always made excellent grades. It was a major accomplishment for me not because I hadn't thought that I could achieve, but because of the hardships I faced along the way.

I was twenty-one the day I earned my high school diploma. After graduation, I turned down the music scholarships and found a job sweeping floors at Stax Recording Studios. I wanted to take a chance on myself as a musician and a singer.

One day, I got it. Music's omnipotent force grabbed hold of me while I was sweeping those floors, and I sang with an urgency that I'd never known before. The owner of Stax, Jim Stewart, was so impressed that he offered to enlist me as a session player, and I excitedly accepted.

It wasn't long before David Porter and I formed the most devastating songwriting duo Stax ever saw. We called ourselves the Soul Children, and the '60s were all ours. We ultimately developed what would become the sound of Memphis and, later, popular music as a whole. In 1967, I released a solo album entitled *Presenting Isaac Hayes*. It was commercially unsuccessful, but not so unsuccessful that it kept me from trying again. I'd overcome so many obstacles in my life; this one was relatively easy to get over. It was music! I knew that if there was anything I could do right, music was it.

The answer for me and for Stax Records was *Hot Buttered Soul*. The album sprang from a river of pain. It had taken me every bit of a year to get over Dr. Martin Luther King, Jr.'s death. I had walked with the brother during the Civil Rights Movement, and we were supposed to meet the very day he was murdered in downtown Memphis. When he died, it seemed like the bottom fell out of everything I was doing. For a long period of time, I simply couldn't create. I was so bitter and angry.

It took hold of me until I really took the time to sort things out in my soul. I became determined. I would become so powerful and so successful that people would have to listen and respect what I was giving. I turned all that fury and rage into the most successful album of the twenty-seven that Stax released that year, easily the most inspired work the label had seen since Otis Redding's untimely death two years earlier.

It was a dream come true. I'd gone from sweeping the floors to being the premier artist on the label. Because I'd accomplished so much in school and overcome the obstacles that I had, I knew I could make it. However, my family had other ideas for me, and none of them included music. It was, "Ike, why don't you be a sanitation worker?" or "You can cook. Why don't you pursue a career as a chef?" or "Why don't you become a bus driver? That's a good job!" Being a musician was thought of as a pipe dream, and they were anything but supportive. I never wanted to pursue any of those jobs because none of them would allow me to be creative. Making the transformation from sweeping floors to what I'd become was another milestone for me. Nobody wanted me to do this but *me*.

See, black folks weren't supposed to have options then. We were supposed to do what was available to us and be happy about it. There was no dreaming allowed unless we were fast asleep. My dream was concrete, and nothing was going to stop me from realizing it. Sometimes you have to follow God's voice, and I knew that He wanted more for me. I just knew it.

Writing was always connected to my life, my spirit, my soul, and sometimes a passing moment in time. For instance, Porter and I were in the studio once, and I was telling him to hurry up and finish a song. At one point, I was yelling at the top of my lungs, and he retorted just as loudly, "Hold on! I'm comin'!" That response ended up being the genesis of a hit for Sam and Dave, but it never would have happened had we not recognized and held on to the moment. Sometimes things sort themselves out in a magical way.

Another majestic moment for me was scoring *Shaft*. It was such a big movie for black folks; likewise, it was an enormous project for me. It meant so much to so many people, and to be an integral part of that was humbling. At the same time, winning an Oscar for it and embracing a movement of empowerment largely inspired by my music made me want to do more. My music made people feel good, gave them a sense of self-respect, and at the same time made me an icon.

All I wanted to do at that point was continue to write songs that painted a picture of black life that other black people could relate to. Our culture was the single most important thing in my mind, career-wise. And it was more or less about everyday living. Dino Woodard called me the Abyssinian Baptist, because I told the truth and spoke to the people in plain language.

So my next album was naturally titled *Black Moses*. The concept behind it was basically centered on how I had been living my life and what I wanted to convey to the people. Black Moses was a symbol of pride. Finally, black men could stand up and be counted. Moses was the epitome of masculinity—a black man who'd reversed the curse of bondage and freed himself and his people. Chains that once represented four hundred years of captivity were now symbols of strength, power, and sexual virility.

To this day, the name still sticks, and honestly, I didn't like it at first. The way I saw it, Moses was a man of God, and that's not to say that I wasn't. I just didn't expect it to catch on the way it did. But I guess that's what happens when the message is clear. The people hear you. So in the end, I always tried to live up to the name and give people music that would set them free. I hope it continues to persevere and offer a positive representation of black people.

I think people's ideals are very individualistic these days. Being black now, as it's always been, is a reflection of the times. Being black to me was all about sacrifice. It was growing up in the country. It was hard living. Tough! My grandmother and grandfather prayed hard and always told me to *do unto others as I would have them do unto me.* My grandmother always read the Bible to me. She and my grandfather taught me how to be a man, to always stand on my own two feet, and to take care of my responsibilities, and I've passed that message along to my children. I've also communicated those messages in my music, and I'm proud to have had such an effect on so many people. I hope that we continue to cherish each other as a people and love each other like we've never loved before.

Remember my music, because it came from the heart.

—Isaac Hayes

Isaac Hayes was an Academy Award–winning soul and funk singer-songwriter, musician, record producer, arranger, composer, and actor. Hayes was one of the main creative forces behind the Southern soul music label Stax Records, where he served as both an in-house songwriter and a producer. In 1971, Hayes earned an Oscar for Best Original Song for "Shaft"; he was also recognized by the Grammy Hall of Fame and the Rock and Roll Hall of Fame for his classic song "Soul Man." He was the recipient of two Grammy Awards and numerous gold and platinum records. Hayes died in August 2008 in his native Memphis. This essay is based on an interview with the late music icon.

♦ Chapter 23

BrookVirgiBadian: My Mixed-In Life

I N MY OPINION, I WAS BORN AT THE PERFECT MOMENT IN HISTORY. I also feel I was born at the perfect intersection of geography. You see, I was born in the Bedford Stuyvesant section of Brooklyn, New York.

At the time, Bedford Stuyvesant was predominantly populated by black folks (negroes or colored, we were often called at the time). It was also sprinkled with shops owned and operated by Jewish people who didn't live in the area. There was Mr. Butler's grocery store at the corner of Halsey (the street where I lived) and Sumner Avenue (now Garvey Boulevard). Sol the shoemaker was around the corner from the Butler store, and Sam Pelner's hardware store was a few doors from them. From what I remember, these shop owners treated their black customers with respect. However, it was a sign of the changing times when Peter Hayes, a black man who was one of Pelner's key salespeople, became the store's owner. Pelner and other Jewish shop owners began to leave the area as the Civil Rights Movement helped black folks realize that they should be owning their shops and doing business with black shop owners.

My mother was Edna Lewis, the daughter of Geneva Booth Lewis and Robert Lewis. The Lewises came to Brooklyn from the small Southern hamlet of Gloucester, Virginia. My father was Eustace Harewood, the oldest son of Clarissa Sealy Harewood and Benjamin Harewood. The Harewoods hailed from the small Caribbean island of Barbados.

Early in my life, this ancestral mixture was a source of great confusion to me. At the time, most black folks in Brooklyn had Southern heritage. In keeping with the adage, "If you don't understand something, criticize it," many Southern-heritage blacks referred to Caribbean blacks in insulting terms. I remember frequently hearing such pejoratives as, "Those damn West Indians," "You goddamn coconuts," or "You came over here on the banana boat." The insinuation was that Caribbean blacks had harder heads than most people, or that Caribbean people had come to America on boats that should have only contained bananas.

There was also a not-so-subtle racist joke that West Indians handled their money better than Southern blacks. More than a few times, I remember hearing (sometimes from my mother's own cousins), "Those West Indians are cheap, just like Jews. They know how to make and keep a buck!" Since my mother was of Southern heritage and my father didn't have an accent, many of these derogatory statements were made right in front of us.

In fact, I often hid my Caribbean heritage, as peer pressure made it more convenient for me to keep those roots to myself. I joined my friends when they tied a Caribbean kid named Gregory to a tree and let ants scurry down his back. I didn't stop them when they chased another Caribbean kid, Basil, all the way home, screaming at him, "Basil, you coconut!" Both situations existed only because their families had different backgrounds than my friends. Hey, the school of thought was that the American blacks were the majority. I look back in retrospect and wonder if what we did was any better than the actions of the Italian kids who fought with us constantly at my racist, predominantly Italian junior high school. Early in my life, I was less than fond of my Caribbean roots and often thought they were of little or no benefit to me.

In spite of the fact that I tried to diminish my mixed cultural heritage, even then I realized some of its benefits. At family gatherings, I often saw Caribbean and Southern people mixing and having fun with each other. Back then, segregation separated more than just black and white, but two of my father's brothers were also married to women with Southern heritage. This opened up my world, as our gatherings included dialogues about Virginia and South Carolina as well as about Bim (as Barbados is sometimes called) and Trinidad.

And the food! We ate Southern fried chicken, collard greens, potato salad, and yams alongside coconut sweetbread, rum fruit cake, meat patties, and codfish cakes. The adults all had fun and got along. A few summers, I traveled "down South" to Virginia and witnessed small-town Southern life. Gloucester was so small, the post office was in the back of the package store. A Dairy Queen with a swing and a sliding board was "the amusement park." The sound of bobwhites chirping and roosters cock-a-doodle-dooing and the smell of my uncle's pigs were a welcome respite from the humid New York summers.

I never visited the Caribbean until I was an adult. My cousin Norman visited Barbados one summer, and his stories, along with his cricket bat, gave me a vision of what the island might be like. It wasn't until I got to college that I really came to realize the great benefits of Caribbean blood. I attended Brooklyn College at a time when Bob Marley's music was beginning to reverberate on American shores. Eric Clapton had a major hit with "I Shot The Sheriff," and white kids began to dig deep to find the origin of the song. The Jamaican kids at school (there were more there than I'd gone to high school with) took up this mantle of power and made it clear: "Marley is our man!"

My entertainment-industry career began at my college's radio station, WBCR. The first radio program I personally produced was a Caribbean music special designed to introduce reggae and calypso music to the campus. Imagine that—I'd never wanted to 'fess up to being West Indian, and suddenly I was a champion of the culture.

The other thing that motivated me to promote my "mixture" was my attachment to a very fine young lady from the small town of Bennettsville, South Carolina. Two of her closest friends in school were very fine young ladies from Jamaica. The Caribbean girls on campus were fine as heck, and it was easier to talk to them if you could put some "patois" into your conversation.

As an adult, I consider myself very open minded when it comes to appreciating folks from different backgrounds. I actively embrace the fact that I am a man with both a Southern and a Caribbean background. I was largely educated at predominantly white schools, and I've lived in New York, Atlanta, and Los Angeles. This emulsion of influences helps make me who I am.

My dad (remember him? Eustace Harewood, the West Indian?) attended the March on Washington, where the great Southern minister Dr. Martin Luther King, Jr., made his famous "I Have A Dream" speech. In college, I became aware of the great Jamaican Marcus Garvey and his credo for blacks throughout the diaspora: "One God, one aim—one destiny!" I now know that we are in this world together, and in spite of our different beginnings, we all are one!

—Kevin Harewood

Kevin Harewood is an entertainment industry veteran who currently resides in Brooklyn, New York.

◆ Chapter 24

A Legacy That Lives Through Me

I'M NOT SURE WHERE THE DRIVE COMES FROM. IT COULD BE MY my father's side of the family tree, where resilient branches stretch toward the sunlight of equality in Arkansas.

My mother, Shirley Whitfield, has told my brothers, my sister, and me countless stories about the leadership of my dad, George Whitfield, with the Students for Freedom (SFF) chapter at the University of Arkansas. Among his accomplishments was helping integrate the school's swimming pool. She also told us stories of how he helped black students receive equal treatment throughout the tumultuous times of the Civil Rights Movement of the '60s. She loved to entertain us with interesting anecdotes of how she would take food to our cousins, Robert (Bob) Whitfield, a director of the Student Nonviolent Coordinating Committee (SNCC) and Ed Whitfield, a member of the SNCC, as they coordinated freedom rallies and other nonviolent protests. Her home often served as a hideaway for Bob when he would need to drop out of sight a while. Or perhaps the ferocity with which I approach my need to talk to our children comes from my uncle Bill Whitfield, who served as minister of education for the Black Panthers.

Since I'm the child of both my father and my mother, maybe my need to talk to our youth comes from my mother's side of the tree. Although she was an educator by trade, she also always played LPs and the radio, making a point of letting us listen to the latest music of our times as well as the music of her past. I like to think that I am a product of both of them, with a few tender branches growing from my own experiences. Regardless of who's really responsible for my deep-seated desire to help our youth, I know that the directive to look beyond my immediate circumstances comes from my parents. It's part of the wealth I want to share with those who come after me.

In this era, where many youth gain their identity from the commercially packaged ideals transmitted through the airwaves and television screens, I find it imperative to dispel the myths of the black man presented in the media: a robber, a thug, a hoodie-and-tennis-shoe-wearing anathema feared by many and always absent from home. I feel a personal directive to help students see the wealth inside of them. I can empathize. I remember what it's like to be a "have-not" often distracted from such a core truth because you're constantly surrounded by "haves." The adults in the community and in the home must reiterate constantly that the road to exterior riches begins with the examination of the riches inside yourself.

When I'm talking to young adults, I tell them about my burgundy Chevy Chevette with the 6 × 9 speakers and the pink fuzzy dice hanging from the mirror, and what it felt like to pull up next to my friend with the brand-new gold 300Z with Bose speakers. I can share my struggles to stay eligible for high school basketball. The school's minimum requirement to play was a 2.5 GPA; while that was fine for my classmates, my parents, who had higher standards and aspirations, would tolerate nothing less than a 3.0. The second my grade point average slipped was the same second I was sidelined for nine weeks. I learned a tough lesson about supporting a team from afar and not living up to the standards set before me. Although these stories are funny now, they have an underlying moral about setting standards higher than the status quo. They allow me to talk about how success is not a sin, and that education and intelligence are not only the birthrights of our Caucasian brothers and sisters. They're for everybody.

I don't have a story about walking through the snow for five miles, milking the cows before I went to school, or not having anything to eat but cold meat and beans, but I can tell you about the baton that's been thrown before us that's there for anyone to grab.

I can talk about how hip-hop started out as a means of telling the black man's story and how the first time I heard Chuck D and KRS-One tell their stories of the streets of New York and the throbbing beats under which their stories were told, I was hooked. I know that hip-hop is the most explosive movement of our times for the audience I seek—kids ages thirteen through eighteen—and how it has become a successful platform from which I can discuss health issues that disproportionately affect the African-American community.

I am a physician, and I have been successful in my career endeavors. I am not ashamed of this success, but I also know that I have a social responsibility to the youth of today to allow them to see adults—specifically physicians—as more than just robots wearing lab coats. We are living, breathing people with hearts that care and hands that heal, but we are also part of the same experience in which they now participate—living. I begin this dialogue with the music played in their iPods—hip-hop.

Hip-hop is not just music; it's a culture. Yes, there are negatives about that culture—the nihilism of gangsta rap, the disrespectful posturing against authority, and the misogynistic treatment of women, but it is an excellent vehicle to reach young adults. My nickname, Hip-Hop Doc, came from these kids. It is a term of endearment that shows they know I care about them. I am able to steer them away from the negative lyrics and the indirect influence of these songs and begin conversations, first about the base level of the beats, and later, on a more serious level, including explaining how drugs and alcohol can kill them. It is not enough that I listen to the music. I must do my homework on the language they use. "Gangsta" may be a type of rap, but when I talk to kids I have to know it's also a term for HIV. Knowing these terms allows me to talk about the impact of unsafe sexual practices in our neighborhoods.

My father has always spoken of "thinking globally, but acting locally." It is through this dialogue that I pass the baton on to our kids. When I teach kids about making healthy decisions throughout their lives, I am affecting locally and, hopefully, lessening globally the number of African Americans who end up infected with HIV/AIDS and dismissing the lore of "sippin' on syrup" and instead making healthy food and exercise choices to reduce the incidence of stroke and heart disease within the community. But I cannot be the only one. We can do so much more together. I put a call out to my peers to do the same as they treat young adults.

It is not enough to just listen to the music and stand before children and speak from the lofty heights of podiums. I have tried to establish a more human presence in the community. This presence not only puts authenticity behind the words, "I care," but it also adds action. After speaking with students at health fairs and school assemblies, I like to hang around for a while and play ball, talk, and share ideas. I'm often found at meetings of Lyrics Anonymous, a program that provides a forum for its participants (mostly young people) to express themselves through lyrics and spoken word; after-school programs that teach kids how to play instruments; and spoken-word poetry classes. As I look around at these meetings, I wonder where the other professionals are. Certainly I can't be the only adult who finds it important to show children that adults care and that we're dialed in to their culture. It is this absence that drives me, and I keep trying harder to fill the void when my peers don't step up.

It is also necessary for me to model learning and show students that education is an endeavor that continues on in all facets of our lives. The presence of more professional adults at these teaching sessions would underscore this message. In these teaching moments, I often have opportunities to answer hard questions about sex and drugs that young adults are often afraid to ask their parents. If these questions are not answered, how can we adults expect that they will learn the truth?

It's not enough to simply achieve the degree of Doctor of Medicine. Doctors must live the requirements of the Hippocratic Oath: "To consider dear to me, as my parents, him who taught me this art; to live in common with him and, if necessary, to share my goods with him; to look upon his children as my own brothers, to teach them this art." To truly put this oath into action, all doctors must step up, step forward, and create a relationship between practitioner and patient. This relationship must exist beyond the confines of our offices and into the community.

As I have attempted to move my brothers and sisters in the community, some within my profession have attempted to pull me back with their negativity. The comparison of blacks acting like "crabs in a bucket" continues to exist. Although I find it an honor to be called the Hip-Hop Doc, some of my peers have criticized me for it. While they laugh, I ask what they're called by the community. Doctor? Sir? Do their patients even understand that they're people, too—people with families, people who were kids once themselves?

I make it a practice not to feed into their negativity; instead, I focus on solutions and invite other doctors to participate along with me. Instead of standing by as statistics are created, doctors can get involved and answer kids' questions before they seek the answers on the street.

In addition to the discrimination that I encounter from my peers, I am also challenged by the economically disenfranchised. Recently, I helped a local rapper give back to his community by distributing $52,000 worth of food, clothes, and bicycles. There, I encountered negativity in a positive moment: I encountered a patient who I had treated as a jail inmate. He stared at me in disbelief, questioned why I dared to be in his neighborhood. Of course, it was obvious why I was there—giving away bicycles to children who had performed well in school—but he wanted to know what gave me the idea that I had the right to be in that neighborhood. I was a doctor, and he was accustomed to seeing doctors only in offices.

After I explained what had brought me to the event, his response reinforced the message I'd heard so many times before. "I never seen no black doctor in the 'hood before." There is a social responsibility for all professionals—*particularly* doctors—to establish a presence in the community. How else can we establish a healthy dialogue with our patients *before* they need life-saving medical intervention? By creating a dialogue with our patients, we can lessen the impact of medical issues *before* they become a threat.

So where am I now? I'm the proud father of a beautiful, intelligent, and funny daughter named Raina. Every day is a balance between career, community, and family. I hope to instill in her the same pride I have in my self-identity and a desire to give back to our community. I take her with me to different speaking engagements so she can experience the same rush of endorphins I get when I share my knowledge with others, and I want her to constantly redefine the wealth she has within herself.

I have used the hip-hop culture to develop a comic book entitled *The Hip-Hop Doc and the Legion of Health,* which features characters relevant to today's youth. The goal of the comic book is to rid the world of disease and improve the health of all Americans by using the culture of hip-hop as a weapon. The aim of my life is to educate our youth about serious health issues through the medium of hip-hop, and I challenge other professionals to stop being part of the problem through their absence. They should instead be part of the solution. It is time African Americans became architects of the future, and "look upon his children as my own brothers, to teach them this art."

Our job is not finished as long as the question, "Is the dream dead?" remains, and the answer is found in the shadows of three nooses in Jena, Louisiana; the spread of HIV among the African-American population; and the disproportionate effects of heart disease and stroke that are so prevalent in our community.

—**Rani Whitfield, MD**

Rani Whitfield, MD, is a Baton Rouge, Louisiana–based family medical practitioner. He is a graduate of Southern University and the Meharry Medical College. Visit www.h2doc.com for more information.

Chapter 25

Bridging the Divide

THE AFRICAN-AMERICAN EXPERIENCE IS A COMBINATION OF ideals. As a community, we've become accustomed to referring to each other as black, but there are a variety of factors that figure into our makeup as a people. First is the creolization of African and American culture. The foundation of Southern culture is an intertwined combination of African, Native American, and European culture, Creole-style. Dr. Hazel Carvey of Yale University termed it the "creolization of America." American Southern culture, according to Dr. Carvey, is essentially American culture that was Africanized by enslaved Africans from West Africa.

My identity as an African American begins with my parents and the black church. Like many black families, mine set out to ensure that I had strong religious beginnings. Both of my parents were from the South, and they brought their culture along when they moved north.

Whenever I said something dismissive of someone else within the community, such as suggesting that he or she had a very conservative or "European" perspective, my mother would determinedly question my logic. Her questions ranged from "What do they bring to the table?" to "Do they offer any positive ideas?" She would remind me that dismissing a perspective or another human being means framing oneself as perfect. Instead, she would insist, in this diverse age, we must search for the common ground among diverse political and theological positions.

My mother was concerned about my generation falling into disunity, like the W.E.B. DuBois–Marcus Garvey trap or the public argument between Malcolm X and Dr. Martin Luther King, Jr. Some believe that having information about our culture defines us as African Americans. However, over the past thirty years, we've learned that having information about African culture does not necessarily translate into an ethic of community service or to a demonstration of love, compassion, or integrity. Information is a part of liberation, but it alone is not enough to liberate our community. We must develop a respect for differences and come to grips with our African past and Creole influences, as well.

Being African American

The climate of this culture simply does not allow for one way of being. Demanding that we all operate, worship, and view the world from a particular perspective is disrespectful of our history. It is a grave mistake and an insult to our ancestors to dismiss people within the African-American community simply because they have divergent views. It is indisputable that America subjugated human beings and dismissed their identity. We as a community ingested this ideal, making such self-destructive statements as, "Don't call yourself 'African!' Define yourself as 'Negro' or 'Colored.'"

In fact, there were laws on the books in South Carolina to prevent people from connecting to their African identity—specifically, from using drums. They feared we would speak to each other in our different tongues and revolt against the brutal system of slavery. No other group of "Americans," except Native Americans, experienced this kind of torture and brutality. We are the seventh generation of sons and daughters of America, and yet we are forced to investigate our past to discover who we were. We are a major part of human history, and our slave experience was just a sliver of a much larger story.

We are a gumbo. We are the Creole culture of America. This is why Creole is such an important part of our understanding. Equally important is properly using the term "gumbo," and understanding what it means to us. It's not just a delicious soup native to New Orleans. It is a metaphor for an entire culture.

If you take two thousand black people with mixed incomes and place them in a fixed community, you'll get certain cultural products.

One family might have a grandmother who watches preschool children during the day. Another family may offer an after-school activity in their living room. A retired coach might assemble a baseball team; a woman might give piano lessons, and so on—all without thought of the monetary gain behind it. This is the idea of extended family—a concept we draw from our Southern and African past.

African-American music traditionally promotes unity and togetherness, bringing together the sacred and the secular. Michelle Williams of Destiny's Child, one of the most popular and successful female groups in R&B history, has transferred those talents to her church with relative ease. To take it a step further, Mahalia Jackson's stirring spiritual performances mirror the blues of Howlin' Wolf and Muddy Waters. The chords are practically identical in some instances; while the lyrics are different, the cultural nuances are not. Go to any dynamic church service and attend any secular concert, and you will notice the same themes in either place.

I believe this source of discontent goes back to DuBois' eloquent statement, "The problem of the twentieth century is the color line." I would add class to that, as well. Our community is full of dirty laundry we do not want to air in public. A lot of what we perpetuate is the result of post-traumatic stress from our experiences in America. It has fractured our spirits and done everything to exacerbate our social, economic, political, and theological plight. But for all that we have endured, African Americans remain strong, polished, skilled, and capable people.

There are those in our community who feel left behind. We must admit there is a level of elitism in our community that is completely destructive to our cause. And among those who *have* made it, whatever that means, there is a feeling of, "I made it. Why can't you?" When we see our brothers and sisters treating each other with anything but love and respect, we should step in at once and work to eradicate the problem. Regardless of social or economic status, we should work to build a movement on a political, theological, and economic level.

Many African Americans, regardless of their socioeconomic status, have embraced unhealthy social values. In the African-American community during the fifties, 70 percent of the men were employed, and most men were married and active parents. As the unemployment rate grew, the statistics began to tell a more volatile, destructive story. As black men lost their jobs, other underground options for income presented themselves. Dope peddling became the first option in many of our neighborhoods, and before we knew it, we'd been reduced to the mind-set of "getting ours" by any means necessary. Truthfully, how different is this mind-set than that of Donald Trump? It's basically the same value system, only Donald Trump has greater resources and the protection of legitimacy in the culture. One is legal, and the other is illegal.

Beyond the surface, people like Donald Trump, Bill Gates, and Ted Turner are building massive enterprises for the sake of their communities. They want to build wealth for the next generation, such as making sure the institutions they graduated from are supported and have the necessary funds to move forward. We have yet to learn about the development of wealth and retention of our resources because we have not established any ethics behind what we are earning. We are first-generation wealth builders in terms of what we are earning for ourselves and our immediate families. Millions of African Americans have middle-class incomes, but we don't necessarily have wealth. This is the difference between our community and other immigrant populations. We have become focused on the idea of "I" as it relates to material possessions.

Reclaiming Our Community

I believe that if African Americans can truly understand that there is something greater than us, we can begin the process of healing our community. That "something" is God and Christ. When you have this value in place, it changes your world view from "me" to "we." Building this broad community effort is the role of the black church. We must incorporate a kind of theology that is willing to critique, engage, and dismantle issues around race and class. And the community has to be ready and willing to embrace constructive criticism that comes along with this type of dialogue.

We should talk to each other with the kind of discourse that is the legacy of men and women like Dr. Martin Luther King, Jr., A.

Philip Randolph, W.E.B. DuBois, Jarena Lee, Fred Shuttlesworth, and Septima Clark. If we do, we'll begin the initial stages of community renovation. We should never forget that our community was built by the good Lord, and unless we pay Him proper respect and reverence, God will have no reservations about dismantling our community.

By no means does this begin and end with my generation, or the next one. The pieces of the puzzle are just now being formed. It is our responsibility as disciples of history to let the next generation know, "This is not about you! This is about people who are not even born! Our duty is to prepare for a generation yet to make its presence known." This is our calling.

One of the first steps is to develop a media literacy campaign in our schools, churches, and civic organizations. Young people are educated by the media—Internet, cell phones, PDAs, text messages, instant messages, television, and radio. Our education system has been subverted by multinational corporations that inculcate our children with destructive ideals and images.

We must also reclaim our space within the education system through charter, contract, and private schools. Traditionally, the church has always provided supplementary education. You did one thing in school, and it was reinforced in the church. Now, they are *competing*, as the value system presented in church is divergent from the values presented at school. Integrity is promoted in church, and social promotion is the norm in schools. Instead of being the supplement, we are now competing with the cultural environment of our children. Once we understand this, we can move forward as a people and reclaim our community.

—**Rev. Otis Moss, III**

The Reverend Otis Moss, III, is the pastor of Chicago's Trinity United Church of Christ. He is a graduate of Morehouse College and Yale University. His father, the Reverend Otis Moss, II, was an active figure in the Civil Rights Movement who worked alongside Dr. Martin Luther King, Jr., at the Southern Christian Leadership Conference.

♦ Chapter 26

A Legacy of Mother-Wit

Moth•er-wit *(noun)*

> A popular term in black speech referring to common sense … not necessarily learned from books or in school. Mother-wit, with its connotation of collective wisdom acquired by the experience of living and from generations past, is often expressed in folklore.
>
> — **Dictionary of American Regional English (DARE)**

> She encouraged me to listen carefully to what country people called "mother wit." That in those homely sayings was couched the collective wisdom of generations.
>
> —**Maya Angelou**, *I Know Why the Caged Bird Sings*

SOME MAY CALL IT COMMON SENSE, BUT IN BLACK AMERICAN culture, it is often referred to as "mother-wit." I believe we are all born with some basic natural intelligence, and when we add the wisdom shared with us by our elders—specifically, the women— that innate gift takes shape and form, both mentally and spiritually. The stories of my maternal great-grandmother and grandmother, my mother, my aunts, and all the other older women in my life taught me to apply this form of common sense to my life experiences at an early age.

My grandmother, whom I lovingly referred to MaMa or MaDear, left my family with a rich legacy of wit steeped in Southern (Louisiana and Georgia, to be exact) tradition. She worked as a domestic all her life, and there was always a smile on her face, even when she was in physical pain from the arthritis that plagued her. One of MaMa's favorite sayings was, "A heap see, but a few know." I didn't understand what MaMa meant by this expression until I was well into my thirties and had lived enough to finally get it. My definition of this oft-used phrase is that no one really knows the situations you face on a daily basis. The grass is not always greener on the other side. Others might see you all smiling, polished up, and looking good and think that's the real you—never knowing the suffering you went through just to put on a game face for the day.

The summer of my eighth year, my younger brother and I spent several weeks in Oakland, California, visiting MaMa. One morning, MaMa brought us along to work. We walked from my grandparents' home to Telegraph Avenue, where we could catch the A.C. Transit to Berkeley Hills (my first time on a public bus). After the bus ride, the three of us walked up steep hills to reach the home of a white family where MaMa worked as a housekeeper and part-time nanny to sisters Missy and Martha. Walking up that winding hill was an adventure for us kids—we counted cracks in the sidewalk and enjoyed the beautiful morning. But it was MaMa's daily routine, and she never complained about the strain.

Once we arrived at the beautiful home at the top of the hill, my brother and I played with Missy and Martha while MaMa cleaned and cooked. MaMa had told me before that the two blond-haired sisters often begged MaMa to take them home with her, and on this particular day, their mother allowed them to go. I couldn't imagine why they wanted to leave their beautiful home, but sure enough, they rode the bus back to Oakland with us.

Missy, the older of the two, admired my hairstyle, with its neat parts, double-strand twists, and colorful hair accessories. Once we were back at my grandmother's house, she let me comb her hair and spray it with Afro Sheen. Martha sat down happily to a pile of MaMa's collard greens mixed with hot-water cornbread.

At the time, I couldn't understand why they were so happy in my grandparents' home, but later, I overheard MaMa whisper to my mother and aunt that "he's been drinking again." Missy and Martha lived what appeared to be a luxurious life, but behind closed doors they and their mother endured angry tirades from their alcoholic father. Some days, he'd throw them out of the house—even in the rain—and my grandparents always offered their home as a shelter.

A heap saw the exterior of their beautiful home, *but a few knew* the pain they suffered behind closed doors. They found warmth and love—the legacy my brother and I were born into—in that little two-bedroom duplex on Porier Avenue that my grandparents called home.

Keep Livin'

MaMa and the other women in my family often said "Keep livin'" as a reminder that as long as you have breath in your body, you'll have good days and bad days. When she'd hear others say something like, "I'm glad I'm not going through that" or "thank God that's not me," she'd murmur, "Keep livin'." It wasn't a prediction of doom; instead, it was a gentle reminder that we all experience both joy and pain as a result of living, and that you can't have one without the other.

The women in my family have always embraced mother-wit and simple words of wisdom shared at the dinner table, on the phone, or during visits as precious jewels and golden nuggets to pass on to each generation. They would always remind us, "Now, you know better than that" when we did something wrong, and we actually did know better—because of the mother-wit instilled in us.

In my opinion, mother-wit is a rare commodity today. Folks just don't exercise common sense like they used to. Perhaps we've become so educated, sophisticated, and liberated that we've lost touch with what used to keep us grounded. I want to keep the legacy of mother-wit alive and well in my family.

That desire became my mission in November 2002, just as I made my last intense push to move my child out into the world. Although I was exhausted, I knew I had just pushed my way into a legacy of women who came before me: I'd become a mother. It was all so quick and frantic from that moment on.

"Push, push, push, Stacey!" The doctor and nurse kept repeating the words, like a mantra.

My husband stood at my side, calmly reassuring me. "You're doing good, honey."

My mother rubbed my forehead, whispering, "Bear down," while she watched in wonder as her child stepped into the role of motherhood.

As the doctor laid my daughter on my chest, the baby looked up at me, her large brown eyes saying, "What do we do now?" In my heart, I knew it was my mission to continue the legacy of the women who'd shaped and formed me. I am blessed to have known my great-grandmother and grandmother, my aunts, and my beautiful mother, who is still here to drop pearls of wisdom in my life even as I mature further into womanhood. Of the many things I wish to instill in my daughter, the legacy of mother-wit is of utmost importance.

In addition to mother-wit, I also wish to grant my daughter the blessing of having different mother types in her life. What ever happened to the days when you had other mothers in the neighborhood watching over you and holding you accountable for your actions at every turn? As a child of the '70s and a teen and young adult of the '80s, I remember what it meant to have many mothers in my life.

Of course, let's not forget my beautiful biological mother, the woman who brought me into this world and would often remind me that she could take me out, as well! Sometimes, Mom never had to utter a word to correct me. A simple glare from behind those dark sunglasses spoke volumes. I'd fearfully defend myself: "I didn't do it, Mommy!"

Then there were the other mothers—your "play" Mom, the mothers at the church, your godmother, and the Mamas-on-the-block—mine were Ms. Clark, Mrs. Johnson, and Miss Brown. They were the women who carefully observed your comings and goings and would always keep you in check if you got out of line. I remember their refrain: "Oh, don't worry. I'll tell your mama for sure." Mamas-on-the-block could be considered nosy or just real observant, but they held us accountable for our actions when we were beyond the watchful glare of our own mothers.

Today, correcting someone else's child could get you arrested. What's that about? I say we go "old school" and leave a legacy of motherhood and mother-wit to the next generation of young girls, some of whom look up to strippers and "video chicks," aspiring to be just like them.

I remember strutting into church one Sunday during my younger days. I was wearing a cute Norma Kamali linen dress, and I *knew* I was looking sharp. An older woman gingerly approached me and whispered, "You need to wear a slip with that dress."

I was embarrassed, but comforted at the same time because of the woman's approach. She didn't publicly lambast me, saying, "Uh, uh, honey. Quit showin' all of your business and go put on a slip!" Instead, she gently pulled me aside and made the suggestion with a kind and discreet approach. Let us lovingly tell a young girl we see on the street to dress more modestly or to quit using foul language.

We must not be afraid to teach our girls how to act ladylike, or to show our boys how to treat a lady. As black women, we must make our foremothers proud by continuing the legacy of encouraging the everyday usage of common sense. Gaining higher education is essential, but using the mother-wit we've been blessed with is one of life's greatest lessons.

—Stacey Evans Morgan

Stacey Evans Morgan is a Los Angeles-based businesswoman and TV writer.

♦ Chapter 27

I Am … African
(No Hyphen! No Hype!)

I was born in Miami, Florida
Both of my parents were born in Haiti
But I've never been there
I mean, I've traveled there, maybe once or twice with my grand-
mother
But I don't actually remember because I was just a baby
What am I?
Well, I guess I'm Haitian, I mean Haitian American
Really just American, since I wasn't born in Haiti
Well I guess … African American, you know, to be exact
Because when I was a little girl, I remember climbing up the stairs
and turning around the corner and …
Wait! Wait!
Why am I explaining myself?
I'm tired of explaining myself!
Minus my self-esteem
Minus the fact that …
My skin … has means … to an end and when
Will I stop explaining myself, denying my African roots
Even if the tree was cut down
I remain the fruit …
It bore
My kinky hair … isn't a style
My accent is my diction
And calling myself an African American … is a contradiction
To the truth … of how we got here
So who am I?

I am … African
No hyphen! No hype!
Isn't it clear to see?
Just look at me …
One-eighth Negro blood clearly runs through me
Clearly I've been caught up in a society that seeks to define me
But deny me … my blood
And since blood is truly thicker than water
The waters that brought me here
Are not the waters that birthed me here
So here is who I am …
I am … African
No hyphen! No hype!
Clicks and surveys cannot downplay that building pyramids … is
my forte
And for me
That's not a legacy; I want to give up … willingly
So call me what I be …
I am … African
No hyphen! No hype!
Black skin
Brown skin
Light skin
Red bone
High yellow
Blue black
Sugarcoat it if you must
But diabetes was never a part of us
For within me
I have the ability
To create the remedies
To incapacitate
The images
You perpetuate
In me
From the white Christmases to the white Jesuses

From white bread to brown pennies
And the black men who are many
In our prison systems …
Listen …
I am … African.
No hyphen! No hype!
And the fight you see in me
Isn't against you
But for my family
So that they can understand that their true … identity
Cannot be smeared like candidates running for presidency
And let it be known that …
I find it a true hypocrisy
That you'd mock the very African woman
That breastfed your babies
This … is … crazy!
But that's okay
That's always been your style
How else can you explain color-coding people's worth, like floor tiles
I'm mild tempered … Only until you test me
So if you want to remain friendly
Remember what's in me
I am … African.
No hyphen! No hype!

—Tracy Pierre

Tracy Pierre is a poet, dancer, actress, and model based in Atlanta, Georgia.

Chapter 28

Growing Up African in America

I WAS ELEVEN YEARS OLD WHEN WE MOVED TO WEST AFRICA. MY parents, who were of Nigerian descent, had no intention to live in the United States beyond just a few years. Time just seemed to fly by, and twenty years later, they found themselves living in South Los Angeles with four kids, a dog, and a house.

The year was 1980. The Sugar Hill Gang and Funkadelic were dominating the airwaves, crack hadn't yet infiltrated our community, and I could still walk around the neighborhood without fear of getting shot by a gang member for wearing the wrong colors. I was a sports addict; baseball was my number one hobby. I lived for Dodger blue, just like every other kid on my block. We played baseball in the street every day until sunset, when the lights would come on, our moms would call our names, and we'd run home to wash up for dinner.

Once I entered our home, my world totally changed. It was like stepping back into Africa. My parents spoke our native language, Igbo, in the house. I learned to understand the language, but my ability to speak it was never as good as I wanted it to be. I always felt a little uncomfortable as a child eating Nigerian food, listening to Nigerian music, and adhering to Nigerian customs in our home. It was tough, because as a kid I wanted to fit in and assimilate into my community, becoming one of the guys. At school, I stood out like a sore thumb because of my last name. It brought me unwanted attention, and it made me different at the exact moment that I wanted to be just like everybody else.

The guys with light skin and green or brown eyes and names like "Rodney Jackson" or "Tony Johnson" got all the girls. They were card-carrying members of the "A" team, and they even seemed to get preferential treatment from the school's teachers and staff. The rest of us brown-skinned brothers had to fend for ourselves and deal with whatever social "scraps" were left. Being on the "B" team never felt very good, and to make matters worse, I had the "African thing" hanging over my head.

My parents sympathized with our struggle, so in the fall of 1980, just before I was to enter middle school, we moved back to Nigeria. They said it was important for us to understand where we had come from and secure a stronger sense of our roots. Man, I didn't want to go. I didn't want to leave all of my friends, and baseball, behind. I'd been very young when I'd made my only trip to Nigeria, so my memories of the land were vague. Like every other black kid in America raised on a healthy dose of skewed African imagery, I thought I'd see wildlife at the airport and be forced to live miserably in a hut in the sweltering heat.

The only part of the equation that was true was the sweltering heat. The airplane ride wasn't bad, and upon arrival, we found the airport to be animal-free. My father, an engineer by profession, had taken a job at a local university, which provided our family with a home that made our house in Los Angeles look like a trailer. My brothers and I enrolled in a nearby school and gradually adjusted to our new environment. We were no longer considered different. Other kids had African names, just like us.

For the first time, I saw people of color in positions of political power—governors, senators, and yes, even a black president. The country was nowhere near as advanced as America, but the people were governing themselves, for better or for worse. There was an air of freedom that was new and different—and appealing. I began to appreciate my new environment. I began to realize the reason I was so ashamed of my heritage was that I didn't understand it. Meeting my cousins, aunts, uncles, grandmother, and distant relatives provided me with a stronger sense of identity and purpose. I began to understand that while I was American, I was definitely African, and it felt great to have a strong affinity for both cultures.

My four and a half years as a teenager in Nigeria were the most memorable of my life. After I completed high school, I moved back to the United States for college, and today I reside in Los Angeles. Now, when I visit Nigeria, it's not as a tourist, but as a proud citizen. When I state my African surname, I state it clearly and with conviction. I speak comfortably and lovingly of both worlds because of my journey home. That is something I hope every African in America can experience in his or her lifetime.

— **Robert Emeka Mark Ajakwe**

A leader in the field of education and youth marketing, Robert Emeka Mark Ajakwe has devoted more than twenty years to the academic and social achievement of America's youth. Having worked extensively with urban communities and school systems, Ajakwe has helped countless parents and youth gain access to educational resources that have proven to be both motivational and life changing.

PART III
RELATIONSHIPS

♦ Chapter 29

Love, Marriage, and Struggle*

OSSIE AND I SPENT DECADES ON THE ROAD PERFORMING AT colleges. In the beginning, all the kids wanted to know, "How do you get into the theater? How do you get to Hollywood? Should I go to New York?"

But over time, as we continued to tour and the years passed, they began to ask, "How did you stay married so long?" I remember looking into the eager young face of a woman who'd asked that question one night after one of our performances. I searched my mind, trying to articulate what I really felt about marital longevity besides the usual platitudes—"Don't go to bed angry," "You've just got to keep God in the equation," or "Try to remain attractive to each other."

There comes a point when you discover what love really is. You don't know it beforehand, but eventually, you arrive at a point when you can say to the other person in your life, *I want you to be the best person you can be. What is it that fulfills you as a human being? Why are you on this earth?* You have to go through resentment, feelings of neglect and jealousy, and all sorts of other emotions before you're free, before you can let somebody go toward their fulfillment. Once you're able to let go and not feel helpless and abandoned, you rejoice in the fact that they are on the road they need to be on. I think that's the beginning of love.

The letting go allows you to rejoice in somebody else's glory and fulfillment. You learn to do that, and it becomes as important as

* This essay is adapted from the book *With Ossie & Ruby: In This Life Together.*

your own fulfillment. So marriage becomes a process, rather than an accomplishment or a fact. It goes on and on. You keep on getting married.

Love is struggle. "I take the risk, even though you might leave me." You know, when you hear about a wife who puts her man through school and helps him achieve some goal, and then he leaves her? That's love, and you can't turn your back on it and not suffer. You've got to learn how to rise above envy, because it's hard *not* to feel less than somebody who seems to be moving way ahead of you.

Ossie and I *did* go through some rough times. Emotions that affect most married people—resentment, anger, impatience, jealousy—affected us, too. How did we ride the rough waves in a relationship long enough for the waters to get calm? When did it sink in that overcoming difficult times gets easier with practice? How did we drag some of the good feelings, good times, and good vibrations into the stormy places?

This letter to Ossie is an effort to put love and marriage under a microscope and into at least some perspective.

Dear Ossie,

I appreciate and acknowledge the fact that you are a good husband. For a while, though, I believed that a truly nice husband could not be achieved without a lot of hard work—if the sista was lucky and the brotha was intelligent and flexible. The idea that a good marriage is made in heaven and swung down on a golden cord like a gift from God did not coincide with my lifelong observations.

Unlike the wedding event, which takes place in a day, marriage is a long process that goes on at some level every day for the rest of your life. You divorce or marry around one issue or another constantly. The percentage of time that you remain married determines your success. We have to *learn* how to live together.

Oh, well. That shouldn't be too tough, if you love somebody.

I thought I loved you, Ossie, when we got married, but I see now that I was only in the kindergarten of the proposition. To arrive at love is like working on a double doctorate in the subject of Life.

I already had myself to take care of; now, with this wedding, there would be *my*self and *your*self. Already a hard worker, I could do a little more, I resolved. It wouldn't kill me. After a while, the drudgery of double duty and babies and more responsibility (even after we could afford help, and I graduated to supervising drudge) left me sorely tested in the love department. You were freer to travel, write, and pursue your heart's ambition. With a wife, the small details of life no longer concerned you—meals, laundry, paying bills, shopping for clothes, etc. I, on the other hand, had to strain and sweat bullets, huff and puff, and be in charge of everything. Something like peace and respite came for a little while, like when I landed jobs out of town or had a baby.

I used to want to shout, "Help me! Help me! Can't you see? So much to be done. You're not a guest in this house! I'm not running a hotel! Didn't your mama teach you nothin'?!" Resentment. Anger. It's not fair! Being a woman is too damned hard. Marriage is for men. A man can take so much for granted. "So, tell me, what's in the newspaper? Can't you see I have no time to read one?"

After some threats, arguments, tantrums, and tears, Ossie, you began to understand. I found out you listened. You just hadn't paid attention to how lopsided the equation was.

You began to say, "I'll make breakfast. I'll wash the diapers. You stay in bed. The children and I, we're going for a walk, maybe to the movies, or to the museum. Take the day, Ruby. Relax." I found myself smiling more and thinking up surprises.

Then, like a quickened pulse beat, the levels of concern in our life together rose, reached through us, took us to a higher level of human concern, hooked us to a deeper blackness, and connected us to other families just like us. We became like everyone else, threatened by newer and scarier dangers, and aware of how the world is wobbling now, bombarded by rampaging "progress."

Both of us already had our feet in the hot waters of Struggle even before we met. As we moved out together to follow those we admired, those who were already way ahead, we plunged in even deeper. We wanted to give a hand, help those on the front line make Justice just, and be part of whatever the Struggle was all about.

Breakfast became more than just a time for food. We eventually learned how to pray together every day, even if only by phone. I don't remember when current political, economic, and social matters became our favorite topics, but I do remember how they stimulated us—especially you. How you loved history, and still do, and your cross-referencing and comparison making.

And how, when the children were very young, you told stories and jokes, and spread your spirit over me, too, like a warm blanket on a cold night. How the newspapers and magazines would accumulate because there was so much to catch up on, and to share. More and more, you and I became part of the Struggle, and the Struggle became a part of us.

I have admired your capacity to interrelate, to see the long arc of events—sometimes in awesome detail, marrying the mundane and the majestic, and the beginnings reflected in the ends. As I listened, I reminded myself again how deeply I love you. Not only because I believe you value me, but also because I believe we have both arrived, finally, at what love is. When you want and pray for someone to be all God created them to be, despite any personal sacrifice it might entail, that is love. Love is overcoming. Love is passion clothed in infinite patience.

There is a magnetism to those who love, who know things, who see, who make connections, and who are committed to the struggles for the wider victories in the world. There is a sensuousness to them, too—as if struggle itself is an aphrodisiac.

Good sex, feeling loved, admired, etc.—all of those things are like a pat on the back, a "go get 'em, girl." They're a nudge to some victory from God, letting you know—and sense—that now you're free to get on with the divine assignment, the mission message, and that you can heed the revelation of why you're here in the first place.

You want to spread the good feeling, want everybody to be happy because working to satisfy that want rounds out your circle, fulfills your equation, and says "yes" to your life. It banishes fear and envy; it is an insurance policy maturing in joy and security as it frees you to stretch, look around, and love beyond your circle.

You can talk now about—think now about—the welfare of others, of worthy ideas to feed into the emotion and information systems. You can love a sunset and watch a sunrise and help feed the hungry and protect the tribe, because you understand love and how it erupts from the deep quiet of ecstasy to the service of divine intentions.

—**Ruby Dee**

Legendary actress Ruby Dee is an Emmy- and Grammy-award winning actress and performer. Her career in acting has crossed all major forms of media over a span of eight decades and includes an impressive eight Emmy Award nominations. In 2007, Dee was nominated for an Oscar for her role in American Gangster.

This essay is adapted from With Ossie & Ruby: In This Life Together *(William Morrow, 1998) by Ossie Davis and Ruby Dee.*

♦ Chapter 30

Living Single

BY MOST ACCOUNTS, I SHOULD NOT BE SINGLE. I'M COLLEGE educated and professionally successful. I'm financially stable and own my own home. I've got no children and no ex-husbands, meaning I'm free to do whatever I want, whenever I want. I am known to be a giving, loving, and honest person and I live my life with the belief that I treat people as I desire to be treated.

As far as physical appearance, many would say I have the attributes that men reportedly seek. I work out four to five times a week, so I keep myself physically fit. My skin has a golden hue, my honey brown hair bounces around and below my shoulders, and my eye color varies according to the day and my mood, anywhere from gray to light brown to a catty green. (And no, they're not color contacts, as I'm often asked.)

The fact that I'm single defies the long-standing myth that the more light-skinned you are, the longer your hair hangs and the lighter your eyes, the more likely you'll be the apple of men's eyes. I've never bought into this notion. I am a strong believer that when all is said and done, it is the content of one's character that determines who is attracted to you, and who you're attracted to. Physical appearance undoubtedly plays a role in attraction, but as my late mother used to say, "Looks will only get you so far." At some point, you have to deal with the person.

I have to admit, however, that I am picky. I do not have it in me to *settle,* because I believe I've worked hard and am worthy of happiness, love, and respect—and nothing less. That's not what my quest for love is all about. No, when I open myself to a relationship, I want someone who is willing to meet me halfway, and who is willing to exist in a mature relationship of mutual respect, love, and honor.

Dating and relationships were not always challenging propositions for me. I had my first "boyfriend" by the time I was thirteen years old, much to the chagrin of my poor mother. After graduating high school at the age of sixteen, I entered into my first serious monogamous relationship; we dated for nearly two years. It ended when he decided to marry a woman closer to his own age who was ready for such a commitment.

Only eighteen, I was on the verge of discovering who I was and who I aimed to be. At that point in my life, marriage was not an option. I moved from my small, rural town in Virginia to Washington, D.C.—sometimes referred to as "Chocolate City." I'd never seen so many sexy and fine black men in one place. They all seemed so mature, so successful, and so self-assured. I was in heaven. I dated men from various social backgrounds, all of them African American.

It never occurred to me that I might one day run out of dating options, because if one relationship didn't work out, there was always another guy waiting in the wings for a date. However, as I entered my mid-twenties, graduated from college, and began my promising career, I started to notice a shift in my dating life and the responses I received from men.

I did not go directly to college after graduating high school, chiefly because my mother died tragically and unexpectedly the year before I was to graduate, and my father was forced to struggle financially to make a life for us. I went to work full time at the age of sixteen for the government, and I earned a good salary. I continued working and had secured a great job opportunity on Capitol Hill by the time I was twenty years old.

After years of being encouraged by my tremendous support system to earn a degree, I decided to apply to college. School had always been a safe haven for me. I loved learning and being in the academic environment. Yet at that point in my life, I had been on my own and could not afford to completely quit working altogether. I made the difficult decision to both work and attend college full time. Needless to say, the demanding schedule necessary to take on full-time work and a full load of university courses left little time for dating, much less a relationship. And at the time, I truly didn't mind. I saw it as a necessary sacrifice and investment in my future. I threw myself into my studies with a vigor I didn't realize I still possessed. For three and a half years, my social life nearly ceased to exist. I thought life would return to normal after graduation, but instead I took on yet another challenge, this time in New York City working on Wall Street.

Working on Wall Street and living in New York City was an exciting time. It was a new adventure for me, and I met a lot of great people. However, as far as dating was concerned, I felt like Rip Van Winkle waking up after a long sleep only to find that black men, by and large, were interested in dating everything *but* a black woman. I first attributed this to the fact that I was in a new city, and on top of that I was treading on the exclusive boys' club environment of Wall Street.

So as I walked the crowded streets of New York, I searched for a pattern of black coupledom to figure out if I was just a victim of my immediate corporate-America surroundings, or if it was something more. Sadly, I saw with my own eyes that countless black men were proudly holding hands with and displaying affection for women who were not black. It soon became obvious to me that this trend was not confined exclusively to the Wall Streeters and other "suit-and-tie" men.

For quite some time, it hurt me so much that I could barely look at an interracial couple. I had nothing in particular against them— rather, I started to ask what was wrong with *me*, with black women. At what point had we become unappealing and undesirable? And most importantly, why?

My friends and I started to talk frequently about the dating situation. Most, if not all, of us were committed to dating black men, but we weren't getting asked out. On the odd occasion that we did get asked out, the dates usually went nowhere. More often than not, there was no real explanation from the man about why the relationship could not continue; the invitations to dinner and phone calls just stopped. Interest in us seemed to be cast aside like yesterday's news, despite what we'd thought was a good dating experience. My friends and I exchanged these stories via e-mail, over the phone, and in person over drinks and/or dinner. It would have been much more comforting to be able to confine the stories to one particular city, with the relief of knowing that this was not a widespread issue, but our stories crossed geographic borders, from Los Angeles to Atlanta to Chicago to New York City to D.C. to Richmond. The list goes on. We were all experiencing the same things, and we were all starting to get used to the idea that we might live out the rest of our lives as single women.

Aside from not having an active love life, these women and I had some other things in common. We are all successful, college-educated, financially independent, and attractive women. We are many shades and complexions, with varied hair textures, from petite to tall, late twenties to late thirties, and slim to voluptuous. It appears that we're in a crisis of equal-opportunity singledom.

Even many of the glamazon, have-it-all celebrity sisters in their thirties, such as Tyra Banks, Nia Long, Sanaa Lathan, and Tracee Ellis Ross, don't appear to be in committed relationships. We're constantly barraged by images of black men on television and film whose love interests are anything but a black woman. We have few images reflected in these mediums of positive, loving, and committed relationships between black men and women. This attitude is reinforced by what we see daily in real life. It's almost as if black women are being phased out as suitable and desirable mates.

I still have hope, but that hope exists beyond the limitations of only seeking a black man. I still treasure my brothers, but I will no longer wait for them. The last guy I was interested in was still hung up on a (non-black) woman with whom he'd been in a difficult off-and-on relationship for the last two decades. They have two children together, one of whom is an adult. When a good friend introduced us, I wasn't looking for anything. In fact, after we went out that first time, I never expected to see him again. But he called and asked me out again and again. Eventually, I grew to like him, and I thought he was a decent guy.

Yet as the months wore on, it became obvious that this guy was a very long way from recovering from his relationship. He simply wasn't in an emotional place where he could sustain even a platonic dating relationship. He constantly double-booked himself when we had dates—to the extent where plans almost always changed at the last minute. He often talked about other women he'd dated or had been intimate with when we went out or talked on the phone. He always found a way to incorporate a mention of the mother of his children into our conversations, with the mentions sometimes extending into a full-blown discourse about their relationship. And this was just within six months of our being introduced. On top of everything else, he was discovering that even though he was fifty years old, he was still figuring himself out and coming to understand his needs. Needless to say, I made the decision to move on.

Given the constantly reported statistics about the legions of unmarried black women who are likely to stay that way, some may question why I didn't give this guy a bit longer to pull himself together. He's what some would call the complete "package," after all. Master's degree from an Ivy League school. Attractive. Prominent career position. Thought-provoking conversations. Well connected in certain society circles. In the end, it wasn't worth it for me to invest any more time with a man who did not—could not—appreciate me in the way that I appreciated him.

So where does this leave me? And the rest of us sisters? I'm not really sure. There is good news, however—*great* news, in fact. There is a powerful, striking image of a black family we're apt to be seeing more of as time goes on. The entire world has witnessed the meteoric political rise of Barack Obama and his beautiful, strong, and unmistakably African-American wife, Michelle. Along with their two lovely daughters, they've appeared together on the presidential campaign trail, at events, on television, and in countless media. One can pray that the image of Barack and Michelle Obama's positive, intact family unit just might give the black community the jumpstart it desperately needs to repair relationships between our men and women.

For my part, I've become comfortable being a single woman. I'm happy with me, and I no longer think there's something wrong with me—that I'm not pretty enough, thin enough, or smart enough. Do I want to eventually find a partner? Yes, absolutely. I believe that the person for me is out there, somewhere, and I'm willing to wait as long as it takes. The difference now is that if that right guy doesn't come in the package of a black man, it's okay with me. I encourage other sisters out there to be a lot more open-minded about their choices, as well. It's not to say that we should turn our backs on black men, but we should certainly be a lot more open to other possibilities.

—**Gilda N. Squire**

Gilda N. Squire is the founder of Gilda Squire Media Relations, based in New York City. Prior to starting her agency, she served as a director of publicity at HarperCollins Publishers. She was responsible for overseeing publicity and book tours for the company's Amistad imprint, as well as several titles under the publisher's flagship HarperCollins imprint. Squire began her publishing career at the G.P. Putnam and Riverhead imprints at Penguin.

Chapter 31

Modern Black Love: Phase Three

I need to stay away from the modern black women of my generation in order to make the most of my life, because they will ultimately bring me down and drain me.

THIS IS THE MIND-SET OF MANY OF MY BLACK MALE PEERS. IT is a new state of mind for me. Before I say anything else, let me say that at my core I seek love, companionship, affection, and romance. My thoughts on relationships, although dark, are set so clearly now simply because I have tried (to no avail) for eleven years to build strong, loving, passionate, and healthy relationships with modern black women.

Now I am left bitter, emotionally paralyzed, cynical, and disillusioned to the point where I no longer believe that what my parents and my grandparents achieved will happen for me. Furthermore, as a means of self-defense, I've resorted to burying myself under a lukewarm blanket of shallow relationships that help me pass the time, satiate my lust, and remind me on a regular basis why I can't get any closer to these lovely, deadly creatures who pack heaven between their legs and hell in their lungs.

I'm in Phase Three of my journey into relationships. It'd have been nice if I could have stayed in Phase One. Phase One is when I was innocent, naive, and believed in love. What makes my situation different from most is that I grew up around a lot of love from a big family. For most of my childhood, the only message I ever got was that couples stuck together. They had their problems, but they worked them out, one way or another. I'd wake up hearing my parents yelling at times, and sometimes my father would speed off out of the driveway, angry as all hell—but at the end of the day, they worked it out through hard work and dedication toward one another.

My dumb ass thought this was how every relationship should be. I looked down on friends who would fuck girls and lose interest. Lose interest? You've got to be kidding me. Black women are the most beautiful, intriguing things on this planet. I love having someone special with me on my journey through life. When I used to meet women I clicked with and felt attraction to, I could spend all day laughing with them, learning with them, or just sucking on their titties. I adored them in every sense of the word. Any problems that came up were well worth an unlimited investment of time, thought, and energy. For the most part, that resulted in me being loved in return—deeply. However, I've learned that being loved and being treated lovingly are two entirely different things. The former is an emotion we are all innately capable of, and the latter is a skill that must be learned.

Thus brings us to Phase Two, where my spirit was dismantled. My father once told me that he wished we (my brother, my sister, and I) were still children. I asked him why, and he said because we had a light in us back then. As we got older and withstood the hardships of life, we lost our light, and that saddened him, he told me. It took several relationships with several different types of black women to finally break me. I didn't give in easily. It took bruises, scars, busted-down doors, the police, and an abortion to make me stop and think that maybe—just maybe—loving the modern black woman is the most dangerous thing I could do.

Now I've landed in my current phase—Phase Three, the bitter phase. Most of my male friends have been there for years. They learned the first time they had a negative experience with a woman and began to adapt then, in many cases as far back as in high school.

Convinced that any problem can be solved, and that hard work and dedication were all that I needed, it took me much longer to learn my lesson and give up. I've learned now, and I've accepted things. But I wish I never had to set foot here.

I've cut a woman out of my life for describing to me how she had diarrhea and had to race home from work. I've cut a woman off because she asked me to check on some R. Kelly tickets and also had the nerve to ask if she could stay at my place when I dropped my friend off at the airport. I've cut a woman off because she asked me to come visit her on a day I planned to visit her anyway. That isn't right at all. But I do it because I'm so emotionally drained from being in relationships with modern black women for so long that now I'm unable to spend any time at all to work things out with a woman. Forget about sparking the half a nerve it would take to explain to them *why* I think whatever it is I'm thinking.

I've broken it down to a science. Instead of giving my all to one woman, I give pieces of myself to several women. It's safer that way. One might get my funny, goofy side. Another might get my intellectual side. Still another will get my adventurous side, and so on. One will get an essence of emotion from me, but when that happens, I'm prepared to process and categorize that emotion (which is normal, considering we're genetically predisposed to become emotionally attached to the opposite sex), locate it, remove its source, and give myself some time to let it fade away, like a sand castle by the sea. I've been able to do this for just under a year now, and these have been the most productive and focused times of my life.

Once you claim something, it can be taken away from you. So I'll never claim a woman. Once you get used to having sex with a woman, she can use sex as a negotiating piece when it comes to her demands and expectations of you. So having multiple sex partners keeps me safe.

I tend to turn a woman out if I sense I'm developing feelings for her. I turn her on to one of my friends to see if she might have sex with him, or I take her to a swingers club, see how wild she gets, and later visualize the crazy things she's done to jolt my heart back into its hole.

Wow. Is it *that* serious? When I think about it, it is. Remember TLC's song "Don't Go Chasing Waterfalls?" Loving the modern black woman for all these years has been just that—chasing waterfalls.

I am clearly not talking about all black women when I say "modern black women." I know many black women (including family members) who play positive, nurturing, and wonderful roles in my life, and I admire them for a range of reasons. The modern black woman, as I define it, is based purely upon the select group of women that *I've dated* and not the entire population, by any means.

The modern black woman is completely independent. She has a good job (or at least one that pays her bills and allows her to have some fun). She's intelligent. She's attractive. She's thick-skinned (extremely hard on the outside), but soft on the inside. The final ingredient is the bottomless insecurity that fuels these characteristics.

The modern black woman is damaged. The majority of women I've allowed myself to get close to have had one of two major issues: either the unfortunate consequences of growing up without a father or previous relationships that have left them insecure.

Two women I have loved had no choice but to be the leaders of their households as they grew up because their fathers abandoned their responsibilities. As a result, these two women were trained to fulfill the duties of a man. In my relationships with them, there was no room for me to be a man. I constantly battled with them and found that the relationship problems they brought to the table were more like what a man would bring. For example, they didn't know how to communicate their feelings. Their pride ruled their actions, and they were afraid to accept love. When it came to loving a man, what reference did they have? They hadn't grown up seeing a healthy, cooperative, and loving relationship. How could I expect them to know how to love me?

The insecure women I've loved have a different set of issues. Most have been either sexually assaulted or otherwise completely taken advantage of by a man. One told me she'd adopted the "screw them before they screw you" philosophy. Another told me she treats men like tires. "You need four tires just in case one pops, so you can keep moving." That might sound cute, but what's really going on is that these women have built walls around themselves to prevent any further harm. They won't ever admit to needing a man for anything, including having and raising a baby. Some have resorted to using men as sex objects.

During my first visit to a girlfriend's apartment, she showed me a file drawer where she kept basic information about the men she was dating—their names, where they'd met, their birthdays, and their relatives' names. Just so she could keep track. She told me, "That's how men are, so why not do the same to them?" I'll tell you why. Because you are spoiling your womb, and you are missing out on what a real man is.

I've had to tell each of these strong, resilient, beautiful, good-job-having, modern black women how to treat me right and why it's necessary for them to open up and tell me exactly how they feel in order for our relationship to grow. I've had to teach them how to accept my love, how to break down the walls that are counterproductive to true intimacy, and to trust that I am in no way trying to harm or abandon them.

So I spent half of my time teaching my girlfriends how to love and trust. I spent the other half actually being in a relationship with them (sometimes as they experienced being in love for the first time). That left me not getting back the love and effort I put into the relationship. Although they were passionately in love with me, they didn't know how to treat me *lovingly*. While they learned, I got nothing but negative energy that was nonexistent in the healthy relationships I had grown up around. Their behavior during our trying times was vicious enough for the men who had abandoned them, appropriate for the men who had assaulted them, and just for the men who had taken advantage of and used them. But it was not at all appropriate for me, the man who loved them. A deep lack of empathy and a coldness fueled by vengeance comes from the heart of the damaged modern black woman.

I put myself through it for so long. I have a list of women who will love me forever and (to this day) appreciate what I did for them. However, in the process, I've lost the belief that love is worth an unlimited investment of time, thought, and energy. It has been eleven years. I am hollow.

Now, as I write this, I see why my peers take solace in Phase Three—not feeling for women. Now that the dust has settled from my last, most stressful relationship, I find myself behind my own wall. This wall took my whole life to show up, and I have no hope that it can be moved or circumvented.

I'm not too blind to see that perhaps I attract (or I'm attracted to) a certain type of woman. These women, now that I think about it, might be in *their* Phase Three. Maybe a part of me actually enjoys opening up these women and showing them that it's okay to come out and love a man. "I won't hurt you. C'mon. Take my hand." Perhaps it makes me feel special, and that's the satisfaction I get from it. But when I reflect on it further, I remember that *all* of my ex-girlfriends have pushed for relationships with me, and they were significantly more aggressive about it than I was. I have an innocent demeanor, and that helped me get women I cared about to open up and trust me. Perhaps they thought I could help them get love back into their lives, or help them experience love for the first time.

Until I find a better way to handle the women I allow to get close to me, I'm going to stay tucked away. I hope, for my sake, that someone can come along and show me a better way, but until that day comes, this is where I'll stay.

As I wait for this slim-to-none chance to occur, I lurk this planet as a man in Phase Three—likely causing pain, sadness, and insecurity for the women I use as nothing more than sleeping bags. What makes me even more dangerous than my counterparts is my innocent demeanor—previously used for good—and my omnipresent desire for love. Women sense these signs of warmth and are drawn to me, assuming they can revive me, but they end up heartbroken, disappointed, and drained hollow, just like me.

It's settled now. I play a new role in this cyclic suicide that is modern black love, contributing further to the growing tide that turns women into the insecure, thick-skinned, and scorned women I accuse of doing me such harm in the first place.

Don't get me wrong. Statistically speaking, I'm bound to run into someone who's right for me. If I ever plan to get out of this situation, I have to keep my eyes open. At the same time, who knows if my eyes are seeing properly anymore? Maybe one day, I'll meet that mythological, and perhaps extinct, woman that Andre 3000 sings about in "Behold a Lady." She'll knock my socks off and have my behind all the way back in Phase One again. She'll tell me that it's okay to love her. She'll say, "I won't hurt you. C'mon," and take my hand.

—Muta'Ali Muhammad

Muta'Ali Muhammad is cofounder and CEO of the Raw Report (www.rawreport.com), which produces documentaries and topical news features on the hip-hop industry and the urban community. Since 2003, he has coproduced, directed, and edited pieces featuring T.I., 50 Cent, Ludacris, Rick Ross, Jadakiss, The Game, Mobb Deep, Young Buck, and more. Currently, he is continuing a foray into commercial film, completing his third screenplay, and preparing to direct his first feature film.

Chapter 32

Relationships Matter

NOW THAT I'M FORTY-ONE, I'VE GROWN TO BELIEVE RELATION-ships bring you closer to your greater self. In retrospect, one particular relationship stands out in my memory. In 1994, I met Marcel Combs (MC)* at the radio station where I was an on-air personality. I happened to be operating the board that night for our community affairs program. The topic was gang violence, and MC was the perfect guest. He was an OG who had supposedly cut his gang ties and set out on a mission to save youth. Under his rough exterior—scowling eyes and menacing tattoos that covered his arms and neck—lay a strikingly handsome man with a brilliant mind. Although I didn't initially feel attracted to him, an energy ran through me as we shook hands. I met him again a few weeks later at a community event, and we exchanged numbers. A series of long phone conversations about books, politics, and governmental conspiracies got me to open up. We became friends.

One night, MC called and told me he was in a rut. He needed a place to crash for the evening. I lived in a big three-story house with an extra room, and my roommates and I agreed to let him stay. We sat in the den most of the night carrying on with our usual intellectual talks, and he began to open up about his past. He shared many stories of his unstable childhood and of the dirty deeds he had done as a member of a notorious L.A. gang. MC had been shot a couple of times, and he'd done the same to some rival gang members. These stories, combined with the knowledge that he'd spent most of his life in

* Name changed to protect his anonymity.

and out of prison, should have sent me running for the hills. Instead, I was overwhelmed with compassion. I felt sorry for him and drawn to him. Maybe this was his intent. The next day, he went on his way.

Two weeks passed without word from MC. I thought about him often, and strangely, I was feeling him. Finally, he called.

"This is a collect call from Marcel Combs, who is an inmate at a California state prison. Press '0' to accept."

I accepted, and MC explained that he had been on the lam from the police for a parole violation. He would be out in three months. This was a definite red flag to flee, but by this time, I was in denial. I had fallen for him. I accepted all of his collect calls, wrote him letters every night, and visited him in jail three times a week. I, too, had become a prisoner, locked into a rigid schedule of waiting at home for his calls and standing in line three to four hours just to get a thirty- to forty-five-minute visit with him behind the glass at the county jail. Indeed, it took a toll on my social life, but I didn't care. I had to be there for my man.

Just before he was released, I moved out of the big three-story house and into a small two-bedroom in Encino. Perfect for the two of us. It wasn't long before things changed dramatically. A few days after he came home from prison, I caught him in my bathroom smoking crack. I was devastated. I immediately sent him packing, dropping him off at his preferred location. That was *it*—I wasn't dealing with a crackhead.

Or so I thought. A couple of days went by, and I began to feel bad. I had never dealt with an addict before, so I wasn't sure if I'd done the right thing by abandoning him. So I went looking for MC and brought him back home.

I spent the next two years desperately trying to achieve the impossible task of unraveling someone else's twisted life. I had the audacity to think that I could heal the wounds of his turbulent past by loving it away. I was literally pulling him out of crackhouses and into rehab or visiting him in jail every three months because he repeatedly violated his parole by failing piss tests.

There were times I jeopardized my own freedom and my life by engaging in dangerous situations with this man. I made some downright reckless choices that were almost suicidal in nature. For example, having unprotected sex with a drug-addicted man who's been in the prison system a majority of his life is *crazy*. I'm blessed to have come out of that relationship HIV negative. Also, although he was no longer involved in gang activities, he still had enemies. Thankfully, we never ran into any of them.

I made great efforts to steer that brutha onto the right path, and somewhere along the way, I lost myself in the process. I lost my identity. I neglected my career, my friends, and my family while trying to help someone who didn't want to be helped.

That became the lesson. You can't help anyone who doesn't want to be helped. I learned many lessons in that relationship that humbled me. I used to be judgmental toward women who loved these types of men, boasting that I'd never date a man who's been in prison or in gangs. It's funny how life is. I ended up in the very same situation.

I often asked myself, *"Why did I choose to be in a relationship like that?"* It may not have been my choice at all. I truly believe I had to go through that experience to get to where I am now. I have no regrets about my relationship with MC. In fact, I am grateful for it. It has helped me become more patient, compassionate, and humble, and less judgmental—all things that bring me closer to my greater self.

—Felicia "The Poetess" Morris

Felicia "The Poetess" Morris is an American rapper and radio personality. Her first album, 1992's Simply Poetry *(Poetic Groove/Interscope) quickly established her as a fixture in the L.A. hip-hop scene. She is president of Poetess Media, which produces entertainment content for multimedia outlets, such as mobile, Internet, TV, and radio. In addition, she's a co-host of* The Foxx Hole, *a Sirius satellite radio show hosted by Academy Award–winning actor Jamie Foxx. Her current projects include* The Hip-Hop Report *on Sprint TV, writing feature articles for* Black America Web, *and making a film about the history of West Coast hip-hop. She truly is a Jackie of all trades.*

Chapter 33

Gone.

I HAD A COUSIN. HE AND I USED TO LOOK LIKE TWINS. WHEN HE would visit us in Los Angeles, people often mistook us for Buffy and Jody from the TV show *Family Affair*. At first glance, that is—it was his red hair. There are pictures of us wearing matching striped overalls and his-and-hers blue and pink cowboy outfits, looking very much alike. Curly hair, pale skin, freckles, and lopsided smiles showing tight white rows of baby teeth.

Certainly, I adored and admired him, most especially when we were little. He was a little bit older and very strong—both physically strong and strong willed. Determined and direct, like an exclamation point. He could get into trouble with such abandon, never holding back, never worrying about consequences. I often tossed aside my usually cautious nature to do things with him that on my own were completely unthinkable.

My right knee still has a scar the size of a dollar bill that's the result of a bad fall from a great height. It was a jump my normally bookwormish self would never have attempted without his prodding and his confidence that I could pull it off. As we got older, he could still talk me into doing very stupid things, but I always knew he loved me, in his way. He might throw me from a moving car (and poke my bruises after), but he would fight to the death anyone else who tried to hurt me.

I grew up an only child with few relatives—certainly none my own age. My parents were not married long, and afterward my father immediately moved away. My mother worked and went to school, so I was always involved in activities to keep me occupied and out of the house. Still, an only child with one busy parent spends a lot of time alone.

We did not always live in black neighborhoods, so there were times when I would find myself having to assert my blackness: the preemptive black strike. "Let me tell you, my white friend, that I am black before you tell that racist joke, before you call someone a nigger. Before you say something that makes me lose you as a friend."

It happened more often than I'd like to remember. When I was seven or eight, an old lady who lived down the street once complained to a friend, while I stood by, about the "horrible niggers" that had just moved into the neighborhood. Those horrible niggers were *me*. Well, she was talking about my mother and her husband, but she was talking about me, too—of course, me, too. She looked so angry, that old lady, watering her roses and hating my family. Sometimes it was as if white people were telling me their secrets and sharing things that I was not supposed to tell anyone else. Their hidden hatred. I mean, not all of them had it, the hate, but the ones that did had it bad. And sometimes, but not as often, they still do.

When we did live in black neighborhoods, someone would usually ask whether I was Creole or just from Louisiana, like so many black people in L.A. are. Some would tell me they have a cousin who sort of looks like me. You know, yellow, with freckles and frizzy hair. No one ever teased me or made fun of me; there were too many other yellow people running around. My color, or the lack thereof, was a total nonissue.

There were grandparents here, at home in Los Angeles. One set. My grandmother often tucked me underneath her arm like a little purse, carrying me along to club meetings ("Sit still!"), to run errands ("Keep quiet!"), and to church ("Shut up and sit still!").

She, my grandmother, was half black and half white. Pale as paper and hard as steel. She hated all black people she did not know. For real. Black people who were black, that is. She had plenty of black friends, and she had plenty of black relatives. She loved them, and they were her life. But if she didn't know you, and you were dark—I mean really dark—you were not getting past the front door. That said, she hated, or maybe feared, white people even more.

One day, when I was quite young, I discovered that my mother and each of her sisters were listed as white on their birth certificates. When I asked why, my grandmother got really upset and told me that white people in this country had the power to "line all the colored people up against a wall and shoot them." She listed them as white to make sure that her children, her daughters, would never have that happen to them. She was not joking.

My grandmother often told me how much she loved and missed her mother. How much her mother had loved her, the only girl out of so many boys. How hard her mother had worked. How her mother was barely literate, but she wrote beautiful poetry and was always kind. She never raised her voice or her hand. My grandmother's grandfather, who had been born a slave, would tell her stories about the Civil War and what it felt like to be completely alone, still a boy and on his own, when it was over.

She was full of stories, but I was young and did not want to hear them. I wanted to run and play and ditch my books and aloneness for something entirely different.

My cousin had a completely opposite life, growing up on the south side of Chicago surrounded by family, surrounded by black people. Extremely popular, he was the kid that every other kid in the neighborhood wanted to play with, hang out with, and be like. He had the best of everything: a pool table in the basement, a mostly absentee physician father, a doting stay-at-home mother, a generous allowance, and a monkey. Seriously. He had a monkey. Three dogs, four cats, a half-dozen hamsters, several fish tanks, and Charlie Chan the spider monkey. I have pictures if you don't believe me.

I visited them in Chicago for a few weeks every year. His mother would take us anywhere he wanted to go, take anyone in the neighborhood along, and pay for everything. Skating? Sure. Museum? Of course. Whatever you want, sweetheart.

Staying with them in the summer was a dream of comic books, shopping, bacon sandwiches on white bread, and grape-flavored Kool-Aid. I would sit in my aunt's ridiculously frilly all-pink bedroom, play with her angora cat, Angel, and listen to her talk on the phone with her friends and gossip about this or that relative. These were all things my mother either hated, had no time for, or did not allow—even on birthdays.

His life, my cousin's life, was gloriously—at least to my eyes—full of family. He, too, was an only child, but there was a set of three girl cousins living a few blocks east, another girl cousin a few blocks south, and half an apartment building full of both male and female cousins on the far north side of Chicago. He had zillions of aunts and hundreds of uncles and secondary levels of cousins (both real and faux) sprinkled all over the city. The aunts—especially the old ones—all doted on him. They were always tucking money in his pockets and telling him how they expected big things of him when he grew up.

We would take road trips to Canada, where everything (and everyone) was clean and white. We'd pack up the station wagon and go to Louisiana to visit family. In Shreveport, everyone had a house with a pool and a freezer full of popsicles in the garage; in Baton Rouge, one old auntie had a farm with pigs and lots of shotguns and neighbors who had no window screens and let flies sit on their babies. We'd always spend a few days in New Orleans, where we got dressed up to visit really old people who smelled and smiled and told us that we were lucky. Lucky to be living the good life. Lucky to have so much. They'd rub my face with their shaky brown hands and tell my aunt to keep me out of the sun and put lemon juice on my freckles so they would disappear.

Then, we'd head back to Chicago to buy hamsters, build tents in the basement, and stay outside playing hard, fast, and breathless until the streetlights came on. Later, we'd watch TV (horror movies were our favorite) until our eyes fell shut.

Was I jealous of my cousin? Yes, of course, a little bit. I wanted pets, but we were never really home enough to take care of one. Did I wish my mother paid me more attention? Yes, but by the time I was a teenager, I was grateful that she had other things to do. What I was really jealous of was a feeling that I had when I was there—that I thought he had, too. A feeling that I had people, people and family who were there for me to turn to if I needed them. People who would not ask questions about where I came from, because they were from there, too.

Then, at the start of high school, my cousin's parents moved to the far western suburbs. Their new home was forest green, with a three-car garage and a deck. It sat just across the street from a duck pond. There, in the suburbs, my cousin, their son, fell madly in love with white girls. Truly, madly, deeply in love with blond girls with pale blue eyes, wide foreheads, and bad tempers.

Now, see if you can keep up. Apparently the white girls that liked black guys liked black guys who looked like black guys. The white girls who liked my cousin liked white guys who looked like white guys, so he pretty much became one. A white guy, that is. He gave up his entire family without a thought and, as far as I can tell, without regret.

I would like to think there was more to it. That there was more to his decision to turn his back on his family, his past, and his heritage than just white women. Perhaps he was under too much pressure to be perfect, to be somebody. I know he was reminded of how special he *could be* most of the days of his younger life.

Maybe there was not enough love or acceptance—and certainly there was little respect—from his father. His father believed that his son had it too easy. He didn't have to face the obstacles that he had overcome, and he didn't have to work as hard. He constantly reminded his son that he wasn't as strong or as smart as he was. He also meted out heavy-handed discipline—unnecessarily heavy and, I think, tinged with bitterness.

And definitely there was too much love from his mother. She was always all-forgiving. She gave and gave and gave, and she expected the same love in return. She was disappointed, and sometimes shrill, when she inevitably didn't get it.

Maybe all that family, all those black people, the same ones that made me feel secure, confident, and more myself, made him feel smothered and caught up in a life that was not the one he'd chosen. Maybe that feeling of belonging that buoyed me up dragged him down.

The last time I spoke to him was a few years ago, just after his mother died. His mother was proud of him, but by then, she also really hated him. My aunt treasured and adored all his little blond-haired, hazel-eyed daughters produced by various and sundry wives and girlfriends. As much as she loved them, she missed the love of her friends on the South Side, who lived too far away for her to visit. Time and distance had taken a toll on her friendships and family relationships, and she'd never made friends in the suburbs as she'd thought she would. Not the same kinds of friends, anyway.

My aunt desperately wanted her son to love her. She wanted to be near her grandchildren, and she willingly gave up everything and everyone to stay near him. But she reminded him of what she'd given up for him at every opportunity.

My cousin openly despised his mother. He was abusive and used her as nothing more than a babysitter and a housekeeper. His dismissive attitude made her argumentative and petulant. Her arguments made him increasingly cold and distant. He wanted to be a new man without a past, and she refused to go away.

But I did call him after his mother's death, against the wishes of all the family members who had turned their backs on him, hard, for passing as white, but also for the way he treated his mother. Yes, in the end, she'd become unpleasant and mean. Before she died, she once told me that I had always been selfish and greedy as a child, and that she had never liked me. I chose to ignore what she'd said. Near her death, angry bitterness dripped off her like Spanish moss, and I just happened to be near. She deserved a better close to her life, but she got the life that she'd chosen.

I had to pay that call to my cousin that one last time to honor my childhood memories. In another world, in another life, we still love each other. He is still my family. In this life, however, he could not get me off the phone fast enough.

Now, it's as if he never existed. Without the pictures, with my aunt now gone, the shared bits of our childhood could be something I made up completely.

—Terese Harris

Terese Harris is a graphic-design artist based in Los Angeles.

◆ Chapter 34

Home Is Calling Me:
Blacks, Religion, and Multiculturalism

HAVE YOU HEARD THE NEW TERM THE MEDIA'S FLOATING around—"postracial"? What is postracial supposed to mean, exactly? Does it mean that racial identity no longer matters; that it's no longer important in our society; that there are very few, if any, real barriers to opportunity for African Americans; that racism and prejudice are largely notions of the past?

If so, this is news to me. Despite the recent accomplishments of many blacks over the decades that have passed since the Civil Rights Movement, race continues to strongly influence many factors—for example, the kinds of jobs people have or the places they live. Blacks are more likely to have less prestigious and less secure jobs than whites. Blacks and whites are not inclined to be neighbors. Eighty percent of blacks who live in America's cities would have to move in order to achieve balanced racial integration. Racial profiling and negative stereotyping about blacks is still commonplace.

Other jargon words, such as multiculturalism and diversity, have grown increasingly common in the lexicon of racial terminology lately, becoming central to the public discourse in this country. Multiculturalism and racial diversity suggest something different from postracial, however. They at least acknowledge racial or cultural differences—that people do have distinct life experiences in this country based upon their racial or ethnic identities. All types of institutions are striving to become more multicultural or diverse. Educational institutions are calling for racially and ethnically inclusive curricula, diversity training has become a mandate for many of

America's businesses, and religious leaders and organizations have developed newfound commitments to racial unity.

In my own research as a sociologist, I've always been particularly interested in interracial churches, especially those where blacks and whites worship together. First, church is voluntary. People can go to whatever church they want, for whatever reasons suit them. Given our history in this country, this has meant that churches are mostly racially segregated. Fewer than 10 percent of all churches in the United States are interracial. There is more than a little truth to the old adage that Sunday mornings are the most segregated hours of the week.

However, the voluntary nature of religion in this country also means that people who do attend interracial churches have myriad other opportunities, opportunities that are not restricted by income or education the same way jobs or choices of residence are. Because of this, people who attend interracial churches may be more racially inclusive and supportive of racial equality than others.

The second reason I became interested is related to the first. For African Americans, black churches have been always central to community life. Historically, black churches have been centers of counter-hegemonic social movements. Slave rebellions and the Civil Rights Movement were forged within black religious space. Black churches are places where African Americans, regardless of their formal skills or education, experience opportunity for mobility, becoming deacons, deaconesses, elders, and church mothers. Black churches have served as a refuge from an often hostile world, and as a sanctuary where blacks are free to relax and emotionally and culturally express themselves.

Today, the vast majority of African Americans, regardless of their level of religious commitment, still have some kind of ownership and attachment to African-American churches. Black churches remain the primary social space where blacks have complete reign and are largely free of the influence of the dominant culture. So when African Americans decide to attend interracial churches, they do so among many opportunities to worship in a church where their race and culture predominate. They are willing to sacrifice being a part of the one place in our society where blacks have control.

Given these factors, why do blacks attend interracial churches? I attended an interracial church for seven years myself. I am in an interracial marriage (my husband is white). For me, one of the great benefits of attending an interracial church was that my husband and I could *just be*. We were never stared at or questioned. Most interracial churches have several interracial families—more than in most other settings. This makes you feel a little more normal than usual.

But prior to attending an interracial church, I attended predominately African-American churches. I grew up in an African-American church where the services were long. It was not uncommon for the benediction to come around 3 p.m. My pastor preached with a fiery fervency, often pacing the pulpit as he delivered the message. Tambourines were played as people swayed to the gospel choir's songs. On many occasions, some people—especially one church member whom I will call Sister Hodge, would "catch the spirit." She would holler when something occurred in the service that moved her, and she'd run up and down the church aisle while shouting and waving her hands high in the air.

My research suggests that most blacks who attend interracial churches also grew up in black churches, as I did. And, like me, they attended interracial high schools or lived in interracial neighborhoods in their youth. Many had white friends as teens. So they were socialized in an interracial environment for a part of their upbringing and were accustomed to being around and interacting with whites. They also tend to be middle class, often holding professional jobs. However, few blacks who attend interracial churches are in interracial families. So, most blacks' reasons for going to a racially diverse church have little to do with wanting to feel normal.

Interracial churches are far more likely than either black or white churches to set aside time during their services for attendees to greet one another. There is a greater emphasis on formally welcoming people and making them feel included. Many interviewees have told me that this is the quality they enjoy most about their church. One attendee put it this way: "I just liked the feeling of [the church], the sincerity that seemed to be there in everybody that I came in contact with."

Just like most homogenous churches, blacks are sometimes attracted to interracial churches by the sermons or the pastor. Many told me they found the Sunday messages to be particularly biblical. They also appreciated their pastor because he was very supportive and genuinely interested in them, in their view. Most blacks also expressed that they enjoyed the church's racial diversity. For many, the interracial church was the first environment they experienced where *cooperative* interracial interaction was the norm. Through their experiences, they had come to recognize that they were not so different from their fellow white church attendees. As one person told me:

> [The diversity] helped me to develop relationships with people outside my race where I felt they were my friend and we share Christ in our life and that they have the same struggles as I do and all of that ... I've gotten to know other people on that more personal level where I've said, wow, you know, it's not that much of a difference.

Interestingly, racial diversity was not the primary characteristic that initially attracted African Americans to an interracial church. They came to appreciate it over time, but the church's diversity was not a priority for them. This means that most blacks do not attend interracial churches for their diversity, but instead, they choose them for other qualities that they appreciate about these kinds of churches, or qualities they became disenchanted with at the black churches they'd attended for most of their lives. Nearly everyone mentioned that they still valued the more interactive, effusive worship style they had experienced in black churches. In fact, many admitted they missed it. But a few I spoke with did not. One man explained:

> I wanted to be in a church that was different from what I was accustomed to in a traditional black church and that was really the bottom line and that's what I have found appealing about [my current church], more than anything else ... [I didn't like] the hemmin' and hawin' from the podium. The catching the Holy Ghost, so to speak, and people running around the church and all those kind of different things.

Some of the religious practices of the black church, such as long worship services, were not appealing as well. One woman explained, "I didn't like being in church all day." Others told me they did not want to have to dress up every week to go to church, and they appreciated the freedom to come to church dressed casually. Another person shared that she had had a string of bad experiences in predominately African-American churches before attending her interracial church. These experiences positioned her to be open to other religious alternatives. As for why she left the most recent black church she had attended, she explained, "There were not a lot of genuine things that were done there as far as praise of the Lord but rather praise of man, praise of money and after I became aware of that, naturally I didn't want any part of that."

Blacks attend interracial churches, then, for two main reasons. Outside of religion, there are few contexts in the United States where voluntary, cooperative, and friendly interracial interaction occurs. Several African Americans told me they had never experienced this kind of environment before; they valued these experiences and what they added to their lives.

The most influential reason, however, is that African-American churches did not have the same kind of allure for them that they have for other African Americans. Blacks who attend interracial churches prefer certain religious and cultural practices at their integrated churches that were not commonly practiced in the African-American churches they were familiar with, such as timeliness, less formal dress codes, and shorter services. There may be some African-American churches that meet some of these criteria, but to these individuals, such African-American churches were few and far between. They then must make a choice between a preference for effusive worship or a preference for shorter worship services, for example; most are more willing to sacrifice the former.

I have to say that while attending an interracial church, I missed the feeling of the black church experience—the spontaneity, the freedom to move your body, and the collaborative worship created through informal interaction among the worshipers, the preacher, and the choir. I missed the emphasis on social justice that many black churches still have.

Today, I attend a black church and, quite frankly, I hadn't realized just how much my soul craved being back in its worship environment until I returned. Other blacks may decide to return, as I did. Despite their good intentions, most interracial churches do not represent a balance between whites' and blacks' religiocultural interests. Rather, the interrelations, religious and cultural practices, and organizational structure of interracial churches tend to be more representative of the preferences and desires of whites than of racial and ethnic minorities. Shouting, like that practiced by Sister Hodge at my childhood church, is generally not accommodated; interactive call-and-response with the pastor is rare; and spontaneous swaying or dancing to a gospel beat is not core to the worship experience.

While there is not currently a mass movement of blacks opting for interracial churches, there is an increasingly loud call for a postracial or multicultural America that is encouraging us to make such a decision. I do support interracial worship and racial diversity in general, but I am convinced that neither a postracial nor a multicultural, interracial society is worth pursuing if it means sacrificing who we are as black people, and what we have gained to achieve that identity. To be a part of most interracial churches, blacks must be willing to sacrifice an important part of who they are and what they want.

Of course, African Americans are not a monolithic group. But those who came before us left us with a legacy of struggle and overcoming; of togetherness; of courage; of a quest for true freedom and equality; of steadfast faith in a mighty God; and, oh yes, of foot-stomping, hand-clapping, spirit-building, and soul-stirring gospel music. Maybe one day I will attend another interracial church—that is, if I can find one where I am able to fully embrace my heritage. But right now, I am so glad to be home.

—**Korie L. Edwards**

Korie L. Edwards is an assistant professor of sociology at Ohio State University. She is the author of The Elusive Dream: The Power of Race in Interracial Churches *and coauthor of* Against All Odds: The Struggle for Racial Integration in Religious Organizations.

◆ Chapter 35

R(evolution)

O N PAPER, HE WAS EVERYTHING A YOUNG, SAME-GENDER-loving brother could ask for—a thirty-six-year-old, masculine, bald-headed, brown-skinned, independent, and hard-working professional brother who didn't live with his mama and had all his teeth. As for me, I was thirty-two and mirrored all the qualities he had, except that I was light-skinned and had curly hair. We were both black and both homosexually active yet adept at blending in with the larger black heterosexual community, which was convenient for both of us. Convenient for him because he was a married but separated man with a two-year-old son. Convenient for me because, despite being openly homosexual, I enjoyed socializing with different circles that weren't always associated with what some view as a "gay" scene.

We met on the Internet in 2001 for what was supposed to just be a sexual "hook-up"—an encounter that met our sexual needs but would end up being no more than a one-time occurrence. I had just moved to Atlanta from New York for work, and I felt blessed to live in Atlanta again. Not only was Atlanta still the "black Mecca" I had remembered when I lived there in the mid-1990s, but it had long been known to many of us as the "black gay Mecca" as well. It's a city where there are so many same-gender-loving brothers that it could make one's head spin. Atlanta represented a place where one could realize great economic and career potential, and where it was also possible to start a meaningful relationship with another upwardly mobile black man. While this was the long-term goal, a brother's still got immediate needs, so I didn't mind getting down for some transient sexual healing when the urge hit me. And as good as Atlanta was for meeting brothers for potential long-term relationships, it was even better if you were just looking for sex.

My first encounter with this brother, who I will call "Al," was passionate and more than satisfying, but after the sex was over, I was surprised to find that he wanted to talk for a while. I obliged, and the conversation showed that he had some substance. However, when he told me that he was separated but still married, I wrote him off as someone I could never take seriously in a relationship. And that was fine with me, since I wasn't really looking to settle down anyway.

Fresh from ending a four-year long-distance relationship with a brother in Boston while living in New York, I was still in recovery mode and felt like being single for a while. Al, on the other hand, seemed to want more and more as our conversation progressed. He kept looking at me quizzically as we discussed everything from politics to our respective jobs; later, he even called me from his car, exclaiming, "You know you blew my mind, right?"

Blew his mind? How could this brother tell me I'd blown his mind when, as he was leaving the house, he all but said, "Don't call me, I'll call you." Maybe by blew his mind he meant that he found me relatively interesting and possibly more than just a hook-up. I thought about it for about two minutes and then moved on. He was just a one-night stand, I thought, and I was poised to convince myself that I didn't care.

Despite Al's specific phone instructions not to call him, I decided to dig up his number on my cell phone a couple of weeks later anyway. When I called him, he seemed surprised, and maybe even a little upset that I had not followed his orders. After I reached out to him, however, we began a gradual reconnection process, which, as the months went by became deeper and deeper. The sex was passionate. We began to see each other more frequently, and we always had great conversations as we got to know each other better. Of course, I felt guilty that he was still married, but he assured me that he and his wife were definitely separated—not living together anymore—and that a divorce was right around the corner. This was somewhat reassuring, but I still feared I was falling into a trap reserved for hetero-sexual women on those awful BET or Lifetime made-for-TV movies. I didn't want to be the cliché on the wrong side of a relationship with a married brother. Even worse, I didn't want to be part of a case on *Forensic Files*.

Almost three months into our relationship, Al informed me at an Atlanta Hawks game that his name wasn't really "Al" after all. He explained that he didn't really trust the men he met online, and he was very private about his personal business, but with me he felt comfortable enough to tell the truth. I guess I was supposed to be flattered, but I wasn't—I felt like an idiot, and most of my friends scolded me for not knowing better and told me to leave him.

Despite his revelation, for some reason I was still drawn to Al, and we didn't grow apart. Instead, we began to spend more time together. As the years went by, we slowly became more integrated into each others' lives. We vacationed in Jamaica and Brazil. He met many of my close friends. I met his son at a basketball game. In 2005, he officially completed his divorce proceedings. Things ap-peared to be moving forward for us, and while it wasn't exactly what I had expected, I went along—cautiously.

Over the course of the next few years, Al and I had many break-ups and make-ups. We lived forty-five minutes apart on opposite sides of the city, our jobs kept us both busy, and personal commit-ments to our respective friends and families made it difficult to maintain a consistent relationship flow. During these times, we dated other people, but for some reason we always kept coming back to one another.

Often, my reason for walking away was the fact that he was nev-er as comfortable with his sexuality as I was. Most of his family didn't know he preferred men. His coworkers were surely unaware, and he was suspicious of anything that could potentially expose the degree of his involvement with me—including my idea to display a picture of him in my private office. This was in direct contrast with my ap-proach to my sexuality, which I had successfully integrated into my personal and professional life. My family and heterosexual friends knew I was gay, and I would talk about my relationships with other men with the same nonchalance as my heterosexual colleagues would when gushing about their spouses and kids. It was no big deal to me, but it still was to him, and I often vacillated between accepting him for who and where he was and staying true to my spirit.

Our last break-up was in the fall of 2007, when I felt I was done with the whole damn thing. I had grown tired of slowing down to his level of comfort with his sexuality, so I ended it. He still wanted to be with me, but he wasn't willing to stay in a relationship if I wasn't happy. So he let me go, thinking that I just didn't love him as much as he had grown to love me.

As the weeks went by, I tried dating other people and moving forward, but I really couldn't. Al had become so integrated into my life that he had developed his own friendships with my friends, co-workers, and colleagues. They always inquired about him, and I often found myself reminiscing about trips and experiences we had shared.

After several discussions with myself, my closest friends, and a therapist, I decided that I needed to call him to explain myself and my reasons for ending things. I didn't want him to think that I didn't love him. I *did* love him, but I couldn't deal with his discomfort about his own love for other men. But slowly I realized that I actually missed this man who had, over the course of months and years, become a good friend and a true partner. I wanted him to give me another chance, and I couldn't help but feel that I was remembering him wrong.

Al was receptive to our reconnection, and we had several long discussions that were among the most honest and vulnerable that I have ever had with another person. We revealed personal and family influences we hadn't known about before. We both cried as we expressed how much we had come to mean to one another, and I believe these conversations made us closer. We agreed to not just "get back together," but to take things slower, spending more quality time, and not repeating the mistakes we had made before. I felt good about reconnecting with him. Although I was optimistic about the future, I was still concerned about how we could continue moving forward in a relationship when I knew I still had reservations about our differing levels of comfort with our sexual orientation. Somehow, things had changed, but I felt like I was just putting a bandage over a gushing wound.

Then, something amazing happened. It was New Year's Eve, and Al and I had planned to spend some time together at his place. I'm not a big New Year's Eve person, so I told him I didn't feel like a big party or anything. I just wanted to do something quiet, either by myself or with him. He was fine with that and said we could just spend the night at his place. His brother had been in town with his sixteen-year-old son for the week between Christmas and New Year's, and although he'd been nursing a cold the whole week, Al entertained them along with his own son, who was now eight years old. On top of that, at the end of the holiday week, Al's brother took off for a four-day trip to the Caribbean for some rest and relaxation, and Al was left to entertain both his son and nephew for a week on his own. The day after his brother returned—New Year's Eve—he dropped them off at the airport and immediately came to my house to pick me up.

When he arrived, three of my closest friends were already at the house preparing a New Year's Eve meal; caught up in the sentiment of brotherly love, I decided that I wanted to stay home and ring in the New Year with them. I asked Al if he was okay with staying over at my house for the evening and celebrating with the group. He looked at me strangely at first in response to the sudden change of plans, but he rolled with it and said, "Whatever you want, baby."

The night was typical by New Year's Eve standards—full of laughter, celebration, and drinking amongst close friends. The next morning, we got up early, and Al drove us to his house. Al cooked breakfast for all four of us—scrambled eggs, hash browns, turkey bacon, homemade waffles, and grits. When we were finished eating, Al sent us all away to take naps while he cleaned up and began preparing his world-famous macaroni and cheese for a New Year's Day party we planned to attend later in the day. Not once did he complain or ask for help, and after everything was done, he curled up into bed next to me to catch a fifteen-minute nap before driving us all to the party. Although he felt under the weather and had been taking care of his family all week, he was totally unselfish—flexible about my change of plans and committed to looking out for me, my friends, *and* his friends for the holiday. It was nothing short of extraordinary.

It has been said that the definition of insanity is doing the same thing over and over again but expecting different results. In a previous relationship, I was blessed to love a wonderful brother who loved and affirmed me in various ways—but not in the ways I was expecting or wanting him to. As a result, I often complained about simple things I thought he *wasn't* doing, such as not calling me back promptly whenever I called him, sleeping through movies we saw together, and, like Al, not being as comfortable with his sexuality as I was. I was so busy focusing my attention and criticism on these "negatives" that I ignored the fact that on most Fridays, he'd drive five hours from Boston to climb in bed with me at 2 a.m. on Saturday morning only to have to drive back at 2 a.m. Monday morning so he could report to work at 8 a.m. Although many aspects of this previous relationship were flawed, and neither of us was perfect, after it ended, I realized that my obsession about what he *wasn't* doing instead of acknowledging what he *was* doing had everything to do with our break-up.

As Al curled up next to me on his bed that New Year's Day and the events of the preceding twenty-four hours played out in my mind, I realized what an amazing man I had. I was suddenly aware of how petty it was for me to overemphasize his relative discomfort with his sexuality at the expense of overlooking the many ways he showed me he loved me. We had had enough break-ups and make-ups to realize that I needed to change *my* approach, or our relationship would suffer the same fate as my relationship with my ex from Boston.

So I stopped the madness. I stopped complaining about what he wasn't doing and started recognizing the ways he showed me he loved me. I started just enjoying him for who he was, and our relationship for what it was—something beautiful, and perfectly imperfect.

In the weeks that followed, our relationship flowed a lot smoother simply because I chose to open my eyes and focus on his positive attributes instead of his drawbacks. I began to acknowledge the changes he had made for me on his life's journey. In fact, once I stopped complaining, he gave me a beautiful framed picture of himself for my office.

Al was not the same man I had met on that cool autumn afternoon in 2001, and to keep him confined as my remembrance of the person he was instead of the person he had become would have been tragic. I don't know what the future holds for us, but I can say that Al—just by being himself and by being in my life—has truly challenged me, forcing me to grow and mature in ways I never expected when we first met. And at the end of the day, isn't that exactly what a soul mate is supposed to do?

Being black and homosexual is difficult in America, as neither black males nor homosexuals are rarely celebrated or often affirmed. But life is short, and I have found a spirit in Al that moves me. He has helped me appreciate the simple, loving things life has to offer. When I look into his eyes, I see myself in the truest sense and the complicated beauty of our journey together and as individuals on this earth. I won't take that for granted anymore. Marlon Riggs, the late black gay film director, exclaimed in his documentary *Tongues Untied* that "black men loving black men is *the* revolutionary act." So let the revolution begin.

—**David J. Malebranche, MD, MPH**

David J. Malebranche, MD, MPH, is an assistant professor at the Division of General Medicine at Emory University's School of Medicine in Atlanta, Georgia. He supervises medical providers-in-training at the Urgent Care Center at Grady Memorial Hospital in downtown Atlanta and sees his own patients at the Ponce de Leon Infectious Disease Center, a local AIDS clinic that provides comprehensive care to the uninsured. Malebranche conducts research that explores the racial, gender, age, and cultural factors that influence black men's health, particularly with regard to sexual risk behavior and HIV testing practices.

♦ Chapter 36

Dear Harold,

TODAY, AS WE APPROACH OUR THIRTIETH WEDDING ANNIversary, I remember that Saturday afternoon in December when we exchanged our vows all those years ago. I wanted a winter wedding, and what a beautiful New York City winter wedding we had. The streets were covered with a blanket of virgin white snow unmussed by salt or tire wheels or rushing feet. The invitation of the city was of calm and tranquility. The sun rushed through the windows of St. Peter's Church and reflected off the blond wooden pews and colorful cushions. The warmth of the sun, even on that cold afternoon, said, "Love is here; take note."

Your best friend, Grady Tate, serenaded us with his mellifluous baritone. The string quartet played with such purity of intonation that it was an offering of grace floating up to the heavens. Your daughter Marion, my stepdaughter, was a part of our ceremony, a witness to our new beginning as a family. In Egyptian culture, it is believed that the ring finger has the "vein amoris," the vein of love, which runs straight to the heart. And on December 16, 1978, when you placed the wedding band on my ring finger, I was truly filled with love. It went straight to my heart and today, almost thirty years later, I can say, "Yes, I still love my husband."

Ours was not an easy beginning. We had both survived disappointing marriages and approached each other with caution. We first met in the Fine Arts Department at Howard University in Washington, D.C. I was majoring in voice and you in music composition. You were practice teaching on us lowly freshmen, so you never noticed me, but I certainly noticed you. You were one of the big men on campus, especially with all the fine arts students. These were times of excitement at our historically black college. The Chiffons were on the charts with "He's So Fine," Stevie Wonder was a twelve-year-old sensation, and Sidney Poitier was starring in *Lilies of the Field,* for which he would become the first African-American male to receive an Academy Award.

But these were also chaotic times. It was a time of President John F. Kennedy's assassination, as well as the assassination of Medgar Evers. There was racial unrest, civil disobedience, and Dr. Martin Luther King, Jr.'s March on Washington for Jobs and Freedom, in which more than 250,000 people participated. So years later, when we reconnected in New York, it was still not easy to separate world events from our daily lives. We were conscientious people who still believed in the dream.

Although I had not become the second Leontyne Price, I had become a working actress. Since leaving Howard, I had become a founding member of the Negro Ensemble Company; performed in plays both on and off Broadway; provided voiceover talent for high-profile clients like American Airlines and the island of Jamaica; worked for Joseph Papp at the New York Shakespeare Company; and met legends, such as Langston Hughes and James Baldwin. I was preparing a new role as the stand-in for the female lead in a hit Broadway musical, *Two Gentlemen of Verona,* for which you were the musical supervisor. This job was particularly tempting because if I learned my lines, knew my songs, was comfortable with the blocking of the play, and was within twenty minutes of the theater, I had no work to do. As you know, Harold, my position was called standby because my job entailed standing by just in case the star of the show was unable to perform. Other than that, I was not even required to be at the theater during performances. I received a check—a very lovely check, I might add—every week, whether I performed or not.

And so our paths crossed again. We began as professionals together, you teaching me the music and me being eager to learn, because I wanted you to be proud of my work. I still remembered the Chiffons' "He's So Fine." This was our new time together. A time of witnessing the ending of the Black Arts Movement; a time when Leroi Jones became Amiri Baraka; a time when Lew Alcindor became Kareem Abdul Jabbar; a time when Melvin Van Pebbles was in *Sweet Sweetback's Baadasssss Song*; a time when PUSH was being organized by Rev. Jesse Jackson; a time of the Attica prison riots; and a time when Maya Angelou published her first book of poetry, *Just Give Me a Cool Drink of Water*. It was a time of recognizing my love for you and a time when you became my cool drink, my best friend, my lover, my rock, and my partner through this journey of life. This journey has not always been easy, but the one thing that has remained constant is our commitment to our family and our marriage.

Our family is a two-career family, in professions that are both unpredictable and sometimes require us to be in different cities or on different continents. This, coupled with the demands of childrearing, sometimes forced us to strategize how we would continue to make our marriage work. We made all decisions together, which meant, as you know, some sacrifices on both our parts, each knowing that the most important consideration was our family.

Harold, I often think of the time when a pilot I'd made for a new television series was picked up by the network. I came to you and told you the job required me to be in Los Angeles. At the time, your music jingle business was thriving, your Broadway work was increasing, and our daughter was still in school. Without hesitating, you said, "I can write music anywhere. This is your chance, and you have to take it." Within one month, we had moved to Los Angeles. Had the situation been reversed, I know my response would have been the same. That is what love and marriage are all about.

As I sit reflecting on these thirty years, I ask myself what has made this relationship work. What have we learned on this journey? One of the most important lessons is that love is not static. Love is an active verb. Marriage is a living, breathing entity, and it can be reborn every day. Love is flexible. Rules can change, and what I needed or required from our marriage thirty years ago may not be the same today.

What has not changed? In order for our marriage to survive and our relationship to grow, we must be vigilant about our promise to each other that we would not allow outside influences to come into our home. Sometimes, when the world is in a time of insanity, we might forget our promise, drift into unconsciousness, and cause harm to each other. But thankfully, our blackout is only momentary. We remember what Elleni Amlak, a designer, once said: "You must polish your marriage every day." And that is what we try to do. We remember that in the privacy of love and marriage, we have come to define who we are: wife, husband, parent, professional, lover, and friend.

I am not arrogant enough to assume I have the answers for all relationships, but I have learned some lessons that I wanted to share with you and pass on to our daughter:

- Socrates said that love is the pursuit of the good, but I say love *creates good*, it does not merely *find* the good in us
- To love is an act of bravery
- To love is to gain a sense of ourselves
- To love is to find the best in one's self and to *earn* your lover's love
- When love succeeds, both partners feel better about themselves
- Love is not a feeling; love is an action
- Don't hold too tightly; let each other be who you are
- Be gentle with your love
- Know that your love is divine
- Remember God and spirituality
- Make love
- Dance
- Remember to laugh
- Respect each other
- Form a partnership
- Always communicate, even when it is painful

Wherever I have used the word love, marriage can be substituted, for they are the same.

My darling husband, in these not-so-conscious times of September 11 remembrances, wars, the pull of gravity, the disappearance of my hourglass figure, the graying of my hair—and these miraculous times of my stepdaughter, Marion, and her children, India and Lena, our daughter, Samantha, and Barack Obama's *Audacity of Hope*, we still have the audacity to love. We continue to polish our marriage every day. Love is still here, and for that, I am eternally grateful.

I love you, Harold, and I thank you for being my husband. You will always be my music.

Your wife,

Hattie

—Hattie Mae Winston

Hattie Mae Winston is an American television, film, and stage actress best known for her role as Margaret on Becker. *She also had roles in other television series, such as* Nurse *and* Homefront. *Winston starred in the Broadway hit* The Tap Dance Kid, *and also appeared on Broadway in* Two Gentlemen of Verona, I Love My Wife, *and* The Me Nobody Knows. *She was a member of the Negro Ensemble Company.*

◆ Chapter 37

The Responsibility

WHO AM I? IT'S A QUESTION MANY OF US ASK OURSELVES, but only a few really know the answer. As a black man in America, I can be a convoluted myriad of contradictions and ideologies. My life has been affected by everything from slavery to racial profiling. Yet I still exist.

My existence is based on many layers and foundations. Sometimes I wonder how I have made it this far. What has strengthened me? What has trained and mentored me? I am what I am because of my mentors—most of whom are black males. Although some say black role models don't exist, I know that they do.

My mother and father divorced when I was very young, but I like to think that I'm pretty lucky nonetheless. I've been fortunate enough to have many different guiding figures in my life. However, just the fact that I consider that to be luck strikes at the very core of the everyday existence of the black male.

I grew up in a mostly black neighborhood in Durham, North Carolina. When I was an adolescent, there weren't necessarily gangs per se, there were neighborhood crews, and we had plenty of young black males in our community. As the younger boys would come of age, the older boys would begin testing us, in a sense preparing us for the latter stages of adolescence. Those experiences taught me to stay and fight instead of running.

High school was a hodgepodge of athletics, getting in trouble, chasing the ladies, and making sure I made some pretty decent grades. I was fortunate enough to be mentored by members of my local community, from everyday bruthas to the men of Omega Psi Phi and Kappa Alpha Psi fraternities. Talking with and watching these men in action had a great impact on me, and I knew I wanted to be a leader. I knew I wanted to be where some of those guys were—and I needed to know how to get there.

The true strength of mentoring is that it allowed my young mind to see past everyday issues and focus more on the future. My mind was being groomed, and eventually I pledged Omega Psi Phi in college; there, I learned service, sacrifice, and humility. I began to understand what it meant to think of us as a people and get away from an individual mind-set. It's not just about me. It's about *us*. We owe those who came before us for the knowledge we have acquired.

Once it was time to tackle corporate America, I was lucky enough to encounter other mentors. I've been fortunate to have many great men in my life, and their reasoning and guidance have empowered me directly as a professional and as a businessman. Corporate America is a delicate mixture of opinions and intentions, and any information that can be passed down should be done so and with haste.

Many men have devoted their lives to the advancement of our youth. The names Carter G. Woodson, Arthur Ashe, and Reginald Lewis evoke memories of great teachers as well as men. Reginald Lewis, a Baltimore native, was a graduate of both an HBCU and Harvard who founded the first African-American law firm on Wall Street. He became widely successful as the chairman and CEO of Beatrice Foods, a company with more than a billion dollars in annual sales. But Lewis did not forget others; giving back was part of his life. In 1987, he established the Reginald F. Lewis Foundation, which funded grants totaling approximately $10 million to various nonprofit programs and organizations during his lifetime. Reginald Lewis was a mentor.

I, too, am a mentor. Teaching has always been a huge part of the African Diaspora, and I feel that I'm a part of that continuing legacy. I am a culmination of my life experiences, and I choose to share my knowledge. I believe it to be part of my responsibility, not only as a black man, but also as a *human*.

They say there are no black male role models. I say we are simply overlooked. As we continue to look for change, we must remember that we have always been a part of that change. We must continue to help guide our own. Be a mentor whenever you see the opportunity, because as a black male, I know I needed one.

—**David Horton**

David Horton is the author of the best-selling book Negro Intellect: A Guide for Young Black Males. *His second book,* Negro Diva: A Guide for Young Black Females, *will be available soon. For booking and other information, contact www.negropublishing.com.*

♦ Chapter 38

This Dope Called Hope

The explosions of my emotions got me twisted
Uplifted momentarily
But fluctuations of my feelings be scaring me
Because change is a woman's prerogative
And my bearings be damn near inoperative
Daring me to slip
So all I can grip is my crotch as they watch me pimp-walk along the
strip
Of self-consciousness
Dripping …
With a wit nobody else can get
So I'm launching this barrage of pent-up confusion at the Sun
Who simply smirks in response, 'cause he's browned me
And ancient Kings hover around me with taunts that I am The One
But nobody can see it, so nobody believes it
And I'm beginning to feel the joke's on me
"Have a smoke on me," my homies suggest
So I ingest nature's way of getting me high
Which only brings my bravado closer to the truth
Ever seen a real man cry—I mean boo-hoo, like only a woman's
supposed to—
And don't know why?
So I stumble on to my humble home
With fears that the woman beside me can see the Achilles heel in
my masculinity
So I slap her around as a diversionary tactic, when in fact it's me
who feels abused

Getting used to wearing HOPE around my neck like a noose—
Loose enough for me to breathe the dope I need in my veins to keep me sane
Reigning in the vanity of the insanity running around in my head
It's vital that I cling to the title "victim" instead of "culprit"
The DOPE, it keeps me numb
Too scared to run, I just sit and pray that someone comes and either takes me away
Or takes me out
Because whatever I say still makes me out to be the bad guy
I've had lies hurled at me before, and it's HOPE that makes me hardcore
For no one can understand the fears of a black man except another black man
But we don't stand around holding hands
We hold in our hands cans of Colt 45 or just 40s of whatever to help weather the lies
That drive us to this form of therapy
And HOPE is scaring me into believing there's a better way
Like Run and Darryl used to say, "THE ANSWERS YOU SEEK R N FRONT OF YOUR FACE …"
But what happens if you're faceless?
And nameless?
The DOPE makes the pain less, and the strain stresses my tresses until they lock
And change into dangling reins so the forces can pull me back
Because I can no longer hold my horses due to the fact that my lungs are full of the hay
That I smoke every day to feed what I need to get me through the day
I bleed with each swagger and sway
The daggers don't kill; they merely pierce the wounds of my will
And at best, I just stand still with my arms across my chest and nowhere to turn
While HOPE continues to burn a desire I can't seem to fulfill
It's ill, pictures of me laying at the precipice of … something

Dry humping this concept of being a better man than what I am
Feeling bound, because my bootstraps cannot be found
And who's that making that annoying sound that there's more in
store than what I can see?
HOPE is destroying me
HIP-HOP is b-boy-ing me into a "cool" that's got me trapped
Employing me on a search that is as elusive as that damned G-
spot—
Just when you think you've got it … it moves
And the dope seems to be the only remedy to soothe this aching
soul
That HOPE has a hold of and won't let go
So … I meditate
As I continue to medicate without direction … aimless
The DOPE makes the pain less
And the strain stresses me from within until my blood runs thin
and my skin is hardened
So pardon me and my attitude, I'm just looking for the latitude to
be free
Of these four walls of "cool" that confine me and find me fighting
fallacies of my manhood
I'm strugglin'
Jugglin' these images of me and the man I'm supposed to be
Somebody please save me, 'cause all this DOPE and all this HOPE
Is about to cave me in

—**Malcolm-Jamal Warner**

Malcolm-Jamal Warner is an accomplished actor, director, and musician best known for his role as Theo Huxtable on the ground-breaking comedy The Cosby Show. *He also starred for four seasons on the sitcom* Malcolm & Eddie *and spent two seasons on the cable show* Jeremiah. *As a musician, Warner released his first CD,* The Miles Long Mixtape, *in 2003, and his most recent project,* Love & Other Social Issues, *in 2007.*

PART IV
COMMUNITY

♦ Chapter 39

Actionable Pride

IT'S CHALLENGING TO DEFINE AFRICAN-AMERICAN CULTURE IN one simple phrase or finite interpretation. It encompasses so many wonderful things to me. It's our unifying history, our interconnectedness, our church, our music, and our art. It's how we have survived in this country over several generations. It is, quite literally, all that I am—spiritually, mentally, and professionally.

Reared by a mother and father who were both social activists, I vividly remember participating in my first public demonstration. I was about four years old, and it was my job to help make signs protesting that there were no "colored" bus drivers in Omaha, Nebraska, where we lived. Throughout my childhood, there would be many other public demands for social justice; it's always been a part of who I am. In fact, I remember thinking that all little children went to demonstrations. So, I take pride in who I am—in who we are as a people. It's this sense of being that aids me in developing my viewpoint of our community's current state of affairs.

As we suffered through the close of the two-term presidency of George W. Bush, many things transpired. We are six years into an unjust war that has crippled our international standing. There is dwindling federal support for college grants and our beloved HBCUs. The effects of the inhumane treatment of our brothers and sisters are still being felt, nearly three years after Katrina, and we have mounting unemployment rates. I believe the state of the economy is a source of discontent for all Americans; however, it hits African Americans especially hard.

Right now, the subprime mortgage meltdown is ravaging our community. We were the last ones "in," so many of us, even though we worked hard and didn't live beyond our means. Many of us had never before been creditworthy—until recently. Unfortunately, all of that progress is in jeopardy, and many black people are going through the process of foreclosure or have already lost their homes. You know, sometimes it's better for a person not to have something at all than to experience it and have it taken away. It's got to be particularly devastating for first-time homeowners. Housing troubles, layoffs, and a shrinking job market are combining to make the economy the most pressing issue for black people right now, I think.

The root of the predatory lending practices that birthed this subprime nightmare was a lack of information. When people get detailed, truthful facts in advance, they are capable of making good decisions. However, the lack of knowledge we may have about certain things is often not our fault. Yes, we have to take responsibility for our own affairs, but one cannot ignore the communication gap that continues to put minorities at a disadvantage. We usually don't find out about crucial information until it becomes history! Although this trend dates back several generations, those disadvantages are still alive today.

Of course, I would be remiss if I did not include the role that unbalanced media coverage has had on us. It has contributed to friction among the different communities of the African Diaspora. While we all have differences—whether we are African, Latin, Caribbean, or European brothers and sisters—we also share certain things. Nonetheless, mainstream media often turns it into an "us" versus "them" scenario, with one group's advancements portrayed as taking something away from another. So instead of rejoicing over accomplishments, we are nudged toward envy and jealousy. That's a divide-and-conquer strategy at its ghastly best. In order to fully participate in the global economy, we must form balanced coalitions.

In all fairness, some members of our community are also using black media vehicles to propagate less than complimentary portrayals of our culture. It's no wonder some of our youth are embracing unhealthy behaviors and values, when our own media actively promote them. There are still too many negative images of black people on TV, in magazines, and in the movies. Some black videos underscore the message, "if you take your clothes off and shake your booty, you'll get paid." It's not surprising that some of our young people aspire to do little more. We must pressure black media outlets to provide more positive messages.

In order to protect our history and legacy, we must take ownership of it. It's our images, our news, our chronological story, and our inheritance. We cannot expect other groups, intentionally or unintentionally, to accurately describe, portray, and empower us. We need to document, preserve, and build our own stories, from our own perspectives. A lot of the omission from history books that we classify as racism is actually just ignorance on the part of writers who do not understand our culture. In many cases, it's just easier for them not to tell the story at all. Completely eliminating us from certain accounts and concentrating on their own accounts is often caused by nothing more than a lack of knowledge. Self-preservation is the first law of nature, so each culture looks out for its own first. That's what we should be about, but whenever black people do the same, there always seems to be a cry of alarm. Perhaps guilt is the reason for that concern?

There clearly needs to be a strategy for the empowerment of black people and the black media as a whole—radio, cable networks, newspapers, magazines, and online—as our primary sources of information all play critical roles. Our businesses should become our first line of resources, not simply an alternative.

The mega-churches, which seem to evoke a sense of unity, are still the largest gathering place of persons of African descent in this country. We have to harness that power and transform it into a working coalition. I have learned that once you are able to function in a unified manner within a single organization, you can transfer that energy easily. If we can understand that a cohesive unit doesn't always mean agreement, we can keep working together for the same goal. Once we achieve it, we can use that positive energy in any capacity we desire.

People ask me all the time, "How do you define success?" To me, success is helping somebody, with the result that the world is a little better because I was in it. In this life, you should have two lists. The first list documents all of the people you have helped, and the second notes all of the ones you've hurt. If the list of people you've helped is a lot longer than the people you have hurt, then, to me, you've lived a successful life.

We must not define success in terms of possessions or dollars, but in terms of Godly character and humility. To protect, preserve, and grow our community, we cannot look at pride as a guiding theme. No, true pride is about action. I pray that we will make our African-American pride actionable.

—Cathy Hughes

Cathy Hughes is the founder and chairperson of Radio One, Inc., the largest African-American–owned and –operated broadcasting company in the nation. Radio One is the first African-American company in radio history to dominate several major markets simultaneously and possesses the first woman-owned radio station to rank number 1 in any major market. Hughes is the first African-American woman to own a publicly traded company.

♦ Chapter 40

Not Denise Huxtable

S AN AFRICAN-AMERICAN CHILD BORN AND RAISED IN THE LUX-
urious surroundings of Anaheim Hills, California, I received
more than my fair share of flack from both black and white
peers. As children, my sisters and I recognized the differences among
us and our classmates, as well as our church members, at painfully
early ages.

Let me start by offering an abridged rundown of my home life.
Our parents, both practicing doctors, successfully raised us in a
close-knit hutch while balancing their respective careers around us
and each other. They made certain to instill my sisters and me with
a refined sense of humility from the get-go. Mom and Dad believed
that to be successful in life, we had to be able to understand others
who are different from us—in particular, those who were less fortunate or better off. In the big, bad world beyond our tall blue fence,
we knew some would ridicule us for what we had, what we stood for,
and what our heritage had molded us to be.

I attended a predominately white, nondenominational Christian
school from preschool through eighth grade, just as my sisters did.
Although the school was hailed as a safe and friendly haven, it was
anything *but* safe *or* friendly for us. Spoiled children ran rampant,
perceiving the world as theirs from the very moment they arrived
home from the hospital. Everything had been handed to them on
silver platters by their parents.

I was no less fortunate, but my parents were careful to explain
where our fortunes came from. There was no "When Daddy has

the checkbook, who can tell you no?" for me. I understood from a young age that money was earned. My parents fulfilled our needs and wants, but only through perseverance and hard work.

So life at school was understandably bizarre for my first years of formal education. I couldn't understand why a little girl who threw a temper tantrum would receive a new toy for her troubles. I couldn't understand how a little boy who fired a smart retort to his parents could then be taken out for ice cream as a form of apology. I couldn't understand why most of my classmates looked at me funny when we played make believe as *Sailor Moon* or built towers with Legos in the sandbox.

"Why is her hair so *frizzy?*"

"There aren't any *blacks* in *Sailor Moon!*"

"Get your *own* Legos. I don't want *you* stealing them!"

Yes, I was very confused by the behavior and hostility some of the students displayed, but I would soon be educated.

Second grade was a milestone, as far as revelations go. During lunch one fine summer day, a girl sitting near my circle of friends complained that she had forgotten her lunch at home. I took the initiative to extend an olive branch and offered half of mine to compensate. She flatly told me she didn't share food with "*niggers.*"

Well, needless to say, I was mortified. I had always known I was different, but I didn't think it would matter in the long run. It *shouldn't* have mattered as much as it did. In a desperate act to save face, I quickly ran to the teacher and tattled on the little girl like there was no tomorrow. My school, known for its strict zero-tolerance policy, swiftly took action. For the next few days, I was repeatedly called to the office to testify and verify what had happened. After everything was said and done, the little girl who had shamelessly turned down my lunch was expelled from school, indefinitely.

I would have held my head high and marched straight back into that classroom, gloating over my victory, as the snobbish little girl packed her things for the last time—if I hadn't felt so rotten. It wasn't my intention to get her thrown out of school. My parents had made us aware of that word and its destructive powers before this whole fiasco had even started. So why was I so shocked that something like this happened? Well, I can definitely say that the next few years of school were *nothing* compared to the negative attention I received from our fellow church members.

My family and I are Seventh-Day Adventist, a denomination of Christianity, and our church, located in Riverside, California, is predominately African American. For the better part of my childhood, my church was a horrible place filled with horrible children. Three girls in particular seemed to constantly have it in for me. Thing 1, the leader of a small party of bullies, strode around church as if she owned the world. Thing 2 and Thing 3 followed loyally behind her, supporting everything she said or did—as most young girls are prone to do at that age.

I made do with my small circle of friends. We did everything from naptime to hymnal scribbling together—until *they*, too, turned on me. Eventually, I became convinced I was the only child under the relentless scrutiny of Thing 1 and her crew. They made it their personal responsibility to pester me about my light skin, eyes, and hair well into my teens. The girls pushed me into corners and physically assaulted me after choir rehearsals and Sabbath school. They would pull my long, light brown hair relentlessly, jeering that they could see the "horrible weave" I had.

Not one to simply sit idly by and allow them to torture me, I retaliated by swinging my tiny fists at them, balling my hands in their nappy hair, and pulling *their* weaves out for the world to see. For every crude comment they cooked up, I had a fiery retort. For every hair-pulling session, I left bruises and welts on their dark skin. For every lie they spread about my family, I had an ugly truth about them to counter.

As all this was going on, the other children began to question me as well.

"Are you black enough?"

"Why don't you look like the other members of my family?"

"Why do you have nicer clothes than the other girls?"

Since we lived outside the community, thirty minutes away, my personal life outside of the church spotlight was shrouded in mystery. Other than the few friends I managed to hang on to, the other children wouldn't even look my way when we passed in the hall. In light of my bleak existence at church and my declining social life at school, I began to build an icy wall between myself and the rest of the world.

During sixth grade, I found myself in another bothersome situation. By that point, I'd developed quite a nasty reputation among my fellow classmates as a cruel, bossy, coldhearted little girl with few friends and many enemies. My best friend, R, was the only other African-American girl in school. We were inseparable, and had been for years. It was R and me against the entire student body, it seemed.

Soon, R and I would be graduating into the impressive new junior high building, and we were already planning our ascent into high school together. But then another joined our ranks: B transferred to our school at the very beginning of the year. She was slim, athletic, and black. We hit it off with B just fine, and soon, the three of us were inseparable.

But at that age, children begin to develop their own personalities and styles. B was into sports. I wasn't athletically gifted, but I could write a mean short story. B was a girl who had had a taste of the hard life, and I had survived my share of "moderately uncomfortable experiences."

R found herself at the point that many African Americans in our position face. Those of us who were raised in Caucasian settings reach a moment in our lives when we must find our identities. We can either identify with the African-American stereotype and reject the Caucasian influence, identify with the Caucasian stereotype and reject the African-American influence, or choose to stick it out on our own and develop a unique hybrid personality that takes the good and bad of both influences.

B and I chose the third option, and R chose B. One spring day, as I sat on the school steps waiting for B to finish her last class of the day, R confronted me and told me about her decision. Since she felt she could relate to B better than she could relate to me, she had no need for me any longer.

I was devastated, to say the very least. My best friend had just dropped me for someone else, with no explanation as to why. To this day, I reflect on that time in my life in wonder. How could one minority student blow another off so easily? There were only five African Americans on the entire campus. Why would she jump at the chance to separate us like that?

This taught me a valuable lesson. It didn't matter what race you were or how well you treated people—there would always be something someone else didn't like about you. There was no "protect your own" mentality, as there had been in my parents' day. It was about what you could do for yourself, and that was all that mattered.

That summer, I retreated into myself, refusing to allow anyone near me. Abuse from church members and students at school had finally taken its toll, and R's betrayal was the icing on the cake. I felt that my naïveté and vulnerability had allowed all these things to happen. I was determined not to be hurt again, so I drew inward, where no one could reach me. Reading, singing, writing, and dancing bored me, and they had once been my life force. I became short tempered and quick to snap at anyone unfortunate enough to cross my path. Loneliness spiraled around me, even though I was surrounded by my family and a few loyal friends. Things just became too much, and I decided to take control by shutting out everyone and only allowing myself to experience what *I* wanted to experience.

Junior high came all too soon the next year. I was still stuck with the same classmates I'd been huddled with for the past eight years; the only real difference was that we had smaller lockers. I started the year with hardly any friends. For a little while, I stayed mostly to myself. I tried to focus on my studies, but that only added to my runaway teenage angst, which seems to get the better of most of us during this stage of life. My grades were so-so. *I* was so-so.

Then I befriended two Latino boys who would have more impact on my life than they would ever know. S had transferred to my school the year before, and P had attended school with me since kindergarten. I suddenly began to take notice of them. We had hung out a bit before, during the tail end of sixth grade, but it was nothing to get excited about. I was convinced they'd tire of me, as R and so many others had, and would soon be on their way again.

But seventh grade proved to be a huge turning point in my personal life. S and P, along with a few others in our various classes, formed a solid circle of friendship, and I became a part of it. I almost didn't *want* to believe they considered me a friend, having been on the short end of the friendship stick for quite some time. Day in and day out, we stuck together in our little klatch and experienced life as junior high schoolers. Trips to the beach, endless hours spent watching movies and participating in writing sessions, and long lunches—our devotion to each other began to melt the tension in my heart. I began to trust.

They weren't black—no one in our group was except for me—but that didn't seem to matter any longer. For the first time in a *long* time, I was in a safe place. Of course, we argued. Let's face it, what's junior high without petty arguments? Yes, we fought and argued like there was no tomorrow, but in the end we all came back to each other. That was life.

Today, S, P, and I are still thick as thieves; we call ourselves the Three Musketeers in honor of our undying friendship. Although we went our separate ways for high school, I've managed to snag some amazing friends with whom I'm still close today.

Growing up in an affluent Caucasian setting has taught me some very harsh life lessons. Sometimes the closest people to you are not what they seem. Sometimes the worst enemies can be your own kind. But there's really no question about race for me anymore. I make my decisions about people based on the content of their character—the real determining factor in a friendship. It's not the size of your wallet, the car you drive, or the race you happened to be born into. It's just the depth of your understanding. With my ever-supportive family and my patchwork clutch of friends at my side, I step forward into adulthood with scars to bear and stories to tell. Not stories of my negative views about whites or blacks, but of my struggle to create a personal path in life—one that is unique, God-fearing, and all my own.

—Shelby Powell-Hicks

Shelby Powell-Hicks is currently a journalism major studying at the Department of Communication at Oakwood University.

♦ Chapter 41

My American Dream

I GREW UP IN THE OUTSKIRTS OF RICHMOND, VIRGINIA, IN THE LATE 1950s. The first time I was ever called a sissy was on my first day of school. As I walked alone down the four country blocks and ascended the enormous stairs of Hickory Hill Elementary School, I felt confident and all grown up. I was a big boy now.

Upon entering the classroom, I immediately spotted Hazel, a neighbor of mine and the frequent object of my childish affection. I followed her into the coatroom, but there was a problem—it was the girls' coatroom. Snickers and guffaws followed. The boys taunted, "He thinks he's a girl! He's a sissy!"

The first time I knew that being black meant being different, my Nanny took me to visit a friend of hers who worked for a rich white lady on the other side of town. "What an adorable little pickaninny," the middle-aged woman said.

"I am not a pickaninny," I responded. I had heard the expression before. I'm not sure I knew what it really meant, but I did know that it was associated with black people and that it wasn't a nice term.

For this act of insolence and, shall we say, audacity, I was publicly disciplined and privately rebuked—for my own good, I was told. My parents were well-educated, proud people who were also a product of their time. My father would not bow to the whims of the white neighbors, but he knew his place, and I was taught to know mine. Shined shoes, clean nails, soft hands, clean and well-cared-for clothes, and full articulation—these were the hallmarks of a proper colored man, a bona fide Southern gentleman.

It would be many years later before I knew that, in fact, the boys had been on to something. I am attracted to and love men. No matter how I have tried to escape, hide, or cover it up over the years, it is a truth that I know and own as much as the color of my skin. But the America of my youth had no use for homosexuals. The gay men I knew before I entered college lived secret, and often troubled, lives. They were regularly arrested for having sex in public parks, among other indignities. Theirs was not a life anyone would choose. They were frequently beaten, molested, and, in at least one case, brutally beaten, castrated, murdered, and dumped in a church closet.

At Benedictine High School, I met my first openly gay man. Well, that's what I would say about him today. He was a jock—tall, handsome, and open about his relationship with a male college student. By this time, I was in full denial—at once both attracted to and afraid of this newfound reality.

My family followed the work of Dr. King, and we shared his vision of justice, fairness, and equality. John F. Kennedy was a hero in my house, and we grieved his assassination together on my fifth birthday. When Dr. King was murdered, I saw my father cry for the first time in my life. I grew up believing that the American dream was mine—a dream of a prosperous life with a family of my own, living near my parents in the same neighborhood. College and travel would alter that dream. A failed marriage and fatherhood would challenge my notions of who I was. Nevertheless, the dream would remain.

After my divorce, I moved to San Francisco. Though I had completed my graduate work only miles away, at Stanford University, I had little knowledge of the gay community of the 1970s. It was a liberating but startling reminder of what it means to be a black man in a white man's world.

Always one to be in the center of things I moved to the Castro, otherwise known as the gay district. There, I faced constant discrimination, always being asked for multiple pieces of identification to enter bars. This was shortly after the "Anita Bryant period," which gave birth to a new uniform for gay men: blue jeans and flannel shirts. The dynamics of exclusion I experienced and the cultural hegemony of the urban gay experience became an unsettling reality. The gay community, for all its purported openness and acceptance of differences, really offered little in terms of self-development and individual liberty. Social isolation became the method through which gay culture exerted its hegemony. Not only did I have to concern myself with behaving like an acceptable Negro, but I also had to figure out how to present myself as a legitimate form of homosexual.

I desired men, but I felt totally alienated from the gay culture with which I was supposed to identify. The culture became a weapon of control, one that forced behavior into a predetermined pattern rather than allowing full self-expression. It was an ill-fitting version of my American dream.

In the city by the Bay, I met wonderful men and women of color. But in so many ways, I felt like a visitor. I went to a few Black and White Men Together meetings and checked out the scene in Oakland. None of it seemed to fit. I was free and liberated, but I never felt that I had found my place.

My gay activism began when I joined the board of the Stonewall Gay Democratic Club. I immersed myself in work until I finally found a place for me. Since openly gay black men were few and far between, I suddenly found myself in demand. I joined the San Francisco LGBT Pride Committee and the Host Committee for the National March for Lesbian/Gay Rights the day before the 1984 National Democratic Convention in San Francisco. I found myself on the cusp of an emerging black gay sensibility in the East Bay and places east, including New York and Washington, D.C. The writings of Assoto Saint, Marlon Riggs, and Essex Hemphill inspired and challenged me. I began to integrate the notion of working for racial justice with a more personal sense of accepting myself.

And then, one by one, countless friends began to die, many of them members of our Dignity San Francisco choir. We whispered and speculated that this deadly plague was the result of some behavior that was apart from the rest of us. One day, it became all too clear that it was *all of us*. It was AIDS. As an early San Francisco Shanti Project volunteer, I was again one of the first black emotional-support providers. Fear and anger were the order of the day. Our government had turned from friend to enemy.

In February 1988, I traveled to Washington, D.C., for the first National Black Gay & Lesbian Conference. This would be a life-changing moment for me. Smart, well-informed, civic-minded and ready to work, the black gay men and women I had always read about were all around me, addressing the issues that challenged our community. Once more, I felt at home.

In many ways, this search for identity, this embrace of the seemingly elusive American dream, is a typically American story. Finding a gay community and believing that you have found solace in it only to be marginalized because of your race—unfortunately, it's not a unique story.

America has made a great deal of progress in the past fifty years. We have not fully realized Dr. King's dream of one America, but now a black man will lead our nation. We have come to accept the humanity in every person, regardless of the color of his or her skin, even if we do at times forget to act on that knowledge.

One day, when I was called "nigger" in the schoolyard and a racist teacher singled me out for ridicule, my parents handled the situation beautifully and taught me how to handle it, too. But when one of my mother's church "friends" told me I was turning into a "punk," my mother didn't know how to handle it. She pushed me away, fearing it was true. Too many families have rejected their queer and questioning young people. We see them all the time, seeking a home on the streets or in the arms of strangers who don't care about them.

They are only dreaming the American dream.

In my work, I have always found a place. Today, that work is as a dream catcher—I catch and hold the dreams of black, same-gender-loving, questioning youth. I want to create a world where it is safe for them to realize their dreams, all while walking in their truth.

—H. Alexander Robinson

H. Alexander Robinson is chief executive officer and executive director of the National Black Justice Coalition and NBJC Action Fund, America's only nationwide African-American civil-rights organizations focused on lesbian, gay, bisexual, and transgender issues.

Chapter 42

An Artist's Colorful Palette

S A WRITER AND ARTIST WHO CREATES CONTENT FOR THE children's market, I see the world, and the people in it, a little differently than most. My view on race is skewed by the endless colors of an artist's palette. I see the world in bright, vivid colors, and discrimination based on race, religion, and sexual orientation doesn't exist.

If only we could all think like children. When children play together, they do so without preoccupation about race. What matters to kids at any given moment is whether or not a friend is fun to be around or likes to do the same activities they enjoy. Unfortunately, adults share their personal views about race with their children, thereby influencing their impressionable minds.

If adults would take a moment to remember what it is like to be a child—laughing, playing in the park, or just hanging out with friends of all colors, they would remember that what truly matters is the content of a friend's character, and not the color of his or her skin.

I often wonder how some adults have strayed so far from their childhood thinking. Nevertheless, as time passes and the world continues to grow, we all seek a happy and safe environment for our family and friends. This shared mission is truly the thread that ties us together. Race does not determine who attains the goal.

As a child, I never stayed within the confines of a coloring book's lines. Nor did I adhere to a strict code of using certain colors to express my point of view. How sad it would be to ignore the rainbow of colors in a box of crayons or paint set! As an artist, I am influenced by all colors and feel fortunate that I can express the true beauty of color to children.

When I write for children, I hope to make them laugh, get lost in a good story, and enjoy the artwork—no matter what colors they see. Hopefully, children will also be influenced by my work to create a world bound not by one color over another, but by the richness they create when they mix together.

When children color pictures, they might decide to use a green or purple crayon to depict skin color. If you ask them why, they'll likely respond, "Because I wanted to," or "Because I like these colors." We can learn from these simple answers. After all, we were once children ourselves, and some of us can still embrace a few child-like notions—that pretty pink poodles are possible, green frogs and purple dinosaurs are loved, and the word "race" means nothing more than a game.

—**Bret Eileen Wilson**

Bret Eileen Wilson is an artist and writer. Her background includes a stint as a publicist at the Walt Disney Company, where she was responsible for writing and editing press kits and securing local and national press coverage for all brands under the umbrella of Buena Vista Home Entertainment. Wilson's entertainment experience also includes positions as advertising director and promotion director in the radio industry and work as an associate cable television producer.

♦ Chapter 43

The Courage to Dream

I WAS BORN IN 1941, SEVEN YEARS BEFORE THE CLEVELAND INDIANS won the World Series. A promoter by the name of Bill Veeck, a real P.T. Barnum kind of guy, had purchased the Tribe and promised the fans a world championship. To everyone's surprise, he delivered. When asked how he did it, he replied, "You can do anything you put your mind to. You can even grow up to be the president of the United States."

Bill Veeck wanted to win, and he needed a center fielder who could hit for power. His promotion skills and will to win led him to the Negro Leagues, where he found and signed the great Larry Doby, a seven-time All-Star and Hall of Famer. Doby became the first black to join an American League team—this during the era of Jim Crow, when black people rode in the back of the bus; water fountains, schools, restrooms, lunch counters, and even libraries were segregated; and any white person who dared to befriend a black person would be labeled a "nigger lover."

Larry Doby may have been a centerfielder for the Cleveland Indians, but he was still a Negro. He couldn't eat with the team, stay in the same hotel as the team, or enjoy the perks that all the other major leaguers enjoyed. Although he played the game with whites, he was still, figuratively, in the back of the bus.

He could hit, catch, and run the bases better than anyone on that team. He was the best. He put his mind to it.

As I gradually began to understand what Veeck and Doby had done, I also began to understand my role in life. I was going to be a "first." I was going to be the first black president of the United States, and I was going to rule the world. As I got older, unfortunately, it became clear that I wouldn't be president of my senior class, let alone the country, but I remained determined that I would be the "first black" to do *something*. I put my mind to it.

I don't know exactly how it happened, but I somehow managed to be the first black to manage a Woolworth's store, and that was a big deal in the 1960s. Only months before, the chain's lunch counters had finally become integrated—but only because a few brave "uppity negroes" got up the nerve to sit at the counter of a Woolworth's store in Greensboro, North Carolina. I felt like Larry Doby when I graduated from the company's management training program. I was filled with pride and a sense of accomplishment—that is, until the "big guy" from Woolworth's remarked in his congratulatory speech at the graduation ceremony that I was the best "negra" trainee they'd ever had. With that, he put me right back in my place—the back of the bus.

I went on to be the first black in a series of unremarkable jobs: the first black DJ on a local pop radio station, the first black to head the marketing division of a major record company, and the first black to own a business in Beverly Hills. Every time, I felt that I could relate to Larry Doby. I was happy to be in the game, even though I knew I was still nothing more than the best "negra" to everyone else.

Doby opened the door for other blacks to get in, and I hope I did the same. Maybe Doby and I, and all the other "first" black men, opened the door for a man named Obama to become the first black president of the United States.

Big stuff, just forty years after Jim Crow. I wish Bill Veeck could have lived to see this happen.

—**William "Billy" Bass**

Billy Bass spent twenty-five years as a creative force in the music business as a marketing strategist for superstar recording acts like Blondie, Pat Benatar, Billy Idol, Huey Lewis and the News, Jethro Tull, and the Babys. He also managed Luther Vandross for Alive Enterprises and consulted for the management team of Bon Jovi. Bass has returned to his first love, photography, and his award-winning photographs have been published nationwide. Check him out at www.billybassphotography.com.

Chapter 44

How Long Will We Continue to Allow the Destruction of the Global Image of the Black Woman?

THE GLOBAL IMAGE OF THE BLACK WOMAN CONTINUES TO BE under attack, and the latest salvo is comedian Charles Knipp's character, Shirley Q. Liquor. Liquor, described by Knipp as being "the Queen of Ignunce," is based on his experiences with and interpretations of black Southern women. Knipp, who is white and gay, performs the character—an illiterate, welfare-collecting mother to nineteen children who drives a Caddy and attends Mount Holy Olive Second Baptist Zion Church of God in Christ of Resurrected Latter-Days AME CME—in blackface.

Men who take on roles as female characters for the purposes of entertainment are nothing new, and they've been handsomely rewarded for their efforts. Flip Wilson made a name for himself as "Geraldine," and more recently, Martin Lawrence had great success with the *Big Mama's House* franchise; Shawn and Marlon Wayans lampooned women in *White Chicks*; Eddie Murphy played an obese sister in *Norbit*; and Tyler Perry has built an industry around his popular character "Madea." With the exception of the Wayans brothers, all these examples are black men dressed in drag as black women.

So what's the difference between a black man in drag and a white man in blackface when both are depicting a black woman? Some have argued that black Americans should not complain about Knipp's character because we turn a blind eye towards black actors who also perform in questionable roles.

You'll get no argument from me on that point regarding Eddie Murphy's portrayal of Rasputia Latimore in *Norbit*. In fact, long before the film was in theaters, the billboards promoting it were enough to make me wanna holla and throw up both my hands. While I definitely didn't appreciate Murphy taking on the dreadful stereotype of a fat, angry, black woman for the rest of the world to laugh at, I can't overlook the fact he did it as a black man.

Hattie Mae Pierce, Martin Lawrence's character, is a religious black woman living in the South. While Big Mama is definitely a big mama, at least she isn't mean. And unlike Shirley Q. Liquor, she isn't on welfare, isn't shown guzzling forty-ounce beers, and to the best of my knowledge, she doesn't have nineteen kids, including one named Kmartina. Oh, and like Murphy, Lawrence is a black man.

This brings me to Tyler Perry's character Mabel "Madea" R. Simmons, who is best known for her standard greeting: "Heluur! This is Madea-ur!" Madea is probably the closest approximation to the Shirley Q. Liquor character, considering that she didn't find out that Deacon Leroy Brown was her daughter Cora's father until years later, and she's also known to drive a Caddy. She will argue with anyone, has a penchant for unique pronunciations, and is part of a large family that includes many children and grandchildren. "Madea" or "Madear" is a common black Southern nickname for "grandmother." The term is a shortened form of "Mother Dear." But again, Perry is a black man.

A favorite defense against any black who takes issue with Shirley Q. Liquor is the Wayans brothers' depiction of Brittany and Tiffany Wilson in *White Chicks*—as if somehow two black men taking on the characters of white, blond-haired, and blue-eyed cruise-line heiresses is even remotely the same thing as a white man in blackface assuming the role of an overweight black woman. In his parody song "The Twelve Days of Kwanzaa," Knipp sings, "On the fifth day of Kwanzaa, my check came in the mail. AFDC! Thank you, Lawd! Come on, kids; let's go to the store for some collard greens, ham hocks, and cheese!" I could only wish that when men—white or black—decide to don drag as black women, they do so as beautiful, wealthy, and dim socialites.

The difference between a black man playing the role of a black woman and a white man putting on blackface and attempting to do the same is that blacks don't have the same history of slavery and racial discrimination as whites do. Since black women were brought to America as slaves, we have been forced to endure every form of racism and sexism imaginable at the hands of whites.

First, it was the Massuh we had to contend with. His penchant for darker skin is primarily responsible for the various shades of brown that represent our people today. Janie Crawford, Leafy, Nanny, and Zora Neale Hurston. Ashay!

Then we were forced to take on the role of raising their children, cleaning their houses, washing their laundry, and cooking their meals. In keeping with America's approved racial etiquette, we did all of this while being referred to as "girl" or "nigger" and remembering to never look at whites directly in the eyes. Mrs. Thomas, Lena Younger, Sofie, and Florida Evans. Ashay!

We dealt with Jim Crow and with racist police officers, teachers, landlords, bosses, and bus drivers. Rosa Parks. Ashay!

For many years, we were denied roles in major motion pictures. When they couldn't get away with that anymore, we were denied the same wages as our white counterparts and the accolades bestowed upon them. Hattie McDaniel and Dorothy Dandridge. Ashay!

Now it's 2008, and we're nappy-headed hoes left for dead in shacks—raped, beaten, and urinated on. In addition, just to remind us that we're still black, our asses are being analyzed on live television during tennis matches for the world to see.

Misogynistic lyrics recited by black men and financed by white men continue to portray us as sexual objects—to the point where some of us are so confused that we gladly take on the role.

So I find it ridiculous when anyone, white or black, defends a white man who puts on blackface and an Afro wig, calls himself the Queen of Dixie, and says things like, "I'm gonna burn me up some chitlins and put some ketchup on there and ask Jesus to forgive my sins."

I draw the line at the notion that in 2008 it is okay for a white man, gay or straight, to make $90,000 a year to dress up in blackface for the sole purpose of degrading black women as entertainment for white gay men, rednecks, and their moms.

I draw the line with gay American culture when it can persecute a black actor for his perceived homophobia and at the same time support a self-described forty-five-year-old, fat, gay, white man and his alter ego, Shirley Q. Liquor. Just as there are blacks who embarrass me as a black lesbian woman, there are gays who do the same.

Knipp doesn't make his living at the Apollo Theater in Harlem. You won't see him on BET's *Comicview*. It's not African Americans who sell out his shows from city to city. It's white gay America that keeps Shirley Q. Liquor alive. From nightclubs to pride celebrations, Knipp is still around because the gay community continues to take pleasure in the degradation of the black female—further proving that race is still an issue in America.

Let's be real about this. Shirley Q. Liquor is a black welfare mother with nineteen kids (Cheeto, Orangello, Chlamydia, Kmartina, and so on) who speaks Ebonics. Knipp likes to justify his routine by saying that his character is a tribute to the good Southern women he grew up around. Is Knipp even *capable* of understanding that back in the day after pigs were slaughtered, their intestines—the chitterlings Knipp mocks—along with hog maws, pigs' feet, and neck bones were all that was given to slaves by their Massuhs to eat, because he controlled their food choices?

You might be tempted to laugh at Knipp in his Afro and blackface makeup, but for many black Americans, poverty is reality and not entertainment. Why would a black woman be on welfare in the first place? Let's start there. What role did whites play in blocking the access of blacks to the same institution of higher learning where Knipp earned his nursing degree? Think about that.

Think about the fact that since we were brought to America as slaves, black women have been forced to endure every form of racism and sexism there is at the hands of whites. And that no matter how straight and long our hair is, or how light our skin is, when we speak up for ourselves, we're labeled angry black bitches, or in my case, the *angry black lesbian bitch*.

Consider the fact that generations of strong black women before me—including those gay America likes to quote in an effort to show how diverse it is—paved the way for us sistas today so we could have the same access that came so easy for women with white skin. Some of those women died without ever seeing the fruits of their labor. Some, like my eighty-seven-year-old grandmother, are still living and pushing their children to go further in life than they did.

Think about the black women and *men* who were forced to go to work at the age of twelve to help support their families. Since they never had the opportunity to finish grade school and learn how to speak and write *your* English properly, today they depend on their grandchildren to fill out forms for them and read them their mail. There is *nothing* funny about that.

Yes, this is very personal for me.

And unlike Tyler Perry's films, there is no feel-good lesson of morality at the end of Knipp's performances. It's just a bunch white gay men and women, probably drunk, applauding the performance of one of their own for being able bring to life their own racist stereotypes of black women.

This isn't an argument in defense of characters like Murphy's Rasputia Latimore. Rather, it's an argument that such characters, while demeaning to black women, are not racist. The same can't be said of Charles Knipp's Shirley Q. Liquor character, which is demeaning, disrespectful, and racist. Knipp is a white man in blackface using the most negative stereotypes of blacks to entertain other whites. These stereotypes are based on traits that can be directly traced back to the history of racial discrimination whites have perpetrated on blacks in this country.

Somehow, I find it hard to believe that if the stiletto was on the other foot, and some black comedian was traveling the country selling himself as "a piece of poor white trailer park trash" in whiteface, that he'd be welcomed with open arms by whites. I'll take it a step further and add that if a black comedian impersonated a white gay man in whiteface, it'd be off with his head, literally.

I know it's easy to try and point the finger of blame back at blacks and say that the drag acts of a few black comedians—poor excuses of comedy, all—are the same as Knipp's act, but it simply isn't true. It's not the same. One is just ignorant, but the other, Knipp's character, is an expression of years of covert racism toward blacks by whites. I expected whites to defend Knipp—after all, they make up his core audience, to the tune of tens of thousands of dollars annually. For blacks to do it is a slap in the faces of our ancestors, and all they sacrificed so we could have the opportunities we enjoy today.

—**Jasmyne Cannick**

Jasmyne Cannick is a Los Angeles-based critic and commentator who writes about the worlds of pop culture, race, class, sexuality, and politics as it relates to the African-American community. A regular contributor to NPR's News and Notes, *she was chosen by* Essence Magazine *as one of its Twenty-Five Women Shaping the World. Visit her on the Internet at www.jasmynecannick.com or www.myspace.com/jasmynecannick.*

♦ Chapter 45

I'm Black, but Am I Black *Enough?*

> In an era where black Americans are billionaires, CEOs, owners, venture capitalists, senators, secretaries of state, and quite possibly the president of the United States of America, do black Americans have the right to complain about white America? In the past forty years, black Americans have gained access to most of the opportunities enjoyed by white America—if not more. Isn't it time that instead of saying "Shame on you, white America," they say, "Thank you?"

I F YOU THOUGHT THE PRECEDING PARAGRAPH MADE SENSE, YOU might want to stop reading. But if you thought that little snippet—actually uttered by a white caller on a nationally syndicated talk show—was crazy, try this one: "*I'm* blacker than *you* are."

A Persian woman boldly proclaimed this audacious statement to me and another black woman after we refused to dumb down to her perceived black stereotypes. The conversation went a little something like this.

"All black people smoke weed." *Yes, the Persian woman said this with a straight face, but we* were *in Vegas and she* had *been drinking.*

"I can't believe you just said that." *Not the best comeback, but why waste wit on complete idiocy?*

"What? What's wrong with that? Cultures have a tendency to do a lot of things, like all Persians drink tea."

"All Persians drinking tea and all blacks smoking weed is not the same thing."

"Why not?"

"Because it's degrading. Who cares if someone drinks tea all day every day? It's not illegal. You're basically saying that all blacks are criminals."

"Whatever. It's true. All blacks smoke weed."

"I don't smoke weed, so how much sense does that make?"

"You're not black. I mean, *I'm* blacker than *you* are. *I'm* from Chocolate City."

I knew "Chocolate City" was code for "a suburb outside Washington, D.C." Her idea of black women, made painfully clear by her statement, could be summed up in her ensemble. She wore a cut-up wifebeater, low-rider jeans, a belly-button ring, a saucy "hood" accent, and the icing on the cake, a fat blunt. As an accessory, a stereotypical black girl stood beside her. The black girl's only purpose was to validate the Persian girl: She stood there silently, not uttering a word throughout the entire exchange.

The Persian woman looked down on my friend and me because she couldn't understand why we refused to support her version of blackness. After all, *she* wore it proudly, even if it was for just a night. She was in her last semester of dental school, and we were on our way to law school. She could risk it, because it would never be a lasting image for her, but black women don't have that luxury. Even if we weren't caught by the police, we would be caught by society. We could never risk it.

As a black woman, I take a risk every time I make a decision. *What do people expect me to do? What will it mean if I do this? How will this decision affect my future? Who am I representing when I do this?* I don't know if I'll ever be able to convey the internal arguments that occur inside my head when I grapple with issues dealing with my race and identity, but those two statements—"Isn't it time that instead of saying 'Shame on you, white America,' they say, 'Thank you,'" and "*I'm* blacker than *you* are"—are the closest depiction of this stress. I'm constantly balancing America's images of black affluence, privilege, and power with the degrading negative black stereotypes that pervade the media, streets, and even the minds of black people.

Most of the time, I'm not exactly sure where I stand.

The philosopher Bernard of Chartres once said, "We are like dwarves on the shoulders of giants." For black Americans, it is slightly different. We stand on the shoulders of each individual who came before us, regardless of whether that individual was a giant or a malnourished, undeveloped child. We stand on successes and failures, and yet we never truly know where we stand. Unsteady at best, each one of us forms the Black Unit, an amalgamation of parts. Some are standing, some are kneeling, some are lying down, and some are clawing, dragging, and pulling others down. Some are helping, pushing each other farther than a single person could go on his or her own.

Together, we move as smoothly and as frighteningly as Frankenstein. With heavy steps, we clank from side to side, off balance. We've hastily screwed on a head, and everyone can see the bolts. Our skin has turned a yellowish green, signaling the toxicity inside as it stretches along, exposing the large, strong muscles beneath. You can see the strength and possibly the beauty in each individual part, but together, the image is a mess.

As a black American woman, I never know who they see when they look at me. Do they see Condoleezza Rice, Karrine "Super-Head" Steffans, or some crazy lady at their job? One of the times in my life when I felt this most poignantly was when I lived in Italy for four months. Without the guise of political correctness or the deftness of language to bridge the gap, many things were made glaringly apparent. When my family visited me in Rome, a local man saw us—a group of black people—and said, "What's up, my niggas?" and smiled. He was excited and meant no harm. My mother quickly tried to inform him that what he was doing was inappropriate and could easily get him shot in America. He responded by reciting 50 Cent's lyrics: "You can find me in da club."

What makes this incident so scary is that the man didn't even speak English, but he knew how to "act" and "respond" to black Americans. He'd heard it enough in our lyrics and undoubtedly seen it in the videos. Knowing that this is what they see, was I surprised to see a Senegalese man in Italy wearing a bright red suit, a red fedora, a cane with a golden head, and a golden iced-out chain around his neck—his best attempt to look like a pimp, when every other Senegalese man was wearing a T-shirt and a pair of jeans? Was I horrified when an Italian man decided to show me, the only black woman in a discotheque, a picture of his penis?

YES!!!! Ultimately, it's because I can't make the answer to the question, "Why me?" make sense. Is it really just the rich, chocolate complexion of my skin, or is it something else? The Italian man was obviously a pervert. Maybe he showed his pictures there every night—maybe it had absolutely nothing to do with the fact that I am black. But then again, maybe it had *everything* to do with the fact that I'm black.

Will I ever get to a place where these things happen, and I don't think it has anything to do with my race? When I'm at a nice restaurant in Beverly Hills and someone asks me to clean their table, or I'm walking around a high-end store and no one speaks to me, I assume it's because I'm black. But maybe it's not. Maybe I'm paranoid, but do I not have a reason to be? When I've had people ask me, "Really, your name's Nadia, and you're from South Central? You're lying. What is it, Shaquiesha?" is it wrong if I read into it a little more than normal when nonblacks say, "Your name's Nadia?"

It would be enough if all I had to worry about were how nonblacks received me and what stereotypes they wanted to label me with, but I also have to consider black people who try to label me as something other than black and push me out of the "Black Circle."

I'm reminded of a discussion I had with my college roommate, who self-identified as Creole. She had a problem with the fact that I self-identify as Haitian American (my father is a Haitian immigrant).

She asked, "What does it mean?"

"What does what mean?"

"Haitian."

"Uhh, it's a type of people, with their own culture, history, flag, and country. Like China."

"Yeah, but China's big."

"Okay, then, like Belize."

"So what, do you not think you're black?"

I explained that I was black because my skin is dark, and everyone can see it. Even if I for some reason decided to deny that I was black, believe me, someone would be sure that I understood that I was—beginning with the doctor who pulled me out of my mother's womb and quickly marked black on my birth certificate.

I'm often met with this monolithic view of blackness. Anything that doesn't appear to be exactly like *them* must be questioned. If you speak differently, if you have a different culture or perspective, or if you look different, you become suspect, because you are not the same.

For example, once while pumping gas on the corner of Florence and Normandie in Los Angeles, I was approached by a young black man who asked me for my number. I informed him that I was in a rush on my way to school. He asked me what high school I went to. I told him that I was in college, at USC.

He looked at me inquisitively and asked, "Are you black?"

"What else would I be?" I quickly replied, noticing that we had the same complexion. If anything, I was darker.

"I mean, I ain't never met no black girls like you."

"Go to USC, and you'll meet at least a hundred."

I quickly rushed off, but I did not forget the conversation. I thought about my life, and how this man could not relate to it, even though I had attended elementary school in that exact area, on the same block, for six years. How did we create such a gulf from one another, and how would we unite it? I have to admit, I felt a special pain because he was a black man. I'd like to say that on my journey through life, I've found more black men who stood beside me, rather than across that gulf where he stood, but I'd be lying.

And even when we seem to be on the same side, there's always the threat of a refusal for procreation and love if I'm too dark or too educated. They say it in ways like, "I wouldn't date anyone darker than you," or "She's cute for a dark-skinned girl," and sometimes even more directly. Once, I was talking to an NFL player and casually mentioned that I planned to attend law school.

He looked at me, and in the most sincere way, he said, "You know no man is going to find you attractive after you become a lawyer."

"What do you mean?" I asked.

"You know, a man like me, an athlete or an entertainer, isn't going to want you. They'd rather have a regular girl."

These comments—all of them—never fail to shock me. I'll even admit that sometimes they sting, and other times they hurt. No matter who says them, I always feel that in some way, something has been taken away from me. Whether it's the opportunity to freely explore and play around in the garb of other cultures; to see hurtful stereotypes and feel unscathed, knowing they have nothing to do with me; to be accepted by a good school without someone thinking its because I'm black; or to be spared the stress of walking around knowing that with every year and every earned degree and every success, my odds of getting married and having children decrease—I crave to be the blank slate. I want to wake up in the morning and be able to define my life on *my terms* and not by the measure of Flavor Flav, raunchy videos, and black statistics.

But in some strange way, even after all of this, I love being black. I love it so much that if given the choice today, I would choose it. I can't quite explain it, but although I have so many bad memories associated with my race, I have more good ones. I still feel like my future gets brighter every day. Who would I be if I wasn't black? Would I be as strong, as agile, as adaptable, as funny? What can I do that has not been done before? Everything.

I have made a decision to live my life so that anyone who comes after can stand on solid shoulders and go farther than I did. I have made a decision to work *with* my community to ensure its success as much as my own. I have made a commitment to not view my black community as monolithic. We do not all have the same history, the same culture, the same language, the same dialects, or the same political associations. We must work together, understand each other, and fight for and with one another. Ultimately, I believe that we can establish a united front, synergizing all of our parts into one gliding movement and leaving our Frankenstein past behind. But each of us has to do his or her part.

My dream is to advance to a place where I can dictate media images and help expose the world to a more diverse Black America. Until that day comes, it's encouraging to see the giants in my life— like Oprah, Magic Johnson, and Barack Obama—and know that in some way we're all in it together. Their success is my success, and because that's true for all of us, in some way, big or small, we succeed every day.

—**Nadia Lataillade**

Nadia Lataillade earned her bachelor's degree at the University of Southern California. She began her freshman year at Georgetown University School of Law in the fall of 2008.

Chapter 46

The Complexity of Race and Class

I GREW UP IN THE CITY OF ATLANTA, DURING WHAT IS THOUGHT OF by many as its most rapid and successful social transformation. I had to be one of the happiest, most privileged kids in the city. My parents were among the social elite, working professionals who had conquered many of life's most trying obstacles. Real estate was my father's forte, and his success afforded us a lifestyle most children would have given a month's lunch for. Now, by no means were we rich, but given our middle-class status, I was one of the few black children who attended school in Buckhead, which was commonly referred to as the "jewel of the city."

When I wasn't mixing it up with the rich white people's children, I was on the southwest side of Atlanta at my grandmother's house every day after school. I didn't mind the culture shock one bit. It was my second home, and my parents always instilled in me the ideals of perseverance and pride—no matter who I was with or where I was. So it was nothing for me to be cast into a circumstance where I was expected to thrive in two different worlds. I respected it. I respected the fact that Dr. Martin Luther King, Jr., and Ralph David Abernathy walked the streets that I played on, even if the children I played with were considered "underclass" by social norms. I was grounded with black pride and learned to walk with a distinct sense of identity as a black man—long before I could even drive a car.

It's funny, because I never really knew that all of that would have a positive effect on my life. I didn't expect it at all. I just lived the days as they came and accepted it as my reality. My parents made me feel good about who I was and never discouraged me from thinking freely or thinking *big*. I remember sitting in someone's mansion at a party. It was a massive twenty-three-room home, with more square footage than any group of people—other than a football team—would ever need. But I liked it. I liked it a lot! I thought to myself, *Damn, I wish I had this! This is what I want one day.* And I never equated that with black or white. I equated it with rich or poor. My parents had everything to do with that.

As one might imagine, I am the product of a family that emphasizes the importance of the African-American culture. We reaped plenty from the gains of the Civil Rights Movement, and my parents' friends were at the forefront of that movement. Since they were members of the black professional elite, legends such as Atlanta's former mayor Andrew Young and gospel singer Mahalia Jackson stopped by frequently to visit. They were like family. From as far back as I can remember, my house was filled to the brim with cultured, influential people. It was the breeding grounds for all things "African American," and I was groomed to follow in the path of greatness.

As the son of a proud Morehouse College alumnus, my future was set. I had "legacy" on my side, and when you had legacy on your side, you embraced it. You did your four years, met a nice young lady across the way at Spelman, got your degree, and went about contributing to the family business. Unfortunately, I just didn't see my life playing out that way. I suppose I wanted to create my own legacy. I wanted something different for myself. I had a rooted desire to live in another part of the country and see different things. So, with my parents' support, I broke from the family tradition and enrolled at Princeton University.

I graduated from Princeton's Woodrow Wilson School of Public and International Affairs and went on to earn a Master of Business Administration degree from Harvard Business School. In 1988, I moved to Dallas to begin my career in real estate development as the director of capital markets for Trammell Crow Ventures.

When my father was diagnosed with cancer in 1992, I left the business I had helped build in favor of the one that bore my name. It was only natural. Although I had traveled thousands of miles away in an effort to start anew, it only made sense to return to the place where I imagined it all happening in the first place. Ultimately, I ended up doing exactly what my father wanted me to do, and it was an honor to do it.

The idea that I was never reared to be anything other than what I wanted to be did everything to instill a sense of strength and self-confidence in me, and it made me want to give back. I was raised to believe that black people who did well for themselves and achieved a "position of power" owed a debt to the community, which is why I strive to be a pillar of mine. Once upon a time, there were moral examples in place to prepare our children to carry the mantle of leadership. It was considered an honor to help cure the ills of society and contribute to a better tomorrow. Nowadays, people seem to have gotten off course. Their focus is more materially driven, and thoughts of volunteerism and philanthropy are a thing of the past.

Integration, once considered one of the most pressing issues for us as a people, has done a lot to distort our community views. As long as our finances are up to speed, we can live wherever we want in this day and age. Our neighbors don't look out for us as they once did, calling our mothers if they sense something is wrong. We just don't bear the same responsibility when it comes to helping each other out. My parents and their friends always provided help, support, and encouragement to one another. Those virtues of responsibility are lacking today—in fact, they're almost nonexistent, in my opinion. We just don't seem to care as much about each other.

In fact, a part of our culture doesn't mind being stereotyped. Back in the day, we were uniformly opposed to such behavior. Even though we were relegated to the lowest end of the totem pole, we still strove to climb it. Now, some of us have accepted that position, continuing to claim welfare and other government assistance with no obvious will to overcome it.

But there are many factors that figure into an African American's success and his or her ability to conquer stereotypical behaviors and actions. I was able to defy the odds because of my strong family roots and upbringing. That gave me the confidence to put my best foot forward every day of my life, and I've reaped the rewards tenfold. I excelled in school and extracurricular activities, such as track and basketball. I had options when it came time to pursue higher education, and I became a successful businessman. Those positive exposures produced a career-minded man with values and principles rooted in community and African-American culture.

Given my background and solid upbringing, I learned long ago how important it is to evaluate other people, other ethnicities, and the social politics that engage us all with each other. In some ways, race trumps class, and in some ways, it does not. Nothing can hide the fact that I am a black man, so why would I ever run from who I am? Fact is, I ran and played with underclass kids from southwest Atlanta, and I am damn proud to say that I did. In the same breath, I went to school with rich white kids, and my parents' success opened doors for me that would not otherwise have been available. The fact that I grew up an integral part of the professional business class put me a step ahead. There is no denying that. I was given the gift of access—access to pursue opportunities and live the way I wanted to live. And I've made my personal choices freely, with no regard to what other people think.

For instance, I married an Asian woman. Some people find it ironic that I would marry outside my race considering my parents' strong example of a happy marriage between a black man and a black woman. But my path was always one focused on happiness. As long as I'm happy, why would I fret about what other people think? The true irony today is that one can marry outside his or her race and still be a part of the race. Again, nothing will ever change my blackness or my wife's Asian ancestry. Race has never been a factor in our relationship. In fact, we both share a common perspective on life and strive for the same excellence in life. Those are the things that matter the most to us. Everything else is inconsequential.

In the end, the cycle of life, love, race, and class repeats itself. The same values that my parents taught me will be passed on to my children. It is absolutely imperative that I make my children aware of who they are and who their family is. They will know that they are African American, and people will have preconceived notions about them. It's only natural. That's what society does. But they must live life by their own standards, just as I have, and just as their mother has. Our children are the profound internal voices of society, and we must prepare and teach them well about race and class.

There are no other viable options.

—Harold A. Dawson, Jr.

Harold A. Dawson, Jr., is the president and CEO of the Dawson Company; he succeeded his father, Harold A. Dawson, Sr., in the position. As its visionary and chief transaction strategist, Dawson's astute knowledge of finance and global market trends has been instrumental in the Dawson Company's current growth. As a civic leader, entrepreneur, and respected industry advocate, Dawson has been featured in numerous local and national publications, including Business Week *and* National Real Estate Investor.

Chapter 47

On Freedom

I THINK IT'S SAFE TO SAY THAT EVERYONE WANTS TO BE FREE. Freedom is an innate desire among humans, particularly if there is little of it. Freedom is often defined as lacking restraints that come from the will of others, but the truest freedom is found by living a life of purpose.

The word *freedom* is a relative term that means different things to different people at different times. To some, freedom means a lack of responsibilities; to others, it means ownership of total responsibility. It can mean being free from confinement, or outside interference, or obligation. In fact, the concept of freedom is so situational and subjective that one person's sense of freedom might equate to bondage for another.

The United States was founded on fundamental principles of freedom. The Declaration of Independence served formal notice to England that the colonies would no longer be subjected to its tyranny. The Revolutionary War—a war for freedom—was fought and won, and the Constitution was written to form a new government and a new nation. That Constitution included the Bill of Rights, a document that specifies certain freedoms.

Exempt from all of that, of course, is the history of African Americans in this country. That history began with denial of freedom in the form of physical bondage. The abolitionist movement and Civil War—yet another war for freedom—helped free an enslaved people. But the victory was short lived, as the tenuous freedom from enslavement was followed by retaliation in the Reconstruction era. The period's black codes, bitter ex-Confederates, and the rise of the

Ku Klux Klan virtually wiped away any freedoms the Freedman had temporarily experienced.

Throughout history, people have suffered through oppression and subjugation, but there have always been movements to create change and emancipate—America's Founding Fathers and their fight against England, the abolitionists' movement against slavery, the American Civil Rights Movement against injustice, and Nelson Mandela's long struggle against apartheid rule in South Africa. These movements resulted in greater freedoms and laws of protection for the masses.

But when does one person's freedom end and another's begin? Can all parties enjoy an equality of freedom at the same time? How does freedom relate to liberty? John Stuart Mill described liberty as "the freedom to act and the absence of coercion." Liberty refers to the individual's right or ability to do what he or she wants, but freedom must have built-in restrictions. You are only free to do what you want as long as you do so while respecting the laws of the land and the freedom of others. Inherently, freedom is actually based on restrictions, and restrictions are necessary to ensure that as much freedom as possible can be experienced by as many people as possible. If the proper balance between personal freedom and society exists, there need be only minimal restraints.

Even if laws exist that dictate equal measures of freedom, freedom is not shared equally by all. In 1968, faced with unbearable discrimination and working conditions, the black sanitation workers of Memphis, Tennessee, went on strike, demanding more humane conditions. The strike was originally for better wages and union recognition, but it expanded to include job equality, better housing, and fair treatment by the police. The sanitation workers, poor men with no power other than the power of faith, wanted freedom from discrimination and unfair treatment by their employers. It essentially became a movement that was a matter of dignity, and Dr. Martin Luther King, Jr., joined their struggle.

Conditions were so abysmal that one protest sign declared, "I am a *man*!" The sanitation workers were a living embodiment of an old Madagasy proverb: "Poverty won't allow them to lift up their heads, and dignity won't allow them to bow them down." The sanitation workers marched, arm in arm, step by step, and saw hatred in the eyes of others, hatred inspired by nothing more than the color of their skin. Police showed up with batons, fire hoses, dogs, and guns. The marchers registered the fear in those same eyes and wondered why anyone would be afraid of unarmed marchers. They tried to read their minds: *How dare you say that you are a man! If you are a man, then* what am I?

That's what they saw with their eyes. But their strong yearning for freedom made them also see the other side of the anger. They saw surrender. They could see the men with the dogs, hoses, batons, and guns parting—like the Red Sea—so they could march on. They knew their bodies could heal from dog bites and wounds, but if they chose to do nothing, their souls would never heal.

By the end of the strike, Dr. Martin Luther King, Jr., had made the ultimate sacrifice—his life—but the history of America was changed forever. It was a revolution, just like the American Revolution. Like the Revolutionary War, this was a war for human rights.

At some point, everyone faces a daunting challenge that pushes faith and strength to the limit, driving them to wonder how God could be so unfair. At these times, some give up, and others see an opportunity to grow. The sanitation workers did not bow down.

I grew up in Memphis surrounded by segregation and restrictions in school, in libraries, in public restrooms, and in almost every aspect of my daily life. Fortunately, my parents taught me the meaning of freedom and liberty. My parents explained that despite the racism I faced every day, there were *no* restrictions on my mind. I could achieve, excel, and ascend beyond the shackles of segregation. The United States of America was a free country, my parents taught me; one day, all those restrictions would be stripped away, and I should persevere in preparation for that great day. I thank God for my parents' wisdom and foresight, and for their belief in the virtues of this great country.

Even outside my home, the strong African-American men and women of my church and community reinforced this mind-set. On my Beale Street paper route, I got to know many prominent black doctors, lawyers, and other professionals (including one young lawyer named Benjamin Hooks). All sent me the same messages: *There are no restrictions. You can achieve.* They all stressed the power of education and that with proper planning and preparation, I could achieve great things here in America.

I can't help but wonder how much more greatness could have been possible if the twin obstacles of racism and discrimination had never existed. Such a frame enables you to see just how strong the black men and women who have succeeded against these immeasurable odds have been. Imagine two men running a race. One has the finest shoes and top-notch training. The other one has inferior shoes and shoddy training equipment. On top of that, he also wears weights around both ankles. When the race is over, the men tie for first place. It's clear that the runner who wears the weights is the fastest; imagine how well he could perform without those restraints.

For this reason and many others, I consider invaluable the lessons I learned in my home and among my community on Beale Street. They gave me the motivation, encouragement, and inner strength necessary to have a full and determined sense of freedom throughout my academic life and career, and that, to me, is personal freedom. Personal freedom is the ability to make the decisions necessary to achieve individual purposes, goals, or aspirations. Personal freedom means that you have the choice to act or not to act—but you must also accept the consequences of that free choice. Freedom is the chance to shape your own destiny. It is liberty in action, and it is fundamental to life and the fullness of a person's existence.

Freedom gives you the power to dream big. Freedom of opportunity and self-empowerment allows you to dream and achieve what might seem impossible. You can start from nothing and achieve greatness. You can live a life free of doubt, insecurity, and fear, and one that is overflowing with confidence, courage, and passion. However, freedom without a dream—without a purpose—is like traveling on a road that ends before you get anywhere. You must have a personal vision as a destination for that journey. Every single quest, from the mightiest movement to the most private life transformation, begins with a vision.

As you begin your journey toward recognizing your personal freedom, never take anything for granted, including your freedom of thought. You must also remember that freedom always has its price. For you, that price might be education, determination, steadfastness, or taking risks. Today, we face a crisis. Freedom as we know it in the United States of America is disappearing at an alarming rate. Threats to our national security brought about the establishment of the Patriot Act, which dramatically curbs the rights of all Americans. This erosion of the Bill of Rights means that it is more important now than ever before for people to understand and realize personal freedom and achieve a satisfying life of purpose.

I still believe that this is the greatest country in the world, and we will continue to evolve into a better and stronger nation.

—**Logan H. Westbrooks**

Logan H. Westbrooks is a Los Angeles-based businessman, philanthropist, and minister.

◆ Chapter 48

Pushed to the Edge: Katrina Stories

Monday is the day fourteen-year-old Ashton Pruitt
proved his manhood.
It's the day maintenance man Calvin Burns turned a
tool chest into a life raft.
It's the day Anthony Pierre's hurricane-party joke became a matter of life and death.
It's the day the Heisser brothers demonstrated true
brotherly love.
It's the day eighty-one-year-old Joseph Banks died.

TO KNOW THE STRENGTH OF THE AMERICAN FAMILY, YOU ONLY
have to know the survivors of Monday, August 29, 2005.
As a reporter and television news anchor in New Orleans,
Louisiana, it's my job to tell their stories. My weekly "Quiet Hero"
reports on WWL-TV began long before Hurricane Katrina, but they
have taken on added significance in her wake. The heroes of Katrina
need to speak, and the nation needs to pay attention. They are the
men and women who, against overwhelming odds, not only found a
way to survive but also to rescue their loved ones and even strangers.
They are the men, women, and children of the New Orleans diaspora
who returned home determined to rebuild their shattered lives.

Deborah Pruitt felt relieved when the sun peeked through the
clouds that Monday morning. The family's home in the Gentilly section of New Orleans had weathered the strong winds of the night
before. The Pruitts had two cars in which they could have evacuated when New Orleans' mayor Ray Nagin issued the order, but they
chose to ride out Katrina at home. At first, it appeared that they had

made the right decision. Unlike our neighbors to the south and east, New Orleans had not experience the full brunt of Katrina's fury.

What Deborah, her seventy-two-year-old mother, her older brother, and her two sons did not know is that the levees and flood walls that protected their bowl-like city had given way. Within hours, 85 percent of the city was underwater. The first inkling Deborah had of trouble was a growing pool of water in the street. Then the water began rising from the crawlspace beneath the house, bubbling up through the family's polished hardwood floors. Before Deborah knew it, the water was up to her knees and continuing to rise.

The pressure of the building water prevented the family from opening the front door of their one-story house. The windows were stuck. Deborah's haven had become a death trap. "We weren't able to get out any of the windows. We couldn't get out any of the doors. We tried the attic, but we couldn't get out there. Okay, it's panic time."

But the family didn't panic—because Deborah's fourteen-year-old son Ashton maintained his cool. Just two weeks before Katrina, Ashton had attended a Boy Scouts aquatics camp. He'd learned how to use a pair of pants as a flotation device. He quickly outfitted his family with makeshift life jackets and used his Boy Scout knife and martial-arts sword to pry open a bedroom window. They saw the water rushing everywhere, and knew that it was only a matter of time before the water topped the house's roof.

Another factor that Deborah would later call a miracle was a ladder. Her mother had recently purchased an extension ladder, never dreaming that it would offer the family a means of escape. The Pruitts positioned the ladder on the house next door in order to climb to the roof of their neighbor's house. At one point during the escape, the ladder fell into the murky water, but again, Ashton raced to the rescue. Using the feet-first dive he learned as a Boy Scout, he quickly retrieved the ladder.

Eventually, the whole family—Ashton, his mother, his uncle, his older brother, and his grandmother—made it to the roof of the neighboring house, even though Ashton's brother is legally blind and his grandmother was awaiting double knee-replacement surgery. They leaned on each other, knowing that they'd all see each other to safety. They completed the climb just in time—Ashton captured a picture of the water lapping over the eaves of his house with his cell phone.

The Pruitts spent the night on that rooftop. They were not alone. In the darkness, neighbors cried out to one another from their roofs and attics. They encouraged one another to hang on as they waited and waited for help to arrive. They had no way of knowing there were thousands of people just like them in the pitch-black city and its surrounding parishes, all waiting for the same few rescuers.

———

Many of those rescuers were not professionals—they were ordinary citizens caught up in extraordinary circumstances. Calvin Burns, the director of maintenance for a youth homeless shelter, Covenant House, was on the front lines. The shelter's young residents evacuated in advance of Katrina, but Calvin decided to stay put. He had no way of knowing that he—and the shelter—would play a major role in the chaotic days ahead.

When flood waters engulfed most of the city, Covenant House remained dry. But just a few blocks away, the Iberville housing development—where he knew his young grandchildren were trapped—was flooded. Calvin turned a large tool chest into a makeshift boat and used a piano dolly to pull it across land until he reached water. Wading in water that reached as high as his chest, Calvin pulled his grandchildren from the Iberville to the safety of Covenant House. After he knew they were safe, he made the trip again and again, rescuing anyone that he could. Once he had transported his precious cargo back to the shelter, he set up a bed for a paraplegic man on top of a pool table and fed any and all who showed up, including weary New Orleans police officers.

Afterward, Calvin went searching for his eighty-four-year-old mother. He learned that she had been evacuated from a nursing home to an I-10 overpass. Calvin was shocked at what he found on that overpass. "The sights on that ramp ... the old people ... swollen legs ... swollen limbs ... just sitting there, staring. Hard eyes. Eyes just telling me, 'Please help me. Help me.' I walked three or four blocks down that interstate, and there's my mother, coming down the interstate with a cane. I put her in that boat with that piano dolly and brought her down the ramp."

The scene on the highway was one of death and despair—and total disbelief that this abomination could be happening in the richest country in the world. Calvin wiped away a tear as he recalled the zombie-like atmosphere. "Some of the worst things I've ever seen in my life on that ramp …"

————————

No one could imagine how bad things would get in the city known as the Big Easy. Anthony Pierre threw a hurricane party the night before Katrina. In fact, he put his boat in the front yard of his Seventh-Ward house as a joke. "[At the party,] I got on the microphone and said, 'Here is Noah's Ark. I'm tying it up in front of my house. If the water rises, come here and jump on the boat.'"

When he said those words in jest, Anthony had no idea that the next morning, he would actually step aboard that barge from the second-floor porch of his house. He can't remember how many people he ferried to nearby St. Augustine High School. "Every time I heard somebody hollering for help or waving flags off of roofs [I went to them]. They were hanging on to poles."

One of those he rescued was seventy-nine-year-old Bernadine Irving, who was trapped in her attic. In the wake of the story, Bernadine's daughter Sharon expressed the family's eternal gratitude to Anthony: "We were all so grateful for him for finding Mama, and whoever else's mama he found, because without Anthony, we wouldn't have Mama today."

————————

In another part of town, Troy Williams thought his life was just about over. Unable to swim, Troy had taken refuge in the last place he could find in his small house—he laced his fingers over the top of his front door and stood on the doorknob. Even then, he says, "The water was still up to my neck. I didn't think there was no tomorrow."

Troy stood in that precarious position for hours, shouting and praying for help. Michael and Jason Heisser heard his cries and, as they had been doing all day, they showed up on a life raft to help yet another stranger. The Heisser brothers climbed onto his roof and knocked a hole in it to pull Troy out. Afterward, they took him to their cousin's second-floor apartment, where the other evacuees the Heissers had rescued were huddled. The life raft they used for their seat-of-the-pants operation was one Michael says Jason stumbled across just the night before as they were leaving their parents' home. "... Unexpectedly, like an angel put it there. My brother grabbed it at the last minute and said, 'Man, maybe we ought to take this.' And it worked out."

It worked out, indeed, for Troy and for the others the Heissers rescued with that inflatable raft, but Jason says it was all because of God. "By the grace of God, we got out. And I'm glad Troy got to see another day. I take no credit for that."

In neighboring St. Bernard Parish, Gerald Banks and his eighty-one-year-old father, Joseph, waded as quickly as they could through chest-deep water. Neither man could swim. Gerald hoisted his father up a tree in the backyard. He climbed up next to his father and breathed a sigh of relief. Then, Gerald looked up and saw their neighbor's house drifting towards them. Gerald urged his father to follow him to another tree, but his father refused. Gerald leapt to another tree, terrified; the house stopped just short of striking the tree to which his father still clung.

There was another glimmer of hope. A young woman swimming by offered to bring them life jackets. In amazement, Gerald recalls, "If you could've seen how it was storming. The wind [was] blowing stuff off the roof. You wouldn't think she was coming back, but ten minutes later, here she comes, with two life jackets wrapped about her. I said, 'Boy, look at this here. That's got to be the angel.'"

Unfortunately, Gerald's elderly father refused the offer. "I beg[ged] him, I said, 'Daddy, take the life jacket!' and he said, 'I don't want it, Gerald.'" It was a tragic decision. A few hours later, Gerald watched his father, overtaken with exhaustion, sink to his death. He relived the tragedy again and again, trying to make sense of what happened. "I kept yelling, 'Daddy, Daddy, Daddy, pull yourself up! Pull yourself up!' But it wasn't going to happen."

Gerald doesn't know the name of the young woman who brought him the life jacket, nor does he know who the local men were that ultimately rescued him. His brother, Roy, was also rescued by strangers and taken to a roof. Roy says, "The water was still rising, but we got together and said a little prayer ... white and black ... didn't know each other before Katrina. We weren't even worried about asking each others' names. Nothing like that. Everybody was helping everybody else. It was life or death."

In the nightmarish days that followed, Gerald and Roy joined the effort to rescue their neighbors. I talked to Gerald in April 2006 in the memory-littered yard of the family's flood-ravaged home. Generations of Gerald's family had lived in the Meraux community, but it would now forever be remembered as the place Joseph Banks died. His eyes filled with tears as he told me, "I'm kind of like a hero, but I couldn't save Dad, so to me, I didn't do everything I was supposed to do. That's how I really be feeling."

But Gerald did all that he could, as did so many others. Every Katrina survivor has a story that will be passed down from generation to generation.

Ashton Pruitt's family spent nineteen hours on their neighbor's roof before they were ultimately rescued by a firefighter. Survival wasn't easy. They spent another two days stranded on a highway overpass with thousands of other people waiting for buses to take them to Texas. Deborah Pruitt says there was no order on that overpass—she will never forget soldiers throwing bottles of water and food rations at crowds of desperate people as though they were spectators at a Mardi Gras parade.

But like so many families, the Pruitts proved to be tougher than their circumstances. After a brief stay in Texas, the family returned to New Orleans. They lived in a FEMA trailer for sixteen months as their house was renovated with the help of volunteers who, three years after Katrina, continue to pour into the region by the thousands. Gone are all the old photographs and family heirlooms the Pruitts treasured before Katrina. They have been replaced with new treasures, like a picture of Ashton standing next to President George Bush in the Oval Office.

Ashton met the president when he received the Boy Scouts of America's highest award for heroism, but the soft-spoken young man remains humble. "In the moment, you're not really thinking about what could happen. You're just thinking about getting safe, and protecting the people that you love."

Ashton's grandmother, Lillian Brown, learned a lesson on Monday, August 29, 2005—the same one that strong families have learned throughout history. "I really didn't think I could survive getting out of that window. But survival is a wonderful thing with the help of God. Because we never know what we can do until we're pushed to the edge."

———

In those stunning days after Katrina, many images of New Orleans were burned into the American conscience. Historians will forever examine the failures of both government and the levees, but we must also immortalize the heroic efforts of thousands of ordinary citizens. Katrina survivors were pushed to the edge, and yet, they are still standing.

—Sally Ann Roberts

Sally Ann Roberts coanchors WWL-TV's Eyewitness Morning News, *the highest-rated local morning news program in the nation. In 1994, Sally Ann cofounded the mentorship organization Each One Save One. The nonprofit organization recruits, screens, trains, and places mentors in schools and organizations across the New Orleans metro area. Roberts lives in New Orleans with her husband, Ron Nabonne. She has three children and one grandchild.*

♦ Chapter 49

The Black Community: For Sale by Owners

EVERYWHERE I TURN, I SEE A "FOR SALE" OR "SOLD" SIGN SWINGing on the actions, transactions, and interactions of the faces and places that supposedly represent black leadership in America. Welcome to a land where some of the most highly visible African-American community activists, political decision makers, and prosperous preachers are being bossed and bought.

Ain't gonna let nobody turn me around has been replaced with *I'm not even going*. Folks like the late Medgar Evers, Thurgood Marshall, Shirley Chisholm, and Rev. Vernon Johns have been replaced by lesser models—less committed, less controversial, less confrontational, and less intellectual. Nevertheless, they do have great smiles, great suits, and great cars.

In our darkest days, from Egyptland to Goree Island, the Lord has always had a way of letting us know that help is on the way. That's why I thank God for President Barack Obama and the standard of African-American leadership he represents. It's not because he's somehow Black America's panacea or premier problem solver. At least Obama is informed, equipped, and enlightened enough to propose some healing alternatives for what hurts America—as well as some pain relief for economically and educationally ailing Black America.

Obama, who holds an undergraduate degree from Columbia University and a law degree from Harvard University (also the alma mater of educator, intellectual, and NAACP cofounder W.E.B. DuBois), is an example of a black man who makes Black America proud. He has no cycle of criminal activity, with matching prison names and dates. He has no drama from "baby mamas." He has no significant stints of unemployment or of lying around on Momma's couch "because of the white man."

Obama is a committed black man who is married to his former boss, who is an accomplished black woman in her own right, with her own Harvard law degree. Their family is reminiscent of *The Cosby Show's* Cliff and Clair Huxtable. Finally, we can find a mix of intellect, integrity, and ideas with a heart—all in black—on the front page of newspapers, as well as on CNN.

It's been reported that at age twenty-four, with his juris doctorate in hand and thousands and thousands in school loans, Obama overlooked high-paying jobs to take a job as a community organizer that commanded a yearly salary of $13,000. He spent the next three years driving a raggedy blue Honda "hooptie" and organizing more than twenty congregations for change—challenging them to change their visual landscape, change their economic options, and change their accountability standards.

He is well remembered by his colleagues. "They expressed admiration for him as an organizer who trained strong community leaders while keeping himself in the background and as a strategist who could turn general problems into specific, winnable issues," said Loretta Augustine-Herron, a member of the Developing Communities Project (DCP) board that hired Obama, remembering him as someone who always set a standard.

It was as a community organizer that Barack Obama said he found his calling. "There was something more than making money and getting a fancy degree," he said. "The measure of my life would be public service."

First of all, he purposely stayed in the background. Most African-American leaders want to be in the spotlight; many of them, in fact, have never seen a center stage they haven't liked. In some cases, these "leaders"—obvious climbers among the black celebrity class—suffer from a hero syndrome or a messiah complex.

In his book *Good to Great*, best-selling author Jim Collins reveals how good-to-great leaders "never wanted to become larger-than-life heroes. They never aspired to be put on a pedestal or become unreachable icons. They were seemingly ordinary people quietly producing extraordinary results." That is not the modern-day black experience. To reach fame or fortune, some African-American "leaders" are merely putting their constituencies, community groups, or church members for sale to the highest bidder. In some cases, it's black viewers or black listeners that are for sale, but it's all a twenty-first-century slave trade of sorts.

Collins goes on to describe a top-ranked leader as "an individual who blends extreme personal humility with intense professional will," but where my thoughts actually waltz along with his is when he documents how the highest level of leaders "channel their ego needs away from themselves and into the larger goal of building a great company." Collins adds that what holds back many companies from being great is "the presence of a gargantuan personal ego that contribute[s] to the demise or continued mediocrity of the company." As I was reading, I found myself saying, *preach!*

It's not that leaders of great organizations have no ego or self-interest, Collins writes. "Indeed, they are incredibly ambitious—but their ambition is first and foremost for the institution, not themselves." *You better preach!*

Collins cites President Abraham Lincoln as a leader who "never let his ego get in the way of his primary ambition for the larger cause of an enduring great nation." The quality of top-level leadership puts ambition in the right place: "ambition first and foremost for the company and concern for its success, rather than for one's own riches and personal renown."

That's the missing link among some black organizations, community groups, businesses, and churches. We have leaders who are concerned more with attracting great applause for themselves than making their organizations worthy of applause. Unfortunately, we are held back by some black decision makers who don't have a clue about the type of masterful leadership that Collins suggests. "For these people, work will always be first and foremost about what they get—fame, fortune, adulation, power, whatever—not what they build, create, and contribute," he writes.

Say that! Now I'm about to *open the doors* of the church. (Note to those who are new to the black church experience: Ask someone who knows it well to explain what that means.)

At one point in African-American history, the message of the black church—and what you were able to extract from it and, as a result, transform your life—was more valued than the money collected each week from its congregants. Now, that value has been turned around 180 degrees; it's exactly this condition of value dyslexia that is penetrating and dismantling black institutions today. A growing number of influential African-American community activists, political decision makers, and preachers value the money over the message, and being served over service. Leaders should be serving broken people, but these days, broken people are serving the leaders. It's "I'll serve you if you serve me," or "I'll serve you according to how you serve me," or "I'll serve you back some of what you serve me," when it should be, "I'll serve you, whether you serve me or not."

The term "servant leadership" was coined in a 1970 essay titled "The Servant as Leader" by Robert K. Greenleaf (1904–1990). Greenleaf's premise was clear: True leadership emerges from those whose primary motivation is a deep desire to help others. Truth be told, many black leaders today—whose names and faces are well recognized nationally on TV or in the newspaper—actually don't have a servant's heart.

Furthermore, two questions raised in a later Greenleaf essay, "Trustees as Servants," were quite thought-provoking as they relate to black leadership: "Whom do you serve?" and, just as important, "For what purpose?" The difference between the leaders and decision makers of today versus the African-American transformational change agents of our past is clear: It wasn't about them. In many cases, black leaders of the past were living sacrifices.

- Consider Sojourner Truth, born Isabella Baumfree, who was sold for $100 at age nine along with a herd of sheep. Over her lifetime, she was sold again and again. Yet she risked her life working with abolitionists, preaching about women's rights, pushing the government to give former slaves their own land to cultivate, and enlisting black troops to help free current slaves.

- Frederick Douglass could have been killed for the newspaper he published and the lectures he gave revealing the evil of slavery.
- The same goes for Araminta Harriet Greene Tubman, who as a child suffered a serious head injury when an angry overseer struck her in the forehead with a two-pound weight. After serving for twenty-nine years as a slave, she escaped and obtained freedom in Philadelphia, but she later returned South, spending the next ten years as a "conductor" on the Underground Railroad. During her time there, she made more than twenty trips and rescued about three hundred slaves.

For what cause has one of our contemporary black leaders risked his or her life? Back then, it was a cultural obligation to "pay it back and forward." "Pay it forward" is a term popularized by Robert A. Heinlein in his 1951 book *Between Planets*. In 2000, Catherine Ryan Hyde's novel *Pay It Forward* was published and adapted into a Warner Brothers film with the same name. In Hyde's book, a teacher asks her class to think of an idea for world change and put it into action. One student considers the challenge and responds,

> You see, I do something real good for three people. And then when they ask how they can pay it back, I say they have to *pay it forward*. To three more people. Each. So nine people get helped. Then those people have to do twenty-seven ... to eighty-one. Then two hundred forty-three. Then seven hundred twenty-nine. Then two thousand, one hundred eighty-seven. See how big it gets?

In sociology, this same concept is dubbed "generalized reciprocity" or "generalized exchange." Today, it's developed into a real-life social movement, not just in the United States but worldwide. A Pay It Forward Foundation has been founded to educate and inspire students to realize that they can change the world. What's frustrating about these two catchy, life-changing concepts is that both "servant-leader" and "pay it forward" were once mainstay principles in the African-American culture. In an article titled "Pluralistic Reflection on Servant-Leadership," Juana Bordas wrote:

> Many women and minorities and people of color have long traditions of servant-leadership in their cultures. Servant-leadership has very old roots in many of the indigenous cultures, cultures that were holistic, cooperative, communal, intuitive, and spiritual. These cultures centered on being guardians of the future and respecting the ancestors who walked before.

This is an extremely distressing void, because the needs in the African-American community are so great, but the servant-leader role models and "pay it forward" participants are few and far between on America's shattered and broken streets.

In general, the black community doesn't expect much in return for its allegiance to institutions and individuals. But who is really at fault for that? Do you blame the self-serving leaders who pimp and prostitute the African-American community for profit, or do you blame those who empower the leaders to do so?

Consider our elected officials, for example. Many politicians meet Jesus between September and November, when they're in and out of black churches like fast-food drive-thrus. Where is the accountability? Who articulates or challenges their voting records, which are public record?

It's the same way with the "plant-a-seed" prosperity movement that's afoot in the pulpit. The only thing that seems to be growing is the pockets and pocketbooks of celebrity preachers. More and more sequined and diamond-studded women are pastors and copastors of some of these churches; many of them get their dresses and their sermons from the same place—St. John.

Don't get me wrong. As an ordained preacher and associate pastor myself, I'm not one of those who believe that ministers of the gospel must take a vow of poverty. At the same time, I don't think these preachers are the only ones who should be rich. If God will provide more than enough for the pastor, there should be more than enough witnesses in the pews who can benefit as well.

Now, we have a class of "have-mores" in the African-American community. Many accomplished blacks now are so accustomed to recognition that they stack up sponsor-related plaques rather than hang them up. There are quite a few who vacation in expensive retreats like Nantucket, Martha's Vineyard, or the Hamptons, bouncing back and forth on private jets. This growing class should be extending more hands up to the community, but instead, it's merely another level of black bureaucracy—more rings to kiss.

Did you ever notice that some folks with familiar names in the black community did not initially support Barack Obama's bid for the presidency? There are some folks who believe they own and control the resources and the networks that deliver the black community—if, as Bob Barker would say, "the price is right." Pucker up and "come on down." There most certainly is a price to pay to get some of those folks pictured in Ebony's Most Influential Black 100 list to join or support you. Sometimes it's straight-up money, but other times it's a debt that's meant to be paid back in favors. Some of these leaders live in an adopted sense of entitlement and expectation of privilege and praise, just like slave owners did in the past. They are the new gatekeepers.

These gatekeepers are also great secret keepers, ensuring their "how-to" recipes and "dos and don'ts" become nontransferable, inaccessible shrines. It's as if black leadership dementia sets in.

Don't believe me? Let's play a game.

- *Quick*, name three accomplished leaders in your ebony hue and kente-coated world that you know well, leaders who are not unreachable icons.
- *Quick*, name an African-American leader to whom you can apply the good-to-great leader adjectives like "quiet," "humble," "modest," "reserved," "shy," "gracious," "mild-mannered," "self-effacing," "understated," or "did not believe his own clippings."
- *Quick*, name one or two young people who are learning from the shadows of that leader, being exposed to the ways and the whys of black, white, brown, and yellow folk from a vulnera-

ble perspective. Have they seen the scars? Have they touched those areas numbed by disappointment? Have they learned how to manage failure? Have they had firsthand question-and-answer sessions on "handling haters," and do they realize that some of those haters look just like themselves? Have they been given access to the mantle of proven and duplicated steps, actions, and reactions that have been mastered?

Unfortunately, many leaders in Black America stay in office so long that most of their major accomplishments are as old as they are. If they ever do give up the power or their position, they just hand it over, saying: "Your turn!" According to Collins, leaders "concerned more with their own reputation for personal greatness often fail to set the company up for success in the next generation. After all, what better testament to your own personal greatness than that the place falls apart after you leave?"

Another appalling trend has been "seed-based" leadership. Some-times leaders reach no further than their own family tree, turning African-American nonprofits, political seats, and churches into family businesses. These men and women hand their mantras and ministries over to children and family members who have the same name but often not the same talents, gifts, or commitment. The same name does not mean the same anointing.

There was a time in our history where we were honest with our children, telling them, "You don't have it, so you won't get it!" For the good of the institution, alternative outside leadership was selected. These days, parents are so determined to keep these family dynasties in place that they have to practically leave their name on everything; they also visit the businesses, churches, or offices regularly enough that no one really notices a change at all. Once again, it's all about building, creating, and contributing taking a back seat to fame, for-tune, and adulation. It's still an endless and tireless search for wealth, control, and popularity, as well as political, economic, moral, or spiri-tual power.

Rick Warren opens his best-selling book *A Purpose-Driven Life* with this statement: "It's not about you." Unfortunately, in Black America, it still is.

The views expressed in this essay were not meant to offend anyone specifically; instead, they're designed to encourage everyone to consider another view: Rather than the window, try the mirror.

—**Angelo B. Henderson**

Angelo B. Henderson won the Pulitzer Prize while serving as a reporter for the Wall Street Journal; *he has also served on the reporting staffs at the* Courier-Journal *(Louisville, Kentucky), the* Detroit News, *and the* St. Petersburg Times *(Florida). A resident of Pontiac, Michigan, Henderson travels across the United States on behalf of Angelo Ink LLC, his media-consulting firm, which provides motivational speaking and media services, as well as training and development to professional and aspiring journalists, corporate executives, support staffs, and civic organizations. He's also a well-known Detroit radio personality, currently host of* KISS Sunday Today *on 105.9 KISS-FM (WDMK) and serves as a full-time associate pastor at Southfield, Michigan's Hope United Methodist Church, one of the nation's largest and fastest-growing predominately African-American United Methodist congregations.*

♦ Chapter 50

A Journey into Manhood

THERE ARE MANY WORDS THAT CAN BE USED TO DESCRIBE THE feelings, emotions, and experiences of a young African-American boy born in New York City and currently approaching manhood in Atlanta, Georgia. In my early teen years, I searched my mind to understand and adapt to the emotions that were washing over me. There was the talk of being "on top of your game," exploring sexual feelings and their potential dangers—including HIV-AIDS and the threat of guns and violence. However, whenever I think about my personal future, I see myself as a successful business-man whose dreams and aspirations have been realized as a result of my strong faith, a loving family, and a firm commitment to give back to my community.

As I look back on my life so far, I realize that it's been a good one, largely because of the sacrifices of my family—especially my mother. However, through my volunteer efforts, I have had the opportunity to personally see the much more difficult lives of others. When volunteering at the Atlanta Food Bank, I've distributed food to people who didn't know where their next meal would be coming from. That made me think about—and appreciate—the fact that I have three full meals a day and snacks whenever I want them. At the Atlanta Children's Shelter, I have seen children my age and younger who were thrilled to have little more than a safe, warm, and dry place to sleep. I had the opportunity to play with infants and toddlers and bring some fun to their lives, if only for a short time. It made me feel good to know I was making a difference in someone else's life.

My journey from boyhood to manhood is not complete, certainly, but as I travel along the way, I am learning lessons that will help me become a strong African-American man, including being careful about choosing the people with whom I associate. You have to make clear decisions about what is right and what is wrong. Although what's right isn't always necessarily obvious (or easy), you must remember what your family has taught you. Now that I am in my mid-teens, I understand more about sex and the dangers of HIV-AIDS, and I know it's a real risk for teens. I know that I must make difficult decisions about girls, relationships, and sex. My first kiss certainly felt good, but I also felt a sense of responsibility right along with it. I made sure that I didn't let it go too far. I have plenty of time in my future to experience total commitment and sexual relationships.

As I think about my life, I realize I'm growing into manhood at a great time. For the first time in the history of our country, we have an African-American president. Barack Obama has persuaded many people to believe that he can change our country for the better. I believe in him and in his commitment to change. As a young African-American male on my way from boyhood to manhood, I'm wishing him well. In the true spirit of giving back and being part of this "change process," I volunteered to help his campaign, which also helped prepare me for the success I see in my future and giving back to my community. I will never stop dreaming and will never stop believing!

—James Worthy, III

James Worthy, III, is a thriving college-bound New York native who resides with his family in Lithonia, Georgia.

♦ Chapter 51

Pay It Forward

BY MOST PEOPLE'S DEFINITION, I LEAD A SUCCESSFUL LIFE FILLED with many of the trappings that represent the American dream. However, as good as I've had it, I am keenly aware that a great deal of my success is due in large part to the people who paid forward blessings into my life. I am talking about individuals who, through their direction and love, contributed to my growth and well-being. In return, they only asked that I sow a seed into someone else. People talk about mentors all the time, but from first-hand experience, I know the remarkable impact noble acts can make on one's journey. I truly believe that giving back to others is one of the most powerful gifts that we can share in our lifetime. In fact, it's the ultimate expression of our humanity.

Early on, my parents and older brother provided me with a solid foundation, a belief and value system that said I could achieve anything in life. For as long as I can remember, I was imbued with a strong sense of pride and connection to black identity. My parents—particularly my mother—infused my young mind with a plethora of positive examples about the African, and the African-American, experience. That, along with my mom's ever-present attention to social graces and appreciation for cultural pursuits, grounded me with a sense of the world in which I lived. I always felt that I belonged.

A good part of my character and healthy sense of confidence benefited from the timing of my birth, which coincided with the height of the Civil Rights Movement and the social change that was taking over America at that time. My earliest memories were nourished by messages booming loud from the radio directing me to "say it loud, I'm black and I'm proud," and to understand that "to be young, gifted, and black" was the thing to be. The sum of these experiences informed not only my upbringing but also the way that I view myself as an African-American man.

Of course, as I grew older, society sent other messages that were contrary to the lessons I learned at home. Fortunately, the die cast by my parents was bulletproof, so I countered those discouraging opinions with a self-assured view of my value and purpose. That strong sense of self-love has been a source of power to me in my adult life.

Apart from my immediate family, a great deal of my social development arrived via my relationship with a woman I affectionately call Aunt Janet. Her influence broadened my perspective and view of the world, as well as my reaction to it. For a period of forty years and counting, my Aunt Janet has played a central role in my life and has expanded my perspective immeasurably. It's irrelevant that she is Caucasian and we're unrelated. Aunt Janet, along with her late husband, Martin, long ago made those barriers that often exist between black and white a complete nonissue for me.

Another pivotal moment in my development arrived when I became acquainted with a man who, next to my father and brother, has provided me with the best possible example of what it means to be a black male in America. I was in my mid-teens when I first met Logan, who taught a college-level elective course I took during my freshman year in high school. I was immediately impressed by his debonair and articulate presence, and I soon began hanging around his office every day after school. Before long, he "adopted" me, and I was given chores to do around his office—which gave me direct access to the life of a black millionaire. Although my parents worked hard to provide our family with a comfortable standard of living, up until that point I'd never known any African Americans who possessed true power. By the time we met, Logan had already enjoyed a successful career in the music business and owned several thriving business ventures, including a record label responsible for several chart-topping hits. Over the ten years that followed, Logan expanded my life exponentially by involving me in various aspects of his enterprises, first as an intern and later as an employee. In the process, he enhanced my self-confidence and exposed me to what is commonly called "the good life."

There have been countless others who, in their own ways, have given immense value to my life. By sharing their time, intellect, and life experiences with me, or by simply listening to my dramas and dreams, they've solidified my path to success. People like Michael Gonzales, Marcia Cole, Doug Seibold, and many others have propelled my life forward by simply giving me a chance to grow in my craft and realize my potential. Yes, I lead an incredible life, but I know that it's only by the grace of God that I've been blessed with the boundless generosity that's been extended to me.

In life, I believe that we all benefit from the blessings of others, including people to whom we are related and also those to whom we have no familial connection. Within the African-American community, we all need to recognize this and commit ourselves to act in ways that express the same sentiment. It's a path of love that leads to our community and eventually returns to our own lives.

As I've settled into my life as a journalist, author, and lecturer, my sense of purpose has become firmly rooted in the time-honored principle of paying forward to others the gifts that have been given to me. Through my words and deeds, I use my talent to bring forth knowledge and understanding about the people and the world we live in. That's my gift, and that's how I repay those supportive acts. It's just like the Good Book says: "Do unto others as you would have them do unto you." I'm not trying to sound corny or preachy, but it's really true: by giving to others, your life becomes so much brighter.

—Gil L. Robertson, IV

Chapter 52

Old Times

Let's talk about old times.

When men didn't use any ol' hook lines

When what we said was really on our minds.

Women were shy and sweet, and wore their ponytails back neat. In order for me to be your man

I had to ask your father for your hand.

You'll remember old times, when we played hopscotch, double-dutch, and jacks

Just doing simple things that kids did to relax.

Remember when Slinkies went flip-flop, yo-yos went around the World, and hula hoops were loved by every woman, man, boy, and girl

That was old times

When men believed in strong family bonds

When women were true to their lover, not displaying their breasts, thighs, and hips to any other.

When drop tops were hot and drive-bys were not, and safe sex was a simple grind up against the wall with your girl until she said stop-ppp

I'm just talking 'bout old times, when your mom and my mom had breakfast, lunch, and dinner prepared all the time.

And remember, if you got sick, they would give you some of that nasty castor oil to make you shhh

That was old times, when men didn't commit black-on-black crime

For we were fighting on the civil rights front lines

When Afros were large and picks were in, and brothers pumped their fists as if they could win

Black was beautiful brown was hip yellow was mellow and white folks was acting hip

That was old times. Before our men were sent to Vietnam and came back with drugs on their mind and we went from the progressive '60s to the superfly '70s, and folks started to imitate Daddymack, wearing long chinchilla coats and big-brim hats

Driving in long Cadillacs with the diamond in the back and brothers started smoking herb and drinking Thunderbird and Gilscott. And some poets tried to bring the spokenword but I don't think too many people heard

Because we put our freedom struggle down

That's when old times stop coming around

You'll remember Oldtime. He was the brother that believed in strong family bonds. She was the sister that was dignified all the time. Sometimes when I think about all that's going down, I just wish I could go back and chat with that cat called Oldtime.

—Talib Latif

Talib Latif is a spoken-word artist, poet, and businessman based in Atlanta, Georgia.

◆ Chapter 53

Something Extraordinary, Something Unique—It's All Up to You

WHEN I WAS A YOUNG BOY, NO MORE THAN SIX YEARS old, the local chapter of the KKK held a march in my small Southern hometown. A number of blacks, myself included, stood along the roadway to watch the spectacle. Some watched out of curiosity, others out of fear, but everyone was shocked and disgusted by the vitriolic racial hatred shouted by the Klan toward blacks and Jews.

I didn't understand some of the names we were called, but the tone of their voices and the anger on their faces were very clear—they hated us. At the time, I didn't fully understand why, since I didn't know them, and they didn't know me. It was a real low point in my young life. Now, I can't say how those degrading words affected the others in attendance, but they made me mad and moved me to prove them wrong. I didn't have a plan, just a burning desire to prove them wrong.

I, along with an older sister and younger brother, was raised by a single mother. We worked side by side in the tobacco fields of North Carolina until my mother got a minimum-wage job pressing clothes in a hot laundry. We didn't have material wealth, but our mother taught us values worth their weight in gold—knowing the difference between right and wrong, taking responsibility for our own actions, respecting our elders, and always believing in ourselves. These lessons have served me well throughout my life. I have needed these values to help me fight off the naysayers.

In high school, my guidance counselor told me I wasn't academically suited to attend a major university. My life experiences had taught me never to let anyone convince me that I was less than the best. I graduated from my state's flagship university with honors. I didn't listen to the naysayers.

From early childhood on, I wanted to be a lawyer, but my friends tried to convince me that such a lofty goal was just too much for a country boy like me. After all, they told me, "you grew up on the wrong side of the tracks," and "there are no professionals in your family." Ignoring the naysayers, I eventually graduated from one of the nation's top law schools and started my legal practice in the South's preeminent city, Atlanta, Georgia.

I've always been fascinated by the law and politics. Both professions just seemed like the perfect avenues to give something back to my community. This belief is what enticed me to run for public office. My first race was for a seat in the Georgia General Assembly. The district I lived in at the time was 60 percent white and 40 percent black. My friends told me on numerous occasions to get out of the race. They didn't believe that an African American could win a district with those demographics. The naysayers were at it again. I won that race, and I went on to serve five consecutive terms in the Georgia Legislature. As God would have it, there was still much more to do.

Later, as it turned out, the man who had served as Georgia's attorney general for sixteen years decided he wanted to run for governor. He left his position as the state's top legal officer with about a year remaining on his four-year term. At the time, the governor was authorized to appoint someone to fill the one-year vacancy.

After much speculation about the attorney general's successor, the governor turned to a young African-American legislator who grew up poor on the wrong side of the tracks. He appointed me, and I became the first African American in Georgia ever to be appointed and serve as attorney general. There was, however, a string attached: I had to agree to run for a full four-year term.

At my swearing-in ceremony in the State Capitol, my wife, Catherine, daughters, Jocelyn and Chelsea, mother, Mary, sister, Jean, and brother, Lee, joined the throngs of well-wishers who packed the Capitol for the historic event. I'll never forget the elderly black woman who hugged me, tears in her eyes, and told me she never thought she'd live to see a day like this in Georgia. I knew I couldn't let people like her down. I had to run for a full term.

The naysayers were convinced an African American couldn't run for the state's top legal position and win. Not in the Deep South. Many of my friends suggested that I just leave the job after a year and go back to private law practice. But I didn't believe that God had brought me this far just to abandon me. I was here for a reason, and I was not about to let the naysayers turn me around. I not only won that first statewide election for attorney general of Georgia, I have now been elected to three four-year terms—with overwhelming support.

My colleagues, the nation's attorneys general, have also bestowed a great honor on me. They elected me to be their national president for 2006–2007, becoming the first African American ever to serve the organization in this capacity in its hundred-year history.

Had I listened to my friends, and the naysayers, none of this would have happened. The late Dr. Benjamin E. Mays, former president of Morehouse College, once said, "We're all born into this world to do something extraordinary, to do something unique, and if you don't do it, it may not ever get done." I spend a great deal of my time telling young kids exactly the same thing. I share my life's story with them as a source of encouragement and as a reminder to never listen to the naysayers, even the ones who call themselves your friends.

Our kids must believe in themselves, regardless of where they came from, regardless of how poor they might be, and regardless of how many parents are in their household. They must expect great things, for if they do, great things will happen.

The challenges for America are great, but times are especially challenging for those of us who happen to be African American. We are still trying to find our collective, unified voice among ourselves and the rest of this country's three hundred million people. The search for our collective voice must begin with recognizing the importance of education.

It's never too early or too late to learn. In order to be competitive in this global economy, a good education is a must. I tell our kids that not everyone will be a basketball player, football player, or rapper. They need a backup plan: "E," a plan for education.

We must also find a way to keep our kids out of the criminal-justice system. We've got to give them a chance to realize their potential and succeed in life. As parents, we can give our children that chance by instilling values that will last them a lifetime. Michael Jordan sneakers cost a small fortune, but values don't cost a cent. They just require a little bit of our time to impart them from one generation to the next.

From my vantage point as an attorney general, I have seen a growing frustration nationwide among African Americans over our criminal-justice system. In my opinion, the best way to deal with this would be to get more actively involved in the legislative process and elect people who will deal responsibly with the issues and bring balance to our law-making process. We must always remember that laws order our society, and without laws, we would have anarchy. Moreover, not all laws are bad. Who can argue with the benefits we've drawn from the Civil Rights Act and the Voting Rights Act? Let's not throw the baby out with the bathwater.

The key to success for all of us is to understand that life's "isms" and individual failures are not permanent limits on our chances to do well. In fact, they are opportunities to prove the naysayers wrong. As Dr. Mays said, "Do something extraordinary. Do something unique."

Emboldened by a strong value system and a belief in the Almighty, we can find that collective voice.

—Thurbert E. Baker

Thurbert E. Baker has served as the state of Georgia's attorney general since 1997. He is the first African American appointed to serve as attorney general of Georgia, the first African American to be elected president of the National Association of Attorneys General, and at the time of this writing, the only African-American state attorney general currently serving in the United States.

PART V
SELF

♦ Chapter 54

The Psychology of Beauty

MY FIRST INTRODUCTION TO BEAUTY, LIKE THAT OF MANY young girls, came from observing the women in my life. Watching my mother prepare herself for an evening out with my father was quite an experience. From the lotions and perfumes to the makeup and hair, it was a long, ritualized process. This ritual always culminated with her putting on an amazing dress and suddenly being ready to present herself to the world. In fact, my favorite dress of hers was a green velvet one with brown mink trim on the cuffs and collar. I also have memories of seeing my grandmother heading off to work decked out in beautiful suits and hats. Even though she worked as a maid at a downtown hotel in Buffalo, New York, you'd never know it judging from her attire.

Black women have always had an amazing sense of style, no matter the circumstances. It's part of who we are, individually and culturally. As a young girl, I learned that beauty was about more than just being visually appealing. It was more about personal pride and self-esteem.

It surprises people that I did not aspire to have a career in modeling. Really, my dream was to become a lawyer. Growing up, I was the classic ugly duckling, a nerdy bookworm. I wasn't the Barbie-doll type at all! I was an athlete, swimming competitively and serving as a swimming instructor and lifeguard during the summers. The world of modeling never entered my mind. Like many things in life, it happened by chance. Although I eventually developed a love for the fashion world, my initial motivation for modeling was to make money for college.

As a student at Northeastern University in Boston, I took a job one summer at a clothing boutique. Lily, one of my coworkers, told me that if I ever changed my mind about law school, I should consider modeling. I thought she was nuts! But she gave me the number for a woman who worked in the industry, just in case I changed my mind.

After returning to school, I met some girls from New York City who also mentioned modeling to me. They showed me magazines and went on and on about the kind of money they made—certainly more than I made at the boutique. So the very next summer, I found the number Lily had given me and placed a call.

After being introduced to *Glamour* magazine, I was on my way, but this new direction was against my father's wishes. Clearly, he wanted me to finish school and knew that I had no understanding of the industry. I guess most people would've been terrified, but I wasn't. Charge it to my type A personality, but I had excelled in other areas of my life, so I figured I could do the same with modeling. I had a quiet confidence. As time went on, I knew I had made the right decision. Even my father got on board once he saw that I could continue going to school and work modeling jobs at the same time. Thankfully, the success continued for many years, opening doors and providing opportunities I ambitiously took on.

Without question, appearing on the cover of *Vogue* in 1974 was a life-changing moment for me—professionally and personally. All of the hard work and time I had put into campaigns, runways, and ads around the world came together in this one moment. After the inroads that models like Naomi Sims had made for black models in the industry, the mainstream was finally acknowledging our beauty. Yes, brown skin and unique features had international appeal, and European traits were not the measuring stick that black women had to live up to.

There were all kinds of emotions running through me—joy, satisfaction, and pride. Surprisingly, one of them was anger. I remember thinking, "It's 1974, and I'm the first? Are you kidding me?" Don't get me wrong, it was an honor to grace *Vogue*'s cover. However, it was the 1970s. I felt there should've been more opportunities for black models to grace the covers of high-fashion magazines. Why wasn't there someone before me? But on a deeper level, a light bulb went on. The sociopolitical gyrations the cover had generated started me on a journey of self-discovery. I grappled with our history as African Americans, my identity as a black woman, and what they mean in our global society.

Although beauty is a marketing tool in the fashion world, it is a purely psychological concept. Advertisers are always telling us, "If you wear this dress, you'll feel powerful!" "Style your hair this way, and you'll look trendy!" "Put on these heels, and you'll command attention!" But if you don't see yourself in that magazine, or in that TV ad, how will you, as an African-American woman, ever know that you, too, are desirable? So it became my mission to make black women a part of the beauty world. Through my work, black women would see a version of themselves in the fashion world. If the international and largely European-dominated fashion industry could include me, then sisters were beautiful! Our spectrum of hues is not a disadvantage; instead, it's a powerful advantage.

Professionally, I felt a great sense of responsibility. I stopped doing Virginia Slims cigarette campaigns and liquor ads when I realized what they were doing to our community, even though they were a huge source of income for me. I became aware that I had a piece to contribute to the larger puzzle.

I also began to demand equal treatment. I can remember doing the same modeling jobs for the same number of days and for the same number of pictures, and yet white supermodels got more money. I gathered momentum, determined to make sure that *whatever they got, I would get as well!* I was quiet until I had enough power to open my mouth. I knew that if I could demand it—and get it—other black models would be treated fairly, too.

Currently, we're seeing the fashion industry take a few steps backward in regards to hiring black models. Bethann Hardison, the celebrated agent and industry activist, has been challenging the fashion industry. Over the years, black models have brought additional readership and revenue to mainstream magazines, and now it seems the magazines just want to take the money and run. But we're not going to let them. We're going to stand up and say, "You're doing it again, and we're not going to stand for it!"

It's a different story, but it's still the same story. Even in today's climate—with our systemic progress and the presidency of Barack Obama—bigots, racists, and prejudices still exist. We have to continue to bring awareness and tolerance to those attitudes.

As I look at the future of black women in fashion (and as a whole), it's really about taking control of our own lives and empowering ourselves. We must never be afraid to speak up or demand better treatment. We have to continue creating our own businesses, brands, and media, and continue to educate ourselves. In this way, we don't have to go to any outside source for acceptance.

I see African-American women continuing to create an original picture of who we are. More importantly, we have to be able to look at ourselves in the mirror—not with criticism or comparison, but with appreciation. Sisters, we are the standard of beauty. We just are.

—**Beverly Johnson**

Beverly Johnson is a supermodel, actress, businesswoman, and philanthropist. The first African-American model to grace the cover of Vogue *magazine, Johnson's success forever changed the idea of beauty in the fashion world and opened the door for other black models to work in the industry.*

♦ Chapter 55

To Thine Own Self, Be True

I HAIL FROM THE COUNTRY; THOSE ARE MY BEGINNINGS. WHEN I was born in 1940, my hometown of Louisburg, North Carolina, had roughly 2,000 residents. It was a small town, but we did have a post office, movie theater, grocery and drug store, as well as a city hall. Like many Southern cities, it was segregated, so we lived on the Negro, or "colored," side of town, where there was no electricity or running water. Most people used kerosene lamps that had to be lit with a match. Today, they are collectors' items, but it was our way of life. Of course, we also had an outhouse and a well from which we'd pump water into a bucket and bring it into the house. Without the convenience of a washing machine, my mother used a washing board to keep our clothes clean, and we took our baths in a big tin tub. Today, it seems like a rudimentary way of life, but I never once felt deprived. To me, we had everything we needed.

My parents met in Baltimore, where my dad was playing professional baseball for the Baltimore Black Sox, one of several Negro League teams at the time. My mother was an attractive woman by European standards, with a petite frame, fair black skin, and long, dark hair. (In many ways, I'm virtually her twin.) My father, a graduate of Johnson C. Smith University, was a teacher. He had a strict policy that my mother would never work outside the home in any white people's kitchens (which was customary at the time), so she was a stay-at-home mom who reared me, their only child.

There was always family around. My paternal grandparents lived up the street, and an aunt and many cousins lived nearby as well. I remember such a sense of community amongst all of us blacks—and a hedge of protection. Although Jim Crow was in full swing during this time, my father kept me sheltered from it as much as he could. I understood I was a victim of segregation and racism, but I didn't always feel its sting.

Fortunately, I was raised in an entrepreneurial family, and everyone had a side hustle. In the summertime, my father grew cotton and tobacco in the back of the property that we owned. Of course, I helped pick the cotton and wrap the tobacco. I went with him to the cotton mill and the tobacco market, where he sold his goods. During the tobacco auction, my dad pointed out which kinds were used for cigar wrappers, which were used inside cigarettes, and so on.

We also had a corner convenience store, where we sold canned goods, fruit, cheese, ice cream, pop, and other sundries. My aunt, who became a teacher after graduating from Shaw University, also owned a beauty shop. Even though my mother was a housewife, she sewed dresses and clothes for people in the neighborhood and worked in the convenience store from time to time. This type of self-reliance made an indelible mark on my own future.

Act I: Branching Out

Obtaining a college degree was something I always knew I would achieve, but I also knew that I had the potential for more. As a child, I did well in school, skipped the second grade, and graduated from high school early. While my father was pursuing his master's degree at North Carolina College (which eventually became North Carolina Central University), I went with him to his classes each Saturday. I'd walk around the campus and pretend I was a student, visiting the college canteen to buy soda pop and talk to the boys and going to the library while Daddy was in class. I had become a pro at my typing course in school, so I typed his thesis. My aunt was pursuing a master's at Shaw University, so I tagged along with her, too. So when I enrolled at Central at age sixteen, I majored in business education because I felt confident it was a career path in which I could excel.

Leaving Louisburg was something I was looking forward to. I wanted bigger and better things. I wanted to lead a sophisticated life and experience more of the unsheltered world. Oh, and did I! Luckily, I got to Central right before the sit-ins began. The original sit-ins first occurred at North Carolina A&T State University, which was practically right next door to Durham—about 40 miles away in Greensboro. The very next day, as a new and very inexperienced freshman, I participated in a sit-in at the Durham Woolworth's with other students from Central. Of course, we all got arrested, but we didn't get booked. They just moved us back to the campus. If my parents had known, they would've immediately brought me back home. I definitely had an angel on my shoulder. But this was small potatoes in comparison to what was ahead.

My sophomore year, I took a momentary leave of my senses when I met my first husband, Donald Burke. He was a college basketball player. The "ooh, I'm free" mind-set of the day—and the heady feeling of being out from under the strict supervision of my father—went a bit too far! I dropped out of school, got married, got pregnant, and moved to Monongahela, Pennsylvania. We lived in a house on a hill, and there I had our daughter, Elizabeth. I had moved away from everything familiar to me, away from my own family. I know my parents were disappointed in me, and so was I.

Yet in some ways, I was doing what was expected of me. In those times, a girl was encouraged to go to college, find a husband, marry him, and let him take care of her. Compared with the other girls I had gone to high school with, I had already gone pretty far. There were twenty-five girls who had started elementary school with me; by the time I graduated from high school, only three of us remained. The rest had gotten pregnant and dropped out.

The angel on my shoulder appeared, and her small voice said, "Girl, what are you doing? You had so much potential! Have you lost your mind?" I probably had! But one thing I've learned is that your right mind always returns. I knew I wasn't meant to be stuck in that place, not developing myself—which had always been my goal. I decided that I needed to go back to school to finish my course of study, so I could make something of my life.

I called my mom and dad. They retrieved me and my daughter, and I reenrolled in college and obtained a scholarship and assistantship. My parents sacrificed their time and money by renting a house in Durham for the four of us. My mother watched Beth while I attended school. I finished my bachelor's degree at Central and stayed on to obtain an MBA. My parents would eventually move back to Louisburg with Beth during this time, but I was confident I had successfully gotten back on track and was on the road to making things better for my daughter and myself.

Act II: Meeting Maynard

Meeting Maynard Jackson is something I'll never forget. He was obtaining his law degree at Central while I was pursuing my MBA. We had a mutual friend, Ralph Frazier, whose wife was a sorority sister of mine. He mentioned me to Maynard, and he was interested. So one day, Maynard showed up at my apartment while Ralph and his wife were there. When I answered the knock at the door, I found a big guy in a bulky sweater who immediately said, "Is Ralph Frazier here?" As if he were actually looking for Ralph! What really got me was the tone of his voice—resonant, clear, and confident.

I offered him a drink. He replied, "I'd like some Hennessy cognac." Well, I'd barely heard of cognac, much less Hennessy, but it just so happened that on a recent flight, I'd picked up a little bottle of Hennessy cognac. Always looking for ways to improve myself, I'd also purchased a couple of brandy glasses at the dime store. Offering Maynard Hennessy in a brandy snifter impressed the hell out of him; he later told me that he'd gone straight home and said to his mother, "I met a black woman who actually knows what cognac is!" He thought I was a real lady of the world.

I could see that Maynard was going somewhere and had ambitions. That was extremely important to me. I had goals, so I had to be with someone who had them, too. It was meant to be, I guess. After we both graduated, we moved to Atlanta and got married.

Once we were in Atlanta, Maynard's friend Vernon Jordan helped me land a job at Clark Atlanta University as the secretary to the president. Eventually, I moved on to Economic Opportunity Atlanta. I started out as an administrative assistant, but I moved up quickly and later became its director of planning. After passing the Georgia bar, Maynard took positions with the National Labor Relations Board and the Emory Legal Services Center. His dream was to start his own law firm and become a successful trial attorney.

Acclimating to Atlanta was not hard for me. Atlanta was still segregated back then, and it had not yet become the metropolis that it is today. The black community was as small and tight as the ones I had become accustomed to in Louisburg and Durham. Plus, white people did not intimidate me. I know that's a bold statement to make because of the times, but I had figured out that black people were as smart and capable as we collectively thought white people were. Having worked in predominantly white business settings, I already had experience reporting to people who were less talented than I was. I had a lot of business savvy, and I was technically proficient, well-read, and well-spoken. In short, I was an asset no matter where I landed. That was a happy time for us—I pursued my professional goals and Maynard accomplished his. We were truly a team.

Act III: Hello, I'm "Mrs. Mayor"

Nineteen-sixty-eight was the year that many things in our world changed for the worse or the better, depending upon your point of view. My own experience was no different. Our first child, Brooke, was born right around the time Martin Luther King, Jr., was assassinated. I was in the hospital delivering her on the day King was buried.

Prior to leaving for an extended visit to North Carolina to introduce Brooke to our respective families, Maynard had decided to become more involved with the community. He considered running for the House of Representatives, but during our family visit, he decided starting his own law firm was more important. After he returned to Atlanta, he told his supporters that he didn't want to run. Days later, Robert Kennedy was assassinated. I believe those back-to-back deaths forever changed the trajectory of Maynard's life. He felt a call to serve as a catalyst for social change, and not just an agent of the law.

So he quit his job, borrowed some start-up money, and ran against Herman Talmadge for the U.S. Senate. I thought he had lost his mind! I was still on maternity leave. We had recently bought a house. We had two children to support. All I could think about was how we were going to make ends meet. Again, my mother and father stepped up to the plate. My mother returned to Atlanta with me so I could go back to work, allowing Maynard to run for office full-time.

Of course, this isn't what I wanted, but you have to do what you have to do for your family. I'll admit that I went back to work with a chip on my shoulder because I hadn't planned to be the sole supporter for our family. But eventually, I got caught up in the momentum of his campaign. Although he lost, he carried the city of Atlanta by such a wide margin that it was obvious to everyone he had a future in politics. Subsequently, he ran for vice mayor of Atlanta (and won) and simultaneously opened a law firm in downtown Atlanta—Jackson, Patterson, and Parks. Overnight, I became a political widow. I had no idea what lay in store for me.

Even though Maynard's vice-mayor role was a part-time job, in the eyes of black folk, he *was* the mayor! He was still quite busy running his law firm at the same time. He was never at home, and people were pulling him in so many directions. I used to say that if you want a housewife, you have to be a househusband! Most of the time he was home, he was asleep.

I had our second child, Maynard, Jr., in 1971, and after that I stayed home, playing the wife of a politician and lawyer. Soon after, Maynard was elected mayor. Any outing we had was related to politics, which left no time to enjoy "couple things." We were getting national attention, but that didn't impress me. What did impress me was what I could see, touch, feel, and smell. I couldn't see, touch, feel, and smell Maynard. I had become the first black first lady of a major Southern city, and my husband simply wasn't there.

Of course, transforming into a politician's wife wasn't easy for me. It was a role with too much scrutiny and not enough leadership. No other black woman had done this. It was right at the time of the white woman's revolution. I call it the white woman's revolution, because black women never had that kind of revolution. We were free to cook in somebody's kitchen, but we were not free to be president of Coca-Cola. No matter what our aspirations were, we were always treated worse.

At the same time, it affected my reference point in Atlanta, as white female organizations began to seek me out. How could I represent white women and black women in that role at the same time? They didn't necessarily go together. I just kept saying, "I don't want to be Mrs. Mayor." I wanted to be Maynard's wife, Bunnie Jackson, but I didn't want to be Mrs. Mayor.

Unfortunately, political wives weren't a part of their husbands' administrations in those days. There were no beautification or good-will projects for you to take on. You were supposed to go to Women's League luncheons or pour tea with some ladies' groups while remaining totally in the background—nothing more than a smiling face for a photo op. I wasn't prepared to be in the background of Maynard's career; I wanted *my own* career. I was too young to recognize that I could remain in the background for five years and then come out during the next five! That never occurred to me, because I wanted to get out *right then*. I wanted more than what the role of first lady of Atlanta offered. In my mind, it wasn't my status—it was Maynard's.

I understand that some people might find this ludicrous. There I was, with a mayor for a husband who's well-known, respected, and brings home a more-than-decent salary. We lived in a nice home, we received countless invitations to important events, and we were known throughout the city, state, and country. Why wasn't I satisfied? There was no dream for me in there. There was no dream with my name on it. My spirit wasn't being nurtured. I wasn't accomplishing any of the goals I had set for myself.

When Maynard met me, I was a *Cosmopolitan*-reading working mother and an MBA student. While I loved being a wife and a mother to my children, I needed to explore my talents outside the home as well. Being the mayor's wife at that time was more about celebrity than actual work. I needed to fill my time with something meaningful, which is what I should've been doing all along. Looking back, we probably should've found some role for me in his administration—some community project or initiative to take on. But there simply was no precedent for it.

I did hang in there for his first mayoral run, which had the fever pitch of Barack Obama's successful presidential campaign. By this time, I had started my own business, and we both knew the writing was on the wall. We had grown apart. He had grown into his political career—the law firm was now going forward without him—and

I was still waiting to come into my own. I realized I couldn't do it as his wife. There was no end in sight to the back-burner experiences I was going through as virtually a single mom and a partner in name only. Our divorce was amicable. I don't think I was evil about it—I was never cruel or jaded, and I didn't leave the marriage hating men. I simply needed to be in a marriage where my ambitions could be just as important as my husband's. I understood that you couldn't have everything at the same time, but not having my dream at all was simply not an option. I knew I'd always be Maynard Jackson's ex-wife, and I could live with that.

Act IV: The Name Is "Bunnie Jackson"

I started firstClass, a company that provided guided tours around the city of Atlanta, with a few friends—Anne Allison, Billye Aaron, and Linda Gulley. Our neighborhood was already a tour site for visitors, and I was impressed by one group of white women who were doing city tours on a volunteer basis. I figured we could do it better and turn a profit at the same time. I operated as the client developer, and the other ladies guided the tours.

After we started doing the tours, I began to see another area we could naturally grow into—event planning. For example, the Southern Conference of Black Mayors (currently the National Conference of Black Mayors) was coming to Atlanta, and I figured, *if I'm doing the tour for them, I might as well plan the gala banquet.* The tour business and event planning led us into convention planning. After that, people we knew through our many connections in the city started asking, "Can you get me in the news?" With that, we evolved into a public-relations company as well. It wasn't a discipline taught in schools at that time, but I got to learn it on the job.

From that point on, we were very busy doing tours, events, and conventions, and PR contracts from major corporations, such as McDonald's and the Coca-Cola Company, started rolling in. From there, I began to branch out to handling PR for entertainment clients, such as Yusef Lateef, Donald Byrd, Peabo Bryson, and Brick. We also represented record companies and managed movie premieres held in Atlanta.

After a few years of experience handling publicity for celebrities, I moved into music business management with the S.O.S. Band. After the band's successful hit record, "Take Your Time (Do It Right)" and a few more million-sellers, I had the opportunity to meet Larry Blackmon from Cameo. Larry and I worked together for seven years after I took over management of Atlanta Artist Productions and Atlanta Artists Records. We had a stream of world tours, successful albums, and hit records, including "She's Strange," "Candy," and "Word Up." I found time to teach a course in music business management at Georgia State University for about four years; the university had been looking for a black music business manager with a graduate degree, and needless to say, I fit the bill. To top it all off, WSB-TV started a locally produced music TV show, *The Dance Show*, and hired me to book talent.

Things begin to blur around this time, but I did make time to start another business: BJT, Inc., a game room at the Atlanta Airport. Tollie Hartsfield (the former wife of ex-Atlanta mayor William B. Hartsfield), Janis Alexander Perkins, and I put our heads together to bid on a subcontract with Dobbs-Paschals, and we won the bid. We had the market cornered on pinball, Pac-Man, Donkey Kong—you name it—at the airport. We were a sight to see emptying out those money tubs from the machines and pushing carts full of bags of quarters through the airport.

Eventually, the go-go lifestyle of artist management wore me to a frazzle. I had no personal life, and I only saw my children on the weekends. I had a housekeeper holding everything together (my mother had passed by that time). I had also married Ray Ransom, a writer, producer, and performer with the band Brick, and had my fourth child, Rae Yvonne. Just like my second marriage, my third one suffered because of my work schedule—which inevitably led to my third divorce. Why? Because I'd done the same thing to Ray that Maynard had done to me—I was never home. So I closed the artist management division and settled back into the PR phase of firstClass full time.

Maynard and I had become friends, and once he sent a client my way that proved to be very lucrative. The client wanted to advertise on bus shelters in Atlanta. I didn't think I could do much with it, but

I stuck it out. Once they could no longer afford to pay me, they gave me stock in the company.

We put together a bid on a contract with MARTA, the rapid transit company of Atlanta. Sam M. Cassell, the man Maynard had run against for mayor, was the sitting chairman of the marketing committee at MARTA. I called him up—since he certainly remembered Bunnie Jackson—and asked about the possibilities of creating bus shelters as vehicles for advertising. He told me, "Well, this is a timely conversation. We're just about to put a proposal on the market." My team and I wrote the proposal and won the bid.

However, we didn't realize that part of the deal was securing rights from the city to put "furniture" on the streets. We were forced to get the city to introduce legislation to pass a referendum to allow us to do so; next, we had to obtain permission from the U.S. government and the state of Georgia to place the shelters on federal and state highways. It took us a year to implement the bid we had won from MARTA, and through all this work, nobody was paying anybody anything. In return for keeping things going, I negotiated myself a 25 percent stake in the company. After all, if they didn't get those rights, they'd have no shelters to put up, and the end goal was to sell advertising on the shelters. I finally got the plan through the city council, and it was signed nearly two years into the contract. I ended up with a $6 million company on my hands.

Act V: The Legacy

As I look back on my life, there are lessons I hope my children and grandchildren—granddaughters, especially—will learn from. Reputation is very important, as are impressions, and you only get one chance to make a first one. Whatever it is that you do consistently is how people will perceive you. I hope they understand that in order to succeed, you must work hard—get up early in the morning and go to bed late. You can't get tired and take a nap right in the middle of things!

Most importantly, my girls must learn that they must take care of themselves. I don't want them to grow up mad at men. I want them to love men, but they must be careful when selecting a mate. I don't want them to ever cop out and say, "I'm going to marry this man and let him take care of me." They could end up marrying a man that they'll have to take care of. Your mate is not promised to you. Death, divorce, or even a job may potentially remove him from your life. I want my children and grandchildren to understand that hard work will get them where they want to go.

Last, I don't want them to settle for anything less than their own dream. "I'll become a nurse, but I really want to become a doctor." Go ahead and become that doctor. You can always circle back around and become a nurse later on. You have to believe in yourself and really believe in your own potential! Listen to, and obey, that small voice in your head—the one that only speaks when you're quiet or when you find yourself at a crossroads. That voice is your internal navigational system, which talks you into being right where you should be, helping you take paths and make decisions that will help you become the greatest version of you.

My small voice is always with me. She always has been. Now, instead of guiding me, she and I walk together.

—**Bunnie Jackson-Ransom**

Bunnie Jackson-Ransom is president, CEO, and owner of first-Class, Inc. She has a diverse business background, extensive administrative experience and organizational know-how, and a dedicated commitment to community involvement. A former first lady of the city of Atlanta, Jackson-Ransom is a member of the National Council of Negro Women, the Atlanta Association of Black Journalists, the board of directors of the Atlanta NAACP, the National Association of Media Women, The Links, Inc., the Atlanta Business League, and Delta Sigma Theta Sorority. She is a past president of the Metropolitan Atlanta Coalition of 100 Black Women and past chairperson of the Georgia Human Relations Commission.

♦ Chapter 56

Better than Equal: Love, Community, and Struggle Forged this Manhood

THE DEFINING MOMENTS OF OUR LIVES ARE OFTEN FOUND IN the challenges of love, community, and struggle. Each shapes our life in a unique way that causes us to respond more vigorously than we'd otherwise be inclined to do.

As I was born in the mid-twentieth century, I was shaped by race, as was most everybody born before 1970. Anyone born between 1954 and 1968 is considered a "civil rights baby" who grew up during the height of the Civil Rights Movement. However, those born from 1975 to the present came of age in what is now being defined as the post–Civil Rights Era. The volatile Civil Rights (social change) and Black Power (pro-black radical) Movements framed conflict as a basis for eradicating the politics of accommodation that allowed "separate but equal" de jure segregation to foster racial inequality. The passivity of the post–Civil Rights Era has reintroduced the politics of accommodation. A new notion of "color blindness" has begun to dismiss race as the basis for the continuing social and economic disparities that exist between blacks and whites.

White children can grow up in America without race ever becoming a salient issue in their childhood. There is no such luxury for black children. Black parents have to have conversations about race with their children early and often. It's the best way for them to protect their children from the realities of the world—the principle reality of which has been being at the bottom of the race caste system in America. For black children, it's not *if* race is going to become a salient issue—it's *when* race will become a salient issue.

For me, it was September 15, 1963, the day my mother tried to explain to my sister and me why someone would blow up four little girls attending Sunday school at church in Alabama. We lived in Brooklyn, New York; I didn't even know where Alabama was, or what it represented. We didn't live in the South, but racism and racial assaults were a reality everywhere, so my mother, with tears in her eyes, had to explain to us why this was important—and how it related to us—before we saw it on television.

The defining moment, however, was in the summer of 1964, when I faced my "race initiation." For black children, race initiation is the very first time they are called a nigger. My family was in the process of relocating from New York to California, and somewhere around Texas, a white family got on the train and sat across the aisle from us. Immediately, a young white boy about my age shouted, "Look, Grandma, there's some niggers." The woman shushed the child, but my mother had that irritated "mother-look," the one she usually lasered at her children—only this time, it wasn't directed at us. She was staring at the boy's grandmother, who just matter-of-factly stared back, as if to say, "Well, you *are* niggers." My mother remained irritated for the rest of the trip, but the white boy and I played together in the aisle. Somehow, I knew better than to ask my mother about it at the time. It wasn't until some days later, after we'd arrived in California, that I finally asked my mother, "What's a nigger?"

It wasn't until a few years later that I really understood how deeply ingrained race is in the American fabric. I still remember exactly what I was doing when I heard that Martin Luther King, Jr., had been assassinated. The sadness and anger was unlike anything I'd ever seen or felt before. Yes, I'd seen riots in New York and Watts. Even though I was only eleven years old, I understood that King's murder was something bigger than an assault on a single person. It was an assault on the ambitions of a community and of a people. Everybody in my family, on my block, and in my community talked about it, in a deep and highly sensitive way.

At this point, I understood the impact of social advocacy and the importance of helping others. Like many others of that period, I understood the consequences of fighting power structures, and how a commitment to social change could endanger your life. A persistent fear that black leaders who speak up will be killed still paralyzes black people and black advocacy now, forty years later.

In her anger, my mother pulled us all together and said, "I don't want you all to try to be equal with white people if they would allow something like this to happen to a man like Dr. King. I want you all to be *better* than this. I want you to be *better than equal.*" In the midst of her hurt, she made an impression on me that not only *could* I be better than white people, but I *had* to be better than my white counterparts, just to be considered equal.

The moment I went to college, I realized that being involved and helping others were important parts of my life mission. I joined a fraternity, Masonic groups, and social causes. I always had to be involved in something, and I had to be vocal about it. In the mid-1980s, I joined the local NAACP chapter, and within a few years I had become the youngest president in the branch's history.

The issues were many, but the most volatile were economic subjugation and police abuse. Attacking corporate discriminators and corrupt cops brought a lot of attention to the branch and to me. Suddenly, I found myself being accused of wrongdoing for things unrelated to my advocacy—incidents from years gone by. True or not, the campaign was designed to derail my advocacy. It ended in a four-month jail sentence that most thought was unwarranted and unjustified, and history has proved me right.

The experience of being prosecuted, however, strengthened my resolve to become a truth-teller about injustice. I became a writer and teacher, writing a nationally syndicated column for seventeen years, becoming a college professor, hosting monthly public-affairs forums for the past ten years, and writing books that articulate this new "color-blind" racism of the post–Civil Rights Era.

All of the injustices I called out in the 1980s came to light during the Los Angeles riots of 1992. The federal intervention we called for in the 1980s came about in the 1990s, as scandal enveloped the Los Angeles Police Department (the scandal continued throughout the early 2000s, and today, reform continues under the enforcement of a federal consent decree). Economic subjugation is still an issue, as capital and business opportunities continue to marginalize the black community in nearly every city in America.

History has vindicated me for taking the stands I took twenty years ago. It was important that my community re-embraced me as it has, but it was even more important that I never let fear about what happens to black leaders who speak out stop me. I continued my advocacy in a way that helped my community address continuing racial disparities. My mother once told me, "What doesn't kill me, makes me stronger." My advocacy today is much stronger and more sophisticated than it's ever been. My success has come from learning life's lessons, being true to myself, and advocating for justice and equality for my people.

My biggest struggle, as is the case for most black men, has been in finding love. Finding love is hard for black men, particularly in a society with a high animus against them. Black men are the only segment of American society who can experience the entire life cycle without being loved, living every day of their lives despised and re-jected on multiple levels—work, school, social interfaces, and most notably, in love.

The struggles of life and love are intertwined, as we often don't find happiness when we find love. The more passionate we are about the things we love, the happier (more successful) we tend to be. This is also true with my own love relationships throughout my life. I never knew real love until I was in my thirties. My father never told me he loved me until I was thirty-three years old. I married the love of my life—my second wife—when I was thirty-five.

While I've always loved my children—most were born during my twenties—it wasn't until I was in my thirties that I learned to appreciate them for their own personalities, not just because they were of my own loins. I really didn't feel comfortable about who and what I was until I was thirty-five. It was then that I realized I couldn't care less what other people thought, and that I could never truly love anybody until I fully loved and accepted myself for who I was. Then I could let folk love me for who I was—both the good and the bad. Moreover, I could overcome the desire to be loved that every black man has—not just on an individual level, but on a societal level. Love is what love does, and for me, like many men, that's ever evolving.

Love without passion is okay. And passion without love is just great sex, but in terms of a lifelong relationship, it's not likely to happen. We often call those things "flings." Black male/female relationships are troublesome largely because the expectations are so great—in some instances, even unreasonable. As a result, these expectations tend to go unfulfilled.

The constant pursuit of trying to find Mr. or Mrs. Right comes with a long checklist of physical, financial, and emotional conditions that translate to a well-financed, luxury-car-driving, CEO husband or a sophisticated professional woman who turns into a closet "freak" trophy wife at sundown. We so often get caught up in what society tells us we should have in a mate that we forget what we really want, and what we know is good for us. Society tells us what we should look for in a mate—what he or she should look like, how we should position ourselves to find him or her, and where we can find him or her.

And so we go looking for love in all the wrong places—looking for excitement and passion in the most unlikely places (as the song lyric suggests, "I'm in love with a stripper!"). Inevitably, we come away empty or find ourselves in flawed relationships that we knew from the start weren't going to work. I've certainly had my share of those, including one that led to marriage right out of college. It ended in the late 1980s with a promise never to do it again, but of course, I did it again. The "Exhale" movement of the 1990s was not just for women. Just like women, men hold their breath, waiting for the right one. Men wade through herds of imperfect women looking for the perfect one. The search for a "soul mate" becomes the objective of every woman and man alike, and as we grow, it is about more than just looks.

My soul mate didn't come gift-wrapped, with a big bow and my name inscribed on a tag. The soul-mate complex suggests that there is a connection waiting out there with someone who is perfect for you. It has nothing to do with what they do, what they have, or what they can do for you. You connect, but you don't know why. That's how it happened to me.

My soul mate knew I was the one, and she waited for me to realize that she was the one. I never thought she saw me as the one. I wasn't exactly the catch of the year. I was a self-employed, high-profile community leader in the middle of a very public scandal. I had been recently divorced and was seeking custody of my three small children. Not exactly a "bachelor-of-the-year" profile. Everyone said we were opposites, and that it would never last. We disagreed, given that we were both passionate about family, community, and doing something that is bigger than ourselves. She is Christian, and I am Muslim, and everybody said we were crazy because we were "unevenly yoked." We told them that all we saw in each other was a fellow believer in God, and we trusted that. Then there was marriage.

Forever is a long time, we both acknowledged, but said we'd take our relationship one day at a time. Nineteen years later (sixteen years of which we've spent married, with both great and not-so-great times), we still marvel at how we think alike and how tuned in we are to each other's moods and thoughts. We raised our children together (I finally secured custody of my kids for the last eight years of their childhoods, the hardest teenage years) and put all of them in or through college. Today, we're raising our fifteen-year-old and living out our dreams.

I found the right one, and she found me. It's still a struggle—because life is a struggle—but we've proved that love and passion in the midst of struggle are possible. The lessons I learned growing up became the lessons that guided my interactions with my children. I told my children that I loved them every day of their lives, so they understand my love for them was never in doubt. Today, we end every conversation, phone call, or visit with, "I love you."

My efforts to combat injustice and to educate the uninformed and misinformed are based on a courage derived from faith, and not by fear. Once you've been in the belly of the beast and come back in your right mind, only to achieve greater accomplishments than ever before, you understand God is real only when you have unwavering faith. The fears of the past are not the fears of the future, and you know (as I know) that it is the permissive and preventive will of God that protects us every moment of the day. Nothing happens without God's permission. What God permits, nobody can prevent, and what God prevents, nobody can permit. What you don't have is because God doesn't want you to have it. What has happened to you is because God permitted it. That's how God teaches, molds, and refines us into the tools of success He needs to change the world.

When we learn, we become wise and successful, and we grow. When we don't learn, we struggle until we do learn. If we never learn, we always struggle—sometimes forever, meaning all our lives as individuals, or for generations, as a community. There are some lessons I've learned quite well, and there are others I still struggle with. I've learned a lot, and my success, praise God, is reflective of the wisdom I've obtained from my life experiences—the most significant of which center on love, community, and struggles for justice.

—**Anthony Asadullah Samad, PhD**

Anthony Asadullah Samad, PhD is an award-winning columnist and the author of the three books, including his latest, Saving the Race: Empowerment through Wisdom *(Kabili Press, 2007). His writings can be viewed at www.AnthonySamad.com.*

♦ Chapter 57

What Happens in the Dark

Y MOTHER'S FIRST NAME IS NORMA. HER MIDDLE NAME IS Dolores. That's most of what you need to know about how I became a bona fide cinephile. She was named after my grandfather's favorite actress, Norma Shearer, a slightly cross-eyed blond best known as the lead actress in the MGM film *The Women*. Dolores was my grandmother's choice, in honor of Dolores del Rio, a raven-haired beauty from Mexico who was more of a star than an actress.

Interesting choices, given that my grandparents were working-class Afro-Caribbean Panamanians, but movies were where they went to escape, and in the 1930s that's what lead actresses looked like in the films that made it to their little town of Colon. Norma, in turn, named me after Michele Morgan, a French actress whose biggest Hollywood film, *Passage to Marseilles*, costarred Humphrey Bogart. A few years later, thanks to the Beatles' monster hit, everyone thought I'd been named after a song, but no. In my family, it was always about the movies.

Picking names is one thing, but when I was four and living in Chicago, my parents divorced, and movies became my thing with my mom. We'd go to the theater a lot, but for me the best times were the Sunday afternoons we spent at home watching black-and-white classics from her childhood on television, with the curtains closed and the lights off. I became enchanted by all sorts of odd things— Myrna Loy's Christmas-morning fur coat in *The Thin Man*, Maureen O'Hara trying to mask her brogue in *Miracle on 34ᵗʰ Street*, the male camaraderie of films like *Beau Geste* and *The Three Musketeers*. Oddest of all, I developed an affection for my mother's old crushes—Clark Gable, Errol Flynn, Bogie, Montgomery Clift, and James Dean. It wasn't a pretty day when, at age eleven, I realized that most of my male ideals were dead.

That was also about the time that I noticed these movies didn't have anyone in them who looked like me. I'm pretty sure that it was Willie Best in *The Ghost Breakers* who made me notice. He was always with Bob Hope, but not quite his equal. It's a portrayal that others came to see as demeaning, but I don't think I ever did. Maybe it was because Bob Hope was so bumbling and inept himself. It was as though Best had just chosen a different comic shading. Intellectually, I understood that some characters were exceptionally derogatory, but truth be told, they were usually poorly written characters in inferior films that held no charm on any level.

Nothing interrupted my love of classic Hollywood film. Not my super seventies feminism, and not my black pride. I didn't look for them to be relevant to my daily life. I understood that they were a fantasy confection from a time and place not my own, as outdated as women in white gloves, men who tipped their hats, and married couples in twin beds.

I didn't realize my approach was postracial right away, but once I got an inkling, I reveled in my highly evolved perceptions. And then I got all medieval with it. A cute little blond (and since she wasn't Mary J. Blige, that means white) who I worked with came in one day bemoaning the fact that she'd tuned in to *Gone with the Wind* the night before, but had missed the first hour and a half.

"Does anyone know how it started?"

I jumped in. The highlights of my synopsis were as follows: On a massive plantation called Tara, Scarlett O'Hara's a spoiled little rich girl who is obsessed with Ashley Wilkes. The only person who can put her in check is Mammy (name self-explanatory). War breaks out, and all of the men sign up to defend the Confederacy. Ashley immediately proposes to his beloved cousin Melanie (*hello, cousin*). Scarlett marries the nearest warm body. The men head off to war. Scarlett's husband dies. Melanie is pregnant. Rhett Butler, scalawag profiteer, steps in to woo Scarlett. Scarlett is cool to him, still obsessed with Ashley, but Mammy loves Rhett. Atlanta burns. Melanie goes into labor. Prissy, a slave with a high-pitched voice who had previously bragged about her midwife skills reveals, "I don't know nothin' 'bout birthin' babies!" Scarlett slaps the taste out of her mouth and sends her off to get the doctor. Prissy heads down the street, taking her sweet time, raking a stick along a white picket fence, and humming a tune—clearly in no hurry to deliver a baby she'll have to take care of.

At that point, I realized that my coworkers were staring at me. "Whoa," said one, "I haven't seen the movie in a while, but I don't remember it like that."

I thought about it for a minute. "Yeah, maybe not, but that's just because you didn't see it through these eyes. Trust me, that story is in there."

It's my little thing. Revisionist thinking. No, it's purer than that. Revisionist viewing. Take *Casablanca*. Quite simply one of the greatest Hollywood films ever, it features Sam, a strong black character written as well as any other in the story—no doubt. As played by Dooley Wilson, he's one of the few American actors in the film other than Humphrey Bogart, so he took on an additional significance for wartime audiences. I salute that. But it always leaves me a bit miffed.

Rather than focusing on the movie's main story—Humphrey Bogart's Rick nobly returning Ingrid Bergman to her anti-Nazi hero husband and starting a beautiful friendship with Claude Rains—I worry for Sam. This brother from Texas followed Rick to Paris, and then Morocco, hammering out tunes just to suit Rick's mood. But come the end of the film, Sam's stuck in North Africa with Sydney Greenstreet (who is clearly a falafel away from a heart attack) while Rick is off with his new pal, a Vichy captain with fluid morals. That just plain violates the rules of bromance. But it's also an awesome character study that shows one man's journey to be his better self. Maybe Rick had studied Marcus Garvey and was giving Sam his free trip back to Africa. There. That's better.

I love new movies, too. I love blaxploitation. I love foreign film. Just being in a theater sets my heart a-twitter. But there's something about the old films my mother shared with me. And to a little black girl who became a black woman, it's somehow appropriate that my favorites that are in black-and-white. They're like looking at snapshots of history through gossamer. Images that let you extract, project, and distill. They're shorthand references for both our reality and our dreams.

So what about continuing the family tradition of child-naming? As an adult, I moved to Hollywood, the movie capital of the world, but my firstborn is named Joseph, after a family friend who was a member of Roosevelt's Black Cabinet (an Ivy League–educated lawyer, the closest the original Joseph ever got to Hollywood was attending Cornell with Franchot Tone).

But before you give me too much credit for being a deep thinker, I'd like to introduce you to my younger son. When he was four, the little guy crawled into bed with me once as I watched Ethel Waters and Eddie "Rochester" Anderson in *Cabin in the Sky*. He fell asleep before the film ended, and I didn't think much of it beyond the sweetness of the moment. But two nights later, he came in as I watched yet another black-and-white film. He took one look at the TV and asked, "Are Joe and Petunia (the main characters' names in *Cabin in the Sky*) in this, too?" I had to bite my lip, I was so proud. Since then, I've never been prouder for having named him Sammy. Surely you've seen Mr. Davis's performance in the original *Ocean's Eleven*, or *Robin and the Seven Hoods*?

You can take the family out of Panama, but not, apparently, out of the movies.

—**Michele Edwards**

Michele Edwards is a journalist and interior decorator. She resides in Los Angeles with her husband and two sons.

♦ Chapter 58

Part-Time Thuggin':
Redefining a Generation by
Discarding the Thug Swagger

I wonder if heaven got a ghetto for thug niggas, a street
life, and a spot for drug dealers.

—From Tupac Shakur's "If I Die 2Nite"

ONCE, WHEN I WAS STILL DETERMINED TO GIVE PROPS TO the pool-hall hustlers who raised me on crack-crazed corners in east Oakland in the 1980s, I decided to call my first volume of poetry *Notes from Behind the 8-Ball: Poetic Verses from an Intellectual Thug*.

It seemed at the time to be the only appropriate way to truly capture the dualities that nourished me from wide-eyed toddler to man-child B-boy. But after a lengthy self-evaluation that included seeing so many dead "thugs" on the news and in my own hood, I saw the fallacy in my thinking. I questioned whether I should hold on to the false notion that I could simultaneously act as a warrior for black babies and still be a part-time thug. The light clicked on in my head one day: as much as thugging was in my bloodstream, shrugging it aside was, too.

That is the greatest lesson I take from the tragic shooting death of my brother, Gemini soul mate, and fallen comrade, Tupac Amaru Shakur. I must for the duration of my life follow my gut when defining the real nigga outline of my soul. Life is too short to let others do it for me.

Perhaps that is the saddest part about Tupac's death—he refused to follow his instinct. He remarked that this instinct had repeatedly told him to let "thug life" go. I wish he had shaken it off, so Tupac the actor, poet, and budding black nationalist could have taken over. I can't playa-hate him though. I've done it a million times myself—tried to live up to other folks' expectations and definitions of how I should be and act.

Tupac the man was one of the clearest snapshots I have ever seen of my own wayward generation. At times, the black twenty-something crowd can be fearless, just like him, and at other times it can be utterly inane and self destructive, just like him.

My first knowledge of Tupac was from his early days, when he rapped with another MC named Ray Luv in the Bay Area. But it was in college that I really discovered him. Although I went to college and Tupac went to the streets, we still shared a common frame of mind: always be down with the thugging, but pray and work toward peace. We both had grown up in intense and often violent, crack-addicted homes. We both fled to our creative passion—words—to escape ghetto drama. It was as if Tupac had tapped into me, like the still-open veins that dope fiends were always searching for.

His first album, *2Pacalypse Now*, still ranks as a classic hip-hop ghetto anthem in my head. The beats were wack, but his talent shined through with his uncanny ability to capture the realness of the 'hood's mix of hope and desperation. This was when his lyrics were about something more than death, sipping Cristal champagne, and toking weed.

He sported African beads, rhymed about unconditional home-boy love, and pointed fingers at my own teenage nemesis, the Oakland Police Department. There is a distinct anger Tupac and I developed during our teenage years in the Bay area, where even when you tried to be conscious and down for a peaceful struggle, the police seemed to have it out for a young nigga.

It probably stems from the long-standing history of bad relations between black people and police in the Black Area, especially in that overlooked blue-collar city by the Bay. The Black Panthers had many run-ins with the infamous Oakland Police Department, which my uncles always told me was just the latest chapter in the divided racial saga of our city. I imagined Tupac being inspired by the same environment, it providing ink for his pen and inspiration for his alcohol-induced rap flows.

Every time I heard *2Pacalypse Now*, which touched on themes of black male insecurity and even teenage pregnancy, it reminded me of my own internal battle to stay on the so-called righteous path. I always told my boys that I was just a few steps from a jail record like Tupac. With all my scuffles and excessive drinking, I was always just a few minutes away from letting the anger from my own childhood explode. But the eventual difference between Tupac and me was not just the fame, but also that I simply refused to let the anger take over. Now I know there are other channels for my fury. The fire inside had to be contained, used at the right time, and aimed at the real enemies.

I've finally realized that "keeping it real" is being true to black progress and not embracing thug behavior. Shooting at other brothers and calling women bitches is not an accurate portrayal of the person I am, or want to be. Why are some brothers afraid to stand up and say thugging is wrong in any form? Why can't we expand and then redefine what a real nigga should be? Why do black folks alienate themselves from ways or things they think are somehow un-black?

Since I have jammed on many late nights to the amped-up sound of the group Nirvana and know the lyrics of some Duran Duran songs, am I less of a real nigga? Am I less down with black "upliftment" if I think thug life is backwards? Even Tupac frequently mentioned his love for the writing of Shakespeare and his appreciation for other styles of music.

Maybe Tupac couldn't heed his own call for self-liberation. Near the beginning of the song "If I Die 2Nite," an announcer says: "A coward dies a thousand deaths, a soldier dies but once." When I die, I want motherfuckers to say P-Frank represented what we really need—a Black Nationalist who loved having fun and getting busy, but respected himself and his people.

Living like a soldier for black people means making sure you are in a position to help the cause. Atlanta rap group G.O.O.D.I.E. Mob had it right when they said, "See to me, a G is a person who understands the plan/Can't do nothing in the hands of the Man." Tupac couldn't do anything for us when he was locked up for nine months in an upstate New York jail cell. There should be no cool points given to cats who are on lockdown. Obviously, brothers and sisters who are victims of police frame-ups are different, but any person who truly believes that jail is inevitable is *wrong*. Any nigga bragging on jail—like a few of my own homeboys have done—are wrong, and like thousands of other brothers in jail, they only hurt their families. Dead men, especially dead thugs, do little for us except provide memories of when they were here on Earth. As my homegirl said days after Tupac's death, "Everybody knows that thugs either end up in jail or dead."

To say I did not shed tears for Tupac would be a lie. In fact, I cry often when I realize how many of us are being wasted, every day, all over the country. For weeks after Tupac died, I played the song "So Many Tears" until the CD got scratched and I had to buy a new one. It only proved that after four years of writing stories about slain gang members (mainly black and Latino males), I too wanted to drown my sorrows in sacks of green cannabis or use bottles of Seagram's gin to numb the pain.

It's easy to try to define ourselves in the Big-Willie dreams of Lexus cars and Armani clothes. All those videos showing brothers with guns tucked in their jackets and sisters dancing around in tight vinyl pants make us think that in order to be "the man," you have to perpetrate like a studio gangster and be down with some light-weight thugging to be real. *That shit ain't true.* As music critic Nelson George says, "A studio gangster can't out-rhyme a bullet." A true soldier knows separating himself from the traffic of negativity is more difficult, and yet more valuable to his race and himself, than shouting, "Fuck the world!"

I now have a distaste for thugs. It's not that I'm now a young conservative, or saying that some curse words are out of place, or insisting that hardcore rap is futile. I'm just tired of thugs fucking up my groove at parties, just when I was about to get a number.

I am not there yet. My mid-twenties find me in constant change, but sooner than later, the thug in me will be gone forever. I wish it could happen for every nigga I know, but unfortunately there is still too much willingness among brothers to think that identifying with the criminal—the thug—is what we are supposed to do.

Perhaps it sounds juvenile or stupid, but I often wonder if Tupac went to heaven or hell. Growing up, my elders were always putting that bug in my ear: "Boy, you going to hell if you keep getting into trouble," my grandmother would say.

And if there is a heaven, we should set ourselves up for a proper landing by our actions here on Earth. That means being true to yourself, no matter what the crowd says. I'm not the best of role models, having spent many nights getting bent off alcohol, searching for car keys, and talking shit. But there was a point when I realized that all the posing and trying to live up to the definition the media has carved out for us as out-of-control, angry black men is pointless.

Turn off that television and radio, African boy. You ain't no thug, and I ain't one either. And if I'm not mistaken, *real* bad boys move in silence. We can identify with the thug's pain, but we don't have to be the hard rock to be seen as a real man. 'Pac was so wrapped up in all his outlawesque behavior, pushing brothers in crowds and spitting at the cameras—OK, I secretly dug that shit—that he couldn't let "thug life" go. That "don't-give-a-fuck" attitude most thugs have is what paralyzed Tupac. And his need to live the life of the "Black Scarface" is what ultimately killed him. I hope that is not the legacy of his valuable life, and of this generation of young black men.

We need a few more full-time black men and a lot less part-time thugs. For the brothers who are still here, there's plenty of time to escape the trap of internalizing anything close to a thug mentality. Free your mind from all the drama, and peep at the bigger picture. If you don't, you'll be wondering, like Tupac did, if God has a space reserved for you.

Rest in peace, Tupac Amaru Shakur. We praise your passion. But thug life deserves to die.

—P. Frank Williams

P. Frank Williams is a journalist, television writer, and producer. He won an Emmy for his work on the 2004 Summer Olympics.

Chapter 59

Monica, Katrina, & Michelle:
The Journey to Obama

The truth is incontrovertible.
Malice may attack it.
Ignorance may deride it.
But in the end, there it is.

—Winston Churchill

THE LAST TWO DECADES OF AMERICAN LIFE CAN BE BOILED down to three words: Monica. Katrina. Michelle.

Every American knows the names. We know what they represent. Within this triptych of monikers, lies the legacies—both past and present—of presidents Clinton, Bush, and Obama. Each woman's name represents another battle in the war to win the hearts and minds of Americans—Americans who have increasingly shifted toward a new collective morality and a history-busting mandate to put a black man in the White House.

Our moral compass began to shift en masse in the midst of a scandal so scandalous one could hardly believe it was true. The leader of the free world cheated on the First Lady in the revered Oval Office with a White House intern and then denied the liaison until physical proof was produced—in the form of that pitiful blue dress.

America, Meet Monica

One would think Monica would have been a source of national embarrassment, as she sauntered around our water coolers in all her voluptuous glory, shapely with spectacle and buxom with gall. But President Clinton's job approval ratings didn't budge. In fact, they rose! His smugness thickened, and it's still lathered on his every word to this day.

At the height of Monica's powers, the country's self-appointed moral watchdogs saw her as their way of bringing liberalism down. Wiretap after subpoena after hearing quickly followed—all designed by Republican conservatives to whip up America's outrage and tip the scales. But despite their undeniable prowess in getting elected, Republicans have repeatedly failed to keep America locked inside an old episode of *Ozzie & Harriet*. Rather than the revulsion they hoped to generate, they instead created a monster called Political Entertainment—a new-school version of political theater with less back room intrigue and more general consumer salaciousness.

Yep, in the 1990s, it was becoming quite clear that counterculture was the new mainstream. Things that were once hidden away in the closet became a national pastime, à la *Jerry Springer* and the *National Enquirer*. The trust we once placed in our president was beginning to dissipate, and we barely noticed as it started to disappear, for more deeply rooted than our thirst for spectacle was a clear identification with Clinton's shortcomings. I mean, we all have our own Monica lurking somewhere, right? Some past example of bad judgment just waiting to emerge with a blue dress? In short, America empathized.

Polls conducted during 1998 and early 1999 showed that only around one-third of Americans wanted Clinton impeached or convicted. Completely out of touch with the will of the people, Republicans pressed on in their witch hunt. Clinton was impeached in December 1998 on charges of perjury, obstruction of justice, and abuse of power. Votes fell strictly along party lines, with not one vote for conviction coming from fellow Democrats. He was acquitted two months later by the Senate and remained in office until 2001.

It has been said that the sexual politics around Monica played into America's "isms"—notions of uncontrollable sexuality levied against African Americans, labels of perversion aimed at the gay community, and accusations of promiscuity toward women who follow their passions. All of these groups are labeled as outsiders by conservatism, and they took advantage of the opportunity to rally together as part of a new-jack morality that became integral to the American ideology of the late nineties. Monica brought in a new political dawn, one colored by a great grappling with our own issues of personal responsibility. At least for a while, we shunned blame and repression.

But somewhere within Monica's saga and Clinton's mastery of this new touchy-feely America, the new morality crystallized even further. It took a couple of years for us to connect the dots and gain an understanding that moral open-mindedness need not be anchored to acts of frivolity and ego. We could be forward thinking and resolve our own inner Monicas without lying and cheating to do so, as Clinton had. We could be free *and* high-minded, liberal *and* responsible.

So, just one year after Monica, the majority of Americans changed their tune and declared that they supported the impeachment and disapproved of the acquittal that allowed Clinton to serve out his term. We decided we were all for personal liberation, but not at the expense of our new morality. Monica taught us that, and in doing so, she left the door open for another woman to walk through.

In the wake of the Clinton scandal, the 2000 presidential election understandably centered more squarely on issues of "moral character" and "honesty." Postelection data found that the most significant reason people voted for George W. Bush was for—try not to laugh too hard here—his high moral standards. After the unspeakable horror of 9/11, Bush had the sympathy of the world and the full support of the American people. He cashed in his cultural currency, betting on WMDs and launching two wars in the name of our new grand morality. A bitter, bruised America went along with it. It would take a complete and total breakdown of Bush's so-called morals to shake us from our slumber and cement the public's indictment. Hell hath no fury like a woman scorned.

America, Meet Katrina

If Monica made us face our personal inadequacies, Katrina made us own up to our collective limitations. She blew into our lives with the forces of race and class at her back. She pulled aside the curtain on the illusion that society can reward the wealthy with disproportionate tax cuts while skimping on basic public safeguards, and that all the treasures trickle down. News alert: It doesn't quite work that way.

The collapse of this key tenet of Bush's beliefs was broadcast live and in living color for the world to see. Suddenly, America angrily called into question not only Bush's handling of the hurricane, but his policies overall. More importantly, it called into question the trust we placed in him. Katrina laid bare any reasonable belief in Bush's competence and revealed the hard fact that America had saddled itself with a leader more concerned with an ideological agenda than real-world choices to help real people.

Katrina demanded that we take a long, cold look at ourselves and our leadership. For whatever systemic racism and everyday prejudices "mainstream" Americans held about their darker brethren, white folks were horrified to see dead bodies of black people floating in the streets of New Orleans. They found it unacceptable that black grandmothers and grandchildren were left in the sweltering heat without food or aid. We all heard the national gasp of horror when thousands of displaced citizens were shuttled into the hellhole that was the Superdome.

In 2005, at the beginning of a new century, it was becoming quite clear that "mainstream" America was beginning to admit it had a race problem—and a president problem. As we all know, the first step in recovery is claiming your illness. Things once left in the closet were now the topic of serious discussions both in the press and around the kitchen table. The trust we once placed in our president was deteriorating rapidly, and this time, we noticed. More deeply rooted than our avoidance of real debate about race was a clear identification with those unfortunate souls in the Lower Ninth Ward. I mean, we all have a grandmother we'd give our left arm for, right? A loved one who we'd rather see dead than degraded in the streets, while our president vacationed and palled around with "Brownie," who was doing a "heckuva job"? In short, America woke up.

Polls have steadily tracked Bush's decline in favorability since 9/11. Americans endured eight years of inept leadership, including his war of choice in Iraq, his lies about WMDs, his endorsement of torture, his failure to capture bin Laden, and his piss-poor responses to Katrina and the financial disaster heard 'round the world. In 2008, his last year in office, he earned the worst Gallup quarterly approval rating of any president since 1945: a blistering 27 percent. Katrina became the impetus for this national about-face on Bush. She exposed a systemic effort to distort the will of the people—white, black and otherwise—in the interest of the powerful, privileged few. She allowed us to fully understand the abuse of power and betrayal of trust that we ignored with Monica.

Senator John Kerry, who was defeated by Bush in 2004 only through trickery, put it best:

> Katrina is the background of a new picture we must paint of America. For five years, our nation's leaders have painted a picture of America where ignoring the poor has no consequences, where every criticism is rendered unpatriotic. And if you say "War on Terror" enough times, Katrina never happens. Well, Katrina did happen, and it washed away that coat of paint and revealed the true canvas of America with all its imperfections. Now, we must stop this Administration from again whitewashing the true state of our challenges. We have to paint our own picture—an honest picture with all the optimism we deserve—one that gives people a vision where no one is excluded or ignored. Where leaders are honest about the challenges we face as a nation, and never reserve compassion only for disasters.

America did step up. In one fell swoop, Katrina exposed the contradictions and revealed Bush to be one of the most divisive presidents in our nation's history. Our broken trust birthed a new appetite of rebuilding both New Orleans and the whole nation as well. The public made the concentrated choice it had failed to make with Monica by shifting from the personal invective of "every man for himself" to a belief in a shared endeavor. "What's in it for me" became "What's in it for *us*?"—at least for a while. Katrina sharpened the rallying call, bringing the wars, health care, energy dependence, national security, the environment, and education into focus through the prism of a newer, more inclusive morality. It allowed us to usher in what would become one of our greatest national moments.

America, Meet Michelle

Let's get the scenario in order. A junior African-American senator captures the Democratic nomination after a long campaign against a former president's wife. Next, he goes on to handily win three debates against a war hero and dominate all national polls before claiming a commanding victory to become the leader of the free world.

This story would be astonishing in its audacity and seeming implausibility if it weren't true. As Winston Churchill once said, "The truth is incontrovertible. Malice may attack it, and ignorance may deride it, but in the end, there it is."

Despite the Clintons, McCain, Palin, Wright, Ayers—hell, even despite Joe the friggin' Plumber and all the malice and ignorance, the truth is incontrovertible. Barack Obama is the 44th president of the United States of America. There it is.

In an interview with *60 Minutes* days after his historic win, President-elect Obama offered this nugget to America: "I want to make sure that I can recreate a bond of trust between the presidency and the public that, I think, has been lost." With his eye-popping approval rating, Obama seems poised to do just that.

On November 10, 2008, the most famous dress to grace the White House was no longer Monica's blue travesty, it was the deep red shift worn by Michelle as she toured her new home. Damn being demure! We bringin' power to the people! The sight of Mr. Obama and his wife striding up the White House steps was a transformative image to behold. Even more than the unforgettable Grant Park moment when he declared victory to an adoring, blubbering throng of believers (including me), the first White House visit and the boldness of the future First Lady said it all. This stellar sister and her husband brought a breath of fresh air to the hallowed halls of the world's most famous residence—and to the rusty old game of politics. In one visit, Michelle supplanted the cartoons of Monica, Katrina, and their representative presidencies, ripe with mishandled trust and low morals. In one photo op, she and Barack infused the image of the White House with pride, panache, and polish again. They are a pair to be admired, to be trusted, and, well, um, to be black! Let the church say Amen!

Yep, in 2008, the fact that our new favorite son is black makes perfect sense when you follow the path the American public has traveled, surviving both Monica and Katrina during the past sixteen years. I heard someone say that they'd never seen so many Americans crying together in happiness as they did on the night of Election Day 2008. In the past decade, Americans have huddled together in moments of demoralization and tragedy—9/11 and Katrina leap to mind. They were moments when we huddled together in our anguish, outrage, and pain. But on November 4, 2008, at 11:00 p.m. EST, when the networks announced "Obama elected president," we huddled together in a collective wave of joy. It was a mighty first in the difficult and tragic union that is America. This first ushered in a 20/20 hindsight of our blunders and failings. Election Day was a new day and an even newer morality for America, one in which a collective enlightenment sprang forth from the ashes of untrustworthy leaders, ego-driven embarrassments, racial division, and an overall ambivalence about the American dream.

According to Gallup polls, liberals and moderates tipped the scales for Obama at 88 percent and 72 percent favorability after the election, respectively. These robust majorities proclaim that they have a positive outlook for Barack Obama's presidency, as would be expected. However, close to half of political conservatives—45 percent—also say he will make a good president. That's far greater than the 23 percent who voted for him in the election—radical information! The same folks who wanted to keep America in *Leave It to Beaver*-land, who resisted affirmative action and gay rights, and who tried to block the progression of our nation's civil-rights legislation—these people are now leaning toward the most liberal president in United States history. Oh, and he's black! Astonishing. We have Monica and Katrina to thank for it.

The fact that President Obama inherits a financial system near collapse, a federal deficit that boggles the mind, two wars, and a violent enemy who remains at large after more than seven years doesn't change the fact that he is turning a page for the nation. This page must be turned. He is turning a page for the black community, too. Our story must be retooled and retold, this time, by *us*.

Luckily, our first black president is a black man who knows who he is and, more importantly, who knows who *we* are. Michelle is the magnificent symbol of his self-knowledge. Let's not take for granted that we could have had a very different black man in this position. How would we have felt if Colin Powell or Clarence Thomas were the first black president? Just as proud? I don't think so. If we wanted to be represented by anyone, it was and is by someone like Obama. If we wanted our story retooled and retold by anyone, it would be someone who knows who we are as a people.

Both FDR and Reagan came into office when America was in economic emergency mode. Each went on to reframe the nation in his own image. President Obama now has the rare opportunity, strengthened by a vocal public mandate, to do the same. Imagine that. America shaped in the image of a black man, with a black woman by his side. Michelle is the steady bow of the Obama ship, one that, it seems, all of America (and the world) hopes will steer us to the Promised Land. A ship that will restore our standing in the world and our self-image at home. It is breathtaking that the new leader of the free world, the most powerful man in the world, is a black man. That he goes home to a tight-knit, loving family headed by a black woman is soul-stirring.

Michelle's "real black womanness" isn't lost upon anyone, black, white, or otherwise. There are no blurred lines when it comes to her lips, hips, and hair. Her swagger is all sister, all the time. I don't mean the nonsensical, fabricated cartoon of a black woman's swagger: gum-popping, neck-twisting, and switching. No, I mean the real swagger of a black woman: solid, strategic, strong.

How will the world react, now that the myth of blackness is being transformed by a beautiful black family in the White House? What do we do, now that the trustworthiness of the president is being reestablished by a black man? How do we act, now that the myth of inferior black intellect is destroyed and the notion of nonexistent black discipline is obliterated?

Should we function as the same characters in a new story? We can't. We must change. Whether it's a revolution, an evolution, or just getting our house in order, when President Obama said in his victory speech, "Change has come to America," he meant us, too. If he is remaking America, how are you remaking yourself? Your family? What will be your story? Our story? The story that walks out before us into this nation and around the world. Most importantly, it will be the story that is reflected back in our own mirrors.

We must add a new name to the litany of monikers that will represent this country. No more Monica. No more Katrina. Choose the name of a woman who has changed your life and changed your mind: a woman who represents the best of you. Let's list her after Michelle and begin a new name game, one in which everyone wins.

We're blessed to be living and breathing and loving and hoping in this time. These are glorious days. These are the days that will be immortalized in history books for hundreds of years to come. These are the greatest days of our collective life. We are alive to drink of the sweet nectar of these days. We are here!

The truth is incontrovertible, if we make it so. We are here! And there it is.

—Ava DuVernay

Ava DuVernay is president/founder of DVA Media + Marketing, the parent company to DVAPR, Urban Thought Collective, UrbanEye, and Urban Beauty Collective. Through DVA, DuVernay reaches millions of urban consumers each month on behalf of high-profile clients at Paramount, Warner Brothers, Fox, ABC, HBO, the CW, and Showtime, to name a few. She is also an award-winning filmmaker, having directed and produced the feature documentary This Is the Life *and Showtime's* Saturday Night Life *under her Forward Movement banner.*

♦ Chapter 60

Just Who I Am

"HELLO," I WHISPERED, SMILING AT MY CLASSMATES AS they stared back in silence.

"Ehh, em, hi," I said, a bit louder this time, attempting to get their mouths to engage in the same way their eyes clearly had.

"Uhhh, hellooooooo," I eagerly repeated, shifting in my seat in hopes that I'd elicit a response from at least one of them.

"What did you put in your hair?" inquired a coffee-complexioned boy sitting to my right who stared at my curly mane.

"Uhh, water," I replied, admittedly bewildered by the question.

"I like his eyes," the chocolate-skinned girl whispered to her friend.

"Yes, *bonito*," the friend responded in a thick Latin accent, smiling directly at me all the while.

As the teacher called our ninth-grade class to attention, I sat there wondering what all of this was about. *Is it because I'm quiet that they ask so many questions?* I wondered to myself, trying to make sense of this odd encounter with my new classmates. Deep down, I knew whatever answer I came up with would never sufficiently address what would remain a lingering series of questions that would always be a part of my life: "What are you?"

My answer? "Just who I am."

I'm impressed by the rich detail of the mélange that makes up our diverse African Diaspora. But I'm still aware that where I fit into that mélange is often misunderstood by many. I've been referred to as "Yellow Boy" (my nickname in high school) and "Cornbread" (my nickname since moving to the Midwest). I am keen to take inventory of what we, as people, notice about each other before we ever ask for a name.

Having grown up in northern California and having lived in Atlanta, Boston, Los Angeles, and now St. Louis, I'm accustomed to getting folks up to speed about the who, the what, and the why of my appearance. When I would let my curly 'do grow out, my black female coworkers would often comment, "You know, we sistas would kill for hair like that." Looking to avoid a clichéd response, I often smiled and said, "You've already got me beat, sista." On several occasions during my massage-therapy training sessions, several of my older white female clients would bluntly ask, "So, what are you?" Clearly, they weren't asking if I was a Republican or a Democrat. I respectfully responded, "I am black," and smiled, confident that some didn't believe me. Such directness endears me to seniors. If all people were that honest, we might have a more effective dialogue on matters of race, color, and ethnicity in this country.

Still, as a child growing up in the California cities of Richmond and Oakland, I never thought that my definition of "black" might be different from that of others in my community. With the assorted ancestry that makes up my family, I never understood why people thought my mother's rich brown hue didn't quite go with my twin sister's tawny coating. I am virtually identical to my father, and having taken his very British name, I often ignored the shared African, Irish, and Spanish Creole roots (along with the rumored Hawaiian and Native-American flavors) that make up my family's diverse heritage. Sure, I'd seen pictures of my grandparents, great-grandparents, aunts, and uncles sitting on our mantle like ambassadors at a United Nations meeting. But it never dawned on me that these people made my family unique in some way. My later experiences would teach me that.

In my younger days, these experiences took the form of schoolyard scuffles with brothas afflicted with the I'm-not-going-to-let-some-pretty-boy-take-my-girlfriend-away syndrome. That was my introduction to hater-ade. In junior high school, my experience with white friends and their families exposed stereotypes of immense proportion. One time, while visiting a friend, my friend's sister announced my arrival to their mother by stating that I was "the colored Joe," to distinguish me from a white friend with the same name. My fondness for white friends often led me to tuck away a desire to correct their dated vernacular, a practice that launched my period of isolationism.

As a college student, I met more people who had very little exposure to people of color and wanted to "get to know more" about me. I call this my exhibitionism period. I'll never forget the reactions I received sometime later, during a visit to China with a friend who resembled Shaq. The Chinese saw him as black, but I seemed to fall into some "other" category in their eyes. This, in many ways, was my period of exceptionalism.

The last "period" of my experience seems to have inspired my most strident feelings about how we, as people of African descent, relate to others and each other. My many academic, professional, and personal successes in life, paired with my light skin, seem to have led many people to classify me as an "exception" to some established black rule. This is not to say I'm not proud or deserving of my success, but that's not the point here. It's more of a quiet experience—the same one that led my extremely light-skinned great-grandmother of Creole descent to reject her own granddaughter, in part because she was a "darky." She didn't come around until that same granddaughter showed up on her doorstep with my sister and me in tow. She fawned over us only after confirming with her own eyes that we could, in fact, pass the proverbial "brown-paper-bag test."

That assessment eerily foreshadowed future life experiences. My sister and I were often picked to lead our preschool class in reading exercises, and we inspired people to marvel over how wonderful we were without ever actually doing anything. We (and others "like" us) were touted as future successes before any serious assessment of ability was performed. That unspoken reality was nurtured by relatives, teachers, and peers, and then later reinforced by professors and the opposite sex. In the working world, it continued with employers and prominent leaders. It's the muscle memory that develops in knowing what "rewards" are expected to come your way for nothing more than being born with light skin, curly hair, and light eyes. Those features make many people feel more comfortable and safe. It's what my girlfriend calls the "peaceful brother" factor. *You're an exception ... you're different from the other black guys.*

Don't get me wrong. I'm not condemning those who championed my sister and me while we were growing up, nor am I repudiating the efforts of guidance counselors, selection committees, and bosses who identified something special in me. They all helped me get where I am today. I also don't want to give the impression that I, and people like me, haven't worked incredibly hard, sacrificed much to achieve, and rightly earned our places in the world. Indeed, I can personally attest to triumphing over outright prejudice, rejection, and fury from all different types of people (including ones who didn't believe I should be where I was). In truth, finding success in this world is difficult without having a degree in what I call "ethnic realism." It behooves us all to understand this as we maneuver life's turbulent waters.

Still, this "safe-ism" element still hurts in many ways. It hurts because the harder I work to achieve based on my ability, the more I become one of ten at the good schools, one of five at the top companies, or one of two who've been promoted. Thus, by statistical default, I become "an exception." Although I deny trading on this currency of the color complex, I admit that my successes in the space of the failures of many qualified brothers at times leave me feeling like the proxy for these presumptuous conclusions that exceptionalism breeds.

I love my ancestry, my family, and my life, yet I am often frustrated by the different things it represents to different people. This is part of my challenge in this life. I don't shrink from it. I acknowledge it and hope that when people meet me, they see beyond what is in front of them. I challenge them to get to know who is in front of them. With effort, we all will discover that we're more alike than different. I accept my experiences and the misunderstandings that accompany them, for they are woven into the fabric of my life and have shaped how I fit into the diverse patchwork tapestry of the African-American experience. I have no choice, really. It's just who I am.

—Joseph R. Whitfield

Joseph R. Whitfield is currently a second-year law student at Washington University in St. Louis, Missouri. Prior to law school, he worked in information technology and business development at two of the nation's largest health care companies.

◆ Chapter 61

Staying True to Your Dreams

I NEVER COULD GET AWAY FROM BECOMING AN ACTRESS. IT WAS in my soul and my dreams, and I could not escape it.

I grew up in Camden, New Jersey. My childhood was nothing like the American dream depicted in Hollywood, with its white picket fences, Sunday-morning church services, and charming neighbors. Between the ages of thirteen and twenty-six, I lost several friends to crime. They were beautiful black men who were imprisoned or murdered, or who overdosed on drugs. I was hopeless at that point in my life, too. I dated drug dealers and did my share of dealing, too.

Back then, I didn't believe I would live past a certain age. I felt so hopeless that I could not even envision a future. I thought of college as unaffordable and therefore a pipe dream, so I just gave up and dropped out of school. Somehow, there came a turning point, and I realized that my particular lifestyle was destructive to myself and to my community. Several people entered my life who helped me make the changes I needed to turn my life in a more positive direction. They told me to not be ashamed of my background. In fact, they encouraged me to embrace it and benefit from the wisdom gained by my experiences.

My road to recovery has been a long and challenging one, but I am grateful for the journey. I now know that my childhood experiences gave me a lot of texture and help me live my life today. My personal history has also informed my craft as an actor, affording me a level of skill to achieve success in my profession. Despite my background, I now know that a person can achieve his or her dreams through perseverance and determination. These ideals have been the backbone to my success.

American society has affected the way we African Americans think of ourselves, and thus our actions. If we do not see ourselves as beautiful and successful people, we will forever remain in a downward state of being. The crime, violence, and drugs in our community come from hopelessness. When people do not believe they have any other opportunity in life, they can succumb to failure.

We need an empowerment revival in our community. We need a motivational revival in our community. We need to go in to our schools, and churches and motivate, empower, and inspire the people in our community to see their lives in a different way. I feel education is the number one way to find opportunities. With an education comes the ability to know how to handle a bank account, invest money, and become an entrepreneur. If we can put a focus on education within our community, the rest will follow.

We live in a time where black people are achieving feats we only dreamed of just a generation ago. I think of myself as part of that movement, and I am committed to doing my part to make a difference. Hollywood has a voice that is heard around the world. So as someone who is now a member of that community, I make it a point to speak out on issues that matter to me. An actor's voice is more powerful than people give credit, so we must use our voices to empower others and change their lives for the better.

I am dedicated to using my success to show other black people that all things are possible if you love yourself and believe in God. I am a living example, with my brown skin, big booty, and hair weave. I now know that I have a place to share my uniqueness in this world. I know that we are all part of God's creation, and there is a place for everyone in this world.

—Tasha Smith

Tasha Smith is an accomplished actress, producer, and drama coach with credits on the stage, TV, and screen.

◆ Chapter 62

History Informs Who I Am, or How I Narrowly Escaped Backslapping

Excerpt from the one-woman show For You, *written by Iona Morris to honor the life of her father, Greg Morris, a star of the hit television series of the '60s and '70s* Mission: Impossible. *Greg Morris was one of the first blacks to have a regular role in a hit dramatic television series.*

IONA, AS HER FATHER, GREG, SPEAKS TO THE AUDIENCE: "NOW, I don't know what a father's supposed to do, but I know what I'm gonna to do, and that is make sure my kids know who they are and where they come from. They may live in Beverly Hills, but I'm not raising any spoiled kids. Oh, no, no, no. They will know the contributions that black people have made to this country. That's why I've got them doing book reports on some black biographies due in three weeks, and they will have the poems "Desiderata" and "Myself" memorized by the end of the summer and be able to discuss their content. And be able to tell me about many of the accomplishments black people have made to this world. Isn't that right, Iona?"

Iona: "And I better have an answer ..."

As I waited in the New York recording studio my agent had told me was one of the most highly respected, established, and "old-boy-network" kind of places, I wondered why everyone was walking around me busying themselves with whatever task was at hand and not speaking to me, smiling at me, or acknowledging me in any regard. This was one of my first voice-over jobs in New York, and I was oh-so-green. Nervous and excited, young and tender, 'cause here I was in the Big Apple! I'd done lots of voiceover work in Los Angeles, but I was in New York! Booking jobs and taking names! Oooo! It was such an exciting time.

As always, I arrived five minutes early. I stood by a large, L-shaped wooden desk in the wide-open lobby, the very heart of the studio.

Four or five doors led off from the lobby into recording rooms, and I stood there, waiting for someone to ask me if I needed help. Finally, I stopped one of the gray-haired gentlemen who was moving about and gave him my name, the name of the client I was recording for (it was some big gas company—Shell, Texaco, something like that), and the product the advertisement was for. He left to get someone.

Ten minutes past the time the session was supposed to start, I still sat in the waiting room. I could have spoken up again, but I was young and working in New York for the first time, and I didn't want to rush anyone. I was the only black person in this studio, and I seemed to get the feeling that everyone else was aware of it as well. I didn't want to offend anyone by interrupting—after all, the producer *had* to know I was there. I'm the only one in the lobby area. Wouldn't he have gotten concerned and called my agent to find out why his talent was late?

Finally, I stopped another mature white gentleman I'd seen walking past many times, gave him my name, and repeated what session I was there to record. He immediately turned toward a door not far from the lobby—right off it, in fact, within eight or ten paces, a room I'd seen a couple of other men enter. He opened the door, walked in, and disappeared for a few more minutes. *Really, how long does it take to tell a director or producer that the talent is here? And it's already late. Why isn't someone walking out to get me?*

Well, the door opened, and another white gentleman, the producer of the spot, emerged with a questioning look on his face. He gave me a slight smile and extended his hand to greet me. After introducing himself and looking at me with considerable disbelief, he tried hard not to show what was written all over his face: *She* can't *be the Iona Morris I hired after listening to hundreds of audition tapes!*

"Are you feeling like a Windy today?" "Windy" was the name of the character I'd be voicing, a beautiful, young, and blond white woman. After all, that's what he thought he was getting! His eyes narrowed in on mine to detect the smallest lie in my answer to his question.

With all that I am, I wanted to slap him back into next week and curse him for his nasty, condescending tone with a smile. But my parents taught me to be proud of myself. They had me reading books early on about what black people have contributed to this nation. I sat there across from this white man, who was putting me through the Daily Black Test to prove that I am valuable in this framework called the world. His world, which is really only America, has a very limited concept of who black people are. It's not right, they say, to acknowledge the truth and the history of this fantastic people. Talk about a media blitz, a literal "blackout" of valuable historical information!

My ancestors railed up inside me and shouted, "Mister, you don't know who you are messin' with! She knows she comes from kings and queens, doctors, lawyers, teachers, and wise women and men who have died and worked hard for both of you to be able to stand here and enjoy modern comforts. Only through our blood, sweat, and tears! Black people have never only helped or died for themselves. We are a generous, forgiving people, with magnitudes of knowledge and talent you will never grasp!"

Sigh. But I digress. But you see what was going on in my head, yelling out in anger at this man. I sat there with a big smile on my face and calmly responded, in my educated, perfectly pitched, and ethnically clean voice, "Yes. I feel like a Windy today."

As he escorted me into the recording studio and subsequently into the booth, I passed the engineer who was the owner of the facility and the first man I'd talked to. Hmmm. In the booth stood two older white men, with whom I'd be reading the spot. One was playing a car engine, and the other would be the owner of the gas station. Everyone appeared pissed off, assuming that this session was a wash. As the engineer readied to record and asked us all to give levels (that's speaking into the microphone to check your voice, so the recording is even), I could see clearly on their faces and through their body language that I was now reauditioning.

I wanted to scream at them and tell them that their racist, elitist nature was permeating the room. It had a smell from down South, a heat flare-up in an air-conditioned room making my deodorant work overtime, a historic hurt grabbing at my senses. I was holding on for dear life to not backslap all of them while I instinctually remembered my teachings, but these guys were making me work overtime.

The session began. One man spoke into the microphone, and then the other spoke. Then, it was my turn. You could hear a pin drop in the short span of time it took me to speak. As I opened my mouth, the first man looked at his shoes, and the other kept his eyes on the one-sheet script in front of him, glasses down his nose, looking peripherally at this young black girl who was about to ruin his session and start his morning off with a ghetto sound. He was sure.

Even today, twenty years later, tears well up in my eyes as I think about that moment. My throat tightens, and the tears now fall onto my cheeks, my lap. I sniffle at the surprise of how much this event still hurts, how much it attacks my heart. Wow. I had no idea I would be affected this way. I thought I was just recounting a story. But I am once again reminded that we may forgive, but the cells, the spirit, the heart—they never forget.

I do not remember exactly what I said, for the words are not really important, but when I opened my mouth and spoke, the man who'd been looking down and leaning against the side of the studio perked up, and the gentleman who'd been hiding behind his glasses smiled, a small sigh escaping his body. The engineer, who'd had his head in his hands, slyly looked at the producer as if to say, "Wow! She sounds white. You can't tell she's black." The producer's relief was evident, although he tried to remain calm and cool. He praised me about how great I sounded, and he said, "Let's begin."

Air returned to the room, the ease of the morning returned, and a good session was about to be had by all.

At the end of the session, all the men shook my hand, complimented me, and thanked me for a great session. I left that studio at a dead run out into the cool air, needing to breathe in freshness to help clear my mind.

Test. This is the Black Test. The one we all go through every single day of our lives. Now, I had choices of how to respond. I included some of them above, but the way I handled it was in the best interest of the next black person to walk into the presence of any one of those men—to make it a little easier for him or her. Though it was justified, my anger and hurt would not help any situation. It would have only fueled it, especially when people can easily argue that they hadn't said anything to warrant such a response.

You see, others don't care if you're hurt or angry. They only care about getting the job done and meeting their needs. So I say, get your and their needs met, and create a future. Create a different paradigm. Take back control of who you are, and do not lower yourself into the common response that keeps you at the mercy of any one person!

Exhale, baby. Exhale. And breathe.

Having grown up in Hollywood and Beverly Hills and traveled the world, to many places where people had never seen a black person, I was able to handle this. My parents created a multicultural world around us, and we were fortunate to live in opulence from my later years of elementary school all the way until I enrolled in college. But most people do not see my upbringing. They see my color. Every day, I am aware of being black. But I am also aware of being a part of one of the most dynamic people on the planet. The *original people*. A group of people who have given the world Josephine Baker, Marian Anderson, Ralph Bunche, George Washington Carver, Jan E. Matzeliger, Granville T. Woods, Benjamin Banneker, Dr. Charles Drew—do you know who these people are?

I could go on and on! The list of great black people is long and reaches back to the beginning of time. Read your history. Seek it out. You come from a great people! We invented so many things, such as the original clothes dryer, the typewriter, the mop, the guitar, the golf tee, the electric lamp, the telephone system and its apparatus, and so on. Black people secured patents on the chamber commode, the water closet for railway cars, the fire extinguisher, the fire escape ladder, the elevator, the gas mask, an ironing board, a printing machine, the player piano, the refrigeration apparatus, and so on. These were some of the answers my father wanted me to give him during the summer. These were the things I read about, things I had to know about. I was upset about the fact that all of this *learning* was taking time away from *playing*, but this information straightened my back and helped me walk into rooms where my hue was the only thing darker than mayonnaise. But still, the Daily Black Test is part of my world, too.

I have failed, stumbled, and cried, but mostly, I have passed that test with flying colors to help the test giver of the day possibly think a little differently about black people. I want to be an example of how we can negotiate our way through the fire. Since we all know the Test could happen at any time, why be upset and volatile? Just be ready.

Barack Obama's preelection speech about race was the one every black person in this nation had been waiting for. We had been waiting for so long for someone to say out loud every single thing he "preached," and the one thing missing from his speech that I see too often in us was *anger*. What a blessing of an example.

An angry black person is only destructive to himself or herself. Anger just makes the Test-giver feel that he or she was right all along, but an enlightened black person who manipulates life to his or her satisfaction is a gift to everyone. That is what my parents taught me. That is what I experience in our presences, and that is what I pray you will take away from my story.

I also know some folks who just need to be told about themselves.

—**Iona Morris**

Iona Morris is a Los Angeles-based actress with credits on stage, TV, and film.

Chapter 63

A Black Male Teen in America

BEING A YOUNG BLACK MALE IN AMERICA TODAY IS HARD! TO BE young, male, and black, all at the same time, is very challenging. As the saying goes, you have three strikes against you already! Young black teenagers are often looked upon as failures. Without knowing us personally, many people judge us by the way we dress and the music we listen to. For many people, our visages are the first things that come to mind when they hear about a shoot-out or a fight.

Why is that? Why is it that the face of a young black teenage male is all too often flashed across the television when a crime takes place? Some black teenage males may be involved in fights or even shoot-outs, but most are not. Most of us are trying to make something of ourselves and our lives. This is very difficult, because many people make it hard for us. In too many cases, they make snap decisions about us in a short time, without really taking the time to get to know who we really are. We are not all the same. We are just trying to grow from being a teenager into being a young man.

Although it is hard to be a young black male teenager growing into manhood, there is hope! The love and support of a good family keeps us strong as we grow. For example, my family reminds me I must never stop believing in myself, because they will never stop believing in me. They encourage me to keep my dreams strong and develop my personal gifts and talents.

In addition to my family, there are other things that keep me strong. One has been my involvement with a great organization, Inspiration, Motivation, Preparation, Activism, Commitment, Team-work (IMPACT). IMPACT has helped me to use the arts to express who I am, a young black male teenager, and who I am trying to become, a young black man. One of my special gifts is dancing: I l-o-v-e to dance! IMPACT has helped me use dance in a powerful way, making it my second voice. I am able to express my feelings, hopes, and dreams through dance movement.

Life is full of obstacles to overcome for young black boys grow-ing into manhood. However, we *can* reach our goal of becoming strong black men, by walking with our heads held high with pride, pride in who we are and what we can become with the support of those who see us as we really are. We are young black teenage males struggling to become proud young black men.

—**Bernard Harrison**

Bernard Harrison is a sixteen-year-old African-American male growing into manhood. He lives with his family in Queens, New York. As he writes in his essay, being a black teenager is a challenge. However, as a result of the love and support of his family; his church, Deliver-ance Baptist Church; and organizations like IMPACT, he's equipped to face the challenges of each new day. He has been blessed with talent in the realm of dance, and he performs locally at community, social, and church-sponsored events. Through his talent, he is voicing the hopes and dreams of a young black teenage male struggling to become a positive black man in America.

♦ Chapter 64

Comfortable Being Me

I AM THE PRODUCT OF AN AFRICAN-AMERICAN DAD FROM KANSAS City, Kansas, and a white mom from Colorado. My childhood was both socially and relationally uneasy. As a family, we moved a lot, mainly because we were poor. In fact, we moved every year until I reached the ninth grade. We were also trying to keep a safe distance from my father. He was an alcoholic and was abusive toward my mom.

Still, my childhood memories of the time he spent with my sister and me were actually good. I knew he could be violent, but I was never really afraid of him—just guarded whenever he drank. The fact that we moved around so much had a much greater impact on my early life and how I viewed myself than any of our family issues or being black.

I grew up in Denver, which is known for its large number of interracial couples. However, my childhood was largely spent in all-white environments with my mom and her extended family members. So growing up, I was often the only black person in a world that was mostly white.

Denver wasn't without black culture, though. We had a black radio station, a black mayor, black police officers and firefighters, and one predominantly black neighborhood. We were scattered about, and never the majority. In fact, I never thought there were cities in America where this wasn't the norm, because Denver was all that I knew.

When the time came for me to go to college, I had my heart set on studying dance at UCLA. Attending a black college never entered my mind. After I visited UCLA, I found that it was not what I had envisioned. It was too large, and I felt overwhelmed. I thought I wanted to be in Los Angeles, so I decided to give USC a try, instead.

But when I got back to Denver, my African-American history teacher suggested I take a look at Clark Atlanta University, a school I had never heard of. My teacher knew me well, so I took a leap of faith and traveled to Atlanta. After time spent on the yard, surrounded by a sea of black people, I was ready to sign up! Attending Clark Atlanta changed my life tremendously.

Moving to Atlanta to attend an HBCU was a unique experience for me. Other than a summer spent in D.C. studying dance, I had never been around so many black people in my life. In Atlanta, it was an all-day, every day thing, due largely to the school I attended and where I lived. From the mayor of the city to the business owners and professors—everyone in my world was black. Denver had previously elected a black mayor, but our people had limited roles in other areas of business and politics. Atlanta was the closest I ever felt to living in a black world, but it wasn't all bliss.

During this time, there was a lot of national racial unrest. It was after the Rodney King beating (and subsequent acquittal) and during the O.J. Simpson trial. I was a mass communication major, and many of the students hated how the media portrayed these incidents. It was almost as if they believed white people just sat around and talked about ways to oppress black people. It was hard for me, because of my interracial background and the predominantly white environments I was reared in. I knew firsthand that most white people weren't obsessing with a hidden racial agenda. It felt like reverse racism to me, and it fueled my desire to leave the university.

Growing up in Denver, I hadn't been white enough, and at Clark, suddenly I wasn't black enough. Talk about extremes! Had it not been for my mom insisting I stick it out for the year (and promising me that if I still didn't like it, I could transfer to USC), I would've never given this new experience a chance. Over time, I found my social place and voice at Clark and decided to stay. Yet it was economics, not race, that spoke the loudest to me.

I'm an entrepreneur at heart, and that spirit really hit its stride in Atlanta. In college, I started a female valet parking service and did very well. Atlanta is one of the best cities to live in if you are an entrepreneur. I believe black people support black businesses, and they'll give you a chance. Everyone I associated with at school was savvy about business and young, so I really gravitated toward that. When I returned to California to visit USC, it just didn't feel the same. I guess I had grown accustomed to life in Atlanta, so I returned. I'm glad that I did.

———————

My life is very different now. My husband is a native Atlantan, and his background is just the opposite of mine. He's a fourth-generation college graduate, and achievement runs high in his family. Attending college wasn't a question—it was the rule. His grandfather was a doctor and his mother is a mathematician. By contrast, my mom didn't go to college, and neither did her parents, but we can trace our roots back to the Mayflower, the very signature of our ancestry. In fact, I didn't know many college graduates or married couples when I was growing up. In my present social circle, all our friends are married professionals.

I honestly can't be mad at white people who don't interact with black people, because their life doesn't call for it. In our daily lives, my husband and I don't have to interact very much with white people. We live in a black community. We go to a black church. Our doctors are black. Our attorneys are black. Our accountants are black. Most of the restaurants we patronize are black. My husband is a doctor, I own a real estate company, and we largely employ black people. There aren't a lot of white people in our social or professional circles, and it's not because we planned it that way. For example, my dentist is my sister-in-law's neighbor, and we do business with certain people because my husband grew up with them. I don't consciously think about being surrounded by black people. It's simply our way of life.

However, when we do interact with white people, it's very different from what I remember growing up. My mother was a maid, cleaning homes and preparing meals for the wealthy. By nature, we were treated differently by whites because of our humble existence. I share that childhood experience with many blacks, but it has surprised some people because I have a white mother. Race doesn't always transcend economics. A poor, uneducated white woman with two children and a black woman with the same set of circumstances often find themselves in the same boat, searching for an honorable way to raise their families.

As an adult, my interaction with wealthy whites is quite different. My husband is a doctor, I own a successful real estate business, and with our children, we have created a stable family. On the surface, we have more in common due to our financial similarities. Here, social standing, not race, is where we find common ground.

In my life, class has played a far greater defining role than race. My family didn't have a lot when I was growing up, and that might've been fine had I been around white people in the same financial position as we were. Since we were always around rich white people, I was always self-conscious about not having money.

I think some things become racial because of circumstances. For example, when my son attended a predominantly white elementary school—where he was the only black boy in his kindergarten class—I didn't think anything of it. However, when he came home one day and announced, "Mommy, I want to be white," my husband and I took immediate action. It's not an option for our children to be in an environment where they can't be who they already are. Like most parents, I want my children to be surrounded with positive influences. In order for them to develop healthy self-esteem, the people in their lives and the experiences they have should reaffirm who they are. Of course, if we weren't financially able, we wouldn't have had the option of placing our son in another school. This wasn't a choice for me growing up. Clearly, that's a money issue, as much as it is a question of race.

Over the years, I've learned that it's important to know who you are and what you like. Nowadays, I am definitely more black than white, because I enjoy "black" things more than I enjoy "white" things. The key, for me, is not labeling either way right or wrong, but just accepting that they are different. For example, I prefer black churches because I like a lot of singing and soulful music. Simply put, I know what I like, and I go with it.

For me, there's nothing better than having an experience where you are the majority. I think we all need to feel like we belong somewhere. Attending Clark Atlanta and experiencing the city of Atlanta opened my eyes to this realization. The most important thing we can do as black people—as human beings—is to know ourselves, and to explore, understand, and accept our own individual identities. Loving me, Michelle Falconer, has opened the door to all of the blessings that have followed.

—**Michelle Falconer**

A native of Denver, Colorado, Falconer earned degrees in finance and communications from Clark Atlanta University and is an active member of the National Board of Realtors, the Atlanta Board of Realtors, and the Southwest Atlanta Focus Group. She is the owner of Real Estate Investments, which has closed over $75 million in investment properties, and the management company EHMS, which simplifies rental management for over $10 million of current investment properties for its clients. Falconer lives in Atlanta with her husband, Walter Falconer, MD; her sons, Hunter and Bryson; and her daughter, Ryan.

◆ Chapter 65

Black Like Me?

Dedicated to Nina Simone, and to those who refuse to allow others to define them.

I'VE BEEN BLACK ALL MY LIFE, BUT EVEN NOW, AS I APPROACH MY fifty-fifth year on this earth, I do not know what being "black" means. Is it knowing how to do the "Souljah Boy" dance? Or is it the ability to speak in a unique dialect, using phrases like, "He axed me to go to the store with him," or "I stay with Mamie Charles and she stay up on St. Andrews Place"? Does it mean I am destined to be one of those statistics often reported in the news media—a libidinous woman with several children, all of whom have different fathers? Or a controlling, nagging woman who's got more mouth or sass than anyone would ever need? Or living on welfare? Or turning tricks up in Hunt's Point? Does it mean that whenever I become angry, my hands fly to my hips and I start rolling my neck, telling my aggressor to "talk to the hand"?

What does being black actually mean? How do black folks behave? I'm still not so sure, but sometimes it seems as though these soul-bending images and stereotypes continue to abound, despite black folks' achievements in the twentieth and twenty-first centuries.

However, I am very clear that I am, indeed, a member of the racial group called African American. I prefer the term black because it's how this society tends to view me, and how I also view myself. I love my skin color. It is a gift to me from my dark-skinned father, Donald H. McIver, and my paternal grandfather, Charles McIver, Sr., who was also dark-skinned and so regal in his bearing that as a child, I thought he was what God must look like.

I cannot relate to being an African American. I do not know from which region of Africa my ancestors may have originated, and describing myself as an African American, though it has become politically correct to use this phrase, sounds tragically hip and inauthentic to me. I am black, and that's all there is to it. Besides, the term African American is a strain on my tongue.

I believe all that really matters is how I view myself. I tend to think of myself as a universalist, a free-thinker, a person who is a citizen of the world and who is without limits imposed by others or myself. I am comfortable in my own skin. I am interested in many different things that make up this journey we call life and that nurture our humanity. In this respect, I hope and expect that my skin color doesn't become an issue.

I have tried to live my life in defiance of how others might define me. As a result, it's sometimes been difficult, and often lonely. Sometimes, I'm the only black in the room. But I've learned as I've lived that if I allow others to define me, I might as well put on those shackles my enslaved ancestors worked so diligently and with such courageous hopefulness to remove. Allowing others to define me is the best way I can think of to quash my spirit and freedom of being. For me, freedom of self is almost everything. No. No, thank you.

Throughout my life, I have always been aware that I am black. During my nap times as a child, I would marvel at my hands, at how my palm was pinkish with yellow tones while the top side was as dark as one of those oversized Lindt's 70 percent chocolate bars. Because my family lived in what could be described as a fairly homogenous white neighborhood, mostly comprised of Italian, Portuguese, and one or two Puerto Rican families, I had many white girlfriends during my elementary and middle-school years.

I didn't become what I call a "Revolutionary Black" until I reached high school. This happened, it seemed, almost overnight, fueled by serious, injury-causing clashes among my white and black classmates that broke out following the assassination of Dr. Martin Luther King, Jr. During this time, I remember hearing Donny Hathaway's "To Be Young, Gifted, and Black" wafting across the radio often.

Of course, being the Revolutionary Black that I was, the only reason I applied to Cornell University in my junior year was because

I wanted to go to the same school where black students had armed themselves with guns. Before driving me (I had not yet obtained a driver's license) to my interview with a white Cornell alumna, my loving and always cautious father begged me to "tap down" my 'fro. I refused. I was not accepted. By this time, I fully believed Gil Scott-Heron's warning, "The Revolution will not be televised," and I was waiting for it to come, anticipating the day when, my skin color notwithstanding, I could just be who I truly am. For me, the Revolution was deeply personal.

But I was unaware of how hated I was as a black person in the United States until one spring morning, as I rushed to my CBS office in the granite building known in the TV industry as "Black Rock." While crossing Madison Avenue at East 51st Street, a cab driver totally ignored the fact that I was in the middle of the crosswalk and narrowly escaped hitting me. I can still remember the sound of his brakes as they screeched to a halt. I raised my paper-laden briefcase and slammed it down, as hard as I could, on the hood of his yellow vehicle. The sound of leather hitting metal made a loud enough noise to elicit looks all around.

Startled by the sheer brazenness of my response, the white male cab driver immediately jumped out of his vehicle. With his hands balled into fists, he looked as if he was ready to slam either of them into my face. I will never forget his words, nor will I forget how the redness of his rage toward me crept up his neck and into his face: "*You ... Nigger ... Bitch ...* why don't you go back to Africa?"

My mouth dropped—not because he called me a "nigger bitch," but because I had never set foot in Africa. I couldn't imagine going back to a place that wasn't really a part of my personal history in any respect, except possibly historically and within the romance of my sometimes other-worldly imagination.

Go back to Africa? I was dumbfounded. I looked at the cab driver as if he was crazy. I almost started to laugh—but I realized that it might have pissed him off even more. Did this white male cab driver not know that I was a product of a working-class family who had deep roots in the Lower Hudson Valley of Westchester, New York? My parents had lived in the state all of their lives. My paternal grandfather settled in New York as a young man right after the conclusion of World War I, and my maternal grandmother had ventured north from South Carolina at the beginning of the Great Depression. No, I was not from Africa. I wanted to tell him that I was as much an American as he was. Although I cannot speak for other African Americans (there, I said it), it seems to me that "blackness" has always been an issue—sometimes negative and sometimes even positive. It is not a problem for me, but at times it seems to be so for others.

Case in point: I moved to Los Angeles to participate in CBS Entertainment's prestigious Programming Internship Training. I had a battery of interviews to undergo, and the competition was beyond fierce for the highly coveted, prestigious position. I was flown out to Los Angeles for five days of interviews with CBS Entertainment's top brass; there, I found out I was competing against recent MBA and law-school graduates. I should add that I was a secretary at the time, working as the assistant to the East Coast executive in charge of developing movies of the week and miniseries. I was absolutely determined to secure the internship. I had failed several years before, and I channeled all the disappointment I'd felt then to marshal everything I had at my disposal to win the second time around. Failure was not an option.

And win I did. After securing the internship, I spent the following year attending pitch meetings where producers—mainly white males and some white females—would peddle their latest ideas for new series or movies-of-the-week in the hope of making a lucrative sale to the network. I was on the side with power, possibly for the first time in my life, and I relished being involved in developing new ideas for television; after all, I'd grown up during the heyday of television, and I was now working for the Tiffany Network. It was a major achievement for me professionally.

I remember attending one pitch meeting with a group of producers that included the cocreator of the then-hit CBS series *Cagney and Lacey*. After the cursory introductions were made, with gritted teeth all around and a strong sense of "What is she doing here?," one female producer-writer considered by many in the CBS programming department to be a demigoddess looked me in the eyes and said with the utmost earnestness as she clasped my hand, "I want you to know how great it is to see you here." (*Translation*: "Boy, am

I surprised!! I did not expect to see a black woman in this meeting! Imagine that!")

As she released my hand, I took a deep breath and thought, *How fucking dare you?*

I replied, barely concealing my anger, "I don't know what you mean. I made it here because of my credentials, skills, and intellect. Don't get it twisted. It might look as if it was an affirmative action move to you, but I beg to differ."

With tears in her eyes, she immediately got up from the couch and left the room. The remaining white men in the room tried to shed their unease and continued on with the meeting as if nothing had happened.

Needless to say, word got around. The executive ranks at CBS Entertainment were not pleased. I had the unmitigated gall to speak my mind and let this white woman know that my color—at least for me—had nothing to do with my place in the organization. I got there because I was smart, good, passionate, and determined. The color of my skin was, for me at least, an afterthought.

See what I mean? Being black is not an issue for me usually. I am more than my skin color, more than the sum of my parts. I am being completely honest when I say I don't think about it much. What I do think about is being true to who I am, following my bliss (and I'm serious about that), and exploring a world that, as Henry Miller said, is "throbbing" with all kinds of interesting things.

I like to think that the same spirit that resided in Nina Simone, Josephine Baker, and Bricktop also resides in me. Yes, we may be black, but we are also fully human, full of kaleidoscopic shards of brilliant color that create a full picture, a bold and unapologetic painting framed in gilt, of how we see ourselves.

Black like me? Yes, of course I am …

But am I really?

Not.

In the end I am, simply, me.

—**Denise L. McIver**

Denise L. McIver's work has appeared in numerous publications, including Variety, Upscale, Book, *and* Odyssey Couleur. *Her nonfiction book* Droppin' Science: Straight-Up Talk from Hip Hop's Greatest Voices *was published by Random House in 2002. She is currently working on a novel set in Paris against the backdrop of World War I.*

Chapter 66

Finding My Niche

IEWING LIFE THROUGH A LENS OF PRIVILEGE IS AT TIMES LIKE dimly gazing through glass. You stand there peering, catching only fleeting glimpses of distant shadows flickering on the other side. You never capture a full view. Feelings of one-sidedness may prevail until you wipe the glass clean and realize that, all along, you were focusing on nothing but a smudge. The world was not as you had perceived.

Many of our black elite are victims of this misdirection, simply focusing on smudges rather than cleaning the glass. Cleaning the glass through which our perceptions are filtered requires investigation both outside and inside one's self. Here, the "privileged" black child is forced to observe rather than experience the black community. In many instances, being a black child of privilege places you on the windowsill—neither inside nor outside the room—but precariously positioned somewhere in between.

As the oldest daughter of an actress and model turned child psychologist and a school jock transformed to a responsible family physician, I was blessed with a life free from excessive worry. The safe city of Anaheim Hills cradled me in the lull of upper-middle-class suburban life, with its constant barrage of slumber parties, Jack-and-Jill playdates, private merry-go-rounds, and endless lessons: tennis, golf, swimming, gymnastics, piano, flute, and horseback riding. Being reared in these surroundings sheltered me from the reality of the cultural world around me. Needless to say, I was aware of my blackness, but the hard-and-fast details of this difference were beyond me, until one particular day in school.

That first time I realized my graceless perch in the windowsill of ethnic experience was in elementary school. At that time, the fact that I was somehow different from the blond children in my second-grade class was far from my consciousness. Truthfully, race was always far from my thoughts until a freckle-faced playmate refused to play with me on the monkey bars because I was black. I quickly quipped that I refused to play with him because of his freckles. I meant no harm by the statement, but the ego strength of an eight-year-old is limited and fades quickly.

This incident, though small, was my awakening moment, the first time I had been made bluntly aware of the phenotypic differences between a vast majority of the student body and myself. Being a young and trusting child, I quickly regained my footing and continued to build close bonds that lasted well into elementary and middle school, which possessed its own perils and pitfalls for my ethnic ego.

In middle school, I was accepted for the most part, but always kept on the periphery. A precocious and forward child, I often got into trouble because of my mouth, which could then rarely get me out of it. On one such occasion, I revealed a very mature crush to a particularly gorgeous twelve-year-old classmate. He looked me over, smiled sheepishly, and told me I was very attractive for a black girl, but his parents would simply not abide him bringing home a "n***er."

My mind reeled for a few minutes. I was hurt and embarrassed. Never before had I been called such a name, and I certainly didn't expect to in 1995, in our comfortable 1995 Orange County community. It shook me to the core. I no longer knew where I stood, or who to trust.

Promptly, I turned to friends at my conservative black church. These friends accepted me to an extent, but they constantly harangued me about my designer clothes, my straight hair, my proper diction, and my family's expensive car.

I wanted so much to belong to one of these two groups, but there I was, trapped. I was not accepted wholly by the black community, nor was I accepted by the white community I was more accustomed to. Among my black friends, I quickly tired of epithets like "Oreo" and "white girl." The self-loathing I suffered through has permeated through our community and deeply affects its victims, counterbalancing ourselves—one against another, black-on-black crime at our innermost core. After all, the only way to truly control a people is to break them, to destroy their sense of family, community, and belongingness. Standing in the windowsill of ethnic identity, I was in danger of losing my footing, and a long fall awaited me.

Regaining my footing required many years of masterful maneuvering. I continued stumbling throughout high school, making both mistakes and memories on my journey to finding myself. My saving grace was a small private historically black university in northern Alabama. This small, conservative school nestled in rural Southern mystique helped me find my own identity. For the first time, I was able to realize my birthright. I was able to identify the advantages as well as the setbacks inherent within the life of the privileged black child. Whether we are at school, at work, or in a public forum, we must present an inauthentic shell of our true selves. We are rarely able to express controversial beliefs or perceived injustices for fear of alienating our ethnic "majority" peers. However, in an environment surrounded by other upwardly mobile, educated blacks, I was able to finally express my chagrin with the way things were. I had finally found my niche.

My slow expedition of self-discovery has allowed me to clean the glass through which I see the world. I am finally able to perceive it for what it is—a place of endless possibilities and misfortunes mixed together, forming a mosaic of options. Will I strive for the possibilities or obsess about impending tragedies? These decisions will present themselves throughout life, and a clear perspective is necessary to ensure safe passage.

Although I live in many different worlds—the black world, the white world, the world of academia, and the world of entertainment where I work as a beauty editor—I must consistently readjust my view in order to avoid the smudges and focus on the real. Soon, I will be able to wander uninhibited through the world surrounding me. Soon, I will be free.

—Allycin Powell-Hicks

A Southern California native, Powell-Hicks is currently completing her medical school residency.

♦ Chapter 67

A Multicultural African

BEING AN AFRICAN-AMERICAN WOMAN, AN AFRICAN AMERICAN, or, better yet, an African multicultural person has been a complex journey for this woman, mother, and artist. That's what my birthright has been. In publishing, my latest destiny; in television, where I gained the most notoriety; in film, which I'm still conquering; and in ballet, where I got started—the same thread binds them all together. My identity is not based on one defining characteristic; I proudly embrace them all.

As many of us are aware, there is something that uniquely binds people of African descent. I speak two languages: corporate white American English and black American patois. Although some call it Ebonics, I do not refer to it in this somewhat derogatory manner. Our patois emerged from necessity, not only as a generational offspring of slave language but also because we were denied education for many years. Black American patois is not a language of ignorance, but simply a way in which our family relates to one another. Yes, I can speak with educated, substantive black professors like Henry Louis Gates and Howard Dodson, but at the end of the day, we can sit in a room in a Boston brownstone and *get down* in our own lingo, that patois!

If you compare African tribes and African Americans, there is an innate compatibility between us. It doesn't matter how many times we've been blended into European structure: our authenticity remains intact. Even now, the way a young lady growing up in the projects on the South Side of Chicago wears her hair or adorns herself with jewelry reveals that connection. Our community is not only bound by a shared history but also by a tangible way of being. It is our heritage.

Teaching our children about heritage and pride is a grassroots effort. We have to embrace this responsibility. Our history is not just cross-continent, centuries removed from our current existence, or accurately documented in a textbook. It's very personal, as well. I challenge anyone in America to show me a history book in our schools that details the black experience in Maine, where I grew up, or properly references Malaga Island, a place where the graves of blacks were exhumed because they were of African descent. That's my history, and it's why I was relegated to live in a hospital as a baby and then transferred to an orphanage after my white mother was diagnosed as mentally ill: because black children weren't allowed to be raised by white women. That's the state of consciousness I was born into.

In the same way, black children are faced with challenges to their identity immediately—especially children who attend private schools, as my children have, where they are the minority and are quickly made aware that they are "different." However, they don't have to go to school to be told that; they can just walk into any convenience store in America. Whatever the experience is to them, it was the same for me. I started ballet classes right after the assassinations of JFK, Martin Luther King, Jr., and Bobby Kennedy. As a child, I saw a push for social change, and then I saw the push-back.

I can't shield my children from these harsh experiences, but I can teach them to educate others who don't have clarity or accurate information about our unique culture. Yes, resilience is in our DNA, but our ability to survive the struggle isn't left up to genetic chance. We have to put in the work. All people—black and others—have to work for what they want. Hard work and superior effort cannot be discounted.

I've taken to heart the wisdom of Mahatma Gandhi, to "be the change I want to see." I believe that we are all responsible for positive change and continued growth. It begins with your own corner. It is up to each and every one of us, because we can't expect Big Brother to do it! Unifying one's own fray to bring about change is an offensive, not defensive, action, and it should be applauded. But we've moved away from that mind-set in this day and age, where everything has to be flashy and fast. That's neither realistic nor productive in most of our cases. The things that are real—family and faith—are never out of reach. Yet, we have to hold on to them and sow those seeds so they can grow. These values must be cultivated in the home.

My children have been reared in a blended family inclusive of many cultures as a direct result of my growing up in foster care. I've taught them the truth: that any discrimination and intolerance whatsoever must be taught before anyone else can dilute it!

Without question, I've accomplished many of my goals because of the strong foundation laid for me by the women who raised me. I have always strived to give the best of myself in love and kindness, and through faith and intuition. The greatest gift I hope I've given my children and the world is the act of giving back. That's the legacy I inherited as a multicultural African living in a perfectly imperfect world.

—**Victoria Rowell**

A versatile theater, primetime and daytime television, and feature film actress, Rowell is known around the world for her various roles. She has become an icon in daytime television as the feisty Drucilla Winters on CBS's highly rated daytime series The Young and the Restless. *She has been nominated twice for a Daytime Emmy and has won twelve NAACP Image Awards. She also costarred in the CBS hit primetime television series* Diagnosis Murder *with Dick Van Dyke for eight seasons while simultaneously continuing her role in daytime television.*

Chapter 68

Why Not?

IN A FEW DAYS, MY YOUNGEST DAUGHTER WILL TURN TWENTY-ONE. Where did the years go? Last night, her mother and I were reminiscing about her growing-up years, both the good and the bad. There are so many positive and good things to say about both of our daughters. I admit it, and I am not ashamed. I am proud of what our girls have achieved. However, there was one incident in her young life that we hate to remember. It's haunted us ever since.

This particular incident took place when our baby girl was a sophomore in high school. She came home from school upset. It seemed that other African-American children on the school bus had accused her of "trying to be white" in the way she talked, acted, and performed in school. We were appalled. This was not something we'd taught our girls. We taught them to do their best, to reach for their dreams, and that with hard work and a good education, they could do anything they set their mind to. We still believe that—both for them and for us.

Our daughters attended a high school that was 40 percent African American and 60 percent white. They were honor-roll students with plans to go to college and dreams of becoming a teacher and a lawyer, respectively. They had goals—not to change the color of their skin, but to take advantage of every opportunity this great country offered them. Our eldest is now a high school and junior college teacher. Our youngest is finishing her undergraduate studies and preparing for law school.

Why was our baby girl being teased? Because she could read, write, do math, and conduct an intelligent and articulate conversation. Intelligence does not equate to "being white." Not using Ebonics as a standard means of communication does not equate to "being white." Treating others with respect does not equate to "being white." Achieving goals does not equate to "being white." Getting the best education possible does not equate to "being white."

My wife and I found that experience frightening, and we still do. Where did we, as African-American parents and as an African-American culture, fail our children? Somewhere, somehow, some of our children have gotten the wrong message. Without goals, education, tenacity, and hard work, African Americans like Dr. Martin Luther King, Jr., Oprah Winfrey, Barack Obama, and Shirley Chisholm would not have made an impact on this great country.

I'll be the first to admit that being African American is still not easy in this country. But that's no excuse. Our daughters watched their mother and me work full-time jobs during the day and go to college at night. We had, and have, big dreams. We are both successful, but that success does not depend on the balance in our bank account. We have done everything we could to make a better life for our daughters and ourselves.

My wife and I taught them to know right from wrong, to be honest, to give back, to have self-respect, and to value education. Getting an education is essential, because no matter what happens in life, no one can take your education away from you. These are the values we, as African-American adults, need to teach our children. Instead of saying something's too hard, our children should say they can work even harder.

When I was a younger man, my dream was to get a college education and a good job. My mother had no money to send me to college, so I had to formulate a different plan. I used grants, scholarships, and job-education reimbursement programs to get my college degree. It took a lot of years of going to night school, working a full-time job, and helping my wife raise our children, but my dream came true. The excitement of walking across the stage and being handed a diploma was overwhelming.

Even today, I may be firmly entrenched in middle age, but I still find challenges as a man. Some of these challenges result from the color of my skin. So what do I do? I work hard. I continue to learn. I contribute in the community and at church—and by contribute I don't mean just financially.

Today, I challenge all African Americans to look back and draw strength from the days when we were a proud, resilient, strong, and caring community. It wasn't so long ago; as recently as the 1960s, you felt a strong sense that the *community* cared. I can't pinpoint exactly when we lost our self-respect, but somewhere along the line, we have. Where is the strength and dignity that allowed our ancestors to rise out of slavery and achieve some of the greatest human accomplishments in history (for example, Dr. Charles Drew's discovery that blood plasma could be used in place of whole blood for transfusions)? There is no doubt that we have our work cut out for us, but my family believes we can do it.

I encourage every African American over the age of thirty to reach back and help a younger person rise up and do the best that he or she can, unencumbered by skin color. Guide them. Show them. Teach them. In today's world, it takes so much more than a family or a village to raise an educated, strong, passionate, self-respecting, and achieving man or woman. It takes moms and dads and grandpas and grandmas and aunts and uncles and cousins and churches and schools and civic organizations to help them be successful.

Can you do it? Will you do it? If not, why not?

—**Gerald S. Brooks**

Gerald S. Brooks is the marketing and public relations director for the St. Louis Public Library.

♦ Chapter 69

By Any Other Name

MY NAME USUALLY LEADS PEOPLE TO THINK THAT I'M NOT a citizen of the United States. Store clerks, sales representatives, and bank tellers see or hear the name Hasna Muhammad and have one of several reactions. Some continue the transaction without a skipped beat, blinked eye, or any other noticeable evidence of registering the name. They scrutinize my ID as they do all IDs, and keep any reaction to themselves. Some try to pronounce my name or comment that it is unique. Some ask me where I come from. Most are content to end the chit-chat when I tell them in standard American English that I am a nonindigenous native New Yawka born and bred in Westchester County.

Others fumble through the transaction, "calling in for approval," putting me on hold, or pulling me from a line. When I ask why (and I always do), I am told that it is "normal procedure" or that I was "randomly chosen." That could be true thanks to Homeland Security and the 1 percent shadow of a doubt that I might be a non-American, Muslim, Arabian terrorist. I don't take that lightly. I am already suspect because I am LWB—Living While Black—so I am careful to have my papers in order and always be prepared for deeper scrutiny. My complexion, the texture of my hair, and the shape of my nose and hips testify that I am an African-American woman. My name, however, exposes me to an additional layer of assumptions, questions, and prejudice.

Our names are as close as we can get to ourselves. We use them to define who we are, to claim what is ours. Names keep our ancestors in our mouths and in our hearts, and they connect us to who we have been. They also make us who we are becoming and create the path to where we are going.

My mother named me La Verne after her little sister. I was proud to have Aunt La Verne's name. She was a beautiful, charming woman with a melodic way of calling each of us *daaarling*. My aunt couldn't have children, so I was her line and her legacy. Just like So-and-So Jr. or a III, her genetic torch burned in my name.

We black folks have been self-defining and renaming ourselves and each other for a long time. Colored. Negro. Black. Afro, then African American. Each transition seemed to be made by consensus. Each one was reflective of the time and current consciousness. In the 1970s, when we were black, proud, and beautiful, we reclaimed our African clothes, hairdos, and African ways of life.

For some, that also meant changing our first names to enlightened Swahili, Yoruba, Arabic, or made-up names that were never used at work or on official documents. For others, like me, it meant abandoning our names through a simple legal process that included hiring a lawyer, paying a fee, getting a new birth certificate, and literally being reborn. People change their names for all kinds of reasons. Marriage. Escape. Religious conversions. I changed my name because I wanted to break the last link in the chain of enslavement. I changed my name because I changed my way of life. I changed my name because I became Muslim.

People have asked me why I—a so-called middle-class, English-speaking, educated "American"—would not only become Muslim but would also change my name from La Verne Davis to Hasna Muhammad, an Arabic name that obscures the African-American legacy of my parents, Ossie Davis and Ruby Dee, and immediately evokes invisible fences and obvious obstacles. I was twenty years old at the time. It was in the mid-1970s, and I had just graduated from Sarah Lawrence College. Like most people that age, I was searching for who I was, where I'd come from, and what I was supposed to be doing with my life. Echoed in another language and in an altered rhythm, I found a set of values and a historical perspective on life that looked like me and felt like home. I found Islam.

As I immersed myself in what had actually found me, I began to read the Old Testament, the New Testament, and the Qur'an (the last testament). I began to connect the messages of all the prophets, from Adam to Muhammad. I prayed five times a day and fasted for Ramadan. I went to the *masjid* on Fridays for congregational prayer, and I held Saturdays as the Sabbath. I took purposeful steps away from the established American and African-American societies and found myself in Brooklyn among other like-minded folks. I rejected everything that did not reflect my new way of life, including my name. I accepted instead the name that my imam recommended for me, Hasna, the third and feminine form of Hasan. With it, I accepted the responsibility to live up to its meaning and its inner beauty.

Islam inserted into our family's Baptist traditions a change of perspective that affected our family gatherings and interactions. We thanked God and Allah for the meals that offered two or three versions of everything: collard greens with pork, collard greens with smoked turkey, and for the vegetarians, collard greens with no meat at all. I was called La Verne sometimes and Hasna at others. When I was introduced as La Verne or when my name was mispronounced as *Haz-na*, I would make the correction to *Hessna* by exhaling the H from my gut, hissing the S, lingering on the N, and letting the A fall out of my mouth. Folks would apologize for using my old name or mispronouncing my new one, except for my grandmother, who attributed everything to Jesus and called me anything she wanted. Most often, people would switch back and forth or use them both in hyphenation.

A lot has happened in the past thirty years. I have come to realize that although my name is Hasna Muhammad, I am still La Verne Davis. I may have left my family name on the page of a legal transaction, but my family never let me go. No matter how critical I became of them and their values, they never criticized my decision to become Muslim or change my name.

My conversion to Islam and change of name were abrupt, and they happened without consideration of the ways in which my family would be affected. Had I looked back to see the trail I'd blazed,

I would have seen them mourn the separation and loss of the little sister and daughter they knew. Had I asked, I would have known about the devastation my mother felt when I silenced her sister's name (fortunately, it was later resurrected by my niece). Had I wondered, I would have realized that my father was waiting patiently. That I was able to let go of my family and then reach out and grab them closer as I came full circle is testimony to how much their unconditional love and support made it possible for me to become who I am: a strong, black, Muslim-American woman named Hasna Muhammad.

My lifelong quest for the word of God as peace has been refined by age. My sense of self and understanding of this world and my role in it have brought me from a follower of men with titles to a leader of myself. I wouldn't have come to this greater understanding without my journey through the portals of Islam, and I wouldn't have the same understanding of Islam if I hadn't meditated with Sri Chinmoy in high school or listened to my grandmother talk about being a good Christian and believing in Jesus well beyond the day, one month before her hundred and sixth birthday, when she died with his name on her lips.

Unadulterated by the devastation that some leaders, the media, and ignorance have brought to this earth and its inhabitants, Islam is a state of peace. Peace is the common theme in the messages from people like Abraham, Jesus, Buddha, and Muhammad. Osama bin Laden, Saddam Hussein, *Newsweek*, CNN, and all of the leaders of the Western world have absolutely nothing to do with it. To me, Islam is a state of peace in the inner and outer space between the inhale and exhale of a collective breath of life drawn in unison by all things and released in balance. It is the harmony in one note. It is the stillness in the vibration of atoms and molecules moving. To me, Islam is the time when all inhabitants of the earth are accepting, affirming, and living in peace. I don't think my interpretation of Islam is very common, and it certainly isn't the publicized version. My interpretation is without words, really. Rather, it is eternal dances, closed-eyed smiles, and feelings evoked from spectacular starscapes and deep sea coral valleys.

A lot has happened in the past few years. The Gulf War and post–September 11th modus operandi have brought Arabs, Islam, and Muslims everywhere to the forefront of every news media outlet. Muslims around the world have been systematically profiled, targeted, prejudged, and killed. Some African-American Muslims have shed their Arabic names and uncovered their hair in order to blend in more with American culture and be less exposed to this particular bias. Others of us cannot, or will not, do so. I challenge the Constitution of the United States to protect me from bias, no matter what I believe in, no matter how I live my life, and no matter what my name is.

In 2004, my parents were honored by the Kennedy Center, and our family participated in a weekend of events that required careful listing of our names and Social Security numbers. At the State Department dinner, my place card read Hasna Muhammad, and at the White House reception, my place card read Muhammad as well. At the Kennedy Center, my place card read Hasna Davis. I have never used the name Hasna Davis. Basking on the edge of the limelight at one of the most prestigious national ceremonies, sitting one row behind and two seats to the right of President Bush, I had been given back my family's slave name. Perhaps it was an honest mistake made by a worker who just wanted to get a name on a card and a card on a seat. Perhaps I was being too sensitive to other possibilities. So much for Homeland Security.

Now fifty-something, I am not too naive to believe that I am exempt from prejudice just because I am a citizen of the United States. I am not too inexperienced to believe that my credentials will not be considered because of my name. I am not too trusting to believe that food handlers will not spit in food ordered under my name, or that neighborhood adolescents will not vandalize a mailbox that reads Muhammad. I carry with me daily the reality that the Constitution may fail to protect me from ignorance and the abuse of power, and that my name—like my skin—is still a dead giveaway. I also carry the belief that prejudice and exclusivity will yield to the collective needs of humanity, and that the planet will move us toward a true state of peace.

—Hasna Muhammad

Hasna Muhammad is the author of several collections of poetry, and she is currently working on a collection of nonfiction titled Places to Stand. *Muhammad combines her writing and photography with media, such as handmade paper, fabric, and wood, to create what she calls literary textile art. Muhammad is an assistant superintendent at a public school district and also enjoys swimming, motorcycling, scuba diving, and hot Bikram yoga. Muhammad's future plans include traveling extensively, establishing a line of greeting cards, becoming a pilot, and visiting the International Space Station.*

Chapter 70

Black Enough for Me

THERE WAS A TIME WHEN I WOULDN'T HAVE FELT QUALIFIED TO write an essay about being a black man. How could I? I attended a predominantly white private school in a small, incredibly wealthy suburb that was only technically located in the Bronx. Even there, I never felt cool enough to sit at the designated "black table" or attend the black student union meetings with any regularity. None of the black girls at school, or anywhere else, wanted to date me. I didn't wear the right clothes. My mom wouldn't let me listen to the right music, and she definitely wouldn't spend money on the right kicks. I wasn't the only black kid in my close group of friends, but I never felt a part of the "larger" black community.

I definitely wasn't alone in my thinking. I even heard about it from my family. Why did I have so many nonblack friends? What kind of music was I listening to? It got worse every time I tried to explain why I was taking a year off before attending law school. They couldn't get it. Why did I want to go to China and Mexico? Why did I need to time to "find myself"? Why would I put my education and my scholarship to law school on hold? They didn't care that I'd wanted to be a lawyer since I was ten years old. They didn't care that most students take time off between completing college and pursuing graduate or professional degrees. They would never say it out loud, but I could feel it on the tips of their tongues, "Sure, *but that's what white people do.*"

This is the same problem facing America, and Black America, today. We don't know what to make of black manhood. The most glaring example of this dilemma is evident in Barack Obama's rise to national prominence. Although many Americans of all racial groups were energized by Obama's presidential campaign, others openly questioned whether Obama is "black enough." In fact, Stanley Crouch, a columnist for the *New York Daily News*, has claimed that Barack Obama isn't "Black Like Me."

It's not really clear what the "enough" in "black enough" means. It certainly couldn't mean is he "black enough" to win the Democratic nomination or the general election, because no black person has ever accomplished either feat. According to Debra Dickerson of *Salon*, "Black, in our political and social vocabulary, means those descended from West African slaves." Those who question Obama's blackness also mention that he has a white mother and a Kenyan father. Of course, they fail to mention that any black man that descended from slaves in the New World probably has at least one white ancestor. Is racial purity really how we want to define blackness? Unless we can trace our roots directly back to the Continent, none of us is really in a position to question anyone else's black heritage.

There are also critics who have questioned the racial authenticity of other African-American males with very divergent backgrounds from Obama's. These men are so famous they are known by a single name like Wayne, or a number like 50. Their status as black males is challenged because many of their actions demonstrate a disrespect for blackness and the sacrifices of their enslaved and oppressed forebears. Many rappers have built careers around calling black men "niggers" and black women "bitches." They have been accused of getting rich by selling a negative image of black men to an overwhelmingly white, middle-class fan base. At the same time, they sell to black males the false hope of drug dealing or rapping as the means by which to achieve success.

Even worse, in the end, little of their money finds its way back to the black community. Instead of investing in other black males, they buy rims for their cars or give money to a white jeweler in return for conflict diamonds mined by black Africans thousands of miles away. Their status as black males is questioned because their work is seen as a detriment, rather than a boon, to the black community.

Few would ever think that Lil' Wayne and Clarence Thomas have much in common, but comparisons between black rappers and the Supreme Court justice are not without merit from a critical standpoint. Thomas's status as a black male has not just been questioned—some have officially excommunicated him from the black race altogether. He is viewed as a pariah or a Benedict Arnold because of his conservative views on civil rights, especially affirmative action, and his adherence to the "original intent" of the Constitution's framers.

So where does this confusion come from? If you look at me, my status as a black male is pretty apparent. It's reaffirmed when I have to announce myself before approaching friends at night, or when I stand in the rain waiting while a row of empty cabs passes me by. But I can't let other people's stereotypes define who I am.

So how do we define ourselves? If I believed what the world tells me, I could only be one of two extremes. In reality, I am, and we all are, somewhere in between. I'm no thug, but I can act ignorant and be rude with the best of them. I am constantly mindful of where I am and what I'm doing. When I was a teenager, my friends and I never tipped well; we'd been known to leave a penny or a nickel. These days, I can't leave less than 20 percent whenever I eat out or take a cab because I want to make sure they know that black people do tip well.

By all accounts, I have achieved the American dream and relative success. Despite attending some of the best schools in America, despite my white-collar job and salary, people at my law firm are still surprised to find out I'm an attorney. No amount of success can overcome these stereotypes. Of course, the irony of being a "successful" black male is that for most of my adult life, I have and will continue to profit from the struggles and perceived shortcomings of my black male peers. Employers and academic institutions treat me as though I'm an exception that can never become the rule. Sometimes I feel guilty, but more often I feel motivated—motivated to be the best example of what a black male can be, and motivated to help my cousins and mentees do the same.

The black male population is too vulnerable, marginalized, and flawed for any of us to declare that someone else is unworthy of being called a black man. In 1998, during an address to the National Bar Association, an organization of black attorneys, Clarence Thomas declared that in spite of his viewpoints on affirmative action and "[d]espite some of the nonsense that has been said about me by those who should know better ... I am a man. A black man. An American."

Although I felt marginalized as a teenager, what troubles me now is not that I didn't feel included in the black community. What bothers me is that at sixteen, I thought being a black male had something to do with what I wore, who I dated, and who was playing in my Walkman. I'm not sure that I am any closer to defining what it means to be a black man than I was a decade ago, but now I don't feel the pressure to fit myself into any particular box. I can be thoughtful and well spoken, like Barack Obama. I can be creative and profane, like Lil' Wayne. I can be intellectual and critical, like Clarence Thomas.

Most importantly, though, I can declare with pride that I am a black man, and I am working to become a better one every day.

—**Donald K. Sherman**

Donald K. Sherman is a graduate of the Georgetown University Law Center and an attorney in Washington, D.C. He is also very active in the local community and serves on the boards of D.C. Vote, D.C. Lawyers for Youth, and Be the Change in D.C.

♦ Chapter 71

I Am a New Afrikan

I AM A NEW AFRIKAN. I AM A CHILD OF NEW AFRIKAN PARENTS. IN the early 1960s, my parents adopted an Afrikan lifestyle, incorporating Afrikan food, clothes, and language into our everyday lives and our community. We became the Omowale family, a Yoruba name meaning "this child has returned home." Some people thought we were odd, but everyone respected us. Now that I understand the history of my ancestors in this country—when we got here, how we got here, and why we were brought here—I consider it my duty and responsibility to recognize the birthplace of my ancestors in defining myself.

I was born in the United States of America. When I am asked about my nationality, I respond that I am an American. When I am asked about my race, I respond that I am black. Both answers are based on a prescribed response designated to be used for statistical purposes or used on applications, licenses, and so on. When I am asked how I define myself, however, the answer is based on my experiences, an analysis of the historical facts, and an awareness I have gleaned from those things. The answer is that I am a New Afrikan.

Among my peers, I have always been considered a rebel of sorts. This was because I saw beauty in things we were conditioned to see as ugly, staged protests and encouraged boycotts, did not conform to peer pressure, and mainly because I questioned the unquestionable system—especially things that I deemed unfair. One of my favorite questions has always been, "Why?"

I can play by the rules and regulations of any game, as long as the rules and regulations are the same for everyone. That is one of the conditions for fairness. I think it is unfair that a people arising from a condition of oppression are expected to adequately compete with people who were provided with advantages. I think it is unfair that an oppressor gets to set the standard for the oppressed as to what is beautiful and what is ugly, and for what is good and what is bad. I think it is unfair to have systems of double standards and double-speak, where one thing is said, and another thing is done. Speaking of fair, if light skin is considered fair, does that mean that dark skin is unfair? My question, again, is, "Why?" Why was it necessary to create a perception of negativity around Afrika and all things Afrikan? *Why?*

Afrika has been made to appear backward, uncivil, and unappealing, but Afrika has been raped and exploited of its natural resources for centuries, so much so that now, its people can't feed themselves and the continent is overwhelmed with disease, war, and strife. But Afrika is like a mother to me. If my mother were ravaged with sickness and her richness of life had been erased, I would still love her. I understand that in her purest state, she was strong, able, and proud. I would not deny her because of what has befallen her.

This understanding shaped my worldview, and these are some of the things I considered when I declared myself a New Afrikan. If the rules are unfair and I continue to play by the rules, I will never win or be treated fairly. Therefore, I decided not to allow myself to be defined by someone else's standards; instead, I am defined by my own perception of self. It has been a very liberating and self-empowering decision for me.

During the Afrikan Maafa (holocaust), countless millions of Afrikans were torn from their native lands. Hundreds of ethnic groups were forced into slavery, lumped into a collective pot, and merged into one group. We are Yoruba, we are Ibo, we are Hausa, we are Ewe, we are Akan, we are Kongo, we are Fanti, and we are many, many more. We are an amalgamation—a fusion—of all these ethnic groups. An analogy would be if you take a variety of fruits, like grapes, cherries, lemons, and berries, and squeeze their juices all together. You don't have grape juice, and you don't have lemon juice—you now have a blend. I am now a New Afrikan.

I yearned for the culture of my ancestors. There was a longing in my soul. I always felt like something was missing, and that something was calling me. Just as when a person loses a limb, he or she can sometimes still feel the itch of that lost limb—a phantom sensation—my feelings were like a spiritual umbilical cord linking me to my origin. As New Afrikans, we had to construct a new and improved balancing act, one in which we could experience the uninterrupted rhythm of our genetic heritage and the reality of our present existence. In this context, I am proud of my connection to Afrika and proud of my roots in America. I can be both a New Afrikan and an American, and they are not contradictory positions.

Everything that exists, exists in apposition but not opposition. They are each one half of a whole. They complement each other. Without this, there is no balance. In order for the world to operate as correctly and efficiently as God planned it, there must be balance. I found balance in the cyclical discovery of a heritage lost and found; of death and rebirth; of what was, what is, and what can be. Afrika is waiting for recognition and acknowledgment from all her New Afrikan children to merge old traditions with new ones, reestablishing our connection to infinity. Until then, she sits like an inextinguishable ember waiting patiently for us to return to her and ignite a flame of mutual healing, love, and acceptance.

—**Dee Robinson**

Dee Robinson is a freelance writer, poet, and producer based in Atlanta, Georgia.

Chapter 72

Little Black Girl
In an All-White World

MY FATHER WAS A BLACK ENGINEER WHO CLIMBED THE corporate ladder. His aspirations paved the way for my family's relocation to New England when I was eleven years old. Back in Ohio, we had grown accustomed to diverse cultural surroundings. In our old neighborhood, we had Jewish, black, Indian, and more races all living on the same block. Of course, I knew this wasn't exactly typical, but I was prepared for the new adventure that Merrimack, New Hampshire, our new city of residence, would bring. At least, I thought I was.

As we made the drive cross-country, I remember crossing the state line of New Hampshire. In the distance I spied the beloved golden arches every kid in America has come to revere. Of course, my brother and I were like, "Ooh, let's stop at McDonald's!" My mother obliged, and as we entered, people dropped their forks and stopped eating, literally staring at us the whole time. I didn't want to eat there, so we left the restaurant.

This would serve as my official welcome to New Hampshire, an unpleasant introduction to our new surroundings.

The "MJ" Effect

Merrimack was indeed a small town. In fact, there were only four black families in the small town, and we were one of them. In terms of diversity, we were it! In terms of black diversity, there was none.

But being black in a virtually white world does have some interesting dynamics. We have, what I call, the Michael Jordan Effect.

When white America sees Michael Jordan or Bill Cosby, they're Bill Cosby and Michael Jordan. Follow me? They're not seen as "black." So to everyone in town who knew us, this upper-middle-class, Cadillac-driving family with a track-star daughter and standout football player son wasn't "black." We were the exception, just like Michael and Bill.

For example, I remember one black girl I went to school with (mind you, there were only four black kids in school, and my brother and I were two of them). Her hair was not kept up much at that time, and I remember some white kids making fun of her. One of them said to me, "Well, you're not like her." I said, "Yes, I am! I *am* her." They couldn't understand that I, the black girl they'd gotten comfortable around, was no different from the one they were bullying. It's still the same "black."

Yet, even for the acceptance we experienced, some kids never let us forget that we were different. This is more the norm than the exception. In an all-white world, sometimes you forget that you're black. Not your blackness per se, but rather it as an identifier. Most people treated me like Candi, not *that black girl, Candi.* Unfortunately, one kid in middle school used to terrorize me, often calling me Blackie. It was shocking and jarring that first time. So yes, I understood that I could be a popular, studious, track star with money at home, and still be a Blackie. That's the way of the world.

This Ain't the White House

In spite of, or because of, the environment in which I was reared, people are a bit surprised that I have such a strong sense of pride in being a black woman and such love for our culture and community. Whenever these discussions arise, I always remind people that my dad hails from Dyersburg, Tennessee, and my mother is from St. Petersburg, Florida. They are Southerners to the core. There was never a question of them forgetting who they are—their roots were planted. We resided in a white community, but by no means did we live in a "white house."

Growing up, it was the simple things that most of us can relate to—the R&B music, the black artwork that adorned our walls, the soul food, and every black woman's main concern, keeping that hair done! I remember that my mother cooked Sunday dinner each week. I'm talking collard greens, black-eyed peas, cornbread, macaroni and cheese, fried chicken, and more. That's why I can prepare all of those foods for my own family today. You know, there wasn't a black hairdresser in southern New Hampshire, so she and I would drive an hour and half to Portsmouth every Saturday. Clearly, she was a black woman!

Also, my mother was involved in efforts geared toward our community, such as the Black Women's Business Association. With New Hampshire being an important primary state during the presidential election season, our family worked on a local level with Jesse Jackson, Sr., as he made the rounds.

Socially, my mother sought out black friends, just as I did. She had to have her girlfriends around, a circle she felt a connection with. It was a necessity for both of us. As I look back, there weren't very many blacks in the surrounding towns. But the ones who were there found each other. To me, black is just something you are, not an affiliation you have to announce. I believe my parents were just living their life, being who they were. If they were living in Tennessee or Florida, they would've been exactly the same. Like them, I have always had this innate need to be with my own. The alternative was simply not an option for me.

Beauty Values

Unfortunately, my concept of beauty was ill-shaped by my surroundings. Living in an all-white world, I never thought I was pretty. I thought I was dark and unattractive. My social environment just didn't lend itself to any other way of thinking. I didn't date much at all. It was fine for the white girls to like black guys, such as my brother. However, a young white boy would never date a black girl. And me, I'm a "black" girl—a dark berry, and not fair-looking or high-yellow (no offense intended).

Like many black women, I have full, beautiful lips. However, I've had them since the fourth grade and just grew into them over time. I can remember wanting lip surgery, some form of lip reduction. Even though I had flawless skin, long hair past my shoulders, and a nice build, I just didn't see beauty back then. Sure, Beverly Johnson, Iman, and Grace Jones were in magazines, but you have to see it in your own life. There was no one in my everyday world, other than my mother, who resembled me. My form of black beauty.

It wasn't until I went away to school, to Boston College, that I really got true confidence in my looks. A white guy friend of mine from back home who was attending college nearby at Northeastern University, said to me, "Candi, you are beautiful. There were no black girls in Merrimack, and now I'm in school, and there's all these black women to look at. You are really pretty."

I remember thinking, "Wow—I *am* pretty!" Not just because he'd said it, but because I had really started looking in the mirror. I was an athlete, a size eight with 4 percent body fat, and all those years I had no idea I was halfway cute! When I got to college, brothers were like, "Hey, Candi!" In some ways, that was good, because I was more concerned with developing my mind than what I looked like. However, it was important that this part of my self-esteem developed as well.

The liberating thing about college was that there were so many kinds of black beauty. I saw with my own two eyes that *my* black was beautiful, too.

A Double Life

Now, as a businesswoman, wife, and mother, I reflect on my childhood experiences a bit differently than I did back then. It's a large part of why I strongly believe that you don't have to wear your blackness on your sleeve, announcing to the world in word, action, and deed, "Hey, I'm black!" Look in the mirror, honey, they already know! It's something you intrinsically are—not something you have to prove. Yes, I'm a dark-skinned woman, but you're going to love me for me. Give me an interview, and I'm going to knock your socks off! It's not because of affirmative action.

I think the world is beginning to understand that just because you own a company, it doesn't mean it's a black-only company. Just because you create a product, it doesn't mean it's a black-only product. We're able to create companies, brands, and products that people from all cultural groups can benefit from. People of all colors are enthusiastic and excited about my *Hip Hop Baby* children's educational DVD series.

Personally, I think my upbringing was an exercise in being able to understand the world and how to navigate it. The little black girl in an all-white world has carved out a niche for herself. That, most definitely, puts a smile on my face.

—**Candi Carter**

Candi Carter has a bachelor's degree in broadcast communications from Boston College. She started her television career at CNN and later produced news specials and children's programming at WISN-TV, the ABC affiliate in Milwaukee. There, she won an Emmy for Outstanding Children's Programming. For the past twelve years, she's produced award-winning television for a nationally syndicated talk show based in Chicago, Illinois. Carter lives in Chicago with her husband and two children.

◆ Chapter 73

Memo to Myself:
I Can Grieve Now

I HAVE WRITTEN MANY ESSAYS ABOUT BEING A BLACK MAN IN America. I have looked at this topic from every angle and vantage point, through every prism available, and with broad considerations. I have asked my fellow brothers to join me in looking within to best define black manhood, black sexuality, black love, black responsibility, and black life in general. I have committed most of my life to helping make the black community—here and abroad—a better, more nurturing place.

I marched to make Dr. King's birthday a national holiday. I organized to help bring an end to apartheid. I joined the fight to combat HIV/AIDS in the black community, and I called on my brothers to overcome the stifling grip of homophobia and join in that fight as well. I mentored young men, spoke to scores of at-risk youth, and offered guidance to college students across the country.

I authored a book on volunteerism and encourage all in earshot, black and beyond, to give back. I have done these things and more. Even though there's a ton left for me to do, if I died today, I'd be satisfied and happy that my life was not lived in vain.

But with all of this, there is something I have not done. I have not grieved. I don't know how. My fingers tremble as I write these words, because I don't know where I'm going. I don't have a clue how to say what I feel. I don't know how to grieve.

Let me explain how I came to this understanding. Not long ago, I visited my sister and her family to help celebrate my niece

Deyonna's eighth birthday. She's a talented, talkative youngster who possesses none of the shyness that defined my early years. As she'd requested, I brought along a DVD of an animated children's movie she wanted as a birthday gift, probably the fourth one I've given her over the years.

Once I placed the package in her tiny hands, she dashed up to her room, eager to watch the film I'm sure she'd already seen a half-dozen times on TV. Nonetheless, there she went, and I followed, trying to make small talk and see what was going on inside her little head. I live in Los Angeles, and she lives in my native New Jersey, so we don't get to talk much. She indulged me for a moment, answering my questions politely but without divulging much detail. School was fine, she told me, and she'd enjoyed a sleepover with friends that she'd hosted the night before. I knew her attention was focused on getting the DVD started, so I kissed her on the cheek and left her to it.

As I began walking down the steps, I turned to take one last look at Deyonna. Her face was peaceful; her eyes had become transfixed on the screen as children do, and she paid no attention to me on the stairs. It was a beautiful image, but I was overcome with a deep sadness. In my mind's eye, I stopped seeing my niece and started seeing myself as an eight-year-old child. This was my niece's eighth birthday, and that's how old I had been when my mother died.

As I stood there, looking at myself, I asked the questions that don't have answers. *How was I able to deal with my mother's passing at such a young age? Moreover, why was I made to? How could God allow this to happen? What could possibly replace a mother's love for her only son? How did I manage over the years without her? How would my life have been different if she had not died when I was eight, and she was only thirty-one years old?*

These questions ran through my mind like pages flipping in a book. I wanted to cry, but I didn't. I went downstairs and joined in the family revelry, doing what I have become an expert at—keeping my pain to myself. I kept it all inside. I don't know how to grieve.

My mother's passing is still like a blur. She went from being sick with a headache that wouldn't go away to being taken out of the house on a stretcher, which was the last time I saw her alive. I still can't watch the Don Knotts movie *The Ghost and Mr. Chicken,* because that's what was on the TV when the ambulance came.

Why didn't I run after them? Why didn't I ask questions? Why didn't I grab the stretcher and scream for her? Why did I just lay there under the coffee table, my usual TV-viewing location at that time, and suffer quietly, with tears streaming down my face? My ability to suffer quietly has become a curse.

The events of those sad days are surreal and disjointed in my memory. I can't discern how much of it really happened, and how much of it I've created over the years to help fill the gaps and explain the unexplainable. I remember a collection of vivid images and voices, but the pieces don't always fit. I remember my father giving my sister and me updates about our mother's condition as she struggled in the hospital; they both thought we were too young to visit to her. I also recall him reassuring me that she was eventually coming home, and me telling myself that she wasn't. Somehow, I knew I wouldn't see her again, at least not alive. (How in the hell can a kid that young tell himself his mother is never coming home again and have it not impact his entire life?)

The actual day she passed is the strangest of my memories. It's as if I watched it happen to someone else. My memories of my uncle, my mother's brother, telling my sister and me that our mother had died, and of my aunt, my mother's sister, holding the two of us as we rocked and cried for hours, stand out the most. I remember my dad's face as he tearfully looked at his young son and thirteen-year-old daughter, struggling to say something, *anything*, to console them. Everything from that day is in black and white. Nothing's in color.

The funeral and its aftermath brought a host of family and friends and a fruit basket from my grammar school. There was no shortage of folk who promised to be there for us, people who kept trying to get me to eat, watch TV, go out and play, or stay in and play. I remember it rained that day, and that my father asked me to be strong for my sister. Then it was over, and life kept moving on.

It always seemed weird how things just kept moving forward. I went back to school. Spring turned to summer, and rent was still due at the end of each month. The world didn't stop so I could learn how to grieve, and I took my cue from that.

Over the years, I've convinced myself that my pain was not unique. Many children lose parents at a young age. Some people lose both, and I'm very lucky that my dad is alive and well. Life goes on, as I've told myself and countless others who invariably ask, "How did you handle your mother's death when you were so young?" You just keep moving.

Indeed, as a man—a black man, at that—I must be strong. Our community needs strong men to help turn the tide of the many ills that beset us. There's no time to cry or wallow in self-pity. We black men have to be John Shaft or Malcolm X, with a healthy dose of W.E.B. DuBois and a spoonful of Barack Obama. Who has time to grieve when we have to end AIDS, stop the genocide in Darfur, build businesses, mentor our youth, and beat back the still-lingering effects of racism, sexism, and general intolerance? Does learning to grieve rate as an item on our community's "to-do" list? For most of my life, I didn't think so.

I now know I've been wrong.

My inability to grieve my mother's death has impacted my relationships, particularly those with women. Issues with commitment *(Why love again, when this woman could leave me too?)* and nonsexual intimacy (I'd still rather chew glass than hold hands) have been hallmarks of every romantic relationship I've had, including my marriage. While I have known this for years, I have never done anything about it. If white men can't jump, then black men can't do therapy—or at least I can't.

But something's got to change. I have to break the cycle. If I am going to be truly committed to helping make our community and our world a better place, I have to be just as committed to being the best person I can be. I have to learn to grieve. My personal experience is part of the black experience, and I am equally responsible for both.

I have to find out how this "thing" stunted my development as a person, and how it has allowed me to be hurtful to women, including my wife, for so long. It is frightening to know you need to do something and not know *what* to do. Perhaps the first step is to admit that my pain is unique; it's not better or worse, not more or less. It's just mine, and that's enough.

To be sure, dealing with my decades-long load of grief won't solve all my many character flaws, nor do I blame my assortment of shortcomings on my mom's passing. I'm not that far gone. But it is a major step in my journey for self-improvement. I can finally admit out loud that my mother's death was devastating to me, and its effects, like the aftershocks of an earthquake, resonate to this day. I want to grieve. I don't know how, but I'm finally, at long last, prepared to learn.

In 1972, Elizabeth Louise Cathcart died of a viral infection. Her son, an eight-year-old boy who loved to play football in the street and who loved his mother dearly, packed all the pain and memories of her passing inside a mental box marked "to be opened at a later time."

God willing, that time is now.

—Christopher D. Cathcart

Christopher D. Cathcart is president/founder of OneDiaspora Group, a public relations and media consultancy in Los Angeles. He is also an acclaimed public speaker and writer who has authored a book on volunteerism titled The Lost Art of Giving Back. *A longtime community activist, Cathcart devotes time and energy to such issues as HIV/AIDS awareness, mentoring young people, and encouraging all to give back. For more information, e-mail Chris@OneDG.com or visit www.onediaspora.com.*

Chapter 74

Short Cuts: A Hairstory

THE YEAR WAS 1994, AND TO QUOTE STEVIE W., IT WAS "HOTTER than July." Summertime in New York is *not* a game. If the sweltering heat doesn't do you in, the humidity certainly will. Just the thought of it makes me want to hop in the shower.

At the time, I was sporting a fierce relaxed bob. I thought that if I could just cool off my scalp, my body temperature might follow. But when you're a slave to Dark & Lovely, getting your hair wet immediately triggers anxieties about blow dryers and curling irons— damned if I wasn't hot *already*!

Then I found a picture of Roshumba, who was serving up her own brand of fabulousness with her short crop. Remember how she used to rock that little 'fro, before she landed in Hollywood and went blond?

Well, I called my mother and said, "Okay, turn to the beauty section in *Essence* and tell me what you think."

Her response was swift. "I *know* you're not going cut your hair that short!"

While I was *way* past getting my mom's permission to change my hairstyle, I was surprised by her reaction—which, of course, meant that I had to do it. My goal was to cut out the perm and start over. I wanted to grow my natural hair into a big Afro and, for once, just let it be. It was a goal, I soon learned, that was easier said than done.

Being the punk that I was, I opted to cut my hair in stages while weaning myself off of those quarterly relaxers. The bob went from below my ear to above my ear and finally, a quasi-Halle Berry pixie. I kept telling myself that it was just an experiment, as the ultimate goal was to cut out the perm and grow it back naturally, but the upkeep of short, relaxed tresses requires a great deal of attention and product. By the time it started getting on my nerves, I decided to shave it off.

Wow. Aside from in-need-of-a-touch-up roots, I hadn't seen my natural hair since the age of fourteen. The forehead that I'd once believed was the exact size and shape of a satellite dish wasn't as big as I'd imagined. For once, I could actually see myself. Who knew?

I ended up loving my short hair for so many reasons. First, aside from wearing a scarf to bed—or not—and dabbing a bit of oil on my scalp, I didn't have to do much. Rather than wasting a whole afternoon at the salon, even with an appointment, I was overjoyed at the prospect of running up the street to Diamond Kuts on DeKalb Avenue to get my "buzz on" for $12 and a half hour, tops. As an added bonus, there was always a bevy of cute boys waiting to get lined-up, so I got to expand my Rolodex to boot.

Then I started to think about the original plan. I vowed to stop cutting my hair and to let it grow out. I really thought I could do it, but you have to be extremely strong-willed to look in the mirror and love yourself with in-between hair. Needless to say, I went running back to my barber, Brian, who would crack up laughing whenever I rolled in, wailing, "Oh, p-l-e-a-s-e just cut it off." We went through that exercise many, many times, and although he always welcomed me with open arms and a shiny, black cape, I knew that one day I'd get past the three-inch 'fro mark.

I tried visualization techniques. I taped pictures of sisters with fly Afros and twists to the walls and fridge. I averted my eyes from anyone who sported a short cut. I stocked up on bobby pins, gel, and yards of fabric for those days when I just couldn't get my hair together. I was determined to make it, but growing out my hair turned into a painstaking process. My head wraps soon became my crutch. It got to the point where I wouldn't leave the house without my head swaddled in cloth. But I held on through the bad hair days and even through a short-lived season of braids until finally, one day, I had the Afro that I'd craved.

And I was happy—for a few days.

I'm a creative person, but when it came to concocting new and innovative styles with my newly long natural hair, I was at a complete loss. I had pulled the single-Afro-puff move for more days than I could count, and I was growing bored. I was also between gigs and felt like a twelve-year-old every time I walked into an interview wearing a puff. Had I just endured a year-plus hair-growing process for nothing? Um, maybe.

Clearly, I was tripping. So back I went to Diamond Kuts. This time, Brian played me. When I started with the whole song-and-dance about not being able to stick it out, he said, "Bet." He started with the two-inch blade, front and center. After I regained consciousness, I realized that there was no turning back. I was sitting at square one—scalped, again.

Since then, I've kept my hair short. I've even tried the whole "texturizer" route, but don't be fooled—that ain't nothin' but an ultra perm. No matter what I do to my hair, I always find myself back in the barber's chair, asking, "Can you take it a little lower, but don't edge me up—keep it natural, okay?"

When I moved to L.A. a few years back, many of the folks I met thought of me as "the girl from New York with the Afro." When I returned from one of my infamous month-long trips back east with my hair chopped off, they were initially shocked, but soon they completely forgot what I'd looked like before.

I have to admit that in this land of bonded weaves, bleached-out locks, and all-around fakeness, I often feel like a sister from another planet. Being an individual is a costly process. I love my short hair, but baby, there is hell to pay for not looking like everyone else. But I have to ask myself, *Why would you want to look like everybody else, anyway?*

So, here I am today, nearly a decade after I cut off all my hair for the first time. A month ago, my friend Miguel shaved off my bad texturizer job over the bathroom sink—with a one-inch, no less. I'm thinking about growing it out again, but I know that to do so, I'll have to take it one day at a time and learn to love it during every wonderful, horrendous, luxurious, and semi-suicidal stage. Just like every other time before, I'm determined to do it. I've got my Jill Scott, Angela Davis, and Tamara Dobson (as Cleopatra Jones) pictures taped to the fridge, and I'm trying to stay focused. We shall see. I might find myself back at the barbershop. Or maybe not.

After all, it's only hair, and it will always grow back.

—**Regina R. Robertson**

Regina R. Robertson serves as the West Coast editor for Essence. *As a freelance journalist, her writing has been featured in* O: The Oprah Magazine, Ebony, Giant, Honey, *and* Venice, *as well as on the Associated Press newswire and Africana.com; the latter originally published* Short Cuts: A Hairstory *in October 2003. Robertson's hair is still short and ever-fabulous.*

◆ Chapter 75

Didn't You Get the Memo?
African Americans Come in All Shades!

I T WASN'T UNTIL I MOVED AWAY FROM MY NATIVE NEW ORLEANS, A city known for its long legacy of color issues, that I became aware of our race's preoccupation with skin color.

It caught me completely off guard. After all, I was just a preteen trying to grab a bite to eat at a local hamburger joint. I won't say exactly which restaurant chain it was, but let's just say I expected to have my meal *my way* that Saturday afternoon.

Apparently, the cashier had another idea in mind. After I completed my order and handed over a stack of crisp dollar bills to satisfy my check, she came at me out of left field, as they say, with a pointed question.

"So what are you?" the ebony-hued young woman blurted as she handed over my change.

"What do you mean?" I asked, confused about the meaning of her question.

"What's your race?" she shot back unabashedly.

I stood there speechless for about thirty seconds, overcome with confusion and, quite frankly, taken aback by her candor.

"African American, black," I retorted, matter-of-factly.

To this day, I haven't decided what was more shocking—the fact that this young lady surveyed my creamy skin, copper eyes, jet-black mane (with matching bushy eyebrows), full lips, and petite frame and didn't surmise that I was African American, or the fact that she had the intestinal fortitude to ask a complete stranger such a personal question. I wouldn't feel comfortable asking that question of people I've known for years.

She seemed only partially satisfied with my answer. A questioning look spread across her face, but I didn't stick around to curb her curiosity. As I walked away awkwardly with my food, my internal conversation lingered on.

Exactly what *did she think I was?* I thought to myself. *How come she didn't realize I was black?*

That was one of my earlier initiations into this topic we often refer to as the color complex within the black community. I was baffled by the woman's confusion about my ethnicity. Call it naïveté, but I was only a thirteen-year-old who had recently moved to Atlanta from New Orleans with my mother. I'd often heard people make reference to New Orleans as a city with a long legacy of skin-color issues, but it wasn't until I moved away from my hometown that I became aware of how these issues pervade in the greater black community.

In New Orleans, it was commonplace for me to sit side-by-side with classmates and friends with skin much lighter than mine; many had flowing blondish locks, pencil-thin lips, pointy noses, and gray, green, or blue eyes. Sure, they shared similar physical traits of Caucasians, and the word "Creole" (a phrase often used to describe people of mainly French, Spanish, African-American, and Native American mixed heritage) was thrown around a lot, but never once did I consider these people to be anything but black.

So you can imagine my surprise when I began to get frequent inquiries about my ethnicity when we resettled in Atlanta, a city that was shaping up to be a "black Mecca," like Washington, D.C. Over time, I grew more and more aware of my distinction as a "red bone," a "shawty red," a "light-skin-ded sister."

And then there were the people who just assumed I was biracial or Latin. Maybe it started when a Mexican woman walked up to my mother in the airport asking for directions in Spanish. She seemed perplexed when my mother responded, "No speak Español" and escorted her to the information desk for help. Or perhaps it was when classmates at my middle school would ask casually, "Are both of your parents black?" (I found that one especially funny, considering my father's swarthy complexion.) I took it all in stride at first, but every once in a while, I wanted to yell out, "Didn't you get the memo? BLACK PEOPLE COME IN ALL SHADES!"

This was the late 1980s, long before Beyoncé and Ciara were on the celebrity scene, but Vanessa Williams, with her opalescent complexion and baby blue eyes, had already been crowned the first African-American Miss America, and Prince, with his signature curly mane and hazel eyes, was on top of the pop music world. Both have two black parents.

What about the Cosby kids? Theo and Denise were about as far apart on the color spectrum as Vanessa and Sondra, but they were all considered equal brothers and sisters. You'd think after Bill Cosby's ingenious casting that America—and especially African Americans—would embrace the fact that our hues span the rainbow.

Still, today many of us equate the depth of one's blackness with skin color. Should Oprah be considered blacker than Jada Pinkett-Smith? What about conservative Supreme Court Justice Clarence Thomas? Does his chocolate skin make him blacker than light-skinned social activist/author Michael Eric Dyson? What about caramel-colored brothers, like Will Smith and Tyler Perry? Should they be considered moderate, middle-of-the-road blacks? I think it's a slippery slope to maneuver; to go there is a step in the wrong direction.

Don't get me wrong. I have since learned about the complexities of skin-color issues that persist in New Orleans, such as the "paper-bag" test, where you had to be the color of a brown paper bag or lighter to get into certain social clubs, and the whole "passé blanche" phenomenon of lighter-skinned blacks with more Eurocentric features passing as whites in order to evade the injustices of racism, from slavery to Jim Crow and beyond. I've even heard whisperings of color issues within my own family.

It's saddening that we have allowed these issues to continue to divide us as a race. It's unfortunate that, to some, the mocha-colored singer Lauryn Hill will never be considered as beautiful as tawny-complexioned Rihanna. The worlds of entertainment, politics, and business are overloaded with examples of African Americans with predominantly "white" features being more accepted by mainstream society, but we don't need to support that practice among ourselves.

As I once wrote in an editorial for my college newspaper aptly titled, "Color Me Mad," it is up to us as African Americans to tackle our color issues head on and challenge the divisions so poignantly outlined in the infamous "Willie Lynch Letter." Purportedly written in 1712 by a British slave owner in the West Indies invited to visit the colony of Virginia and teach his methods for dividing slaves to American slave owners, the letter advised, "You must use the dark-skinned slaves versus the light-skinned slaves."

It is up to us to begin questioning the preferences and prejudices so deeply embedded within American society, and to break down these barriers by pointedly celebrating the heterogeneity that makes us a beautiful people. We should all take on the responsibility of educating ourselves and the younger generation about the root of these divisive issues, so we can begin to move past them.

As for me, the inquiries about my ethnicity aren't as frequent, and when they do occur, they don't bother me much at all. In fact, just today, I was posing for a portrait at an Atlanta photo studio when the photographer, a young Chinese woman, assessed my features and bluntly asked, "Are you mixed?" I'm not sure exactly what she thought I was mixed with, but I just laughed if off and responded, "No, I'm African American, black. We come in all shades, you know."

—Chandra R. Thomas

Chandra R. Thomas is an Atlanta-based journalist whose work has appeared in Essence, Ebony, People, Newsweek, *and* Atlanta *magazines. She recently completed a Rosalynn Carter Mental Journalism Fellowship, for which she wrote about mental health issues in the African-American community.*

◆ Chapter 76

Calm within the Storm

I WAS BORN IN LOS ANGELES TO AN INTERRACIAL COUPLE. MY father was white and Jewish, and my mother was African American. Both were in the entertainment business—my father was a record executive and my mother was a singer. We moved to Indianapolis when I was very young, and my parents divorced when I was only five. Shortly thereafter, my father abducted my little sister and me, telling us that our mother had passed away.

We spent the next six years moving from place to place until Pops met and remarried another woman. Trouble seemed to follow us at all stops. My stepmother had substance abuse problems, and we continued to travel for a variety of reasons. Through it all, my sister and I were subjected to intense emotional and physical abuse, and the mental anguish was more disturbing than anything else.

When I was eleven, I learned that my father was diagnosed with stage IV lymphoma. On the day he received his diagnosis, he came home and immediately apologized for telling my sister and me that our mother was dead. He also felt the need to explain how his own "shortcomings" had disrupted his relationship with our mother before telling us that he was dying.

He was an average-sized man, standing five-foot-nine and weighing a hundred and eighty pounds the majority of his adult life. The last time I saw him, he was a fraction of his former self—a sickly seventy pounds—and confined to a wheelchair. He told me that he didn't want me to see him like this, so it would be the last time that we'd ever speak. In our parting dialogue, he emphasized the importance of becoming a man sooner, rather than later. He stressed that I needed to do so in order to take care of my sister, and he gave me $10,000 in cash and a hundred blank checks to carry out his wishes. He instructed me to pay the bills now, but after receiving word that he had died, I was to stop writing checks, and then everything else would make sense.

The Mayo Clinic had given him sixty days to live, but he fought seven months longer than that. All the while, my stepmother lived every day in a drunken stupor. Different men and women frequented the house, and drugs and alcohol were commonplace. We were living in Las Vegas, and I wasn't yet twelve years old.

As one might imagine, my sense of self came early on in life. I credit that to the combination of training my father instilled in me, both consciously and subconsciously. Between the necessary travel and mental games I was forced to take part in, my life was an organized mess. My father was a Reform Jew and my grandparents were Russian Jews, so the rituals and basic ethics he learned along the way were passed on to me. That said, he was still a very progressive thinker.

When news of my father's passing reached my mother, she sent for my sister and me immediately. I didn't want to live with her. I didn't know her. I hadn't seen her in years, and for whatever reason, the chaos I was living in seemed normal. I felt in control. I knew what I was dealing with, and I didn't want to change my environment. I was stubborn. As disordered as my circumstances may have seemed, my father had done pretty well. No matter which affluent area we were living in, we were almost always the only kids of color around. I had it made!

Needless to say, the courts ordered us to move back to the ghetto of Indianapolis with my mother, and my chaotic cycle persisted. She was a functioning alcoholic, as was my new stepfather. There were seven of us living in a two-bedroom house and my problems began right away: one night, my stepbrother tried to molest me, and I struck him over the head with a vase.

The real breaking point for me came when my stepfather ordered my mother to get rid of our German shepherd. He'd come home from one of his drunken binges and wanted the entire household, if not the neighborhood, to know it. My mother was boiling some water for a round of coffee and trying hard not to hear any of it. They argued incessantly until he picked up the hot teakettle and cracked her over the head with it. I followed my natural reaction, to jump in the middle and break it up. I didn't want to be there, and I didn't really know her from him, but this was my mother. Her reaction? "Mind your own business! You are not grown!"

At that moment, I was forced to love them from a distance. I couldn't do it all over again. I'd gone from the relationship my father and stepmother had to *this*? It was the same volatile, reckless, and unstable cycle, and I was all too familiar with it.

When I was fourteen, I spent a lot of time living with friends and found a job working at Kinney Shoes, and then another at Long John Silver. I didn't have a lot of pride and wasn't ashamed of where I came from, but I never wanted people judging me based on who they thought I was. There was a point when I began to think about my circumstances very deeply. I realized just how muddled things might seem from the outside looking in, and even through my own eyes. Often, I thought out loud, *God has to be good. Without him, I would be crazy.*

During my periods of self-reflection, I also realized that I never got any of the emotional support or feedback I needed from my family or people I considered close to me. But that was the norm. People never thought much of disappointing me, I think, because of their own emotional shortcomings.

So I tried to do things objectively. That way, it was okay. If I saved $500, I was making progress. If I got an A in one of my classes, it was a sign that I was okay. If I saved up enough money to go on spring break with my friends, I was just as good as they were. That was the way I could give myself some value and take care of my sister—almost like a daughter—much as my father had instructed me to do. And it gave me purpose. I got more out of giving than receiving. I also realized that once my father had died, everything I had was a blessing and could be gone in a split second. That did everything to shape my outlook on life.

When I tell my story, most people are amazed that I was able to survive so much at such a relatively young age. Even more are startled that I was able to thrive under my circumstances, that I somehow had the intestinal fortitude to do so. When you consider the income disparity, racial differences, and physical relocation that I had to undergo, all at the same time—most people would have cracked under the same pressure.

Strangely enough, I owe all that to my parents and stepparents. In their own way, their dysfunctions helped mold me by forcing me to accept myself for who I was. My stepfather had ten kids of his own, so he never told any of us we were special or treated us any different. We were all the same in his eyes. My parents and stepparents never searched for any special qualities in any of us, or acted as if we were going to be the next anything. It's not like it was a conscious thing that they did, but no one ever made me feel like I was anything more than what I was.

Surprisingly, I was never hung up on where I was from, maybe because I am halfway creative or somewhat of a dreamer. I always tried to visualize where I wanted to get to and where I wanted to be, rather than concentrating on what I was doing or where I was at the moment. So many people find themselves stuck on representing a certain city or neighborhood or block. For me, that was never the case. I always tried to pull the best qualities out of worst-case scenarios and use them to make myself a better person.

For example, my stepmother was unfit and emotionally abusive. But that was just the mask that life forced on her. Underneath all that, she was a polished woman, and from her, I learned about etiquette. My mother was extremely honest and bore a real sense of who she was. My father had the business savvy of a multimillionaire, and although my stepfather would drink a fifth of Old Granddad every night, he would still get up at four-thirty every morning to go to work.

In high school, I realized how great life could be. I excelled socially and academically, even though my existence at home was horrible. But when I got to college, I struggled to compete academically and athletically. I'd earned scholarships, but it didn't matter; I almost flunked out my first semester. On top of all that, my athletic career went down the drain.

So after graduation, I went to work at General Motors. I made $50,000 a year with overtime. This was back in the '80s, and to me, that was a lot of money, especially considering my mother was making $12,000 a year. Considering what I'd come from, it was something of a success story. But one day, an older friend of mine gave me some advice that changed my life. She told me that she knew her life would never move beyond the place it was at that moment. She implored me to seek something else and find "something more meaningful" to do with my life.

It got me to thinking, so I went back to school, this time to Notre Dame. This time, I went for me. I didn't go there to be a lawyer. I went to learn. In law school, grading is anonymous. You go through it wondering whether or not you deserve to be there. Many people just assume that anyone who's black is there simply because of affirmative action; no matter how much confidence you have, if you are a minority, some people will make you think you don't deserve to be there. So imagine their—and my—surprise when I graduated from Notre Dame's law school, the first African American to graduate with all honors. It was the biggest moment in my life.

It did more for my self-confidence than anything else in my life had before. I was in a top-twenty law school surrounded by the brightest students in the country, and I was in the top tenth of my class. It was objective validation. It told me that no matter what, I could compete against anybody, no matter who they were, how much money they had, where they came from, and so on. I learned about the importance of being a great professional throughout that entire ordeal. In order to keep clients for the long term, you have to have substance. My clients would later teach me a lot about hard work, respect, integrity, commitment, perseverance, resilience, and patience.

As I've maneuvered the snags and triumphs that have transpired along the way, I've come to realize that I am motivated to help people even though I've never been able to rely on anyone but myself. I never had a rich uncle to go borrow money from if I was unable to pay my bills. In order to pursue a law degree and graduate with top honors, I had to embrace the process. There are people with far more resources to hang on to who would not have taken the risks I have taken.

I know you hear this in church all the time, but God was preparing me for whatever he was going to put in front of me. That said, I will tell you this: the best thing that could have ever happened to me was being poor. I found happiness in having nothing. I never had to have material things; I didn't need to find myself immersed in the affluent trappings of life to be happy. I was internally motivated and wanted my children to have a better life than I had.

At the same time, I was a little naive, because if you do not know what you are missing or the downside of things, you're more willing to take risks. As a Christian I can back all this up, scripturally speaking. As a human being, emotionally, I can look back on my life and say, "God has never failed me."

What I have right now has come as a result of my constant praying for opportunities to be challenged. After spending many years as a successful executive in the music business, I needed a new challenge, but I found myself struggling for two years, searching for what I would do next. There was nothing new for me to do in that industry, but I didn't really know what I wanted to do next.

The last thing on my mind was becoming a part of NASCAR, the second-largest sport in the world, but one with very few African Americans in it! But it's been every bit the blessing that I prayed for. Living in Charlotte, North Carolina, has been an ideal situation for my family, and I can honestly say that this position has forced me to use every skill I have ever developed—marketing, business, law, and leadership. It's a win-win situation.

Having confidence in my abilities is the primary reason why I am where I am today. I don't think I am any different from any of the people I grew up with, but I do think there are things that are unique and special about me. Some of the kids I grew up with were smarter than I, but they decided to hustle instead of becoming successful. This isn't one of those corny soliloquies, but if *I* can do it, *you* can do it. If you look at where I came from, what I've done, and how I've done it, there is no other explanation. I believe that I was destined to be the man that I am today. I also believe there is a divine component to my life, and it's allowed me to go further than I ever imagined.

I believe our biggest handicap today as African Americans is not having the luxury of being able to focus. A lot of the time, we are just trying to survive. There are so many distractions and things going on, you do not have the luxury to try to learn. We are busy trying to stay alive, working double shifts at Dairy Queen to pay our bills. Simply put, our access to information is limited, because we do not know "somebody who knows somebody." I was fortunate enough to have good luck and an angel on my side to guide me through the process.

Interestingly enough, I never had any difficulty balancing my black and Jewish heritage. In fact, it has helped me relate to people from all walks of life. There are things I picked up from my Jewish heritage that I didn't even realize. What it did teach me is that we all have something in common. When you connect with someone about what you have in common, you can celebrate your differences.

People like to say that I make leaping over high hurdles look easy, but it is truly a survival technique. My secret is that I take it one day at a time. I actually battle with my wife about this all the time. She is a big-picture person who tries to solve all problems at once. I like to chip at the atoms, one at a time. I try to take on life and issues in small jumps. I will approach a problem that might look insurmountable, but I know the only way to get there is one step at a time.

In the end, I would like to be seen as someone who has substance. I would like to be thought of as someone you can respect. Whether you like me or not, you can respect me and feel I've done something to help others.

—**Max L. Siegel**

Max L. Siegel is the president of global operations at Dale Earnhardt Inc., the top motor sports franchise in NASCAR. As one of the most influential executives in the entertainment and sports industries, Siegel recently made history when he became the highest-ranking African-American executive in NASCAR.

◆ Appendix I

Important Dates in African-American History

1619   The first Africans arrive in Jamestown, Virginia.

1662   Virginia law establishes that a mother's status determines her child's freedom.

1773   Phyllis Wheatley, who is considered to be the founder of African-American literature, publishes her first book, *Poems on Various Subjects, Religious and Moral.*

1789   The U.S. Constitution designates African Americans as only three-fifths of a person.

1803   The Louisiana Purchase increases the size of the United States, opening up the argument about admitting slave states and free states.

1810   The busiest period of the Underground Railroad begins.

1815   The African Methodist Episcopal Church (AME) is established.

1818   Frederick Douglass is born.

1820   Harriet Tubman is born.

1827   The first black newspaper, the *Freedom Journal*, is launched.

1831   Nat Turner leads a slave rebellion in Virginia.

1850   The Compromise of 1850, which includes a Fugitive Slave Act requiring the return of runaway slaves to slavery, is passed by Congress.

1856   The first African-American owned and operated university, Wilberforce College, opens.

1856   Booker T. Washington is born.

1857   The Dred Scott decision designates slaves as property, not citizens.

1859   Harriet Wilson publishes *Our Nig.*

1861   The Civil War begins.

1863   President Abraham Lincoln signs the Emancipation Proclamation.

1864   George Washington Carver is born.

1865   The Civil War ends, and the Freemen's Bureau is established. Congress ratifies the Thirteenth Amendment, abolishing slavery.

1867   Madame C. J. Walker is born.

1867   Reconstruction begins.

1868   W.E.B. DuBois is born.

1868   Congress ratifies the Fourteenth Amendment, making African Americans full citizens.

1870   The first African American in history is elected to House of Representatives, Joseph Rainey of South Carolina.

1870   Congress ratifies the Fifteenth Amendment, which prohibits preventing any U.S. male citizens from voting based on race, color, or previous slave status.

1877   Reconstruction ends.

1889   The National Baptist Convention is established.

1896   In *Plessy v. Ferguson*, the Supreme Court sanctions the "separate but equal" doctrine of Jim Crow.

1902   The first African-American professional basketball player, Harry Lew of the New England Professionals, takes the court.

1903   The first play to star African-American actors on Broadway makes its debut—*In Dahomey*.

1907   The Church of God in Christ is established.

1914   The period known as the Great Migration begins.

1916   Marcus Garvey brings his Universal Negro Improvement Association to the United States.

1923   Fritz Pollard becomes the first African-American football coach in the NFL.

1926   Carter G. Woodson begins Negro History Week, which becomes Black History Month in 1979.

1927   U.S. tennis star Althea Gibson is born.

1935 Students from the HBCU Wiley College participate in—and prevail in—a debate with white students from the University of Southern California.

1939 Hattie McDaniel wins a Best Actress Oscar.

1941 President Franklin Delano Roosevelt bans racial discrimination in government employment, defense industries, and training programs.

1942 Johnson Publications is founded.

1942 Reginald Lewis is born.

1943 U.S. tennis star Arthur Ashe is born.

1945 *Ebony* magazine is founded.

1947 Jackie Robinson joins Major League Baseball.

1948 President Harry S. Truman desegregates the military.

1950 Gwendolyn Brooks becomes the first African American to win a Pulitzer Prize, for her poetry.

1951 *Jet* magazine is founded.

1953 Willie Thrower becomes the first African-American NFL quarterback.

1954 *Brown v. Board of Education* decision rules that "separate is unequal," ending school segregation.

1955 Fourteen-year old Emmett Till is murdered.

1955 The Montgomery Bus Boycott begins.

1957 A white mob prevents nine black students from integrating Central High School in Little Rock, Arkansas. President Eisenhower later sends in federal troops to escort the students into the school.

1958 Willie O'Ree of the Boston Bruins becomes the first African-American NHL player.

1959 Motown Records is founded.

1960 Student sit-ins begin in Greensboro, North Carolina, to integrate restaurants.

1963 Sidney Poitier wins a Best Actor Oscar.

1963 Medgar Evers is murdered.

1963 Dr. Martin Luther King, Jr., delivers his "I Have a Dream" speech.

1963 Four young black girls are killed in a church bombing in Birmingham, Alabama.

1964 Congress passes the Civil Rights Act of 1964. Three civil rights workers are found dead in Mississippi during the Summer of Freedom.

1965 Malcolm X is assassinated.

1965 Dr. Martin Luther King, Jr., leads a march across Alabama, from Selma to Montgomery.

1965 Congress passes the Voting Rights Act of 1965.

1967 Carl B. Stokes becomes the first black mayor of a major to mid-sized U.S. city (Cleveland).

1967 Thurgood Marshall is appointed to the U.S. Supreme Court.

1967 Edward Brooke of Massachusetts becomes the first African American to be elected to the U.S. Senate.

1967 Robert Hayden is named the first black poet laureate of the United States.

1968 Dr. Martin Luther King, Jr., is assassinated in Memphis.

1970 *Black Enterprise* magazine is founded.

1970 *Essence* magazine is launched.

1970 Charles Gordone becomes the first African-American playwright to win a Pulitzer Prize for drama; the play is called *No Place to Be Somebody*.

1974 Beverly Johnson becomes the first African American to grace the cover of *Vogue*.

1977 *Roots* premieres on national television.

1979 Radio One begins broadcasting.

1980 U.S. tennis star Venus Williams is born.

1980 Black Entertainment Television debuts.

1981 U.S. tennis star Serena Williams is born.

1983 Vanessa Williams is crowned Miss America.

1984 *The Cosby Show* debuts.

1986 *The Oprah Winfrey Show* debuts.

1990 Lawrence Douglas Wilder becomes the first African American to be elected governor of a U.S. state (Virginia).

1991 Clarence Thomas is appointed to the U.S. Supreme Court.

served from December 26 to January 1 each year. Featuring activities such as candle-lighting and pouring of libations and culminating in a feast and gift giving, the holiday was created by Ron Karenga as a means to help African Americans reconnect with their African cultural and historical heritage by uniting in meditation and study of "African traditions" and "common humanist principles." Each of the seven days of Kwanzaa is dedicated to one of the following principles, as follows:

- Umoja (Unity): To strive for and to maintain unity in the family, community, nation, and race.
- Kujichagulia (Self-Determination): To define ourselves, name ourselves, create for ourselves, and speak for ourselves.
- Ujima (Collective Work and Responsibility): To build and maintain our community together, to make our brothers' and sisters' problems our problems, and to work to solve those problems together.
- Ujamaa (Cooperative Economics): To build and maintain our own stores, shops, and other businesses, and to profit from them together.
- Nia (Purpose): To make our collective vocation the building and developing of our community in order to restore our people to their traditional greatness.
- Kuumba (Creativity): To always do as much as we can, in the way we can, in order to leave our community more beautiful and beneficial than we inherited it.
- Imani (Faith): To believe with all our hearts in our people, our parents, our teachers, our leaders, and the righteousness and victory of our struggle.

Watch Night (New Year's Eve): A mainstay in black communities across America, Watch Night is a gathering of the faithful in church on New Year's Eve. The service usually begins anywhere from 7 p.m. to 10 p.m. The importance of these celebrations can be traced to gatherings on December 31, 1862, when African Americans gathered to await the news that the Emancipation Proclamation had become law. However, prior to that date, it was equally important to slaves who lived on plantations across the South, because many own-

1993   Supreme Court Justice Thurgood Marshall dies.

1993   Toni Morrison becomes the first African American to win a Nobel Prize for Literature.

1995   The Million Man March on Washington takes place.

1997   Tiger Woods wins the Masters tournament, the first African American ever to do so.

1999   Franklin D. Raines becomes the first black CEO of a major corporation (Fannie Mae).

2000   Retired U.S. general Colin Powell is appointed U.S. secretary of state, becoming the first African American to serve in that role.

2001   Bob Johnson becomes the first African-American billionaire.

2004   TV One debuts.

2005   Rosa Parks dies.

2006   Coretta Scott King dies.

2006   Ground is broken on the National Mall for a Dr. Martin Luther King, Jr., Memorial—a first for an African American or a civilian.

2007   Johnson Publications founder John H. Johnson dies.

2008   Barack Obama wins the Democratic presidential nomination—and the U.S. presidency.

African-American Holidays

All Saints'/All Souls' Day: All Saints' Day is observed on November 1 by members of the African-American Creole community and other African Americans of the Roman Catholic faith in honor of their loved ones who have reached heaven and are reunited with God. It is immediately followed by All Souls' Day, which commemorates the departed faithful who are still in purgatory and have not yet been purified to reach heaven.

Black Family Reunion Day: The Black Family Reunion Celebration is a two-day cultural event celebrating the enduring strengths and traditional values of the African-American family. It is sponsored by the National Council of Negro Women. In 2009, it will be held September 12–13 on the National Mall in Washington, D.C.

Black History Month: Established by Carter G. Woodson as Negro History Week, this celebration evolved into a month-long remembrance of important people and events in the history of the African Diaspora. It is celebrated annually in the United States and Canada in the month of February, and in the United Kingdom, it is held during the month of October.

Black Music Month: Black Music Month is celebrated in July of every year in recognition of the outstanding contributions that African-American singers, composers, and musicians have made to the culture and heritage of the United States.

The Bud Billiken Parade and Picnic: This annual parade is held on the second Sunday of each August in Chicago, Illinois. The largest African-American parade in the United States, the event was conceived by Robert S. Abbott, the founder of the *Chicago Defender,* to focus on the betterment of African-American youth in Chicago.

Children's Day: Children's Day observations first began in the United States in the mid-nineteenth century. Officially recognized by George W. Bush on June 3, 2001, the holiday celebrates children and also promotes child welfare.

Hilton Head Island Gullah Celebration: Presented by the Native Island Business and Community Affairs Association of South Carolina, this festival, held each February, celebrates the Gullah/Geechee tradition and the legacy of African slaves who settled along the Atlantic coast.

Jackie Robinson Day: This holiday is celebrated on April 15 in the United States to mark the day Robinson broke the color barrier in major league baseball. The Robinson signing is widely regarded as a pivotal event in advancing equal rights for African Americans.

Juneteenth (also known as Freedom Day or Emancipation Day): A holiday celebrated on June 19, Juneteenth commemorates the announcement of the abolition of slavery in Texas. The holiday originated in Galveston, Texas, and was celebrated there and in Wilmar, Arkansas, for more than a century before becoming popular in other parts of the country. As of February 2008, twenty-six states have recognized Juneteenth as either a state holiday or a state holiday observance; these include Texas, Oklahoma, Florida, Delaware, Idaho, Alaska, Iowa, California, Wyoming, Missouri, Connecticut, Illinois, Louisiana, New Jersey, New York, Colorado, Arkansas, Oregon, Kentucky, Michigan, New Mexico, Virginia, Washington, Tennessee, Massachusetts, and North Carolina, as well as the District of Columbia.

Dr. Martin Luther King, Jr., Day: The U.S. holiday commemorating the birth of Dr. Martin Luther King, Jr., is observed on the third Monday of each January (King's actual birthday was January 15). It is one of four U.S. federal holidays that commemorate an individual person. Ronald Reagan signed the holiday into law in 1983, and it was first observed in 1986. It was officially observed in all fifty states for the first time in 2000.

Kwanzaa: Kwanzaa is a week-long festival celebrated primarily in the United States that honors African-American heritage. It is obers of enslaved Africans tallied up their business accounts on the first day of each new year. Human property was sold, along with land and furnishings, to satisfy debts, and families and friends were often separated, possibly never seeing each other again in the earthly world. Thus, December 31 was often the last opportunity for enslaved and free Africans to be with their loved ones.

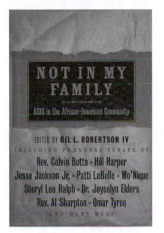